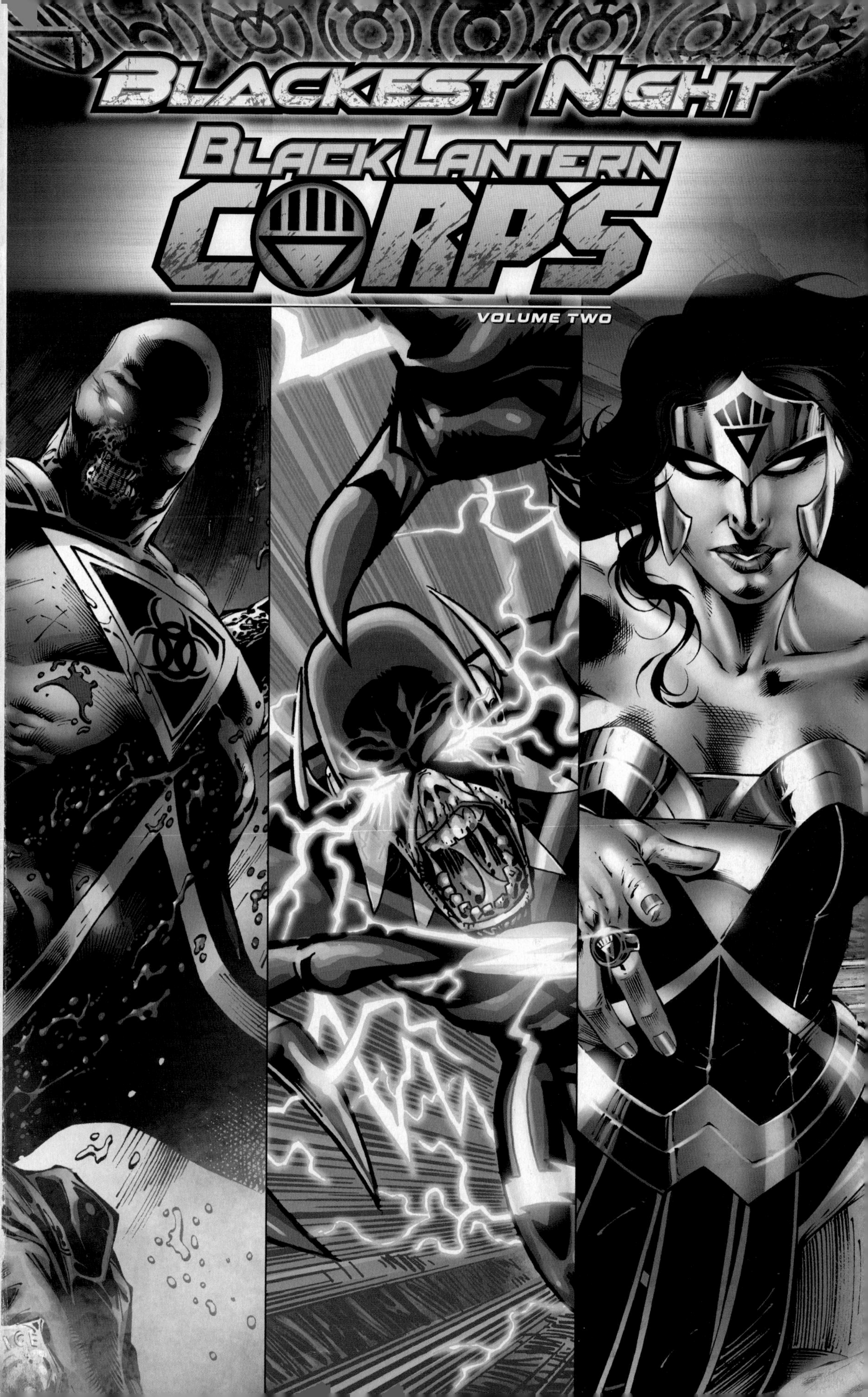
BLACKEST NIGHT
BLACK LANTERN
CORPS
VOLUME TWO

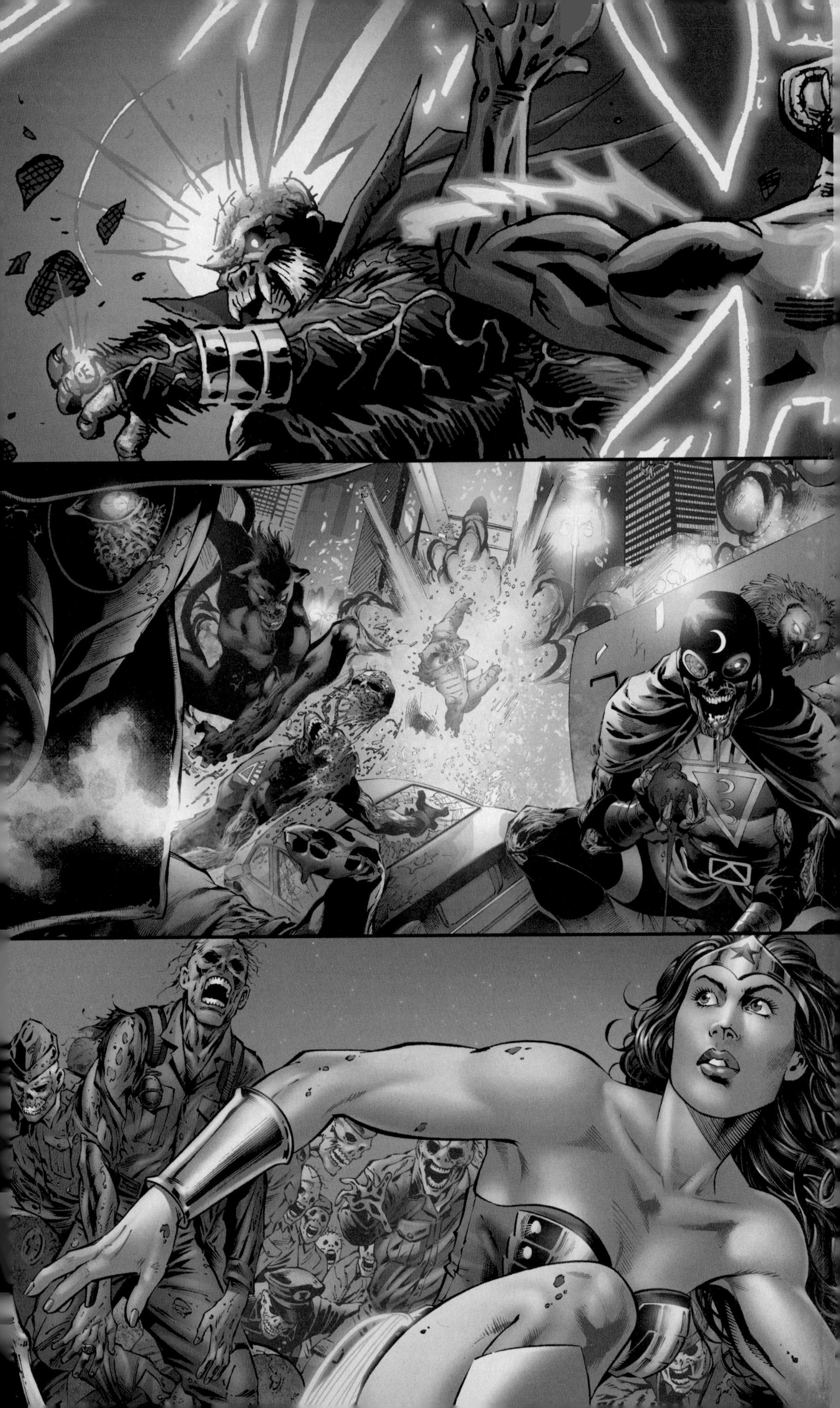

BLACKEST NIGHT
BLACK LANTERN CORPS

VOLUME TWO

THE FLASH

GEOFF JOHNS
WRITER

SCOTT KOLINS
ARTIST

MIKE ATIYEH
COLORIST

TRAVIS LANHAM
ROB LEIGH
LETTERERS

JSA

JAMES ROBINSON
TONY BEDARD
WRITERS

EDDY BARROWS
MARCOS MARZ
EDUARDO PANSICA
PENCILLERS

JULIO FERREIRA
LUCIANA DEL NEGRO
RUY JOSÉ
EBER FERREIRA
EDDY BARROWS
WAYNE FAUCHER
SANDRO RIBEIRO
INKERS

ROD REIS
COLORIST

JOHN J. HILL
LETTERER

WONDER WOMAN

GREG RUCKA
WRITER

NICOLA SCOTT
EDUARDO PANSICA
PENCILLERS

PRENTIS ROLLINS
JONATHAN GLAPION
WALDEN WONG
DREW GERACI
EBER FERREIRA
INKERS

Eddie Berganza   Adam Schlagman   Brian Cunningham *Editors-original series*
Rex Ogle *Assistant Editor-original series* / Bob Harras *Group Editor-Collected Editions*
Sean Mackiewicz *Editor* / Robbin Brosterman *Design Director-Books* / Curtis King Jr. *Senior Art Director*

DC COMICS / Diane Nelson *President* / Dan DiDio and Jim Lee *Co-Publishers*
Geoff Johns *Chief Creative Officer* / Patrick Caldon *EVP–Finance and Administration*
John Rood *EVP–Sales, Marketing and Business Development* / Amy Genkins *SVP–Business and Legal Affairs*
Steve Rotterdam *SVP–Sales and Marketing* / John Cunningham *VP–Marketing*
Terri Cunningham *VP–Managing Editor* / Alison Gill *VP–Manufacturing* / David Hyde *VP–Publicity*
Sue Pohja *VP–Book Trade Sales* / Alysse Soll *VP–Advertising and Custom Publishing*
Bob Wayne *VP–Sales* / Mark Chiarello *Art Director*

Cover by Rodolfo Migliari

DC COMICS 1700 Broadway, New York, NY 10019 A Warner Bros. Entertainment Company

Printed by RR Donnelley, Salem, VA, USA. 6/16/10. First printing.

HC ISBN: 978-1-4012-2785-2
SC ISBN: 978-1-4012-2807-1

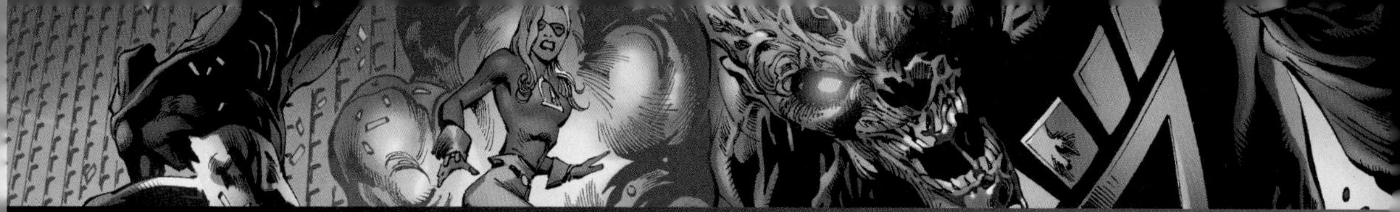

THE STORY SO FAR...

Billions of years ago, the self-appointed Guardians of the Universe recruited thousands of sentient beings from across the cosmos to join their intergalactic police force: the Green Lantern Corps.

Chosen because they are able to overcome great fear, the Green Lanterns patrol their respective space sectors armed with power rings capable of wielding the emerald energy of willpower into whatever constructs they can imagine.

Hal Jordan is the greatest of them all.

When the dying Green Lantern Abin Sur crashed on Earth, he chose Hal Jordan to be his successor, for his indomitable will and ability to overcome great fear. As the protector of Sector 2814, Hal has saved Earth from destruction, even died in its service and been reborn.

Thaal Sinestro of Korugar was once considered the greatest Green Lantern of them all.

As Abin Sur's friend, Sinestro became Jordan's mentor in the Corps. But after being sentenced to the Anti-Matter Universe for abusing his power, Sinestro learned of the yellow light of fear being mined on Qward. Wielding a new golden power ring fueled by terror, Sinestro drafted thousands of the most horrific, psychotic and sadistic beings in the universe, and with their doctrine of fear, burned all who opposed them.

When the Green Lantern Corps battled their former ally during the Sinestro Corps War, the skies burned with green and gold as Earth erupted into an epic battle between good and evil. Though the Green Lanterns won, their brotherhood was broken and the peace they achieved was short-lived. In its aftermath, the Guardians rewrote the Book of Oa, the very laws by which their corps abides, and dissent grew within their members.

Now Hal Jordan will face his greatest challenge yet, as the prophecy foretold by Abin Sur in his dying moments finally comes to pass...

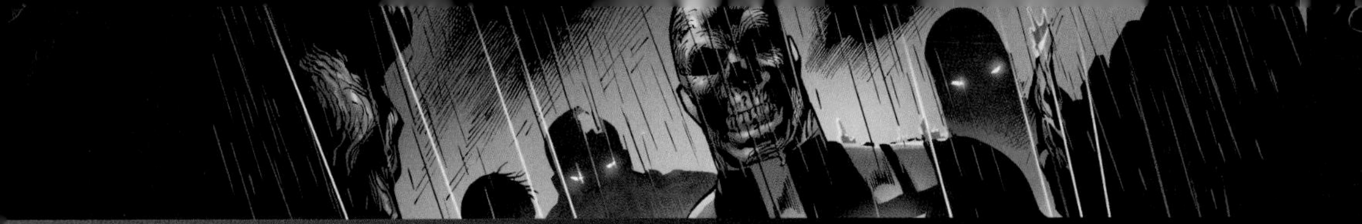

The emotional spectrum has splintered into seven factions. Seven corps were born.

The Green Lanterns. The Sinestro Corps. Atrocitus and the enraged Red Lanterns. Larfleeze, the avaricious keeper of the Orange Light. Former Guardians Ganthet and Sayd's small but hopeful Blue Lantern Corps. The Zamarons and their army of fierce and loving Star Sapphires. And the mysterious Indigo Tribe.

As the War of Light ignited between these Lantern bearers, the skies on every world darkened. In Sector 666, on the planet Ryut, a black lantern grew around the Anti-Monitor's corpse, using his vast energies to empower it.

The first of the Black Lanterns, the Black Hand, has risen from the dead, heralding a greater power that will extinguish all of the light—and life—in the universe.

Now across thousands of worlds, the dead have risen, and Hal Jordan and all of Earth's greatest heroes must bear witness to Blackest Night, which will descend upon them all, without prejudice, mercy or reason.

BLACKEST NIGHT: THE FLASH 1
Cover by Scott Kolins with Mike Atiyeh

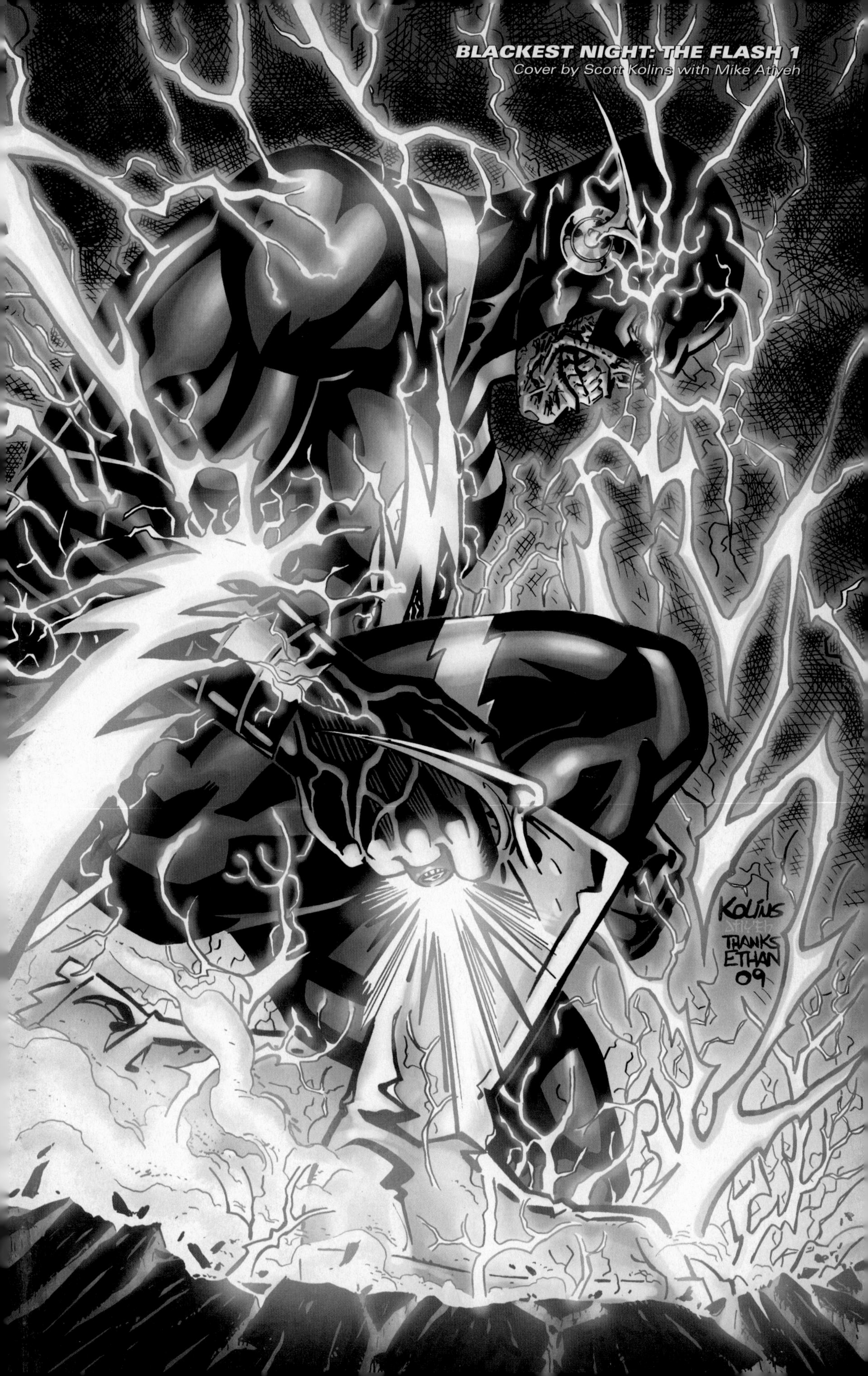
KOLINS
THANKS ETHAN
09

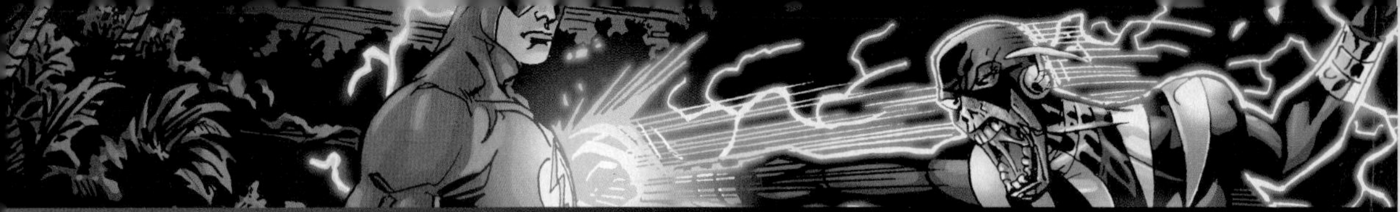

BLACKEST NIGHT: THE FLASH
CHAPTER ONE

GEOFF JOHNS
WRITER

SCOTT KOLINS
ARTIST

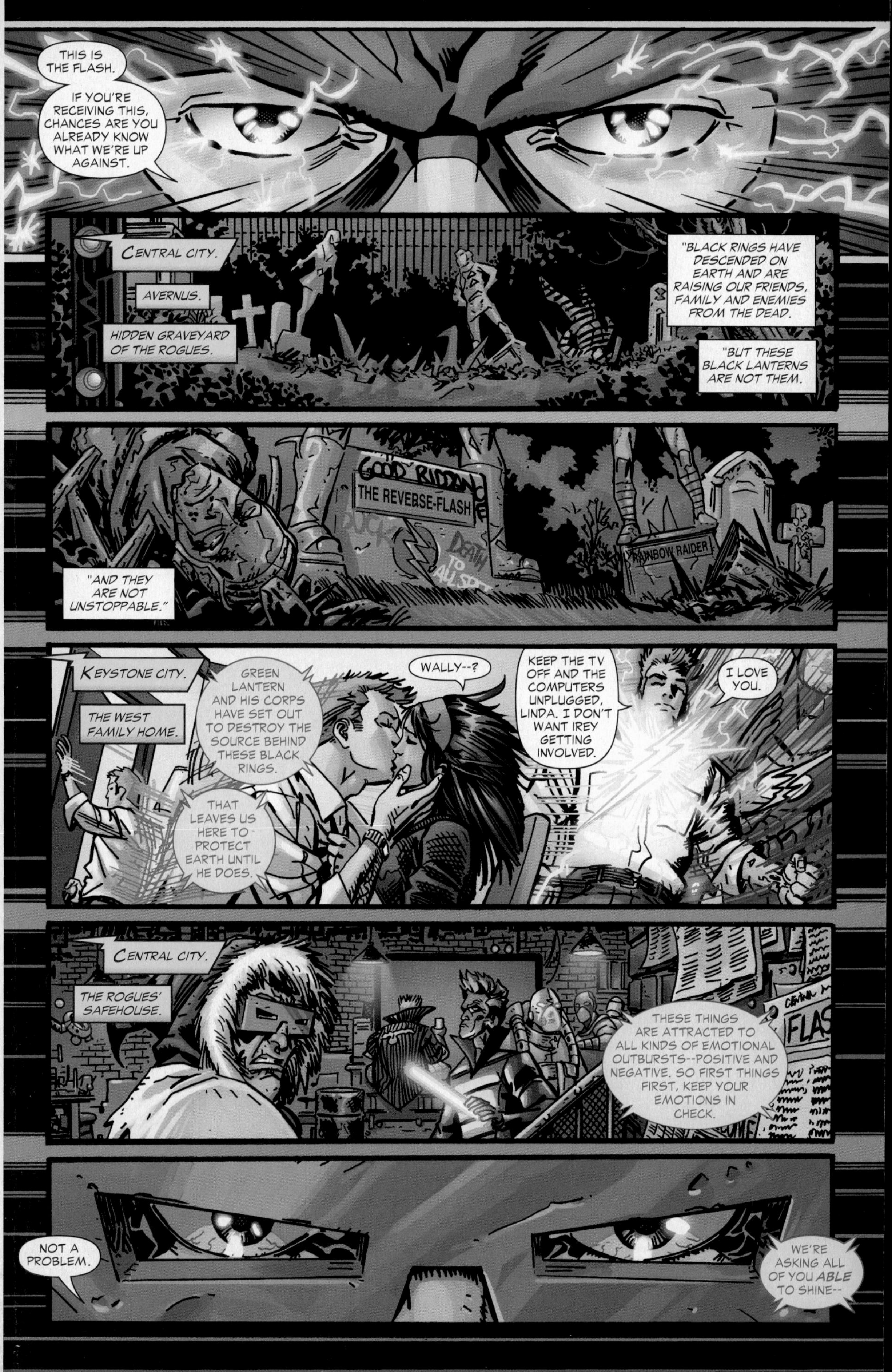
THIS IS THE FLASH.
IF YOU'RE RECEIVING THIS, CHANCES ARE YOU ALREADY KNOW WHAT WE'RE UP AGAINST.
CENTRAL CITY.
AVERNUS.
HIDDEN GRAVEYARD OF THE ROGUES.
"BLACK RINGS HAVE DESCENDED ON EARTH AND ARE RAISING OUR FRIENDS, FAMILY AND ENEMIES FROM THE DEAD.
"BUT THESE BLACK LANTERNS ARE NOT THEM.
GOOD RIDDANCE
THE REVERSE-FLASH
DEATH TO ALL SPDT
RAINBOW RAIDER
"AND THEY ARE NOT UNSTOPPABLE."
KEYSTONE CITY.
THE WEST FAMILY HOME.
GREEN LANTERN AND HIS CORPS HAVE SET OUT TO DESTROY THE SOURCE BEHIND THESE BLACK RINGS.
THAT LEAVES US HERE TO PROTECT EARTH UNTIL HE DOES.
WALLY--?
KEEP THE TV OFF AND THE COMPUTERS UNPLUGGED, LINDA. I DON'T WANT IREY GETTING INVOLVED.
I LOVE YOU.
CENTRAL CITY.
THE ROGUES' SAFEHOUSE.
THESE THINGS ARE ATTRACTED TO ALL KINDS OF EMOTIONAL OUTBURSTS--POSITIVE AND NEGATIVE. SO FIRST THINGS FIRST, KEEP YOUR EMOTIONS IN CHECK.
NOT A PROBLEM.
WE'RE ASKING ALL OF YOU ABLE TO SHINE--

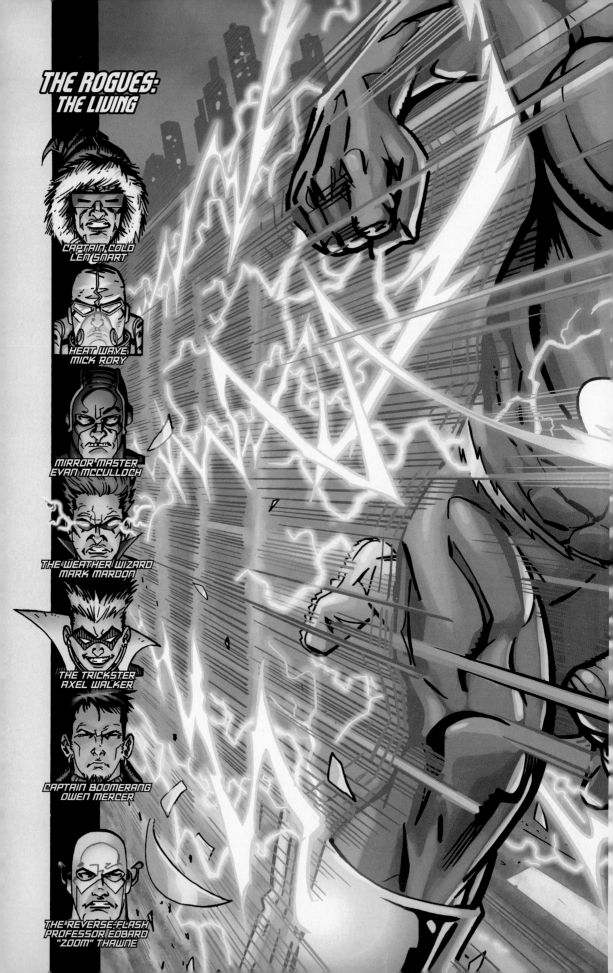

THE ROGUES:
THE LIVING

CAPTAIN COLD
LEN SNART

HEAT WAVE
MICK RORY

MIRROR MASTER
EVAN McCULLOCH

THE WEATHER WIZARD
MARK MARDON

THE TRICKSTER
AXEL WALKER

CAPTAIN BOOMERANG
OWEN MERCER

THE REVERSE-FLASH
PROFESSOR EOBARD
"ZOOM" THAWNE

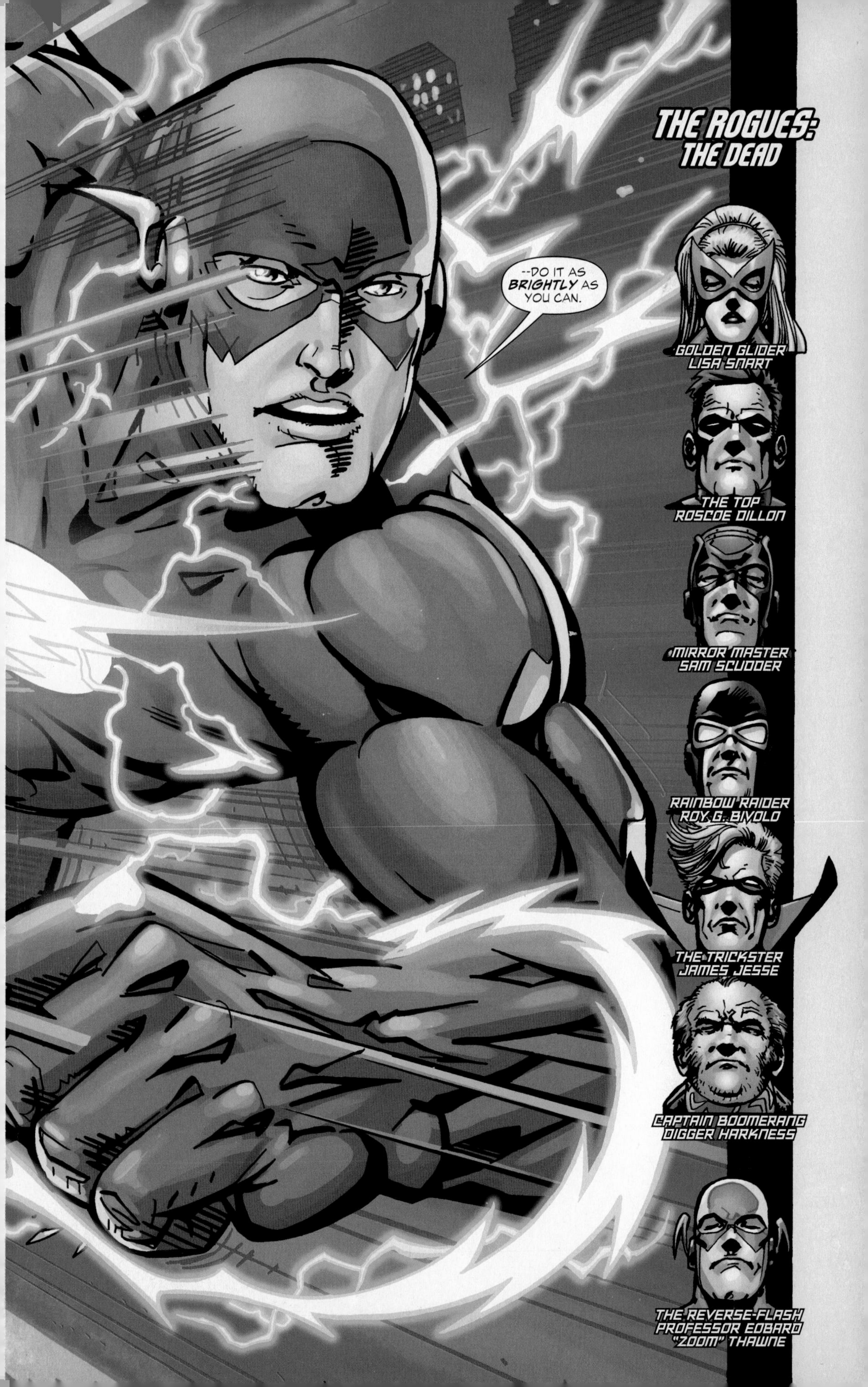
THE ROGUES:
THE DEAD
--DO IT AS BRIGHTLY AS YOU CAN.
GOLDEN GLIDER
LISA SNART
THE TOP
ROSCOE DILLON
MIRROR MASTER
SAM SCUDDER
RAINBOW RAIDER
ROY G. BIVOLO
THE TRICKSTER
JAMES JESSE
CAPTAIN BOOMERANG
DIGGER HARKNESS
THE REVERSE-FLASH
PROFESSOR EOBARD
"ZOOM" THAWNE

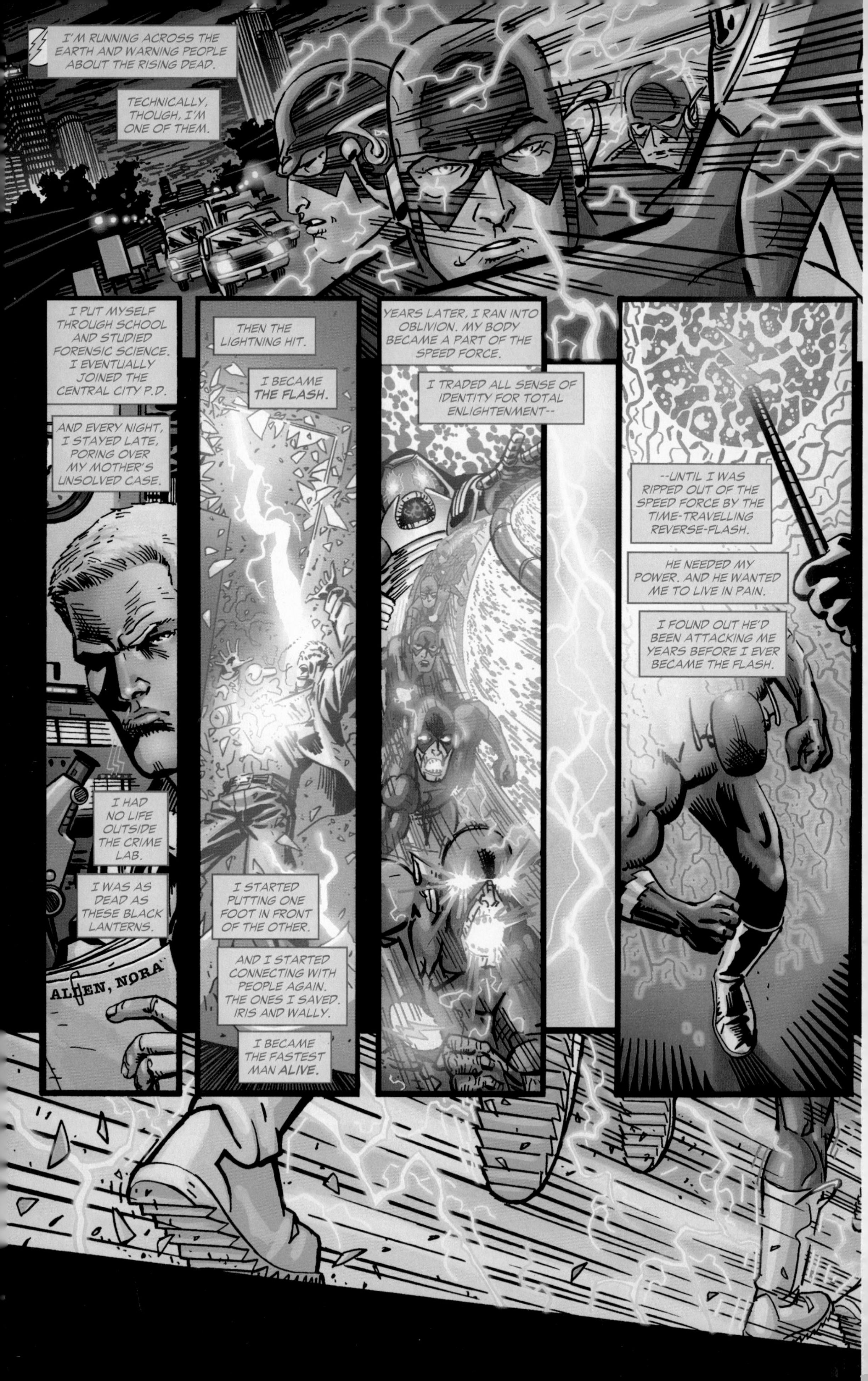
I'M RUNNING ACROSS THE EARTH AND WARNING PEOPLE ABOUT THE RISING DEAD.
TECHNICALLY, THOUGH, I'M ONE OF THEM.
I PUT MYSELF THROUGH SCHOOL AND STUDIED FORENSIC SCIENCE. I EVENTUALLY JOINED THE CENTRAL CITY P.D.
AND EVERY NIGHT, I STAYED LATE, PORING OVER MY MOTHER'S UNSOLVED CASE.
I HAD NO LIFE OUTSIDE THE CRIME LAB.
I WAS AS DEAD AS THESE BLACK LANTERNS.
ALLEN, NORA
THEN THE LIGHTNING HIT.
I BECAME THE FLASH.
I STARTED PUTTING ONE FOOT IN FRONT OF THE OTHER.
AND I STARTED CONNECTING WITH PEOPLE AGAIN. THE ONES I SAVED. IRIS AND WALLY.
I BECAME THE FASTEST MAN ALIVE.
YEARS LATER, I RAN INTO OBLIVION. MY BODY BECAME A PART OF THE SPEED FORCE.
I TRADED ALL SENSE OF IDENTITY FOR TOTAL ENLIGHTENMENT--
--UNTIL I WAS RIPPED OUT OF THE SPEED FORCE BY THE TIME-TRAVELLING REVERSE-FLASH.
HE NEEDED MY POWER. AND HE WANTED ME TO LIVE IN PAIN.
I FOUND OUT HE'D BEEN ATTACKING ME YEARS BEFORE I EVER BECAME THE FLASH.

I WAS TWELVE WHEN MY MOTHER WAS MURDERED. THAT WAS THE DAY I STOPPED LIVING.

AND THE DAY I STOPPED MOVING FORWARD.

I WAS STANDING STILL FOR YEARS.

HE CLAIMED RESPONSIBILITY FOR EVERYTHING "BAD" THAT HAPPENED TO ME.

STARTING WITH THE MURDER OF MY MOTHER.

HE TOOK REVENGE ON ME IN REVERSE. I'M SURE HE THINKS HE WAS "CLEVER."

NORA ALLEN IN LOVING MEMORY

THE MANIAC.

I COULD'VE SNAPPED HIS NECK ALL OVER AGAIN.

BUT THAT'S JUST IT. BEFORE I WAS LOST TO THE SPEED FORCE, I KILLED THE REVERSE-FLASH DEFENDING THE PEOPLE I LOVE.

HIS BODY WAS LATER STOLEN BY THE ROGUES AND DESECRATED.

GOOD RIDDANCE THE REVERSE-FLASH
DEATH TO ALLSPEED

CAPTAIN COLD AND HIS SUPER-THUGS HAVE A THING AGAINST SPEEDSTERS, NO MATTER WHAT SIDE OF THE LAW THEY'RE ON.

BUT THAT MEANS THE REVERSE-FLASH THAT BROUGHT ME BACK--

--WAS FROM SOME POINT IN TIME AFTER HE'D RETURNED FROM THE DEAD.

I HAVE A RESURRECTION OF MY OWN IN THE DAYS AHEAD, BARRY. THANKS TO A GOOD FRIEND OF YOURS.

I HAVEN'T MENTIONED IT TO HAL OR WALLY, BUT I CAN'T HELP BUT THINK:

Welcome to
CENTRAL CITY
THE FASTEST CITY IN THE WEST

IS THIS WHAT LEADS TO THE RESURRECTION OF EOBARD THAWNE?

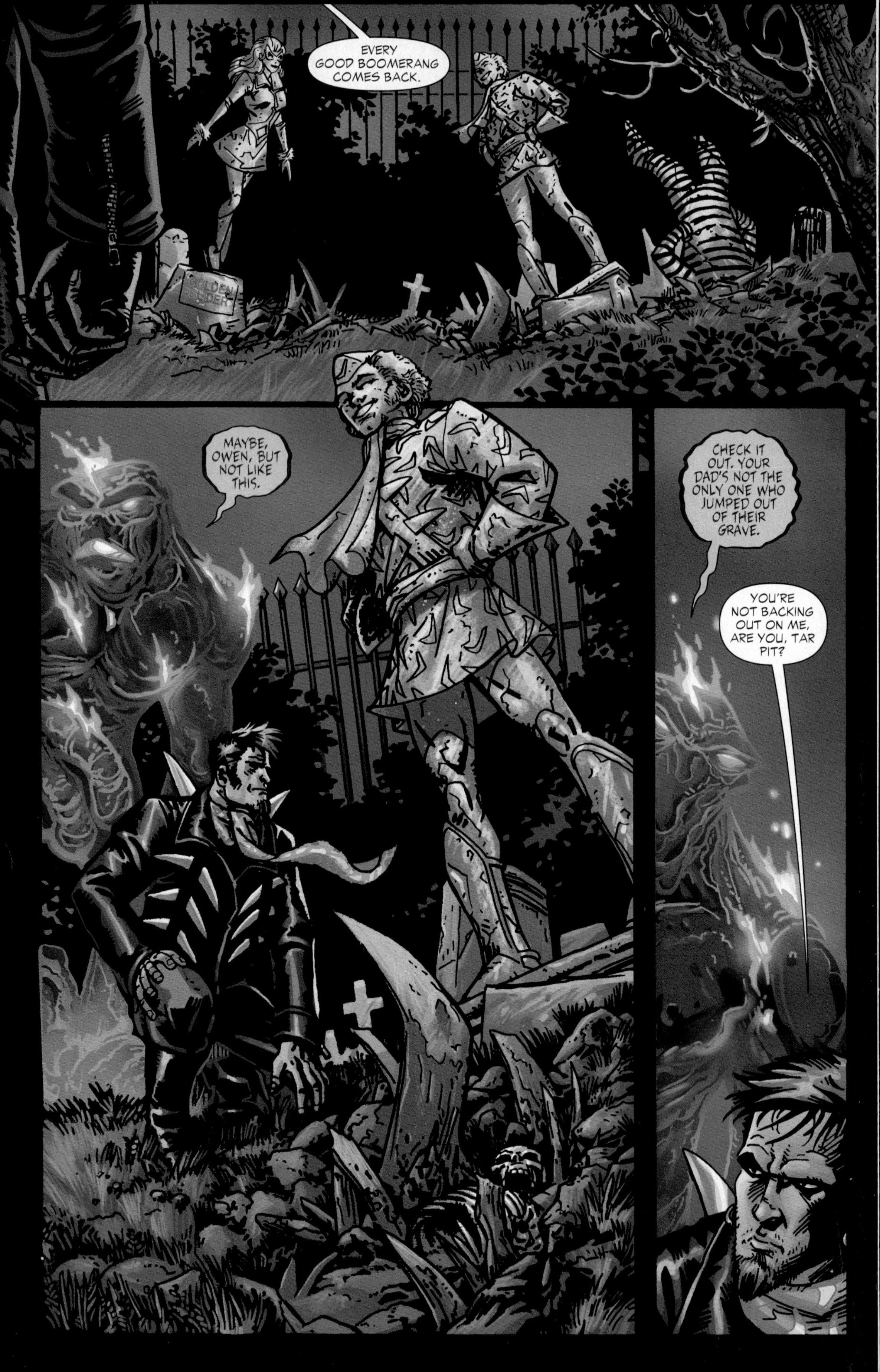
EVERY GOOD BOOMERANG COMES BACK.
GOLDEN GLIDER
MAYBE, OWEN, BUT NOT LIKE THIS.
CHECK IT OUT. YOUR DAD'S NOT THE ONLY ONE WHO JUMPED OUT OF THEIR GRAVE.
YOU'RE NOT BACKING OUT ON ME, ARE YOU, TAR PIT?

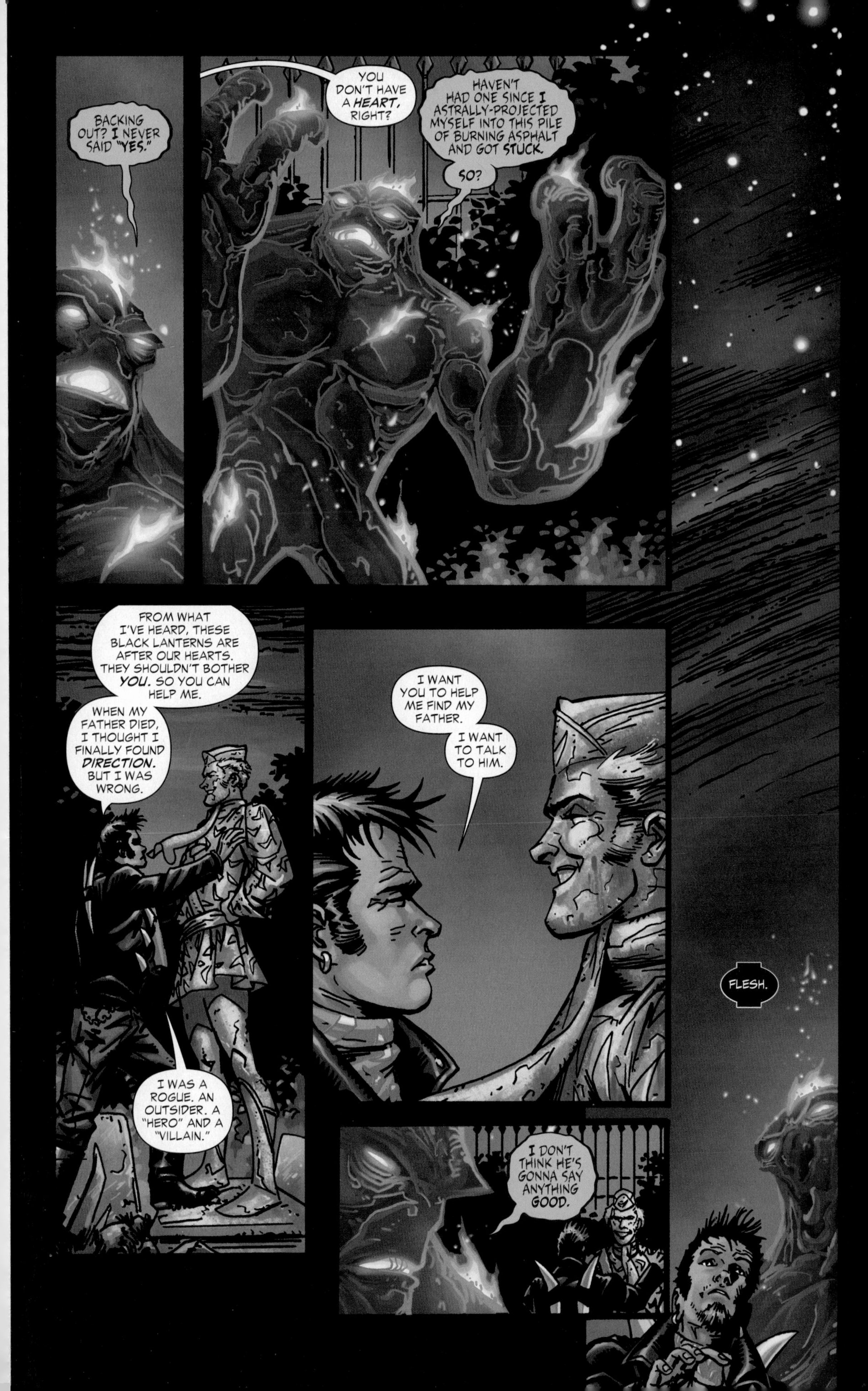
BACKING OUT? I NEVER SAID "YES."
YOU DON'T HAVE A HEART, RIGHT?
HAVEN'T HAD ONE SINCE I ASTRALLY-PROJECTED MYSELF INTO THIS PILE OF BURNING ASPHALT AND GOT STUCK.
SO?
FROM WHAT I'VE HEARD, THESE BLACK LANTERNS ARE AFTER OUR HEARTS. THEY SHOULDN'T BOTHER YOU. SO YOU CAN HELP ME.
WHEN MY FATHER DIED, I THOUGHT I FINALLY FOUND DIRECTION. BUT I WAS WRONG.
I WAS A ROGUE. AN OUTSIDER. A "HERO" AND A "VILLAIN."
I WANT YOU TO HELP ME FIND MY FATHER.
I WANT TO TALK TO HIM.
FLESH.
I DON'T THINK HE'S GONNA SAY ANYTHING GOOD.

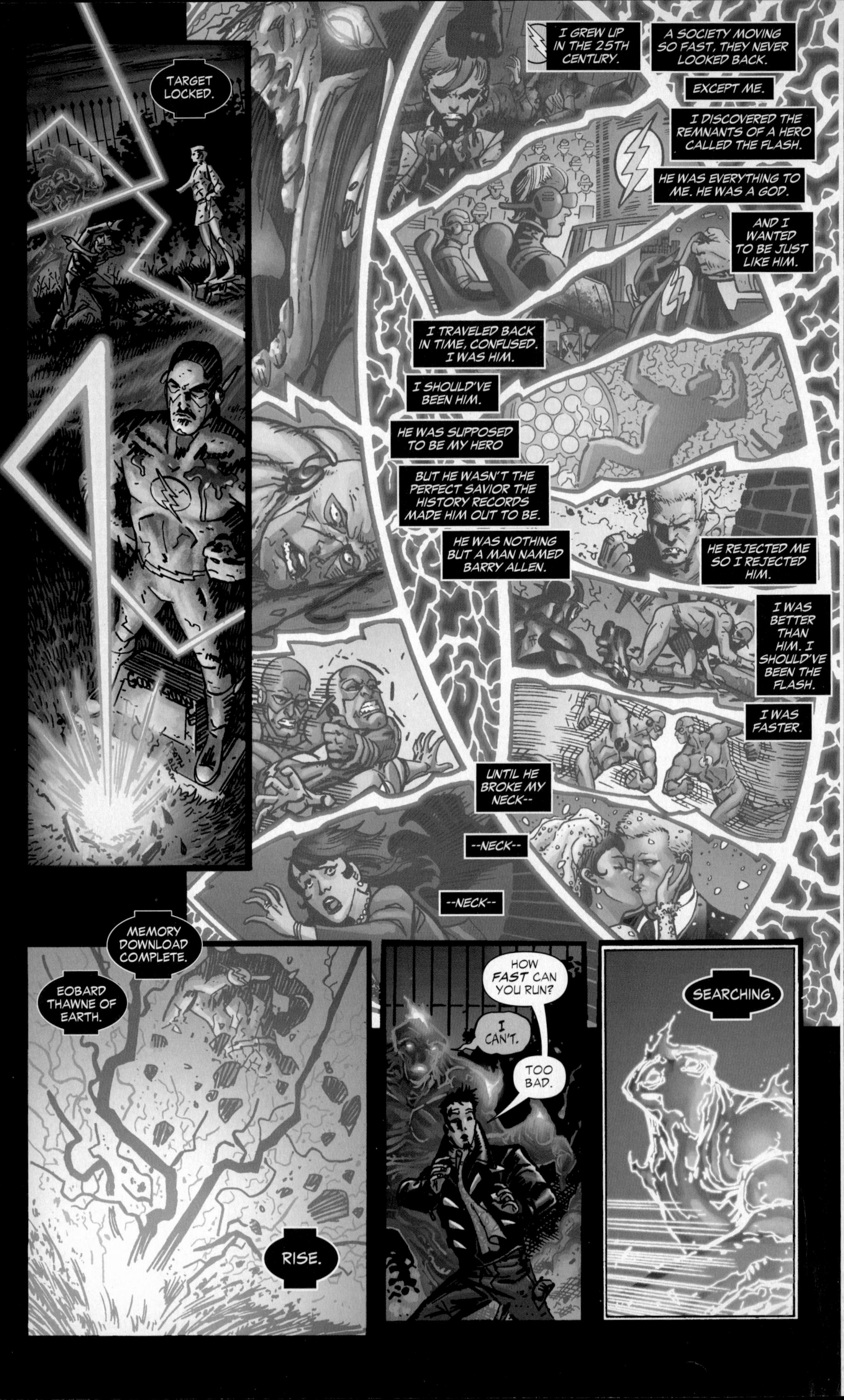

TARGET LOCKED.
I GREW UP IN THE 25TH CENTURY.
A SOCIETY MOVING SO FAST, THEY NEVER LOOKED BACK.
EXCEPT ME.
I DISCOVERED THE REMNANTS OF A HERO CALLED THE FLASH.
HE WAS EVERYTHING TO ME. HE WAS A GOD.
AND I WANTED TO BE JUST LIKE HIM.
I TRAVELED BACK IN TIME, CONFUSED. I WAS HIM.
I SHOULD'VE BEEN HIM.
HE WAS SUPPOSED TO BE MY HERO
BUT HE WASN'T THE PERFECT SAVIOR THE HISTORY RECORDS MADE HIM OUT TO BE.
HE WAS NOTHING BUT A MAN NAMED BARRY ALLEN.
HE REJECTED ME SO I REJECTED HIM.
I WAS BETTER THAN HIM. I SHOULD'VE BEEN THE FLASH.
I WAS FASTER.
UNTIL HE BROKE MY NECK--
--NECK--
--NECK--
MEMORY DOWNLOAD COMPLETE.
EOBARD THAWNE OF EARTH.
RISE.
HOW FAST CAN YOU RUN?
I CAN'T.
TOO BAD.
SEARCHING.

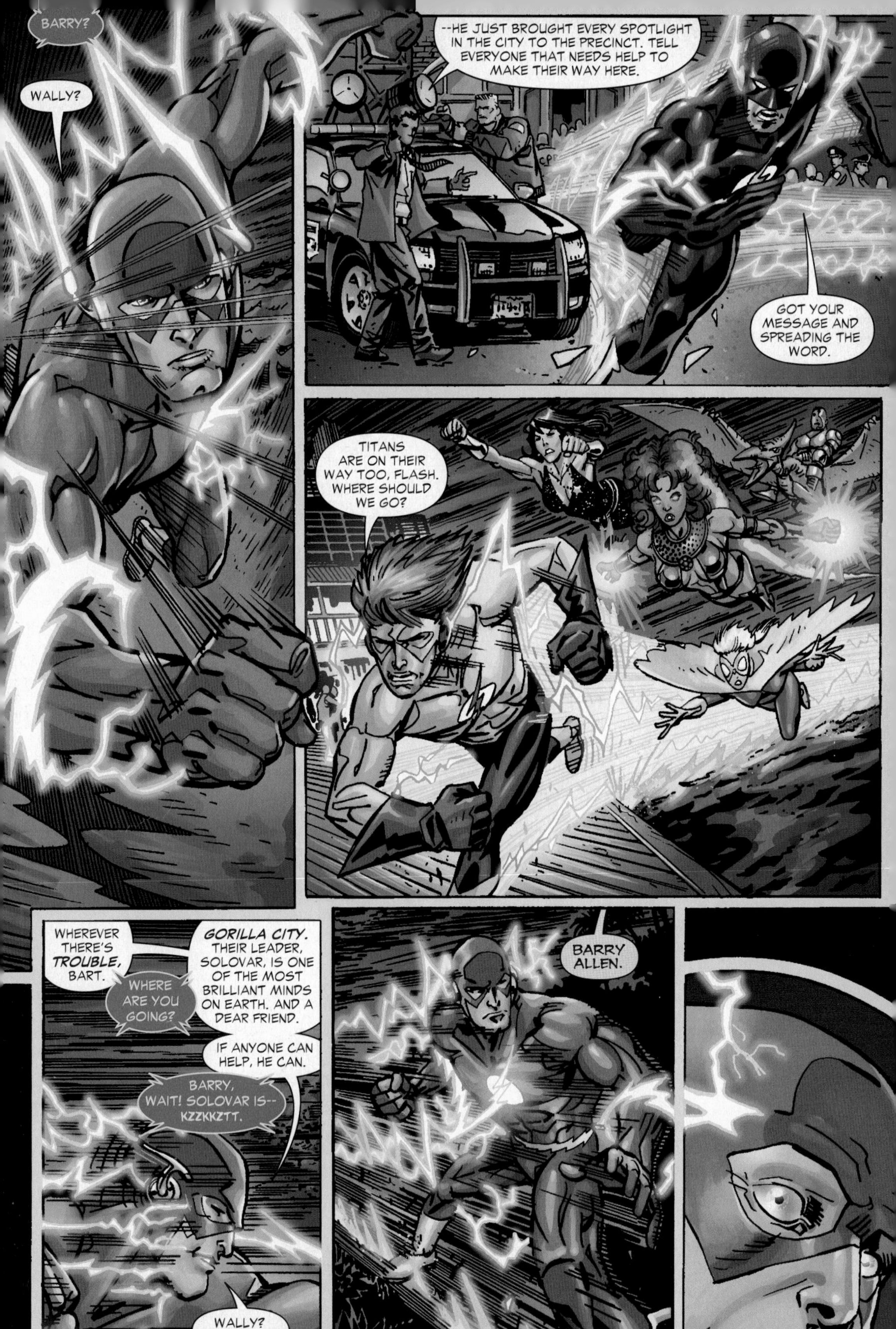
BARRY?
WALLY?
--HE JUST BROUGHT EVERY SPOTLIGHT IN THE CITY TO THE PRECINCT. TELL EVERYONE THAT NEEDS HELP TO MAKE THEIR WAY HERE.
GOT YOUR MESSAGE AND SPREADING THE WORD.
TITANS ARE ON THEIR WAY TOO, FLASH. WHERE SHOULD WE GO?
WHEREVER THERE'S TROUBLE, BART.
WHERE ARE YOU GOING?
GORILLA CITY. THEIR LEADER, SOLOVAR, IS ONE OF THE MOST BRILLIANT MINDS ON EARTH. AND A DEAR FRIEND.
IF ANYONE CAN HELP, HE CAN.
BARRY, WAIT! SOLOVAR IS-- KZZKKZTT.
WALLY? YOU THERE?
BARRY ALLEN.

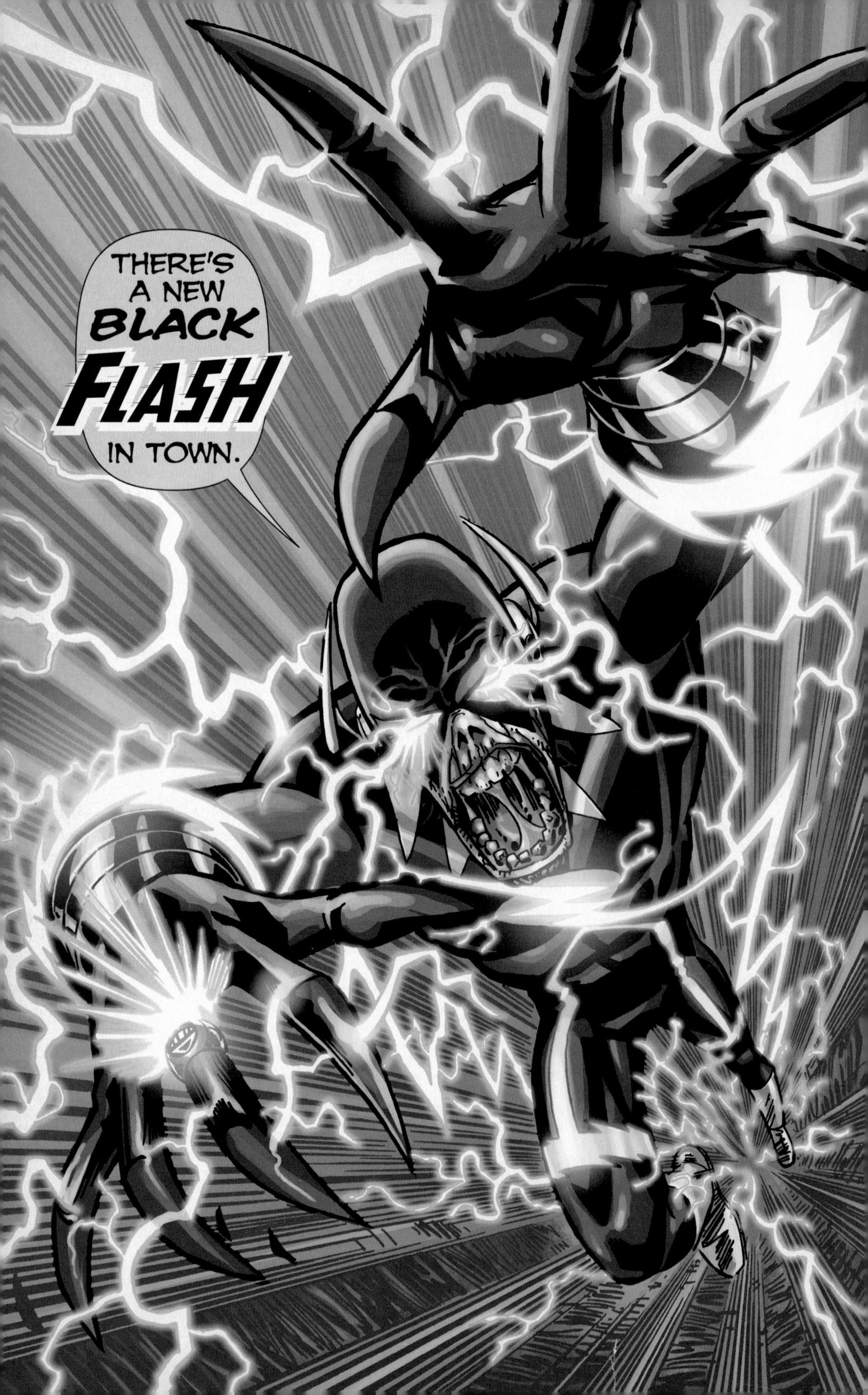
THERE'S A NEW BLACK FLASH IN TOWN.

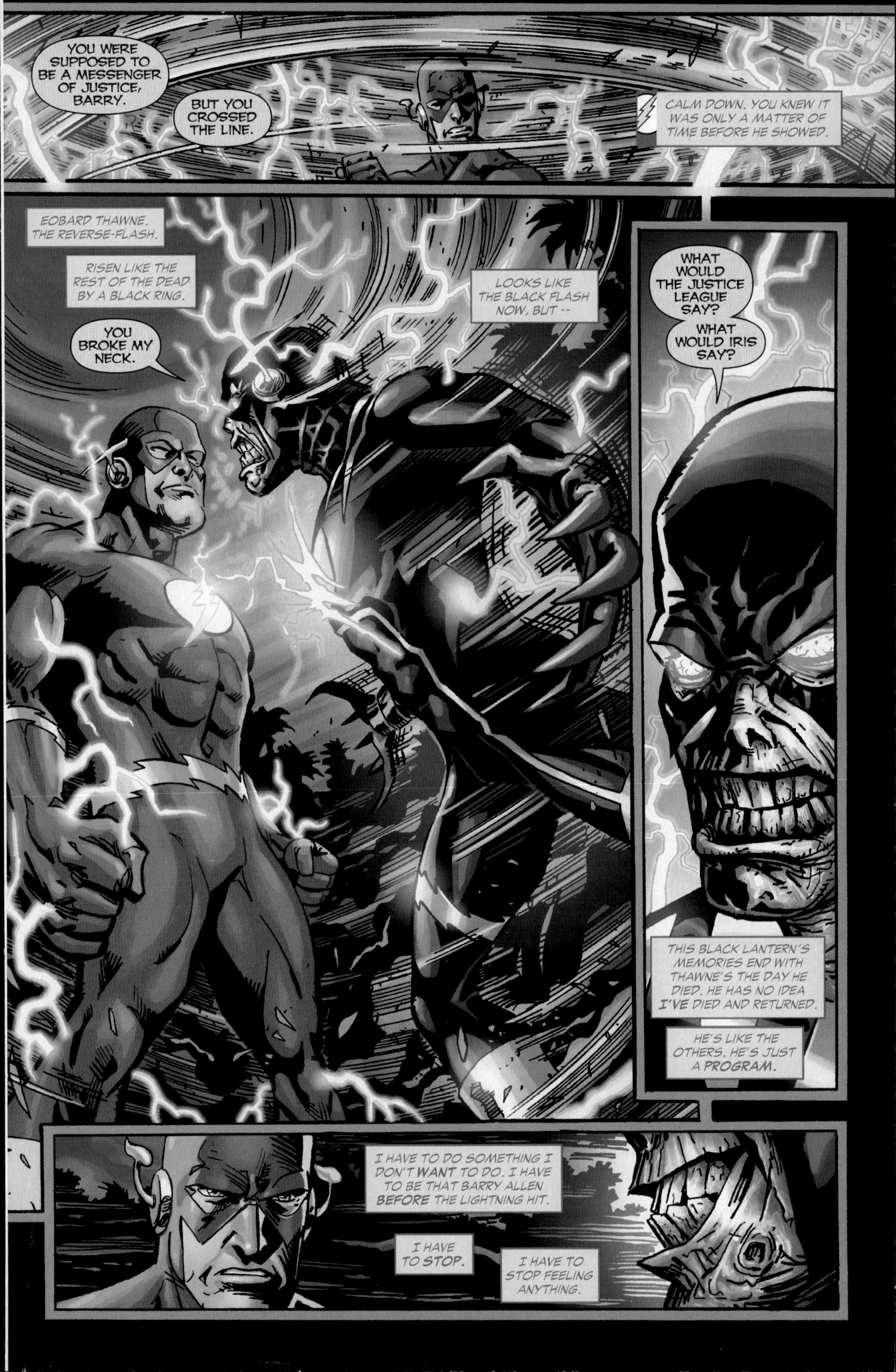
YOU WERE SUPPOSED TO BE A MESSENGER OF JUSTICE, BARRY.
BUT YOU CROSSED THE LINE.
CALM DOWN. YOU KNEW IT WAS ONLY A MATTER OF TIME BEFORE HE SHOWED.
EOBARD THAWNE. THE REVERSE-FLASH.
RISEN LIKE THE REST OF THE DEAD BY A BLACK RING.
YOU BROKE MY NECK.
LOOKS LIKE THE BLACK FLASH NOW, BUT --
WHAT WOULD THE JUSTICE LEAGUE SAY?
WHAT WOULD IRIS SAY?
THIS BLACK LANTERN'S MEMORIES END WITH THAWNE'S THE DAY HE DIED. HE HAS NO IDEA I'VE DIED AND RETURNED.
HE'S LIKE THE OTHERS. HE'S JUST A PROGRAM.
I HAVE TO DO SOMETHING I DON'T WANT TO DO. I HAVE TO BE THAT BARRY ALLEN BEFORE THE LIGHTNING HIT.
I HAVE TO STOP.
I HAVE TO STOP FEELING ANYTHING.

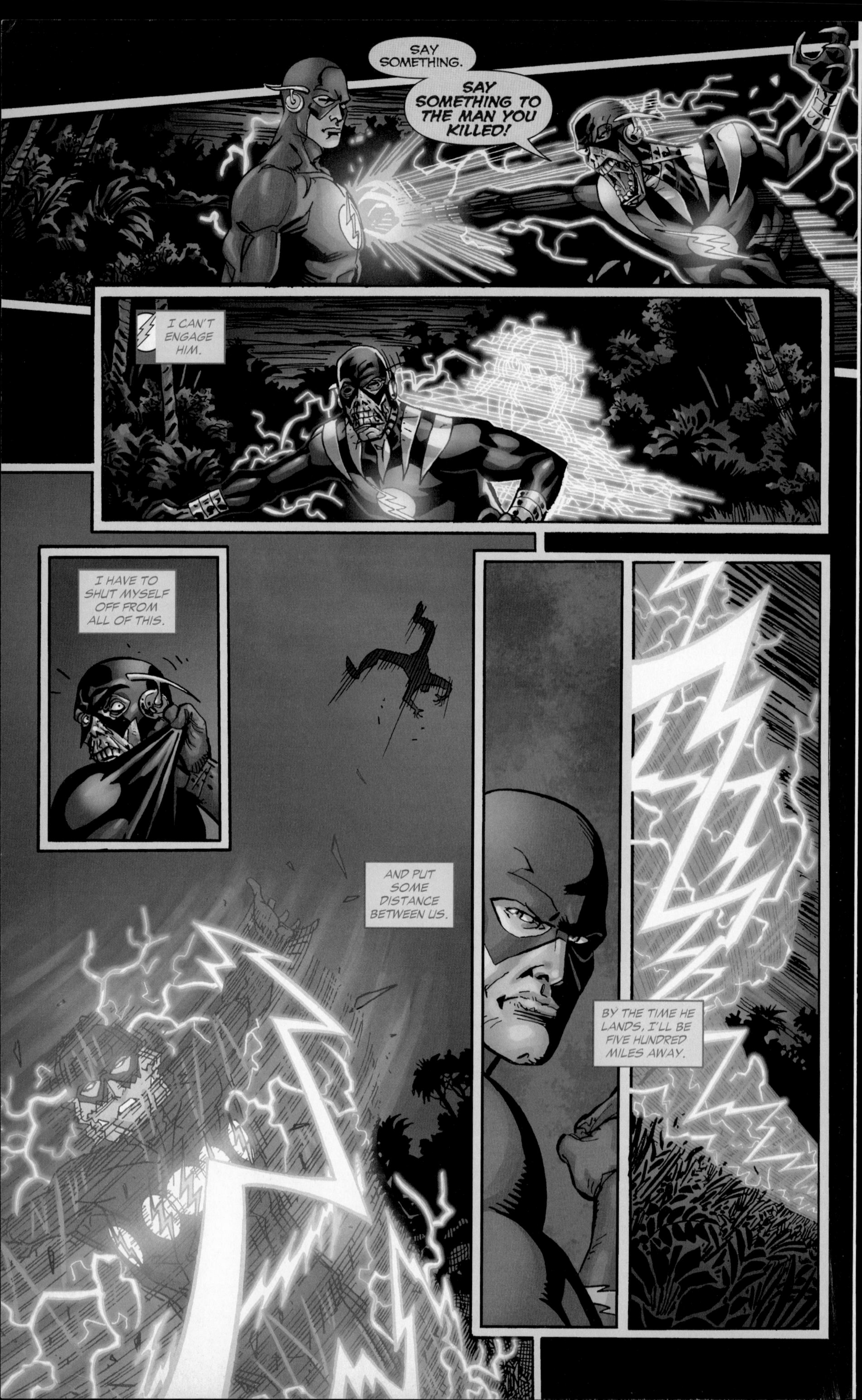
SAY SOMETHING.
SAY SOMETHING TO THE MAN YOU KILLED!
I CAN'T ENGAGE HIM.
I HAVE TO SHUT MYSELF OFF FROM ALL OF THIS.
AND PUT SOME DISTANCE BETWEEN US.
BY THE TIME HE LANDS, I'LL BE FIVE HUNDRED MILES AWAY.

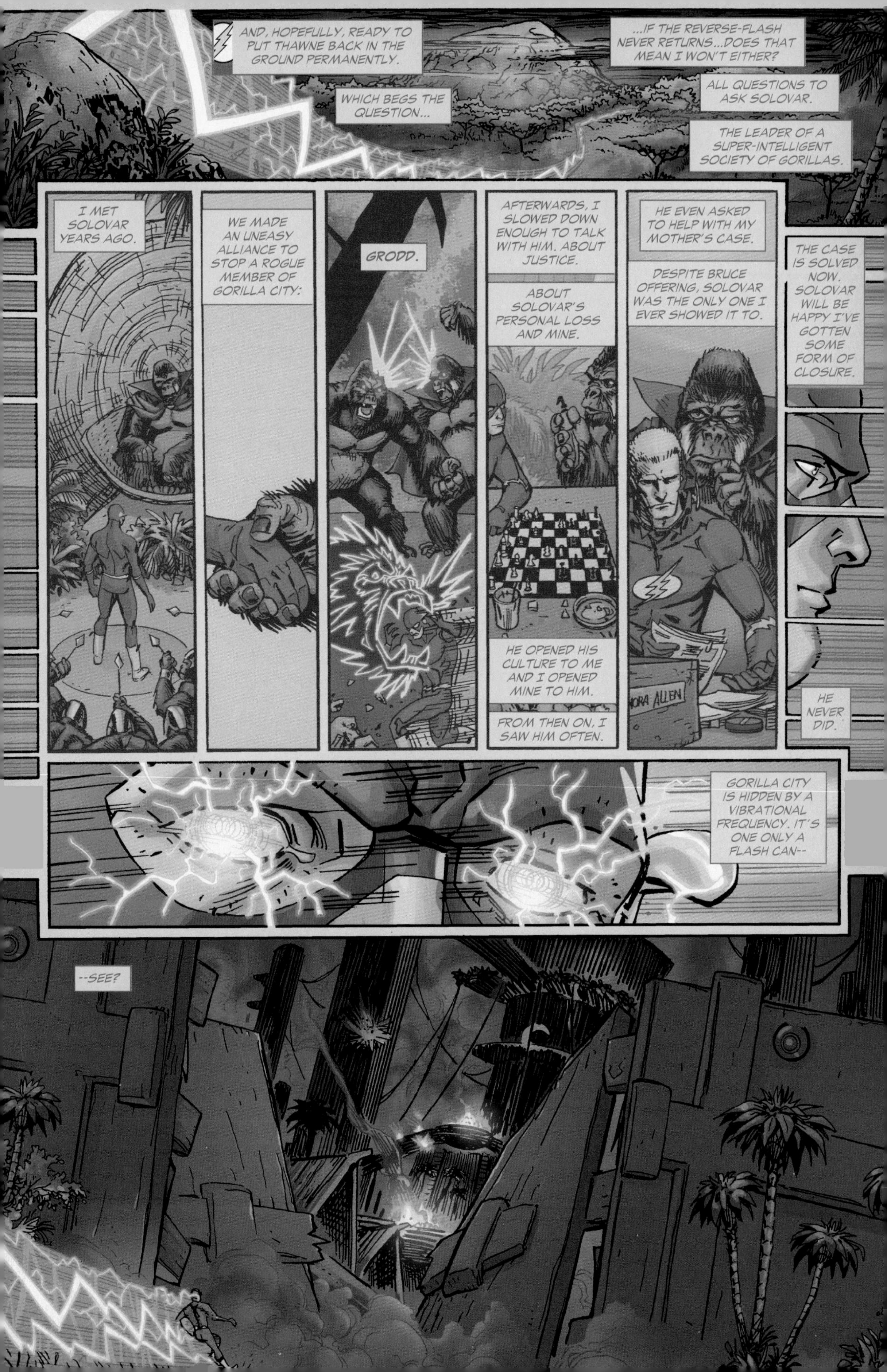
AND, HOPEFULLY, READY TO PUT THAWNE BACK IN THE GROUND PERMANENTLY.
WHICH BEGS THE QUESTION...
...IF THE REVERSE-FLASH NEVER RETURNS...DOES THAT MEAN I WON'T EITHER?
ALL QUESTIONS TO ASK SOLOVAR.
THE LEADER OF A SUPER-INTELLIGENT SOCIETY OF GORILLAS.
I MET SOLOVAR YEARS AGO.
WE MADE AN UNEASY ALLIANCE TO STOP A ROGUE MEMBER OF GORILLA CITY:
GRODD.
AFTERWARDS, I SLOWED DOWN ENOUGH TO TALK WITH HIM. ABOUT JUSTICE.
ABOUT SOLOVAR'S PERSONAL LOSS AND MINE.
HE OPENED HIS CULTURE TO ME AND I OPENED MINE TO HIM.
FROM THEN ON, I SAW HIM OFTEN.
HE EVEN ASKED TO HELP WITH MY MOTHER'S CASE.
DESPITE BRUCE OFFERING, SOLOVAR WAS THE ONLY ONE I EVER SHOWED IT TO.
NORA ALLEN
THE CASE IS SOLVED NOW. SOLOVAR WILL BE HAPPY I'VE GOTTEN SOME FORM OF CLOSURE.
HE NEVER DID.
GORILLA CITY IS HIDDEN BY A VIBRATIONAL FREQUENCY. IT'S ONE ONLY A FLASH CAN--
--SEE?

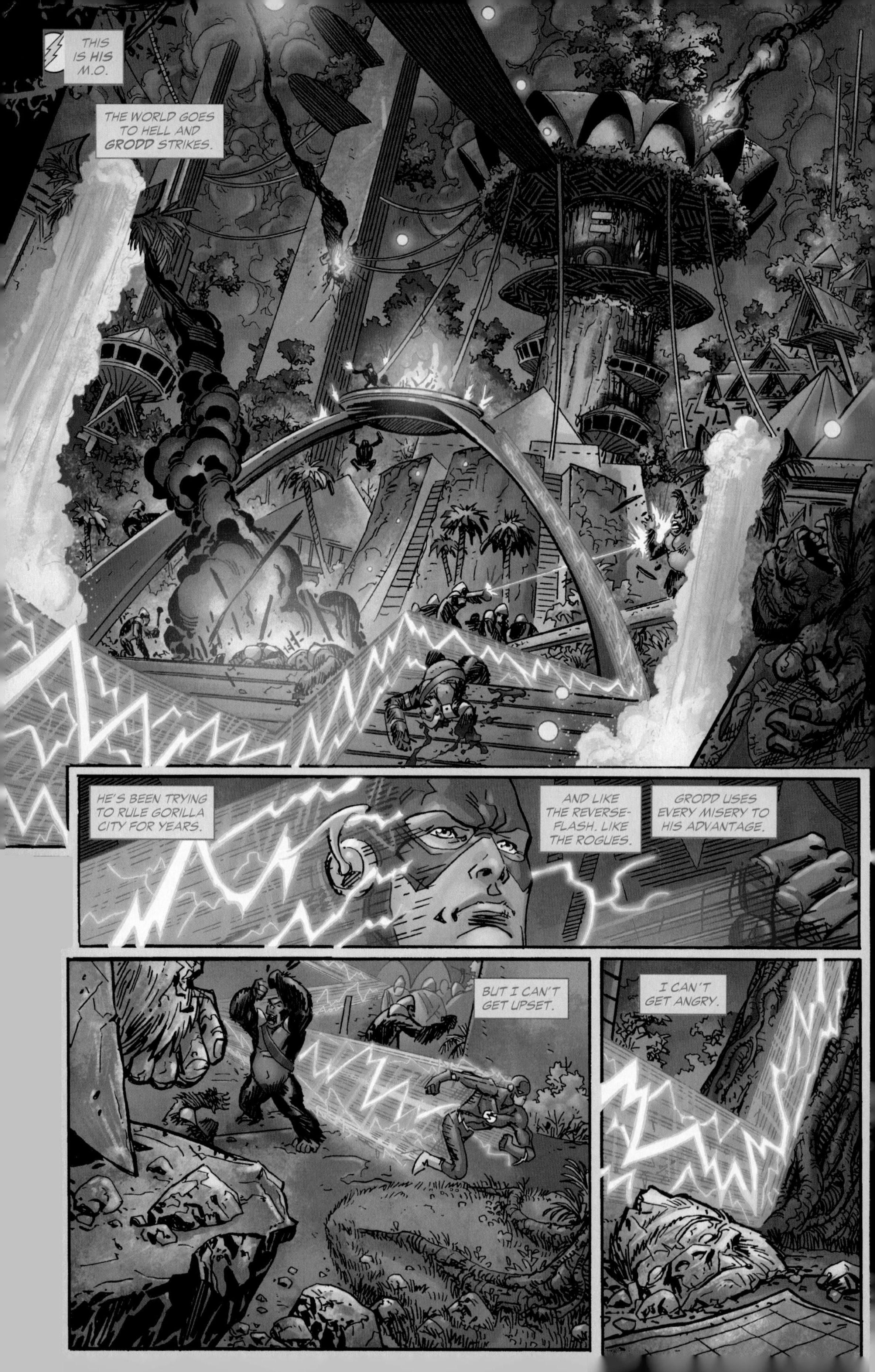
THIS IS HIS M.O.
THE WORLD GOES TO HELL AND GRODD STRIKES.
HE'S BEEN TRYING TO RULE GORILLA CITY FOR YEARS.
AND LIKE THE REVERSE-FLASH. LIKE THE ROGUES.
GRODD USES EVERY MISERY TO HIS ADVANTAGE.
BUT I CAN'T GET UPSET.
I CAN'T GET ANGRY.

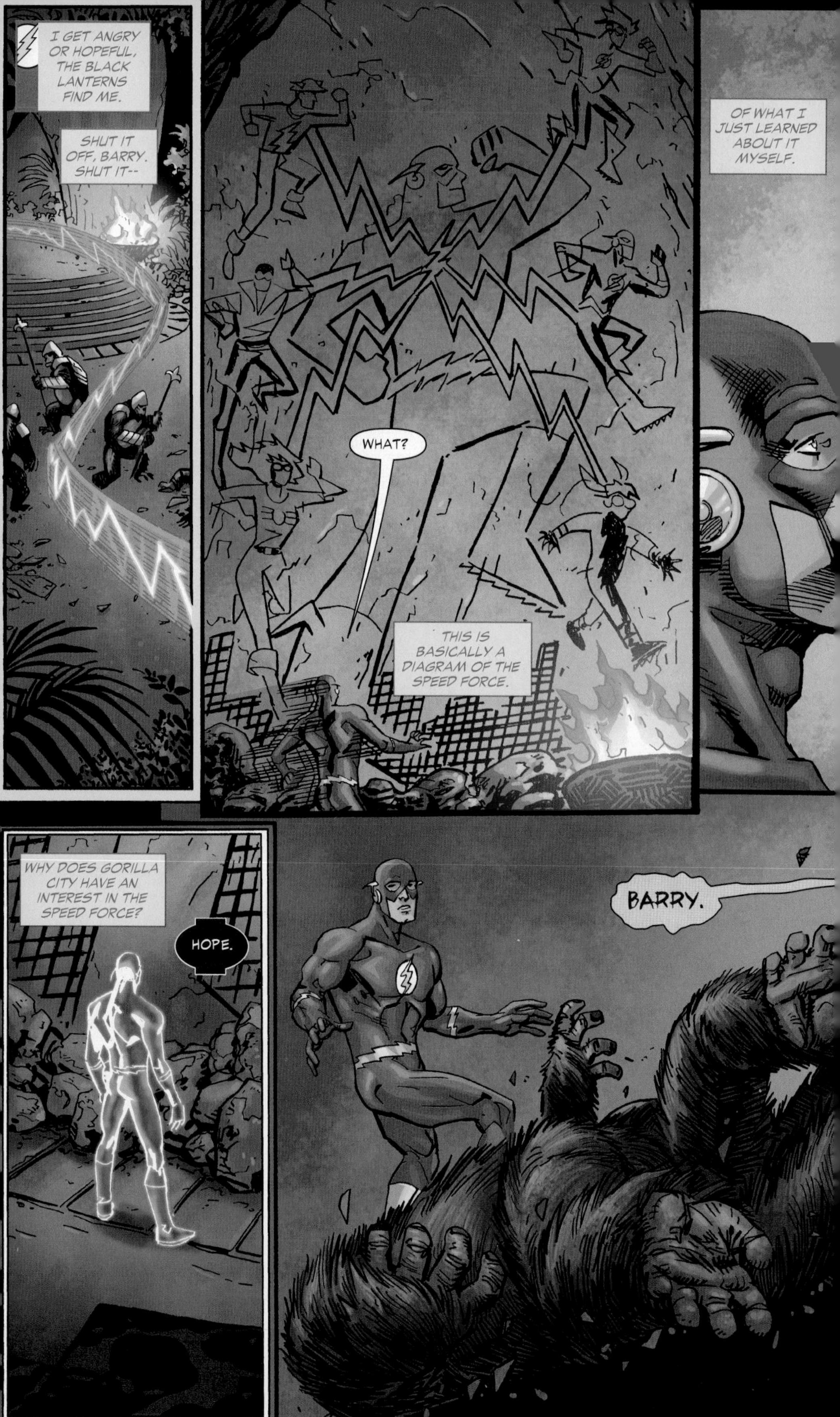
I GET ANGRY OR HOPEFUL, THE BLACK LANTERNS FIND ME.
SHUT IT OFF, BARRY. SHUT IT--
WHAT?
THIS IS BASICALLY A DIAGRAM OF THE SPEED FORCE.
OF WHAT I JUST LEARNED ABOUT IT MYSELF.
WHY DOES GORILLA CITY HAVE AN INTEREST IN THE SPEED FORCE?
HOPE.
BARRY.

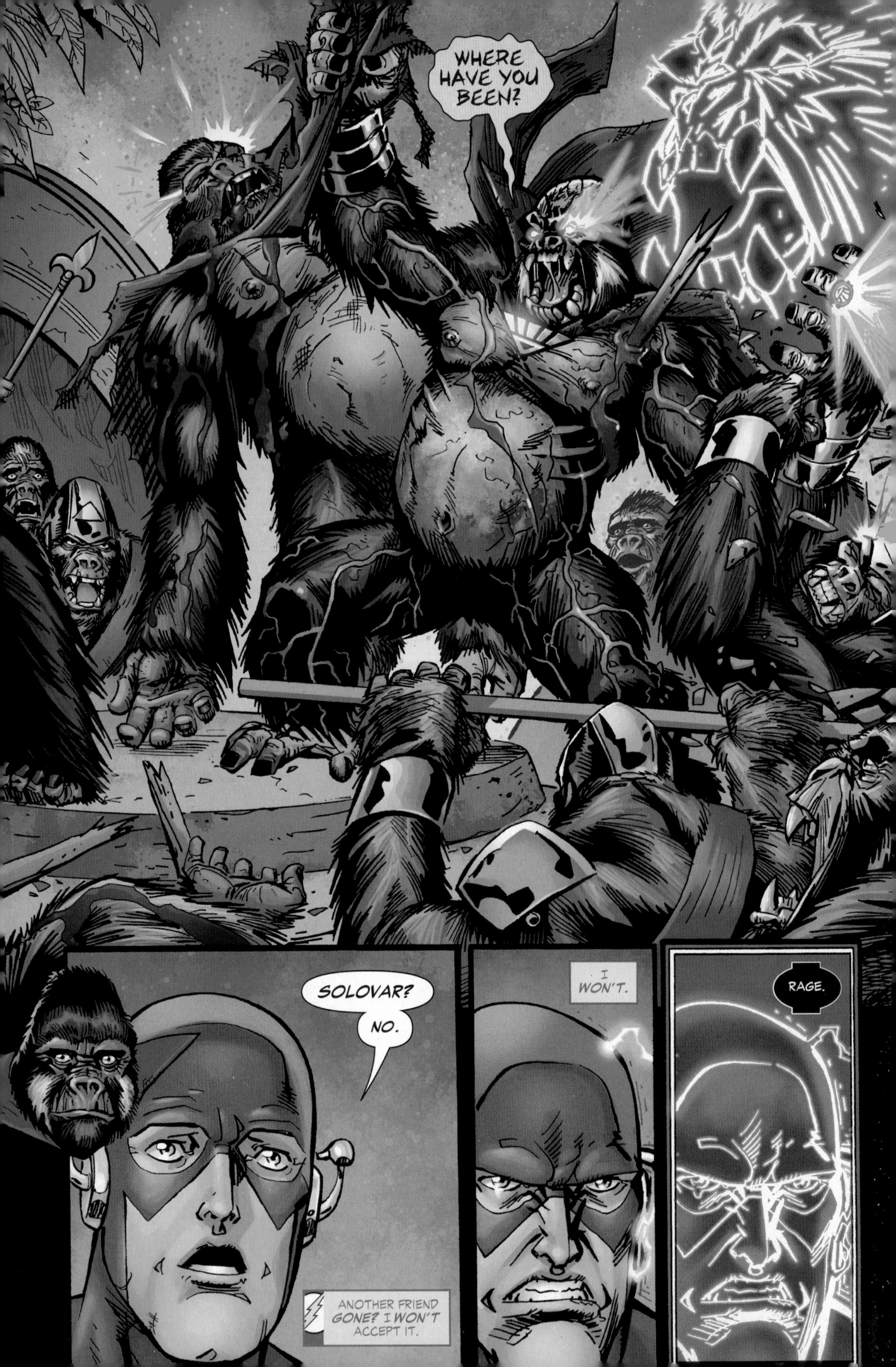
WHERE HAVE YOU BEEN?
SOLOVAR?
NO.
ANOTHER FRIEND GONE? I WON'T ACCEPT IT.
I WON'T.
RAGE.

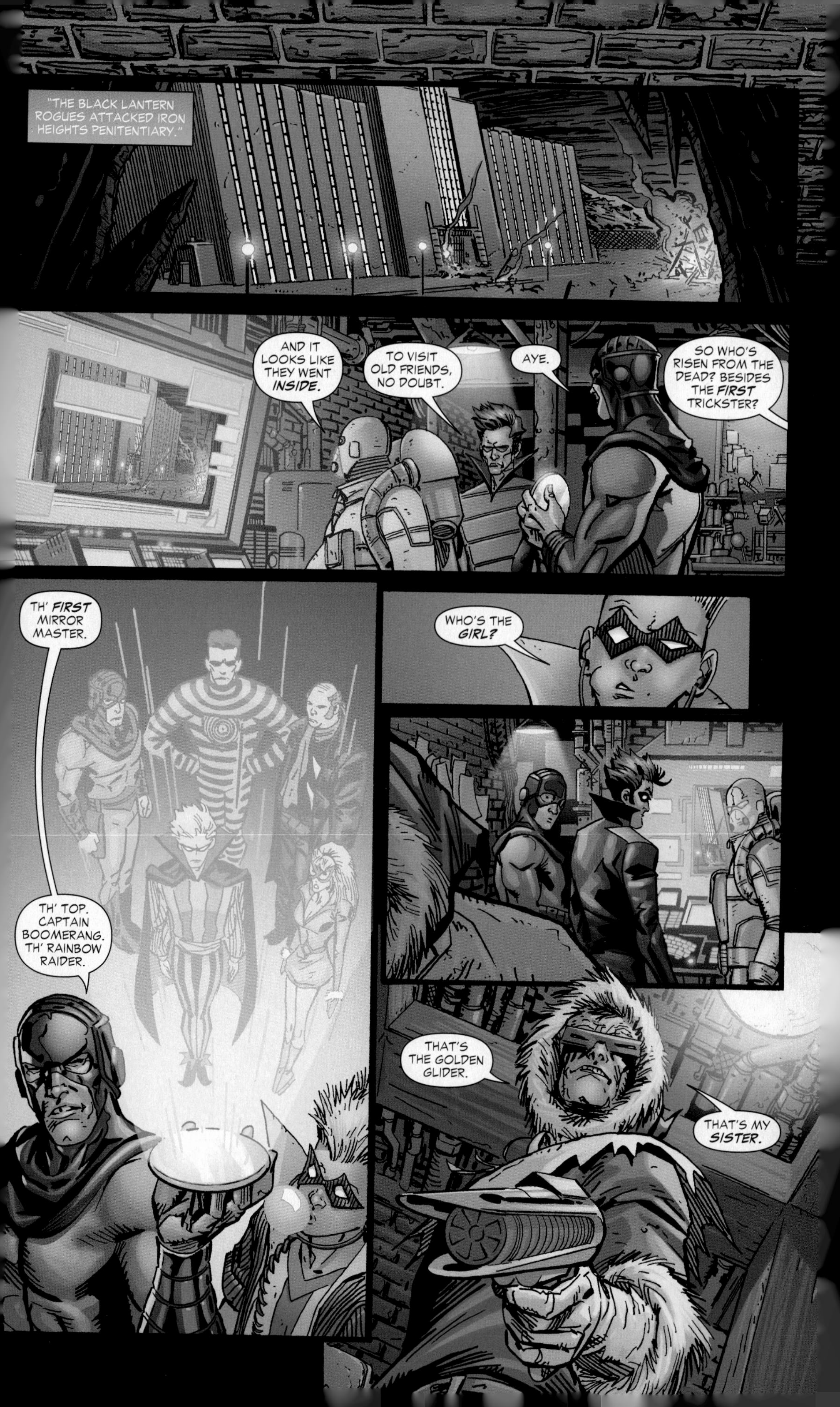
"THE BLACK LANTERN ROGUES ATTACKED IRON HEIGHTS PENITENTIARY."
AND IT LOOKS LIKE THEY WENT INSIDE.
TO VISIT OLD FRIENDS, NO DOUBT.
AYE.
SO WHO'S RISEN FROM THE DEAD? BESIDES THE FIRST TRICKSTER?
TH' FIRST MIRROR MASTER.
TH' TOP. CAPTAIN BOOMERANG. TH' RAINBOW RAIDER.
WHO'S THE GIRL?
THAT'S THE GOLDEN GLIDER.
THAT'S MY SISTER.

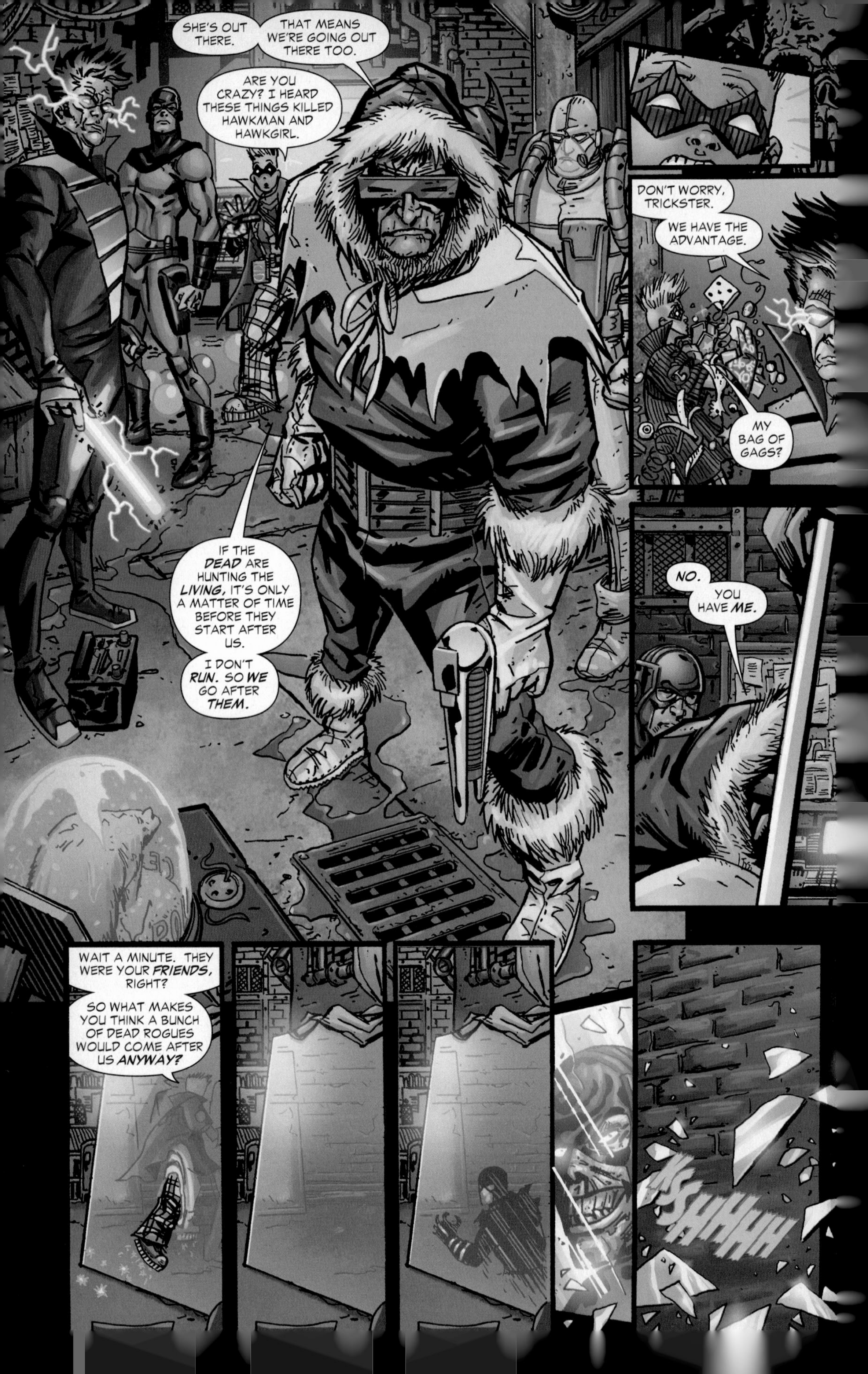
SHE'S OUT THERE.
THAT MEANS WE'RE GOING OUT THERE TOO.
ARE YOU CRAZY? I HEARD THESE THINGS KILLED HAWKMAN AND HAWKGIRL.
IF THE DEAD ARE HUNTING THE LIVING, IT'S ONLY A MATTER OF TIME BEFORE THEY START AFTER US.
I DON'T RUN. SO WE GO AFTER THEM.
DON'T WORRY, TRICKSTER.
WE HAVE THE ADVANTAGE.
MY BAG OF GAGS?
NO.
YOU HAVE ME.
WAIT A MINUTE. THEY WERE YOUR FRIENDS, RIGHT?
SO WHAT MAKES YOU THINK A BUNCH OF DEAD ROGUES WOULD COME AFTER US ANYWAY?
KSSHHHH

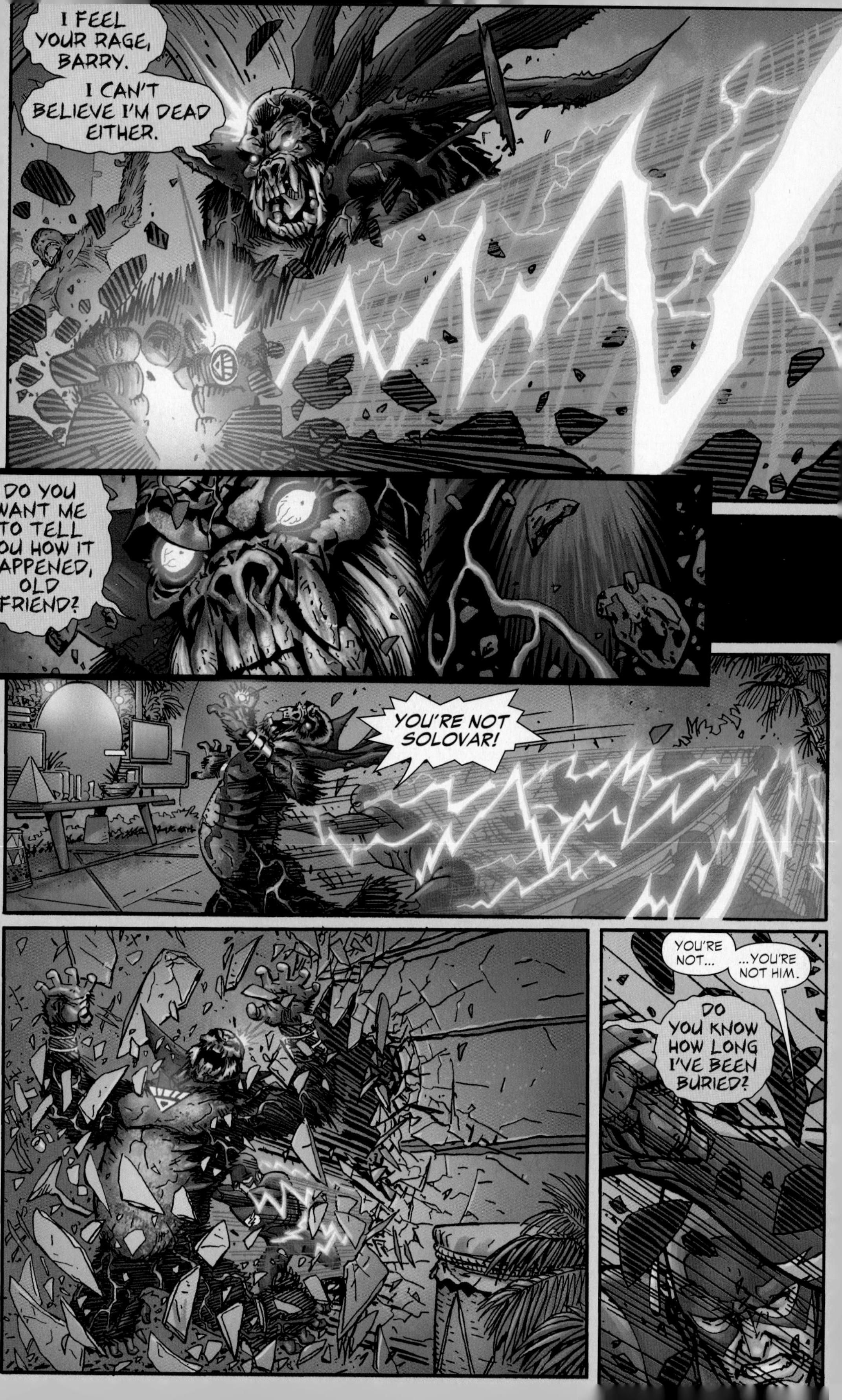
I FEEL YOUR RAGE, BARRY.
I CAN'T BELIEVE I'M DEAD EITHER.
DO YOU WANT ME TO TELL YOU HOW IT HAPPENED, OLD FRIEND?
YOU'RE NOT SOLOVAR!
YOU'RE NOT...
...YOU'RE NOT HIM.
DO YOU KNOW HOW LONG I'VE BEEN BURIED?

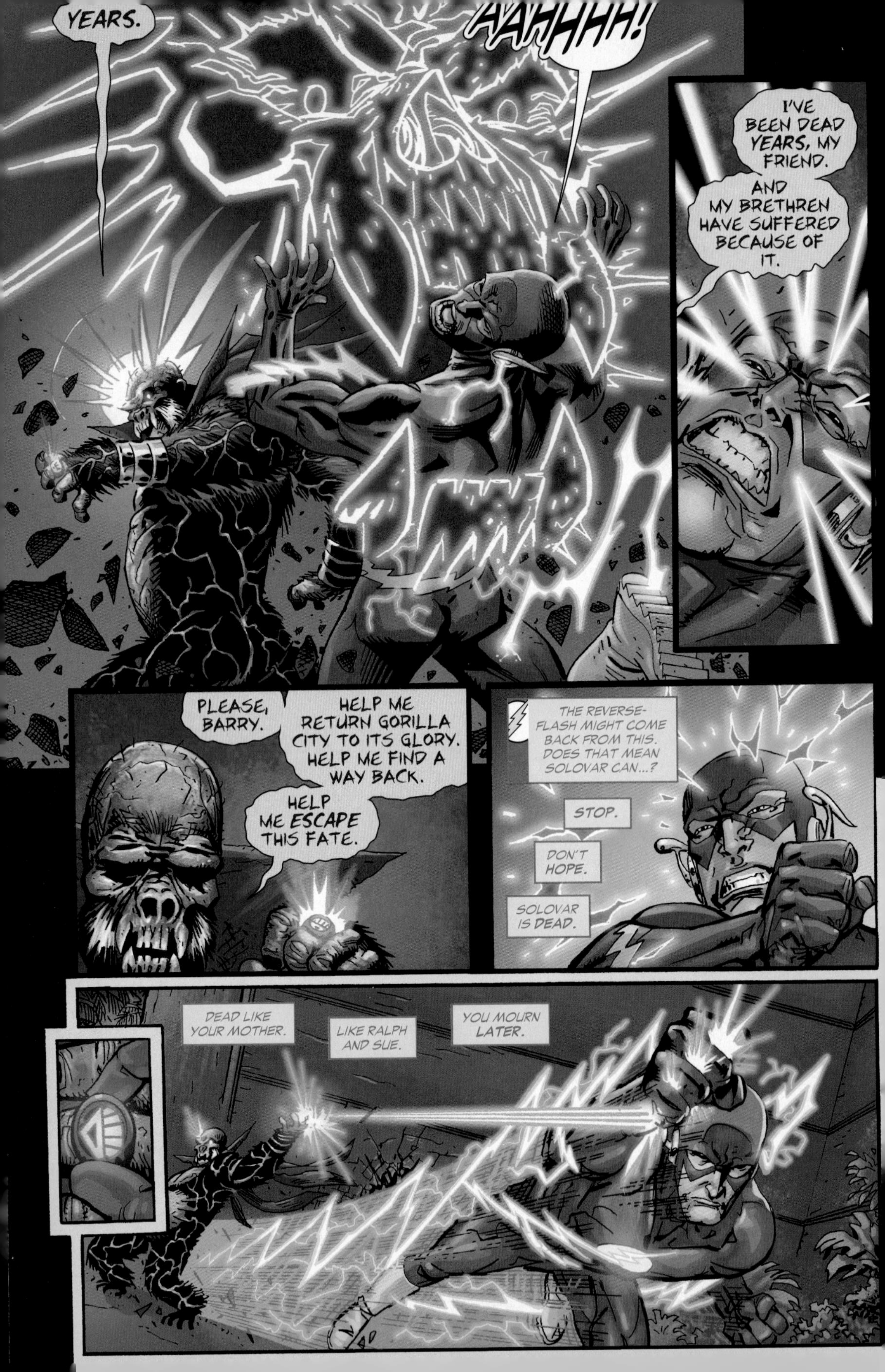
YEARS.
AAHHHH!
I'VE BEEN DEAD YEARS, MY FRIEND.
AND MY BRETHREN HAVE SUFFERED BECAUSE OF IT.
PLEASE, BARRY.
HELP ME RETURN GORILLA CITY TO ITS GLORY. HELP ME FIND A WAY BACK.
HELP ME ESCAPE THIS FATE.
THE REVERSE-FLASH MIGHT COME BACK FROM THIS. DOES THAT MEAN SOLOVAR CAN...?
STOP.
DON'T HOPE.
SOLOVAR IS DEAD.
DEAD LIKE YOUR MOTHER.
LIKE RALPH AND SUE.
YOU MOURN LATER.

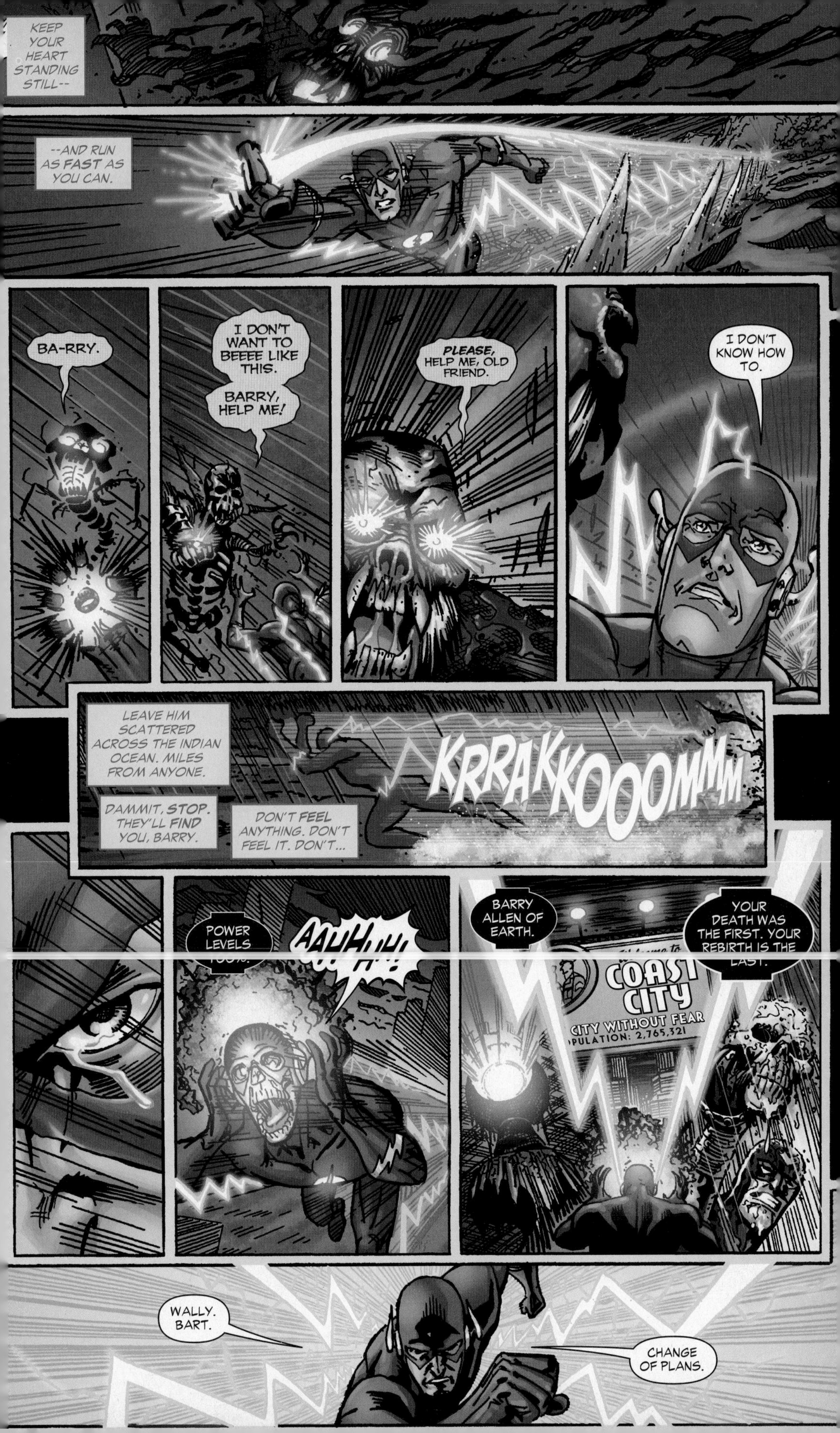
KEEP YOUR HEART STANDING STILL--
--AND RUN AS FAST AS YOU CAN.
BA-RRY.
I DON'T WANT TO BEEEE LIKE THIS.
BARRY, HELP ME!
PLEASE, HELP ME, OLD FRIEND.
I DON'T KNOW HOW TO.
LEAVE HIM SCATTERED ACROSS THE INDIAN OCEAN. MILES FROM ANYONE.
DAMMIT, STOP. THEY'LL FIND YOU, BARRY.
DON'T FEEL ANYTHING. DON'T FEEL IT. DON'T...
KRRAKKOOOMMM
POWER LEVELS
BARRY ALLEN OF EARTH.
YOUR DEATH WAS THE FIRST. YOUR REBIRTH IS THE LAST.
COAST CITY
CITY WITHOUT FEAR
WALLY. BART.
CHANGE OF PLANS.

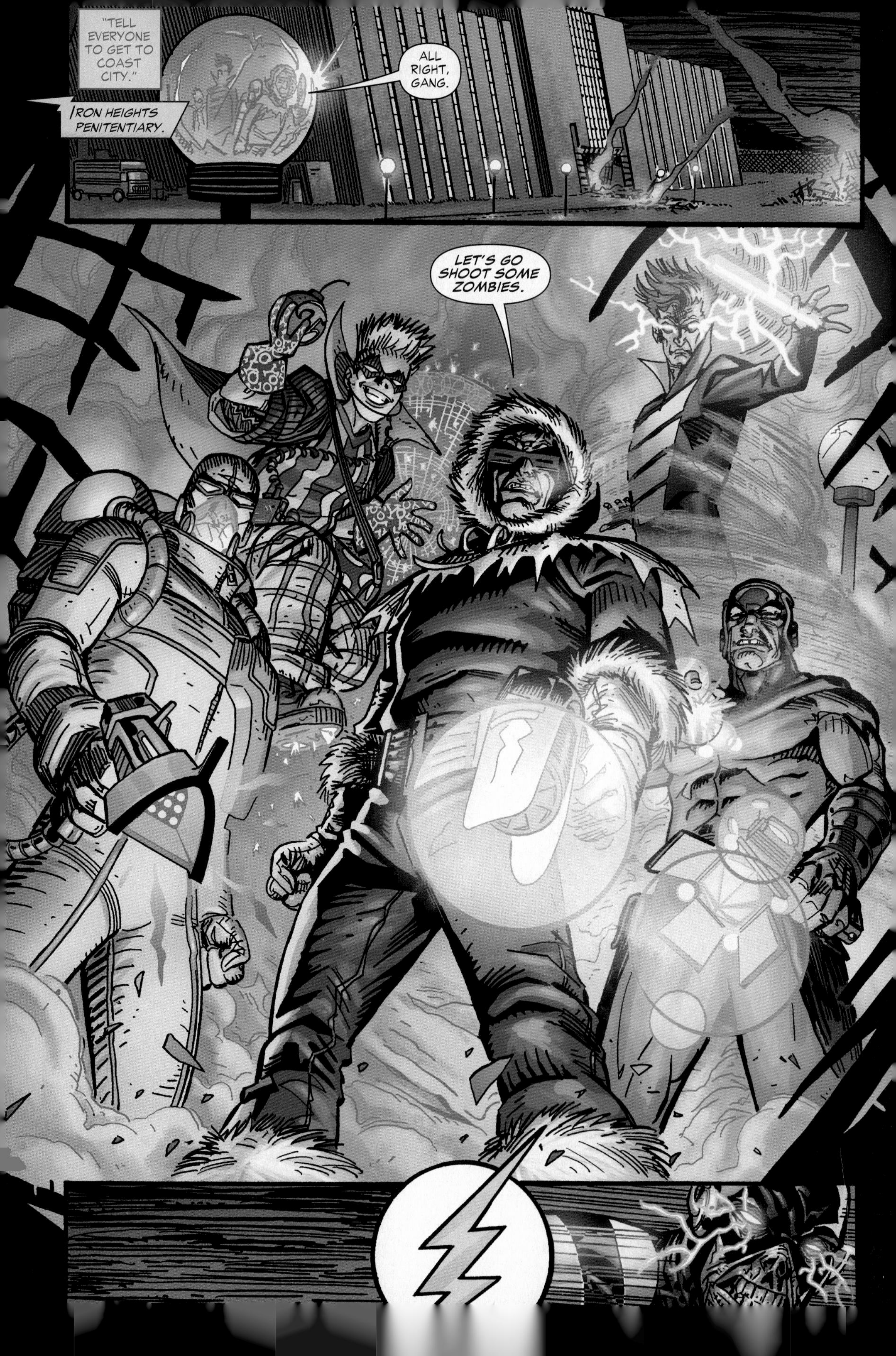

"TELL EVERYONE TO GET TO COAST CITY."
IRON HEIGHTS PENITENTIARY.
ALL RIGHT, GANG.
LET'S GO SHOOT SOME ZOMBIES.

BLACKEST NIGHT: THE FLASH 2
Cover by Scott Kolins with Mike Atiyeh

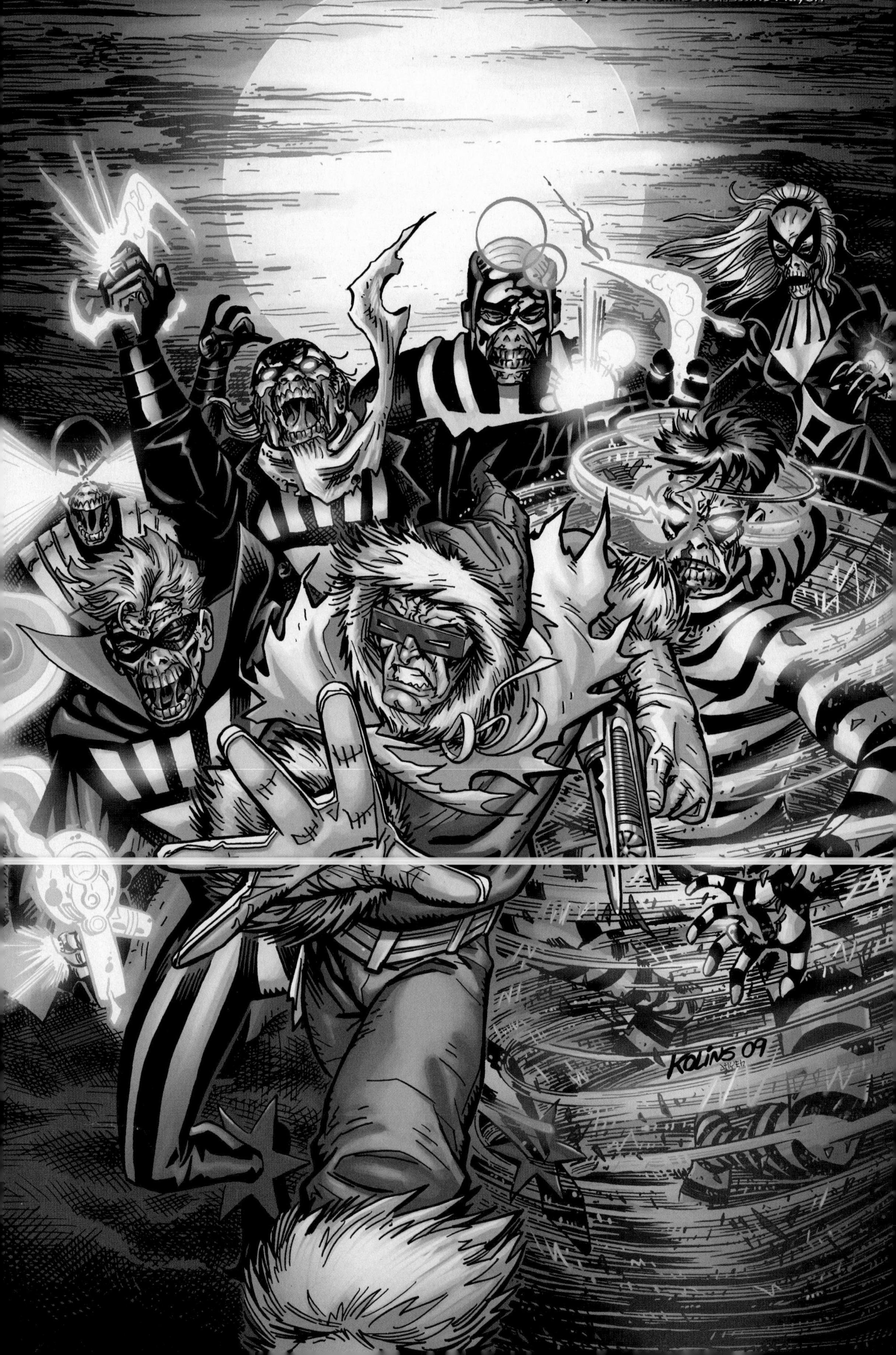
KOLINS 09

BLACKEST NIGHT: THE FLASH
CHAPTER TWO

GEOFF JOHNS
WRITER

SCOTT KOLINS
ARTIST

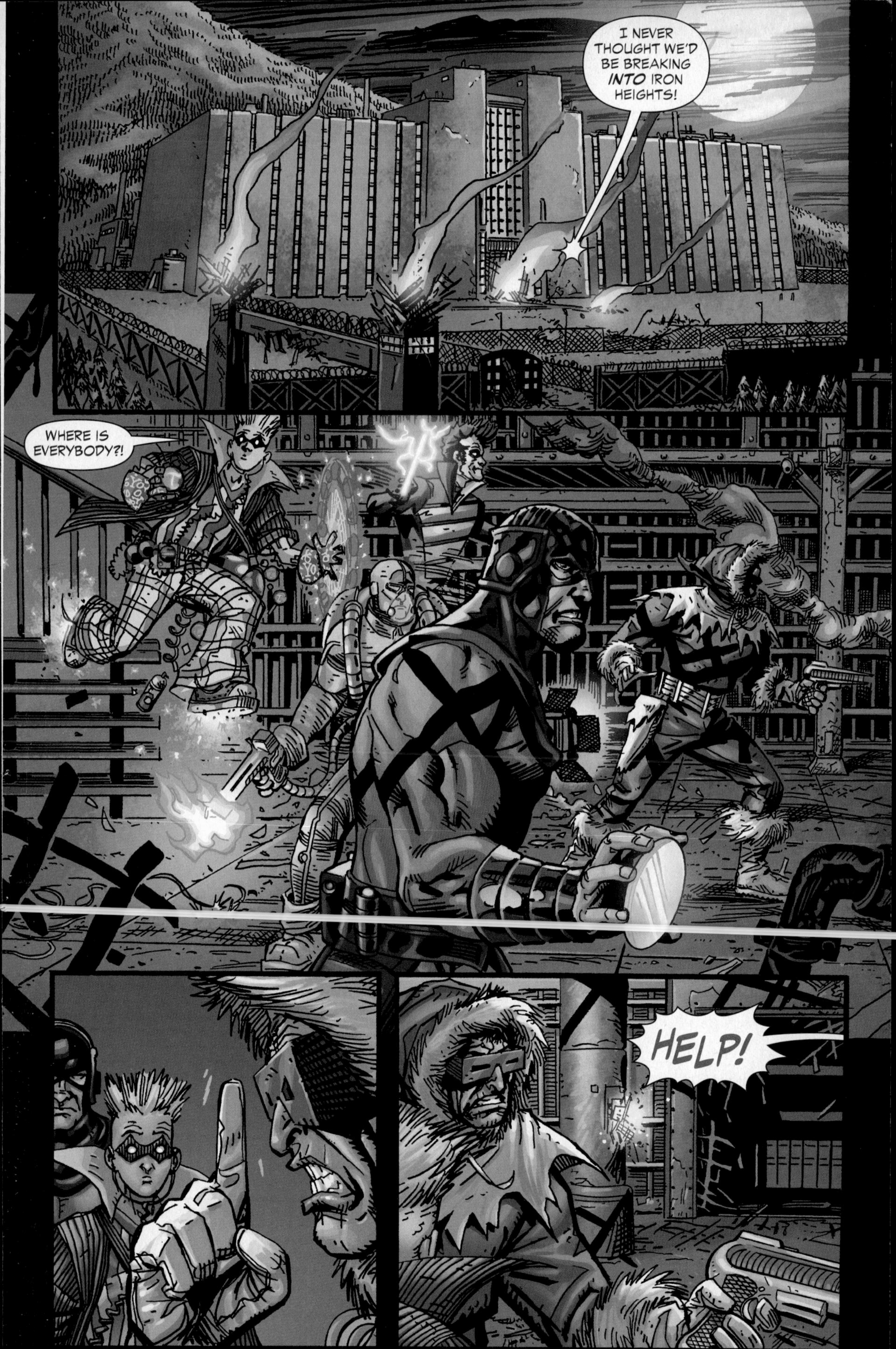

I NEVER THOUGHT WE'D BE BREAKING *INTO* IRON HEIGHTS!
WHERE IS EVERYBODY?!
HELP!

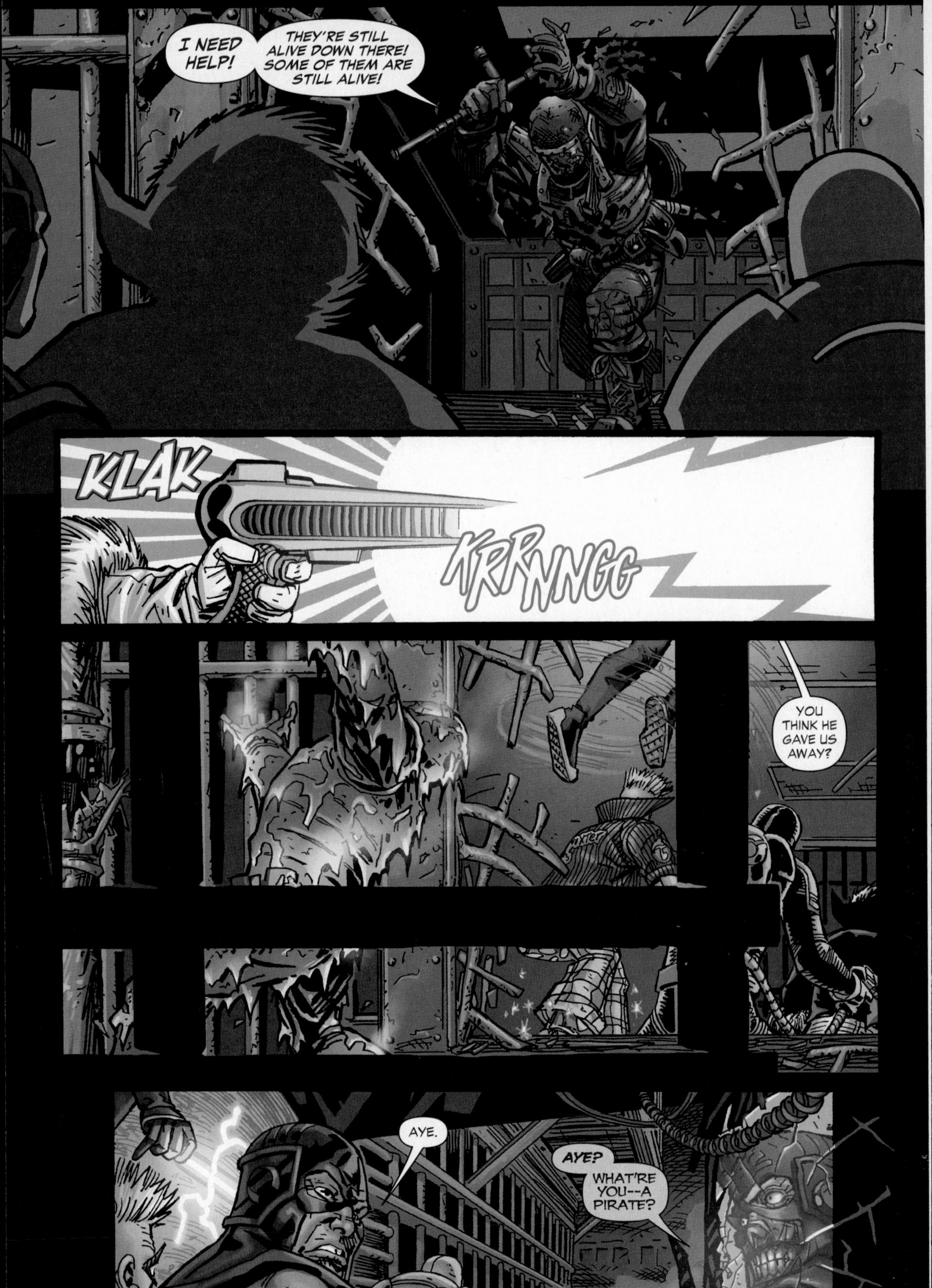
I NEED HELP!
THEY'RE STILL ALIVE DOWN THERE! SOME OF THEM ARE STILL ALIVE!
KLAK
KRRNNGG
YOU THINK HE GAVE US AWAY?
AYE.
AYE? WHAT'RE YOU--A PIRATE?

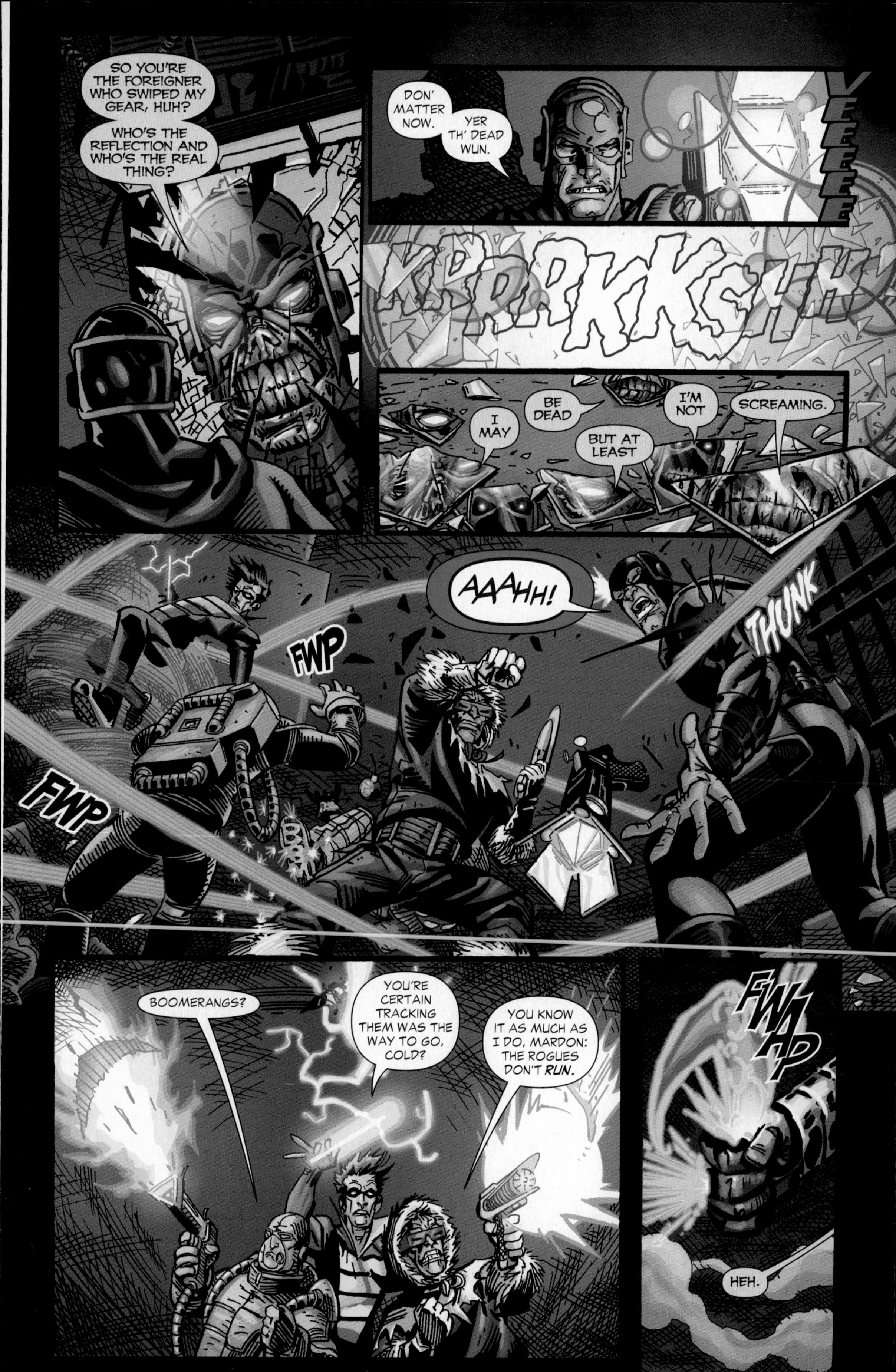
SO YOU'RE THE FOREIGNER WHO SWIPED MY GEAR, HUH?
WHO'S THE REFLECTION AND WHO'S THE REAL THING?
DON' MATTER NOW.
YER TH' DEAD WUN.
VEEEEEE
KRRRKKSHH
I MAY
BE DEAD
BUT AT LEAST
I'M NOT
SCREAMING.
AAAHH!
THUNK
FWP
FWP
BOOMERANGS?
YOU'RE CERTAIN TRACKING THEM WAS THE WAY TO GO, COLD?
YOU KNOW IT AS MUCH AS I DO, MARDON: THE ROGUES DON'T RUN.
FWAP
HEH.

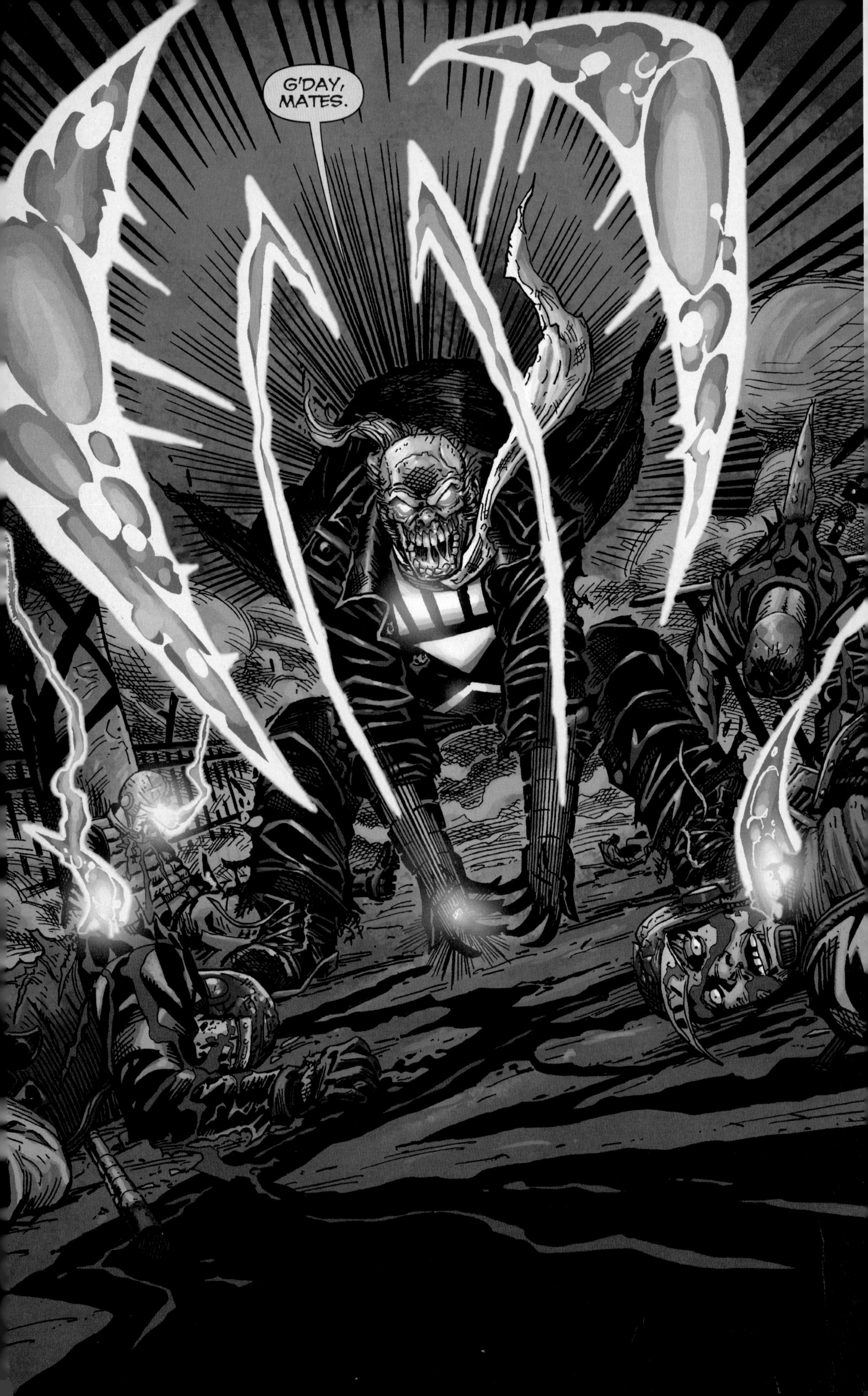
G'DAY, MATES.

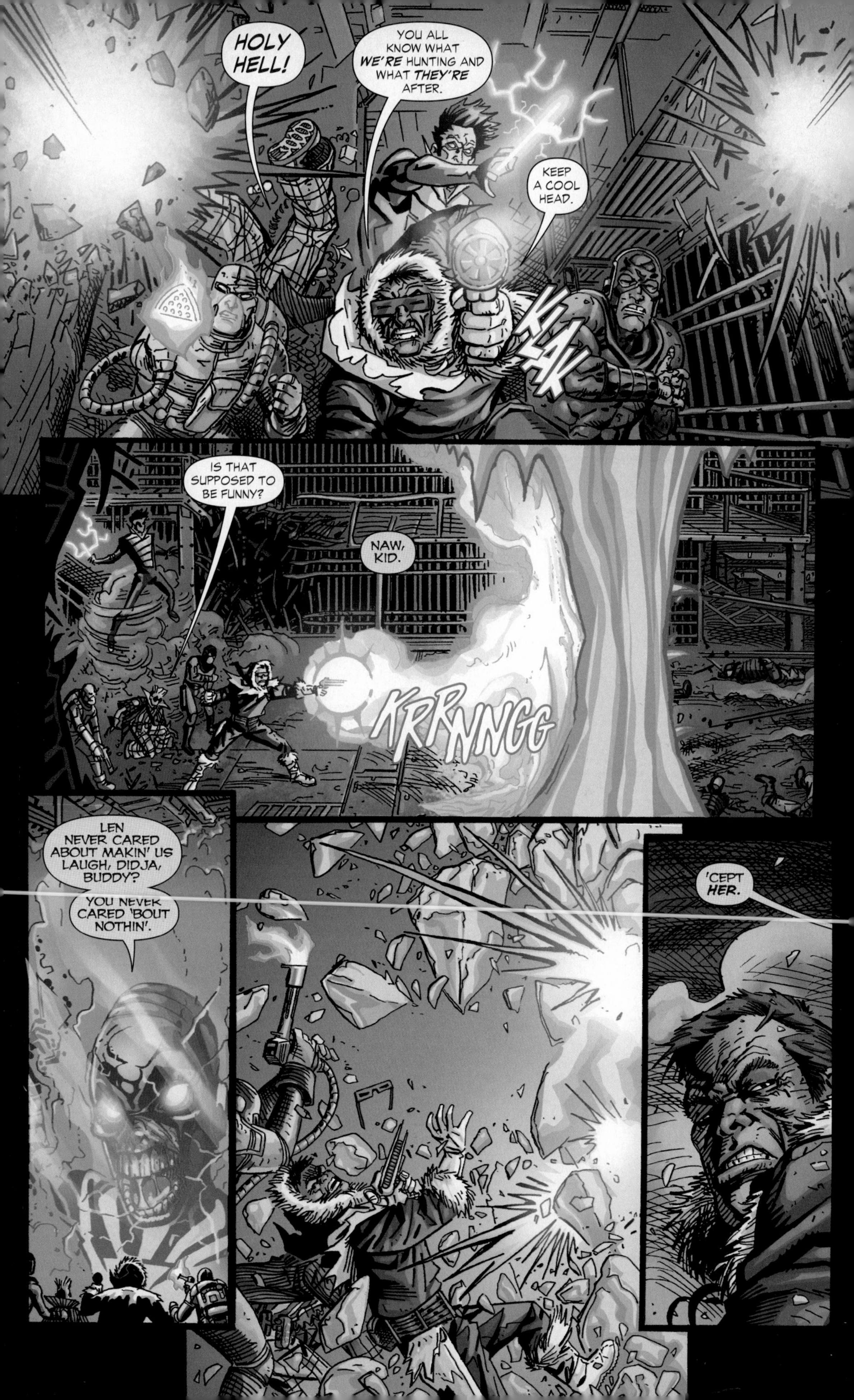
HOLY HELL!
YOU ALL KNOW WHAT WE'RE HUNTING AND WHAT THEY'RE AFTER.
KEEP A COOL HEAD.
KLAK
IS THAT SUPPOSED TO BE FUNNY?
NAW, KID.
KRRNNGG
LEN NEVER CARED ABOUT MAKIN' US LAUGH, DIDJA, BUDDY?
YOU NEVER CARED 'BOUT NOTHIN'.
'CEPT HER.

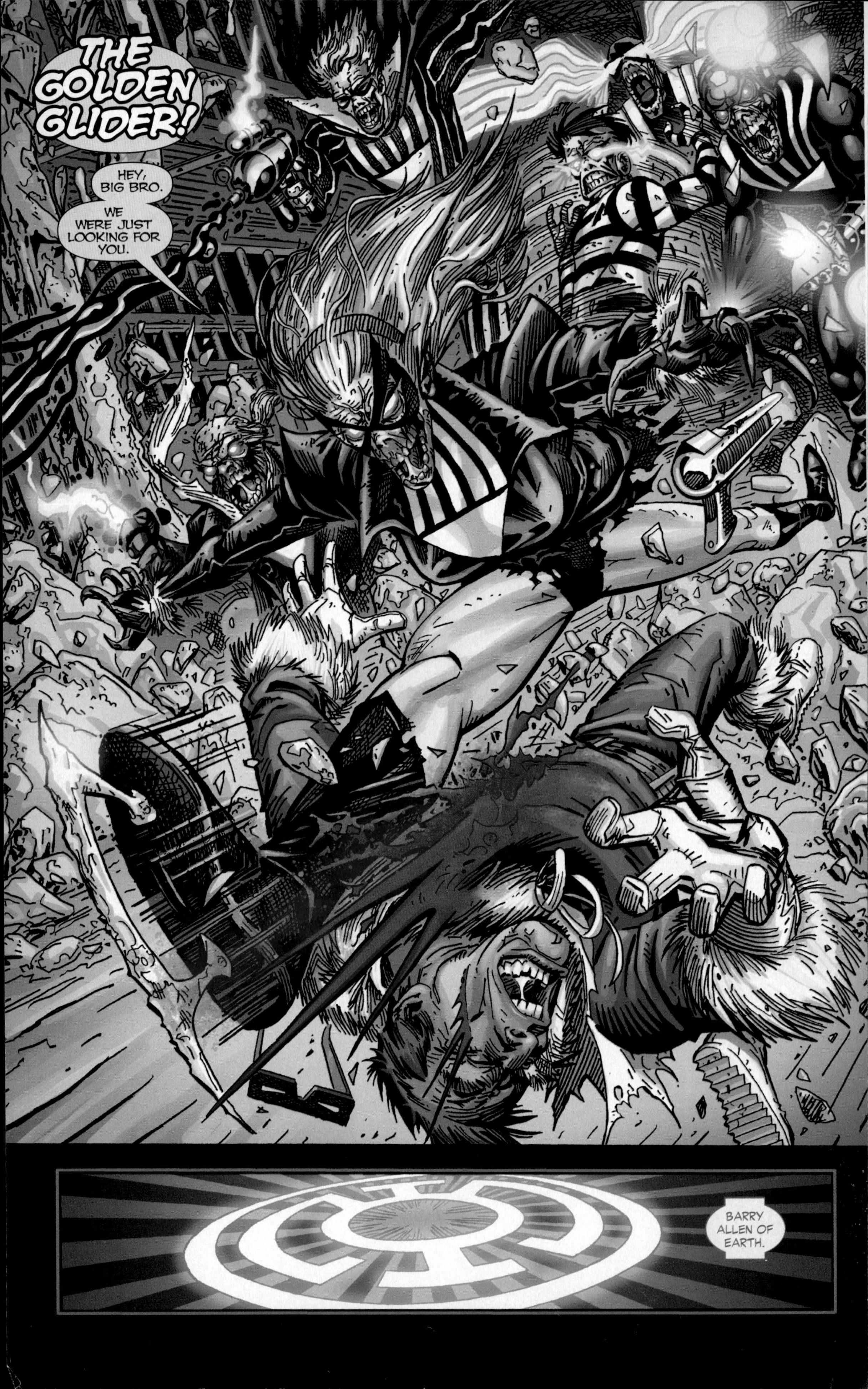
THE GOLDEN GLIDER!
HEY, BIG BRO.
WE WERE JUST LOOKING FOR YOU.
BARRY ALLEN OF EARTH.

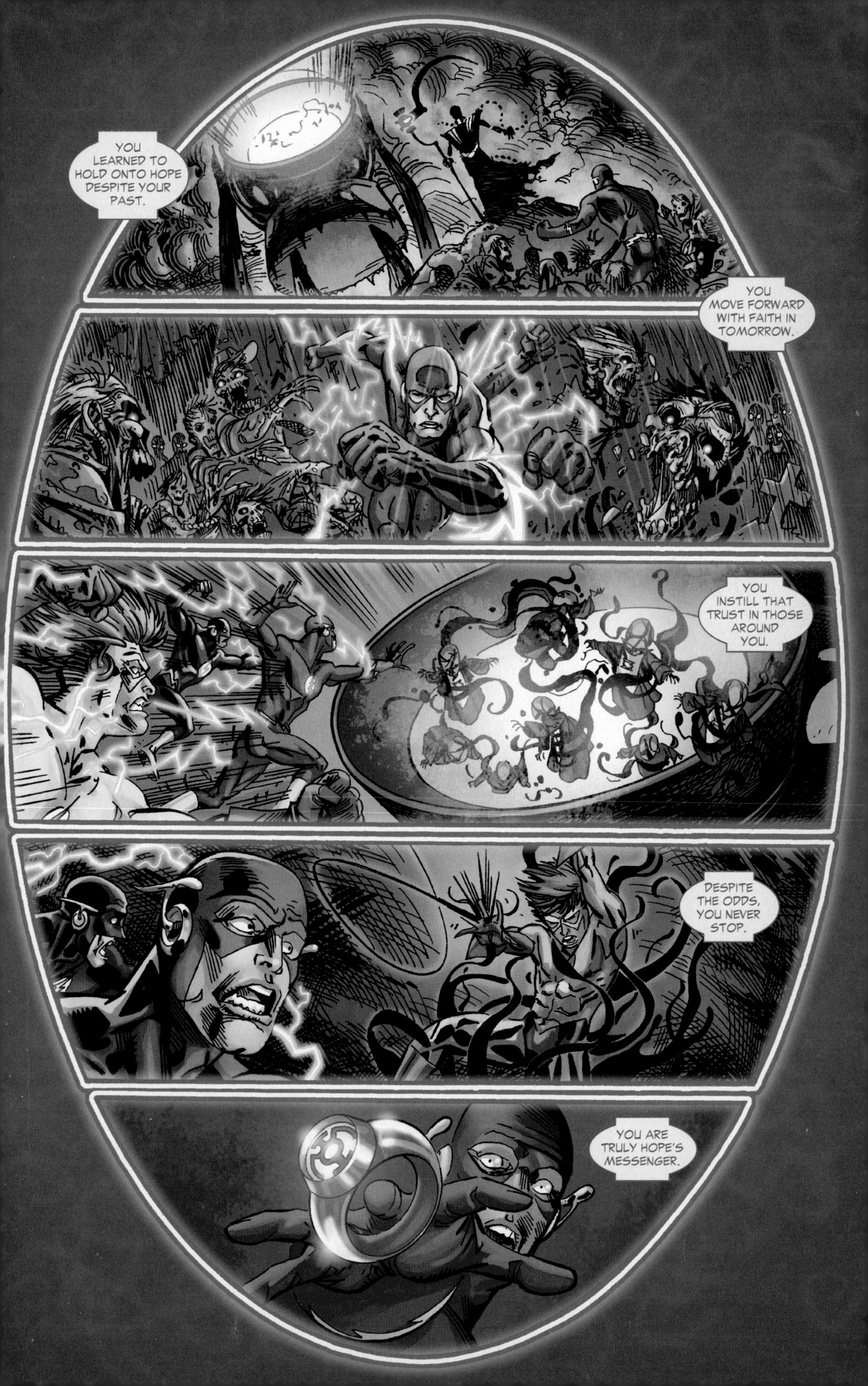
YOU LEARNED TO HOLD ONTO HOPE DESPITE YOUR PAST.
YOU MOVE FORWARD WITH FAITH IN TOMORROW.
YOU INSTILL THAT TRUST IN THOSE AROUND YOU.
DESPITE THE ODDS, YOU NEVER STOP.
YOU ARE TRULY HOPE'S MESSENGER.

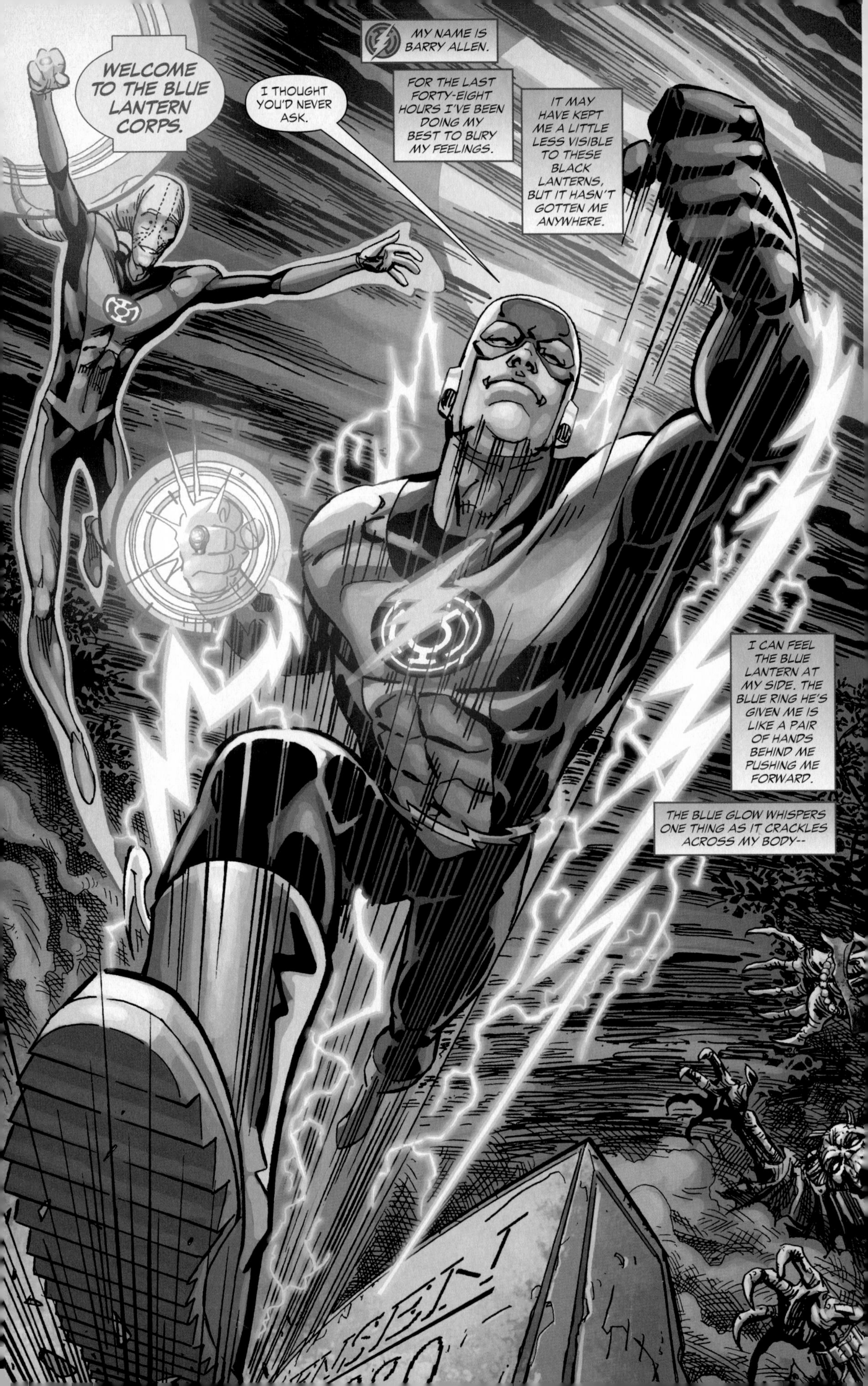
MY NAME IS BARRY ALLEN.
FOR THE LAST FORTY-EIGHT HOURS I'VE BEEN DOING MY BEST TO BURY MY FEELINGS.
IT MAY HAVE KEPT ME A LITTLE LESS VISIBLE TO THESE BLACK LANTERNS, BUT IT HASN'T GOTTEN ME ANYWHERE.
WELCOME TO THE BLUE LANTERN CORPS.
I THOUGHT YOU'D NEVER ASK.
I CAN FEEL THE BLUE LANTERN AT MY SIDE. THE BLUE RING HE'S GIVEN ME IS LIKE A PAIR OF HANDS BEHIND ME PUSHING ME FORWARD.
THE BLUE GLOW WHISPERS ONE THING AS IT CRACKLES ACROSS MY BODY--

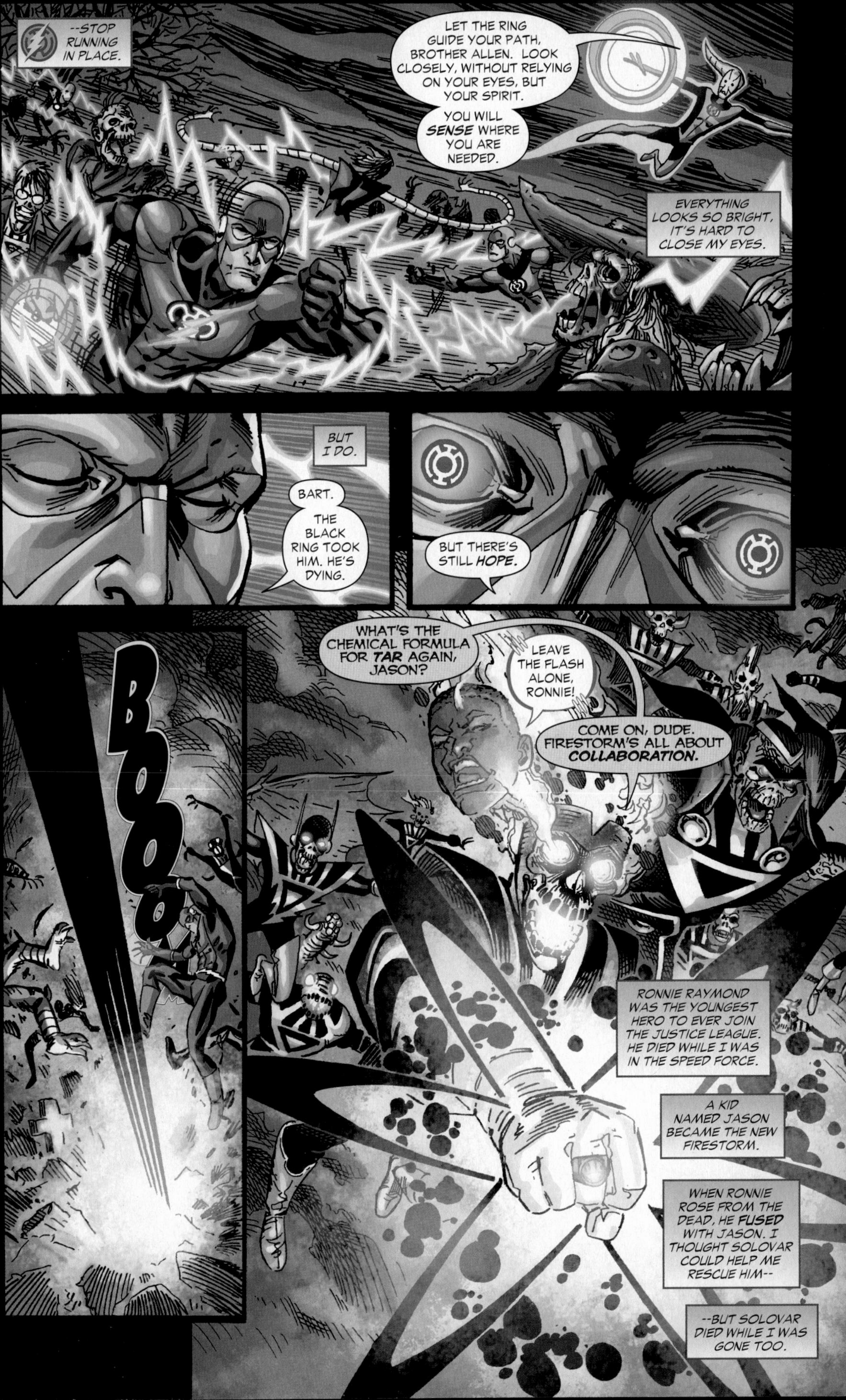
--STOP RUNNING IN PLACE.
LET THE RING GUIDE YOUR PATH, BROTHER ALLEN. LOOK CLOSELY, WITHOUT RELYING ON YOUR EYES, BUT YOUR SPIRIT.
YOU WILL SENSE WHERE YOU ARE NEEDED.
EVERYTHING LOOKS SO BRIGHT, IT'S HARD TO CLOSE MY EYES.
BUT I DO.
BART.
THE BLACK RING TOOK HIM. HE'S DYING.
BUT THERE'S STILL HOPE.
BOOOM
WHAT'S THE CHEMICAL FORMULA FOR TAR AGAIN, JASON?
LEAVE THE FLASH ALONE, RONNIE!
COME ON, DUDE. FIRESTORM'S ALL ABOUT COLLABORATION.
RONNIE RAYMOND WAS THE YOUNGEST HERO TO EVER JOIN THE JUSTICE LEAGUE. HE DIED WHILE I WAS IN THE SPEED FORCE.
A KID NAMED JASON BECAME THE NEW FIRESTORM.
WHEN RONNIE ROSE FROM THE DEAD, HE FUSED WITH JASON. I THOUGHT SOLOVAR COULD HELP ME RESCUE HIM--
--BUT SOLOVAR DIED WHILE I WAS GONE TOO.

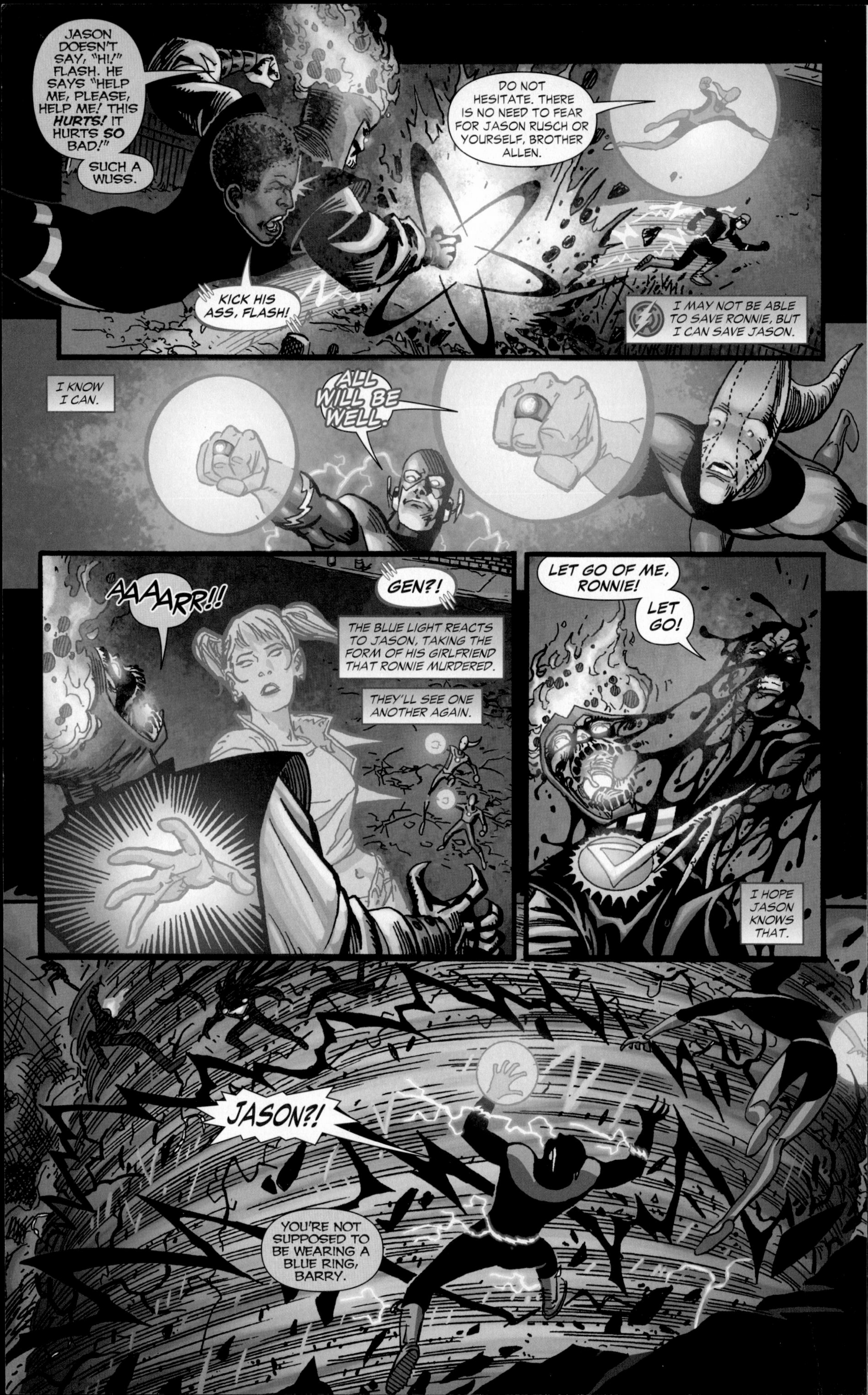

JASON DOESN'T SAY, "HI!" FLASH. HE SAYS "HELP ME, PLEASE, HELP ME! THIS HURTS! IT HURTS SO BAD!"
SUCH A WUSS.
DO NOT HESITATE. THERE IS NO NEED TO FEAR FOR JASON RUSCH OR YOURSELF, BROTHER ALLEN.
KICK HIS ASS, FLASH!
I MAY NOT BE ABLE TO SAVE RONNIE, BUT I CAN SAVE JASON.
I KNOW I CAN.
ALL WILL BE WELL.
AAAARR!!
GEN?!
THE BLUE LIGHT REACTS TO JASON, TAKING THE FORM OF HIS GIRLFRIEND THAT RONNIE MURDERED.
THEY'LL SEE ONE ANOTHER AGAIN.
LET GO OF ME, RONNIE!
LET GO!
I HOPE JASON KNOWS THAT.
JASON?!
YOU'RE NOT SUPPOSED TO BE WEARING A BLUE RING, BARRY.

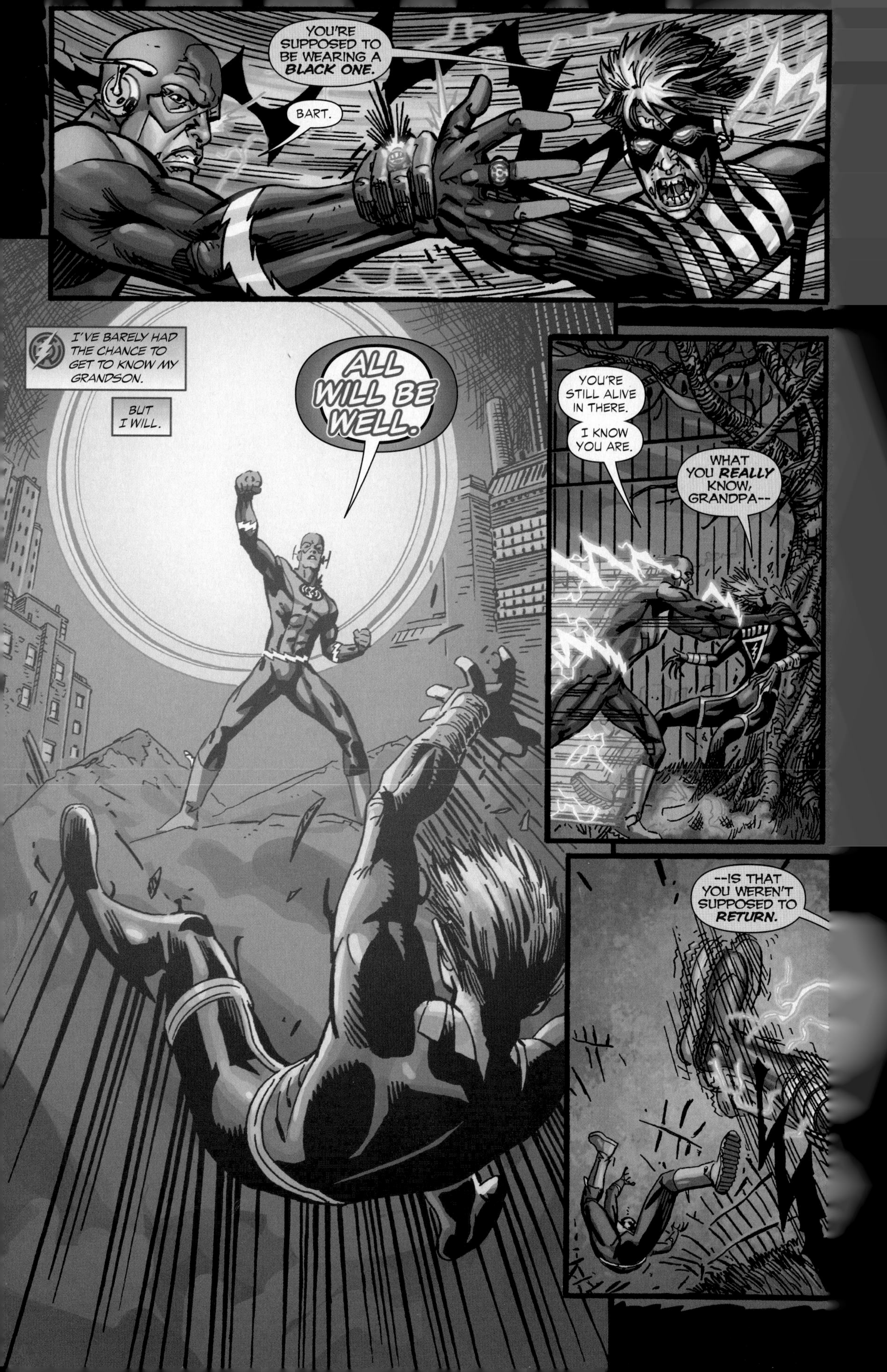
YOU'RE SUPPOSED TO BE WEARING A BLACK ONE.
BART.
I'VE BARELY HAD THE CHANCE TO GET TO KNOW MY GRANDSON.
BUT I WILL.
ALL WILL BE WELL.
YOU'RE STILL ALIVE IN THERE.
I KNOW YOU ARE.
WHAT YOU REALLY KNOW, GRANDPA--
--IS THAT YOU WEREN'T SUPPOSED TO RETURN.

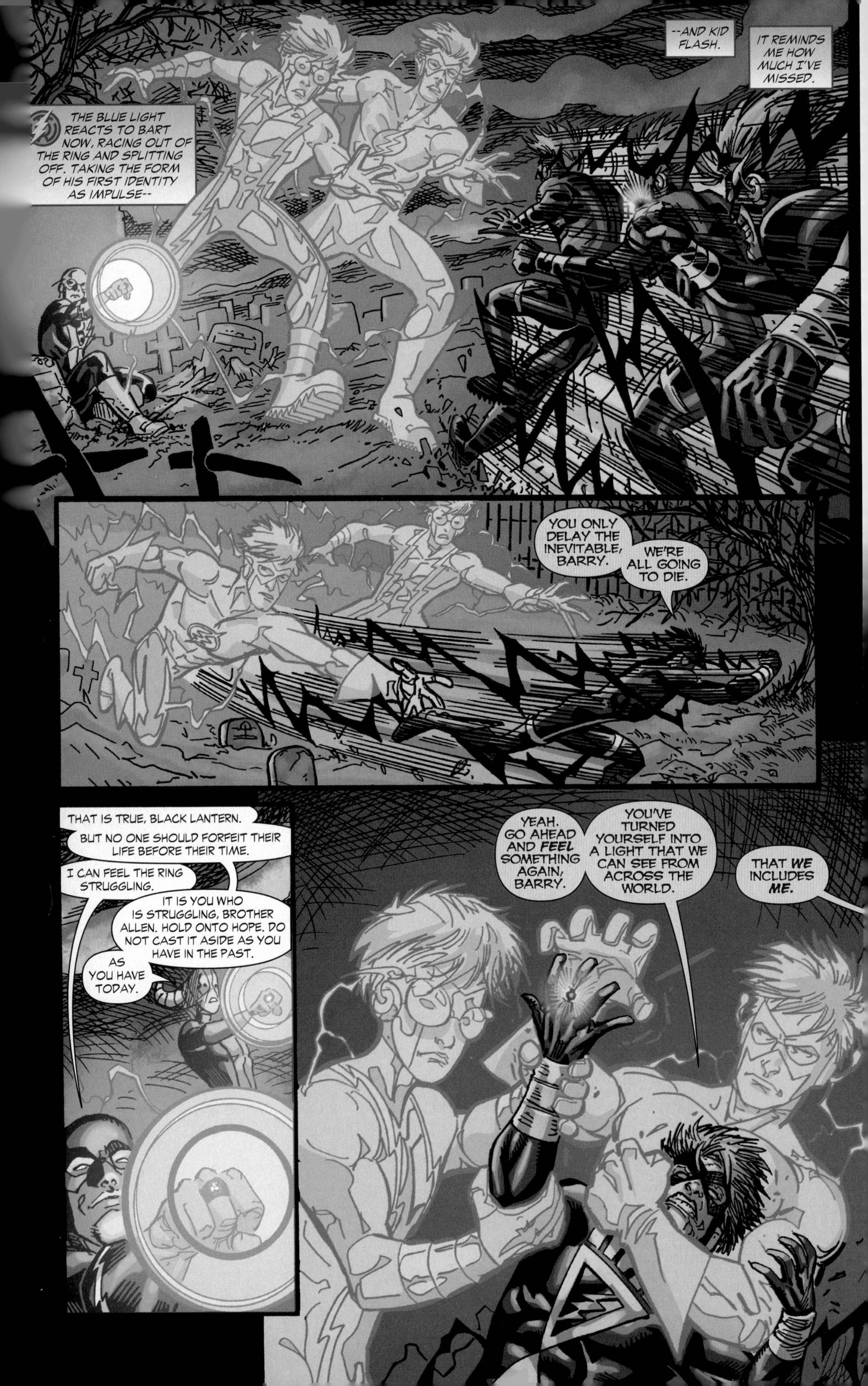
THE BLUE LIGHT REACTS TO BART NOW, RACING OUT OF THE RING AND SPLITTING OFF. TAKING THE FORM OF HIS FIRST IDENTITY AS IMPULSE--
--AND KID FLASH.
IT REMINDS ME HOW MUCH I'VE MISSED.
YOU ONLY DELAY THE INEVITABLE, BARRY.
WE'RE ALL GOING TO DIE.
THAT IS TRUE, BLACK LANTERN.
BUT NO ONE SHOULD FORFEIT THEIR LIFE BEFORE THEIR TIME.
I CAN FEEL THE RING STRUGGLING.
IT IS YOU WHO IS STRUGGLING, BROTHER ALLEN. HOLD ONTO HOPE. DO NOT CAST IT ASIDE AS YOU HAVE IN THE PAST.
AS YOU HAVE TODAY.
YEAH. GO AHEAD AND FEEL SOMETHING AGAIN, BARRY.
YOU'VE TURNED YOURSELF INTO A LIGHT THAT WE CAN SEE FROM ACROSS THE WORLD.
THAT WE INCLUDES ME.

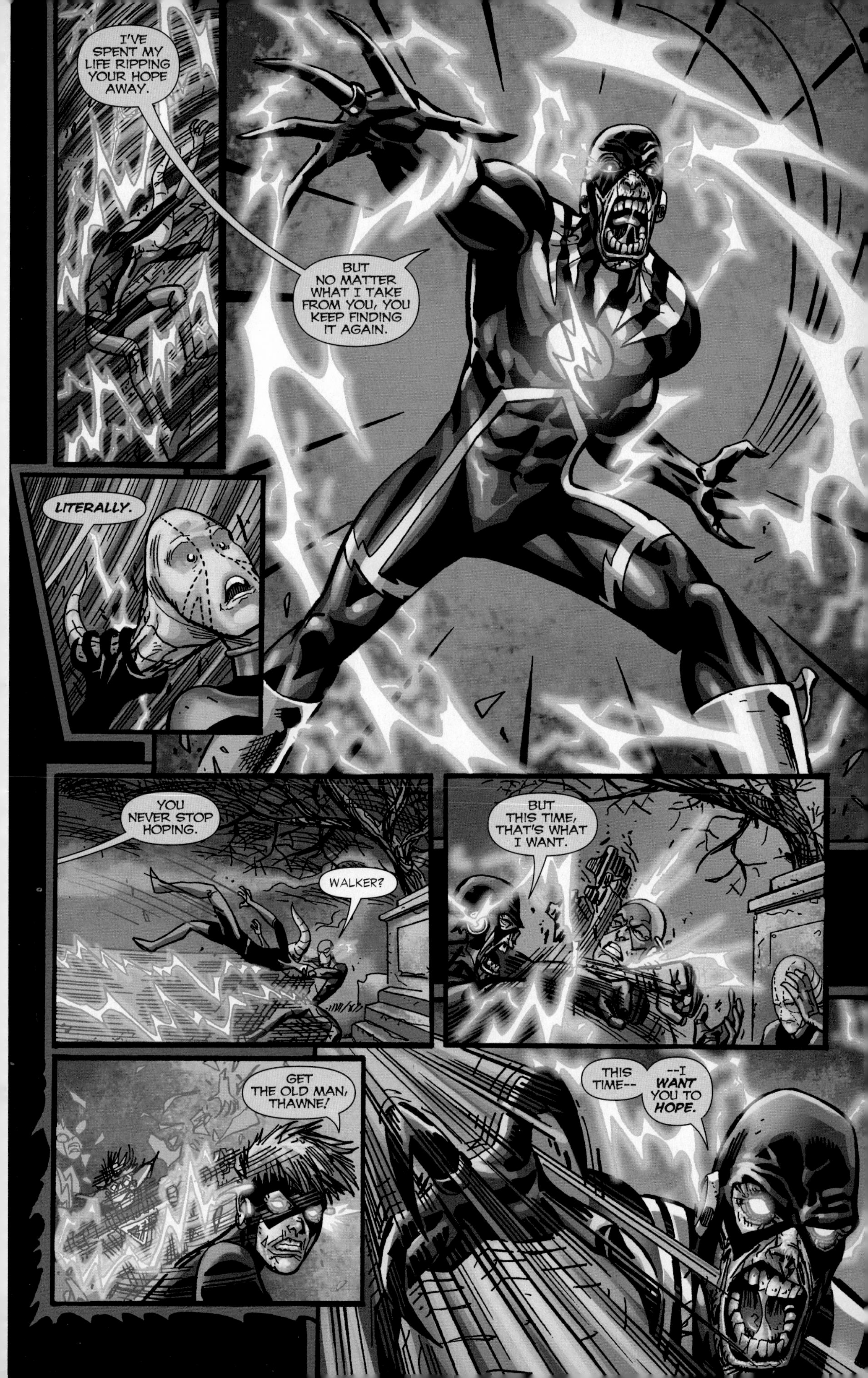
I'VE SPENT MY LIFE RIPPING YOUR HOPE AWAY.
BUT NO MATTER WHAT I TAKE FROM YOU, YOU KEEP FINDING IT AGAIN.
LITERALLY.
YOU NEVER STOP HOPING.
WALKER?
BUT THIS TIME, THAT'S WHAT I WANT.
GET THE OLD MAN, THAWNE!
THIS TIME--
--I WANT YOU TO HOPE.

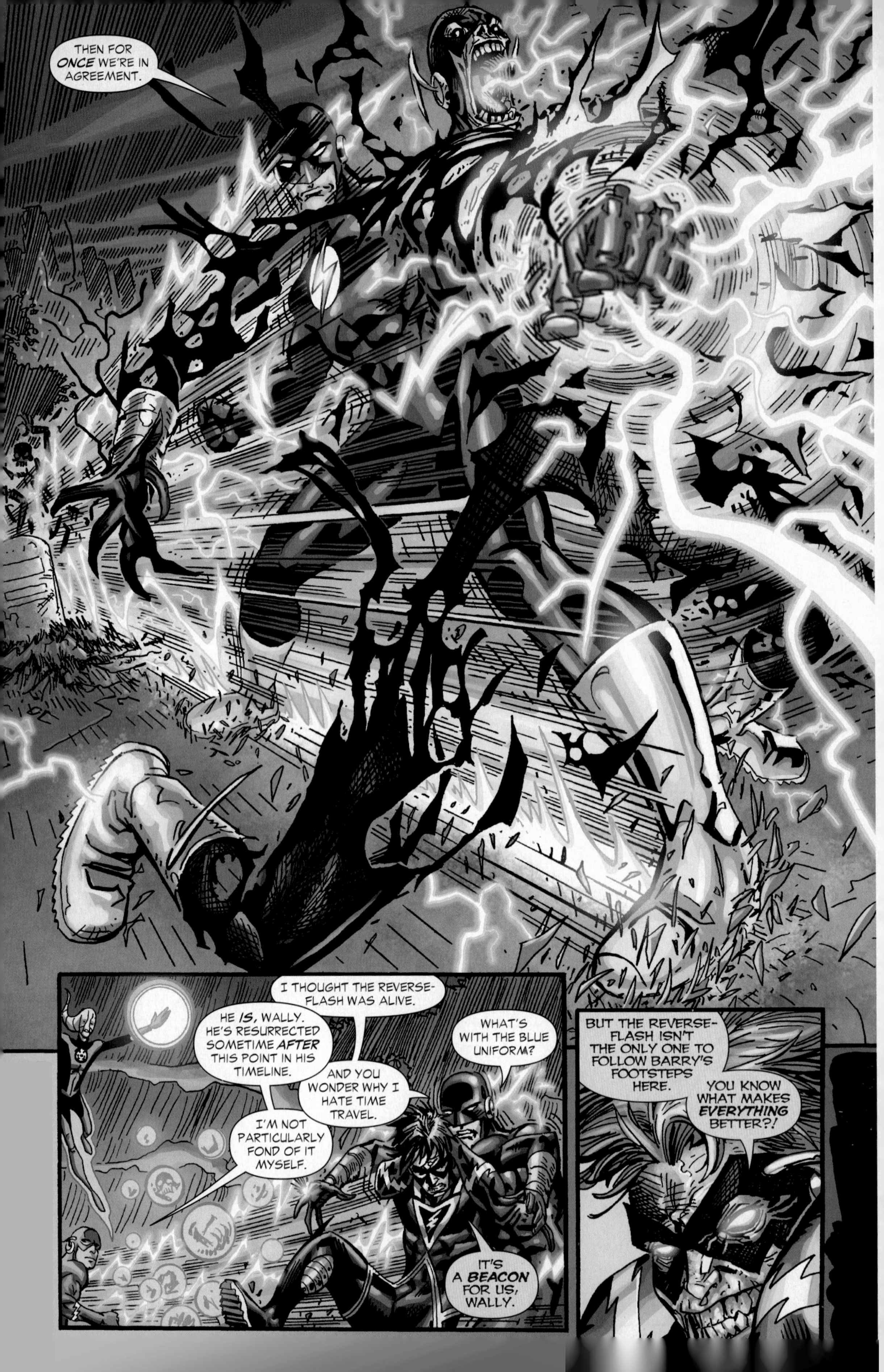
THEN FOR ONCE WE'RE IN AGREEMENT.
I THOUGHT THE REVERSE-FLASH WAS ALIVE.
HE IS, WALLY. HE'S RESURRECTED SOMETIME AFTER THIS POINT IN HIS TIMELINE.
AND YOU WONDER WHY I HATE TIME TRAVEL.
I'M NOT PARTICULARLY FOND OF IT MYSELF.
WHAT'S WITH THE BLUE UNIFORM?
IT'S A BEACON FOR US, WALLY.
BUT THE REVERSE-FLASH ISN'T THE ONLY ONE TO FOLLOW BARRY'S FOOTSTEPS HERE.
YOU KNOW WHAT MAKES EVERYTHING BETTER?!

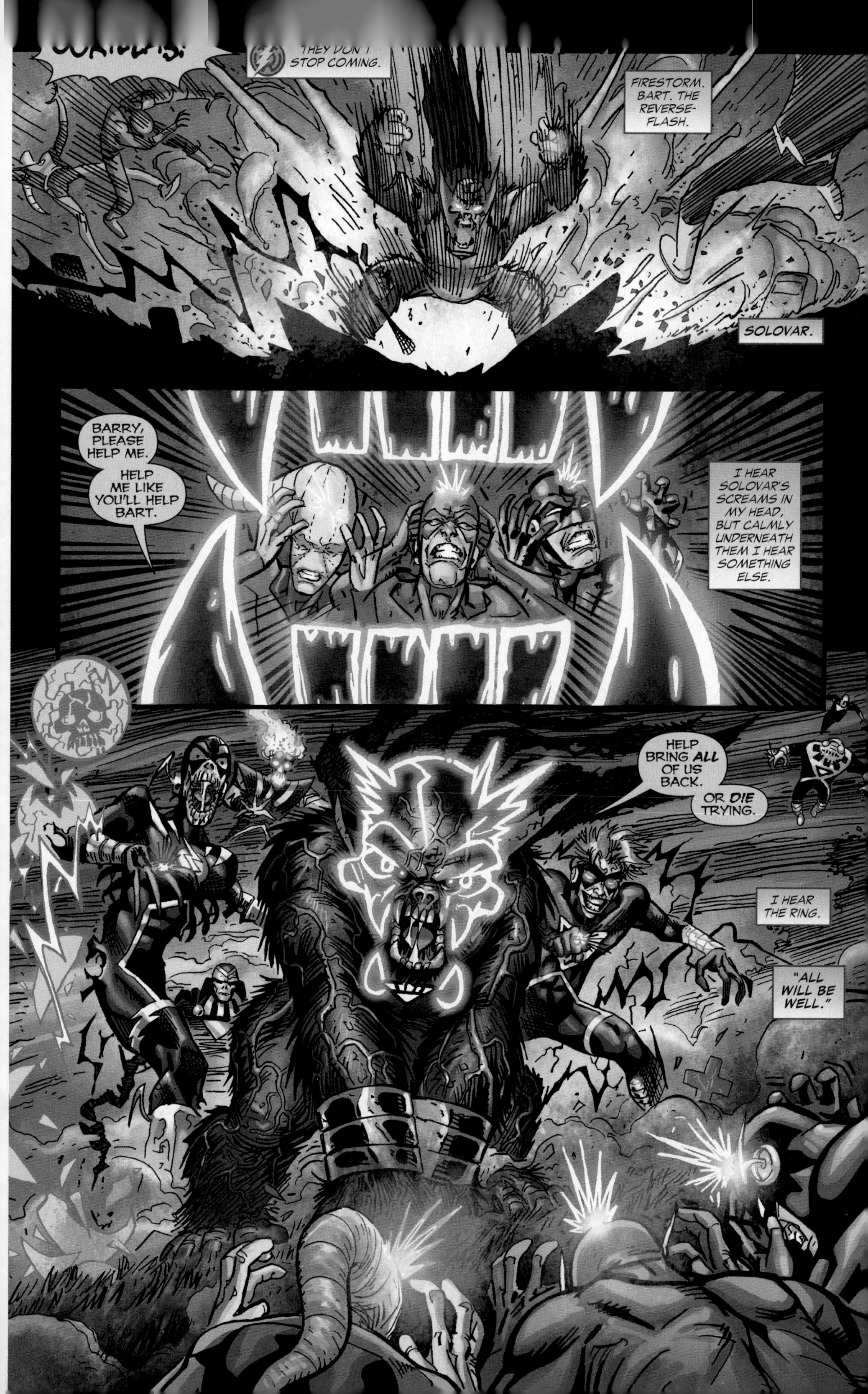
THEY DON'T STOP COMING.
FIRESTORM. BART. THE REVERSE-FLASH.
SOLOVAR.
BARRY, PLEASE HELP ME.
HELP ME LIKE YOU'LL HELP BART.
I HEAR SOLOVAR'S SCREAMS IN MY HEAD, BUT CALMLY UNDERNEATH THEM I HEAR SOMETHING ELSE.
HELP BRING ALL OF US BACK.
OR DIE TRYING.
I HEAR THE RING.
"ALL WILL BE WELL."

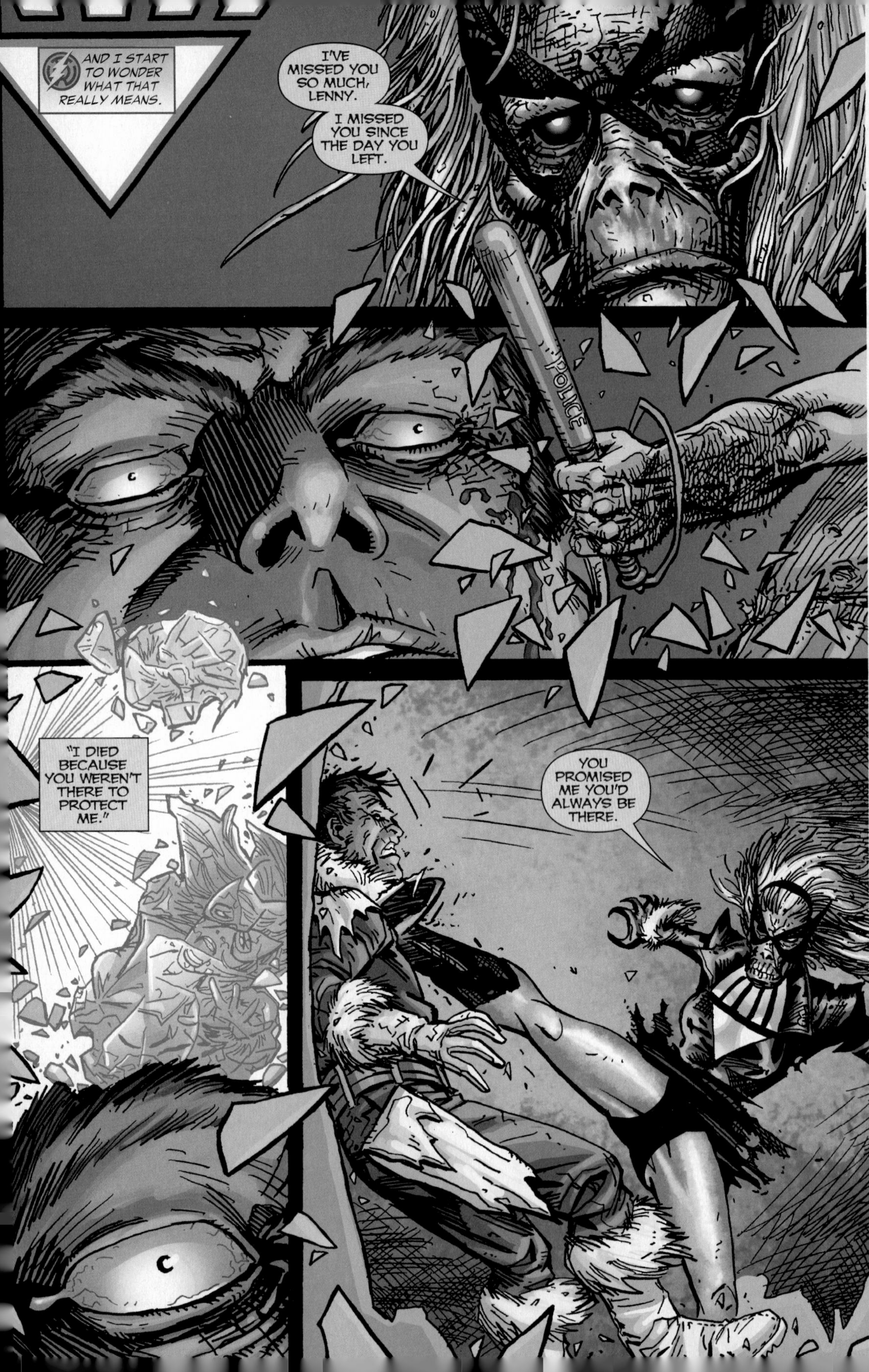
AND I START TO WONDER WHAT THAT REALLY MEANS.
I'VE MISSED YOU SO MUCH, LENNY.
I MISSED YOU SINCE THE DAY YOU LEFT.
POLICE
"I DIED BECAUSE YOU WEREN'T THERE TO PROTECT ME."
YOU PROMISED ME YOU'D ALWAYS BE THERE.

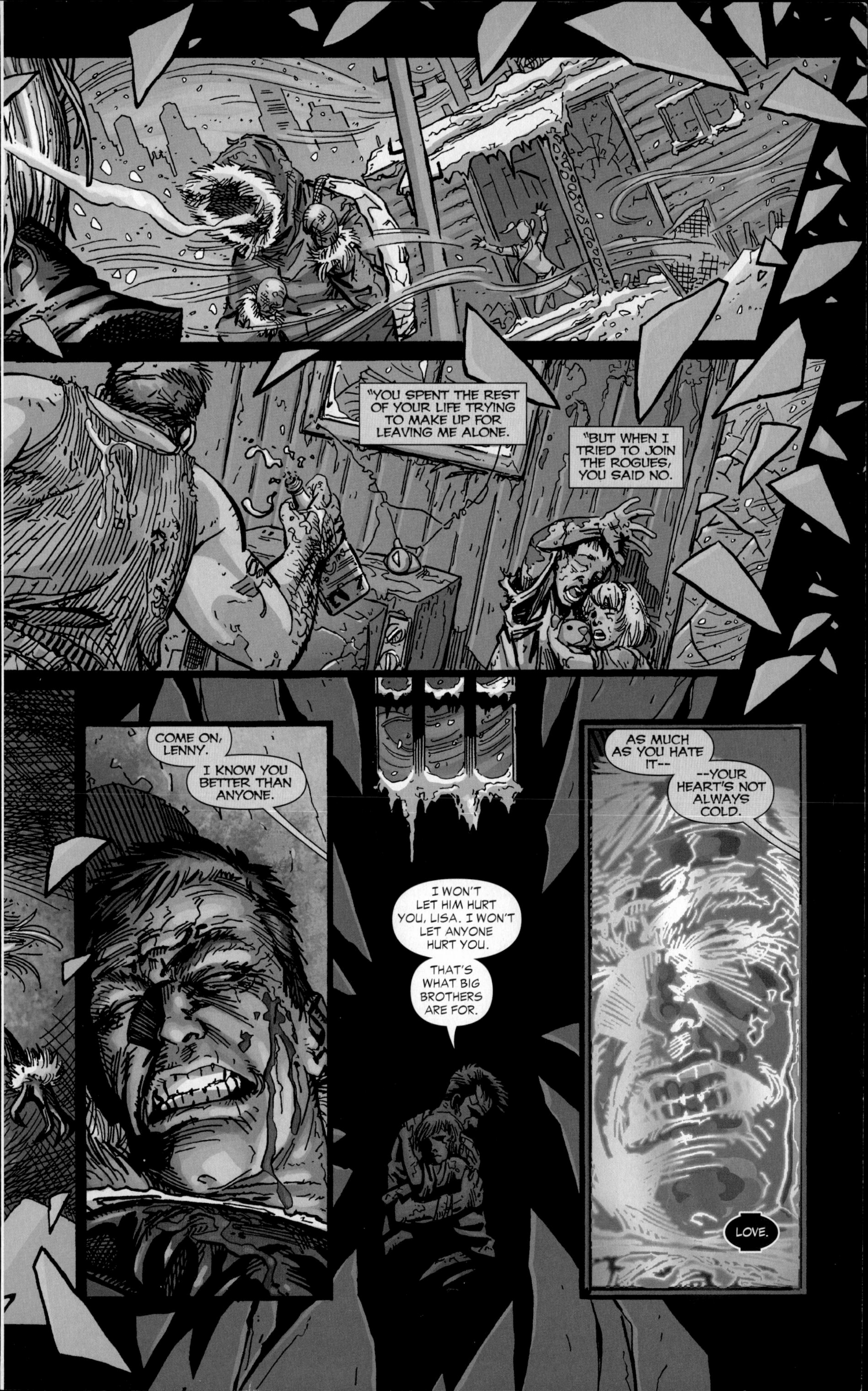
"YOU SPENT THE REST OF YOUR LIFE TRYING TO MAKE UP FOR LEAVING ME ALONE.
"BUT WHEN I TRIED TO JOIN THE ROGUES, YOU SAID NO.
COME ON, LENNY.
I KNOW YOU BETTER THAN ANYONE.
I WON'T LET HIM HURT YOU, LISA. I WON'T LET ANYONE HURT YOU.
THAT'S WHAT BIG BROTHERS ARE FOR.
AS MUCH AS YOU HATE IT--
--YOUR HEART'S NOT ALWAYS COLD.
LOVE.

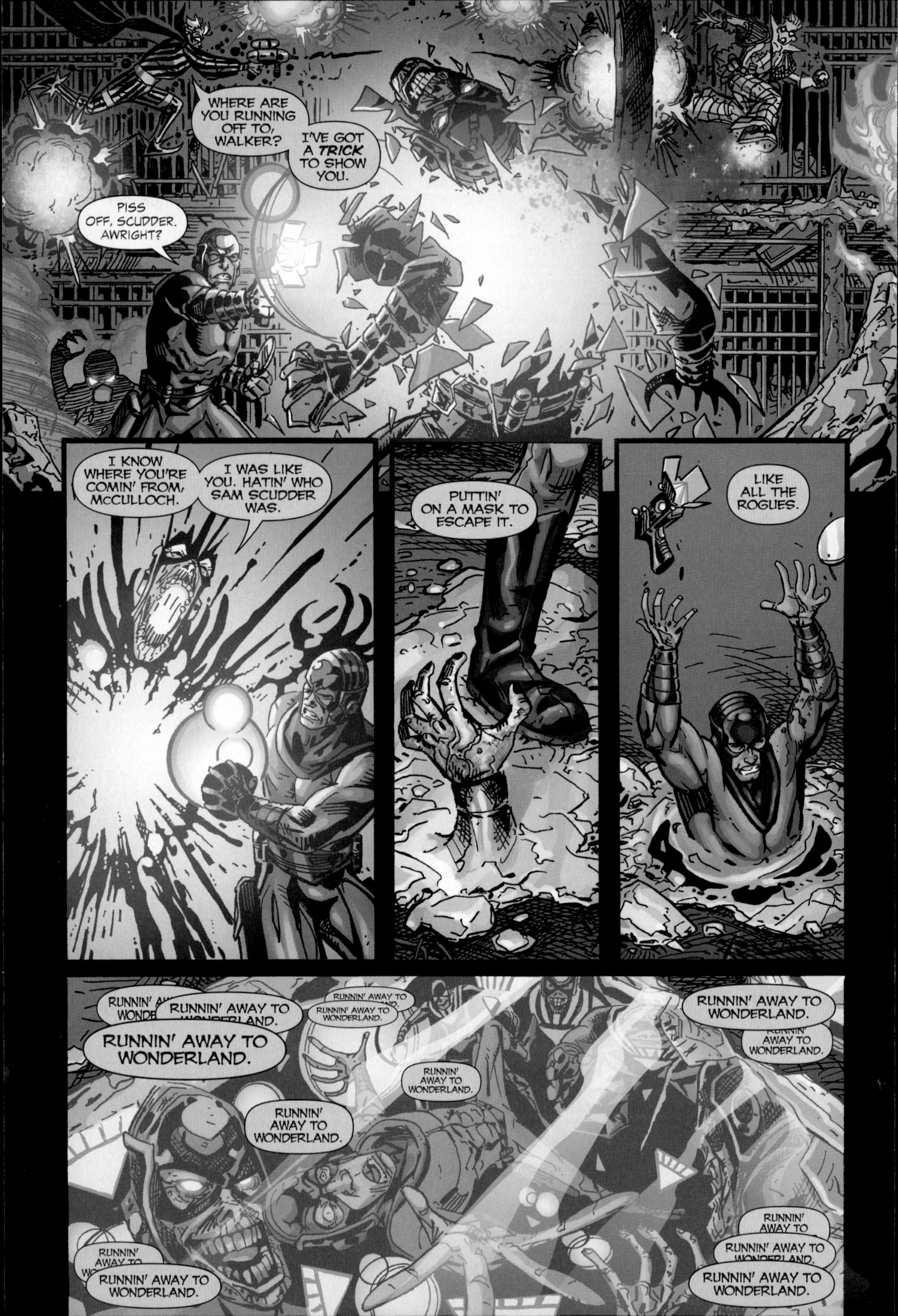
WHERE ARE YOU RUNNING OFF TO, WALKER?
I'VE GOT A *TRICK* TO SHOW YOU.
PISS OFF, SCUDDER. AWRIGHT?
I KNOW WHERE YOU'RE COMIN' FROM, McCULLOCH.
I WAS LIKE YOU. HATIN' WHO SAM SCUDDER WAS.
PUTTIN' ON A MASK TO ESCAPE IT.
LIKE ALL THE ROGUES.
RUNNIN' AWAY TO
RUNNIN' AWAY TO
RUNNIN' AWAY TO WONDERLAND.
RUNNIN' AWAY TO WONDERLAND.
RUNNIN' AWAY TO WONDERLAND.
RUNNIN' AWAY TO WONDERLAND.
RUNNIN' AWAY TO WONDERLAND.
RUNNIN' AWAY TO WONDERLAND.
RUNNIN' AWAY TO
RUNNIN' AWAY TO
RUNNIN' AWAY TO WONDERLAND.
RUNNIN' AWAY TO
RUNNIN' AWAY TO WONDERLAND.
RUNNIN' AWAY TO WONDERLAND.

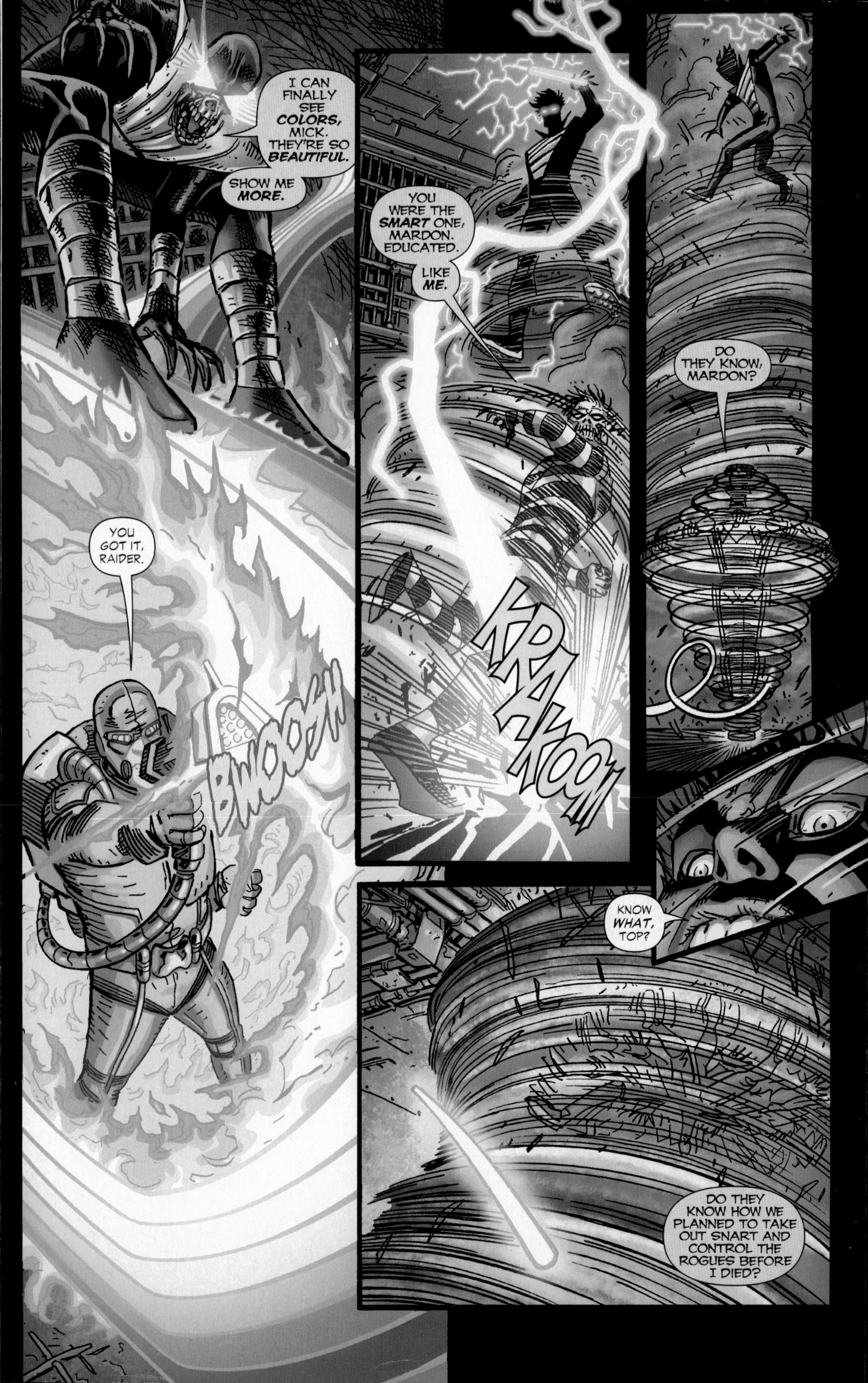
I CAN FINALLY SEE COLORS, MICK. THEY'RE SO BEAUTIFUL.
SHOW ME MORE.
YOU GOT IT, RAIDER.
BWOOSH
YOU WERE THE SMART ONE, MARDON. EDUCATED.
LIKE ME.
KRAKOOM
DO THEY KNOW, MARDON?
KNOW WHAT, TOP?
DO THEY KNOW HOW WE PLANNED TO TAKE OUT SNART AND CONTROL THE ROGUES BEFORE I DIED?

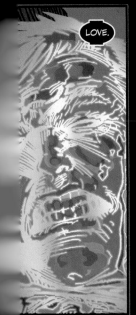

LOVE.

NO. NO, THAT'S IT.

WHAP

KRATCHH

I LEARNED A LONG TIME AGO, SIS.

WHEN LIFE HITS YOU HARD, YOU GOTTA SHRUG IT OFF...

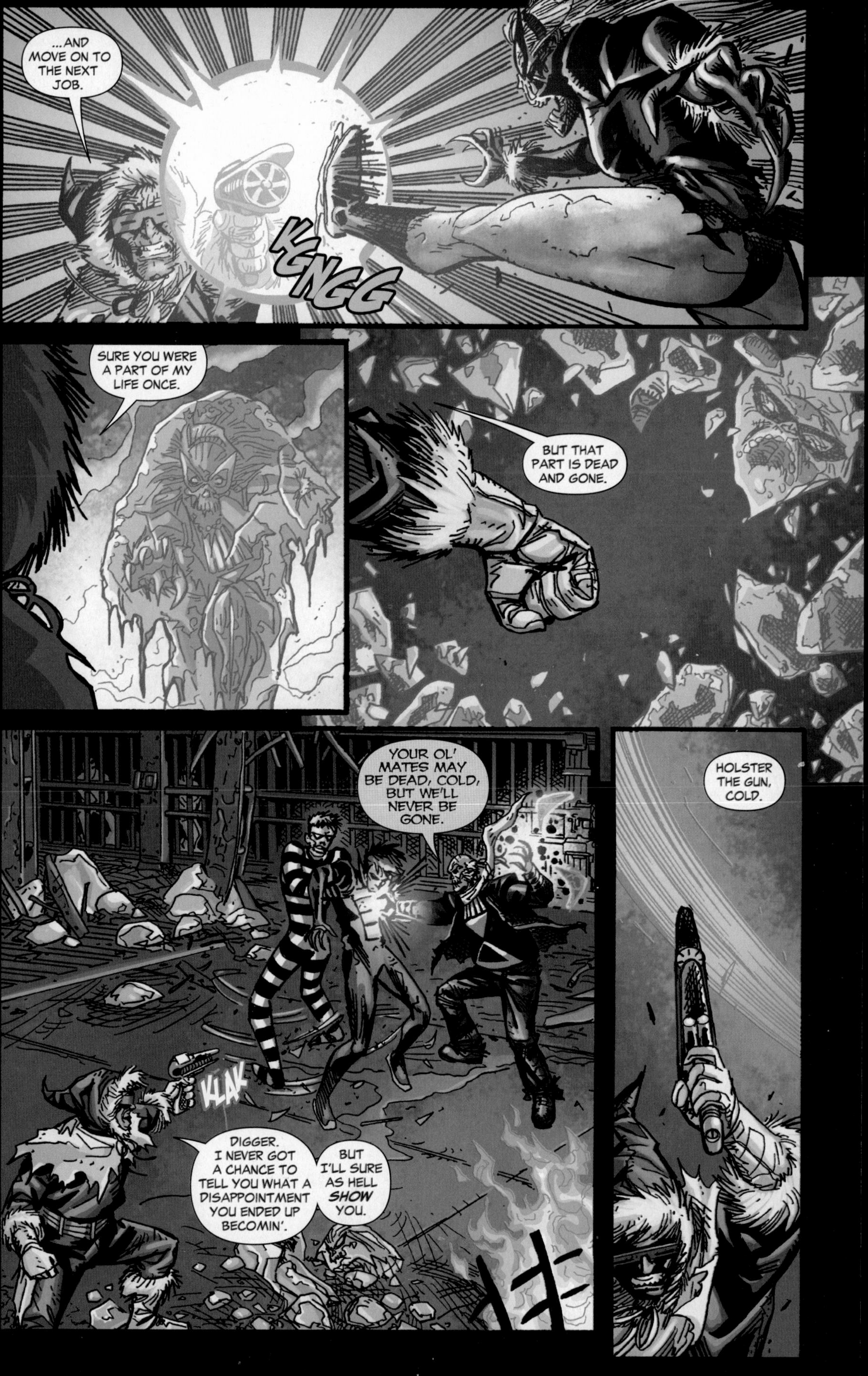
...AND MOVE ON TO THE NEXT JOB.
KGNGG
SURE YOU WERE A PART OF MY LIFE ONCE.
BUT THAT PART IS DEAD AND GONE.
YOUR OL' MATES MAY BE DEAD, COLD, BUT WE'LL NEVER BE GONE.
KLAK
DIGGER. I NEVER GOT A CHANCE TO TELL YOU WHAT A DISAPPOINTMENT YOU ENDED UP BECOMIN'.
BUT I'LL SURE AS HELL SHOW YOU.
HOLSTER THE GUN, COLD.

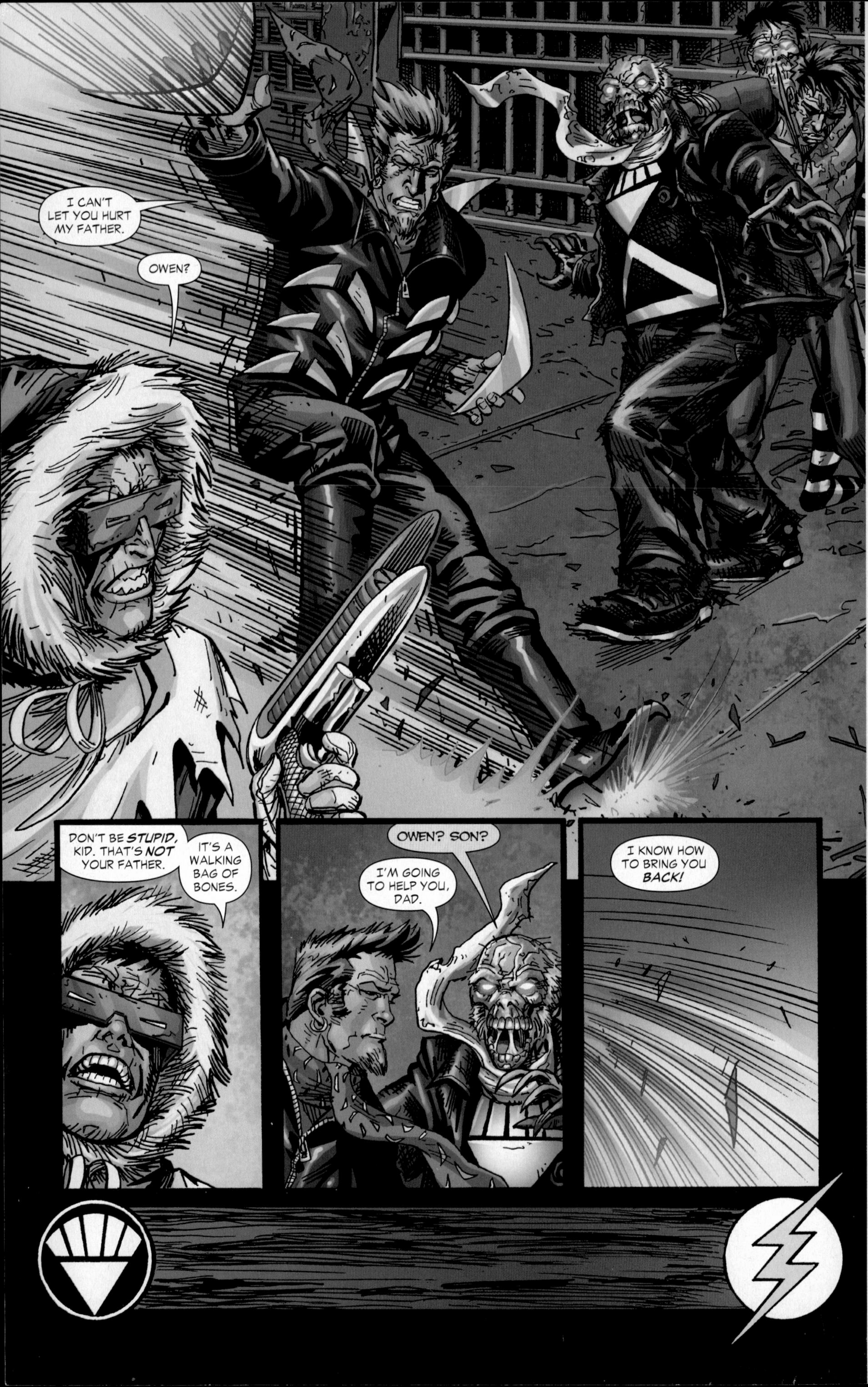
I CAN'T LET YOU HURT MY FATHER.
OWEN?
DON'T BE STUPID, KID. THAT'S NOT YOUR FATHER.
IT'S A WALKING BAG OF BONES.
OWEN? SON?
I'M GOING TO HELP YOU, DAD.
I KNOW HOW TO BRING YOU BACK!

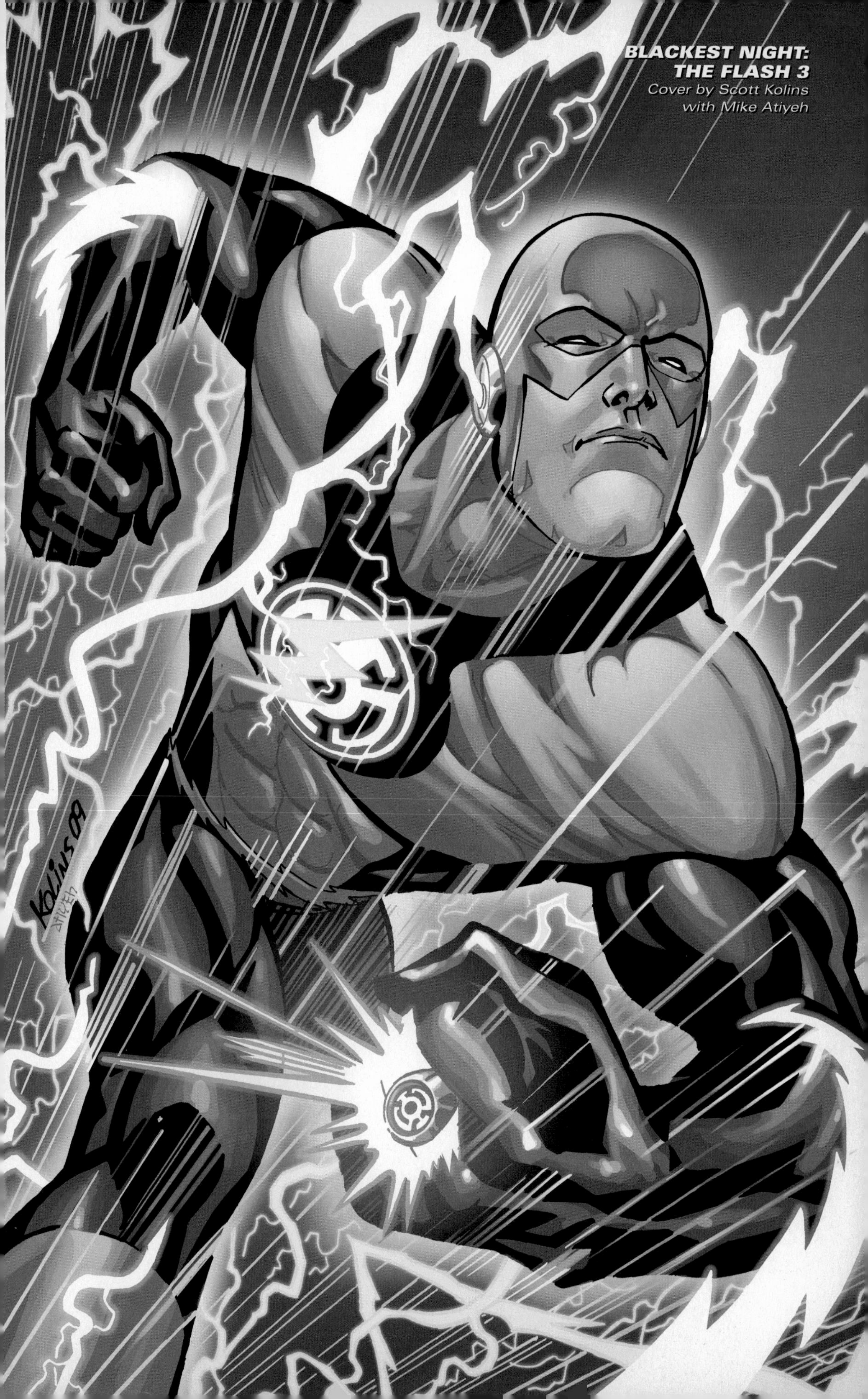

BLACKEST NIGHT:
THE FLASH 3
Cover by Scott Kolins
with Mike Atiyeh

BLACKEST NIGHT: THE FLASH
CHAPTER THREE

GEOFF JOHNS
WRITER

SCOTT KOLINS
ARTIST

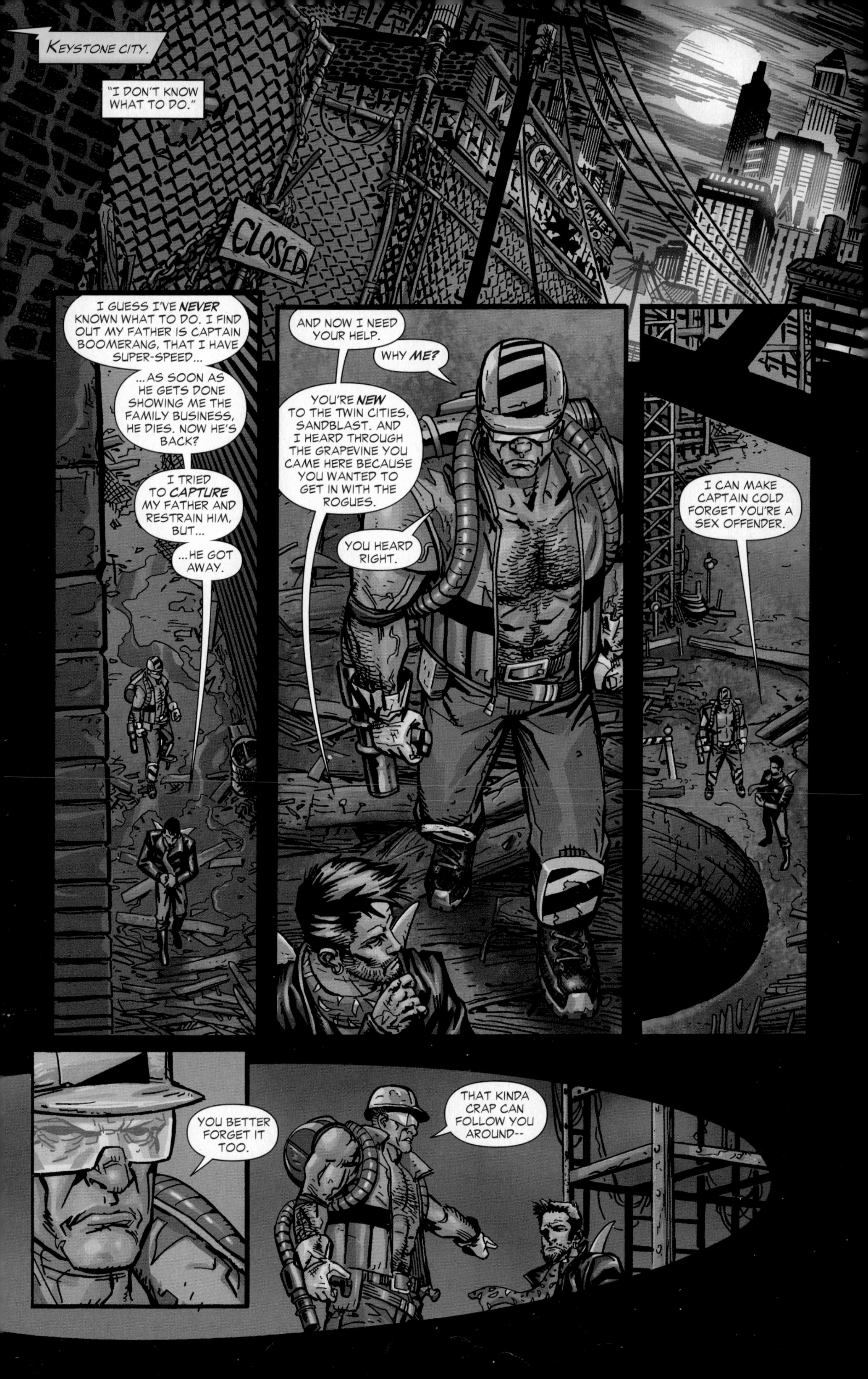
KEYSTONE CITY.
"I DON'T KNOW WHAT TO DO."
CLOSED
I GUESS I'VE NEVER KNOWN WHAT TO DO. I FIND OUT MY FATHER IS CAPTAIN BOOMERANG, THAT I HAVE SUPER-SPEED...
...AS SOON AS HE GETS DONE SHOWING ME THE FAMILY BUSINESS, HE DIES. NOW HE'S BACK?
I TRIED TO CAPTURE MY FATHER AND RESTRAIN HIM, BUT...
...HE GOT AWAY.
AND NOW I NEED YOUR HELP.
WHY ME?
YOU'RE NEW TO THE TWIN CITIES, SANDBLAST. AND I HEARD THROUGH THE GRAPEVINE YOU CAME HERE BECAUSE YOU WANTED TO GET IN WITH THE ROGUES.
YOU HEARD RIGHT.
I CAN MAKE CAPTAIN COLD FORGET YOU'RE A SEX OFFENDER.
YOU BETTER FORGET IT TOO.
THAT KINDA CRAP CAN FOLLOW YOU AROUND--

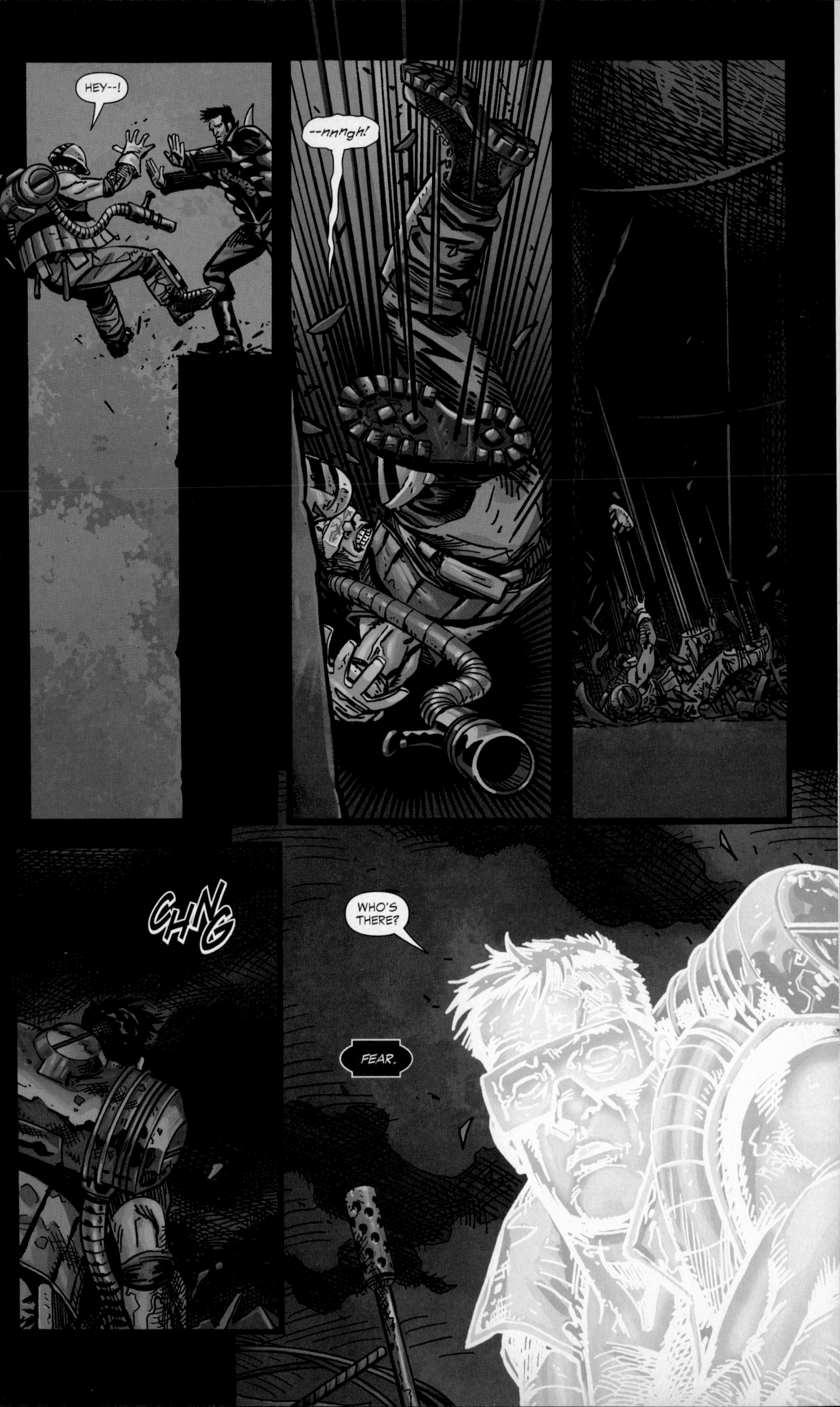

HEY--!
--nnngh!
CHNG
WHO'S THERE?
FEAR.

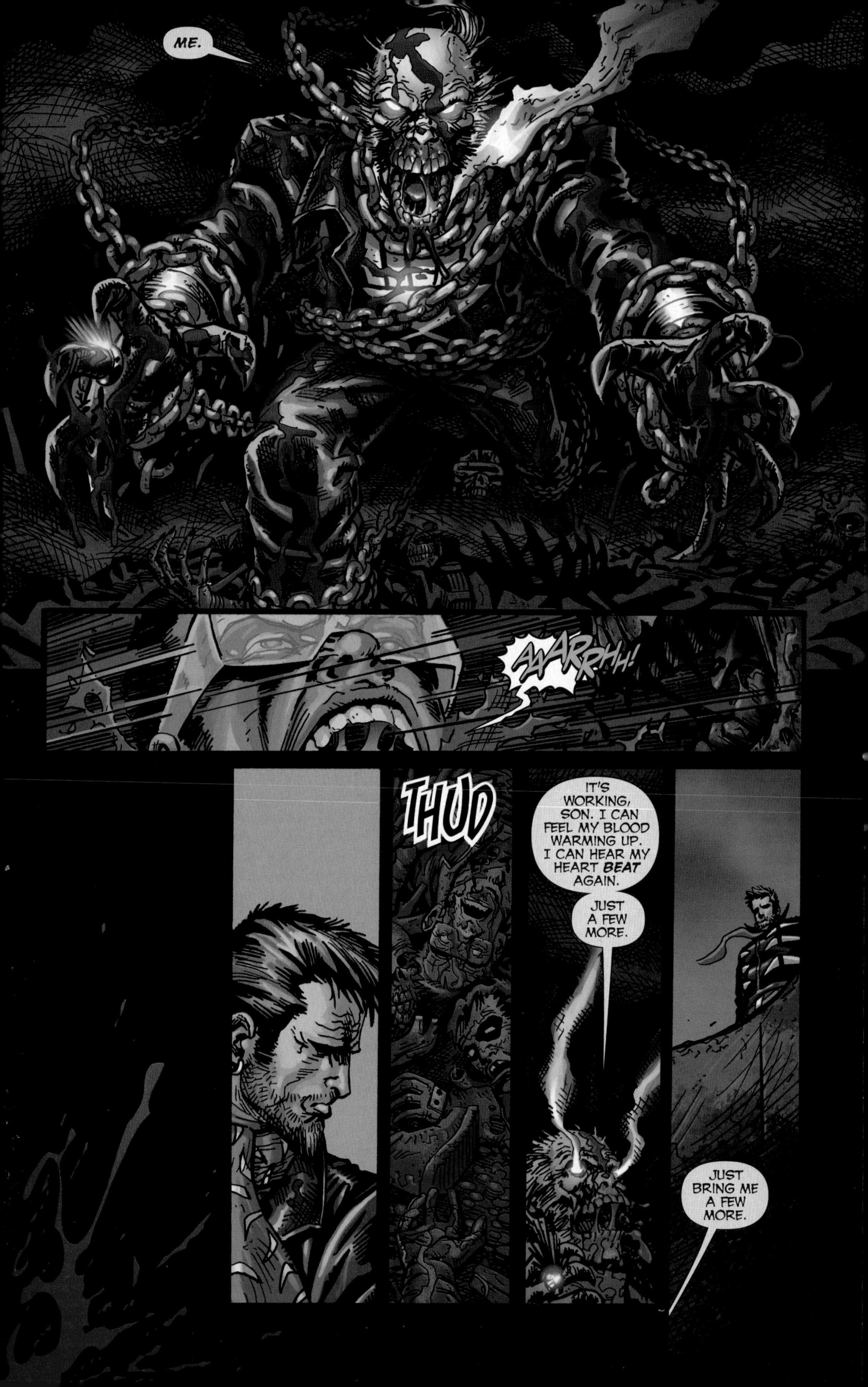
ME.
AAARRHH!
THUD
IT'S WORKING, SON. I CAN FEEL MY BLOOD WARMING UP. I CAN HEAR MY HEART *BEAT* AGAIN.
JUST A FEW MORE.
JUST BRING ME A FEW MORE.

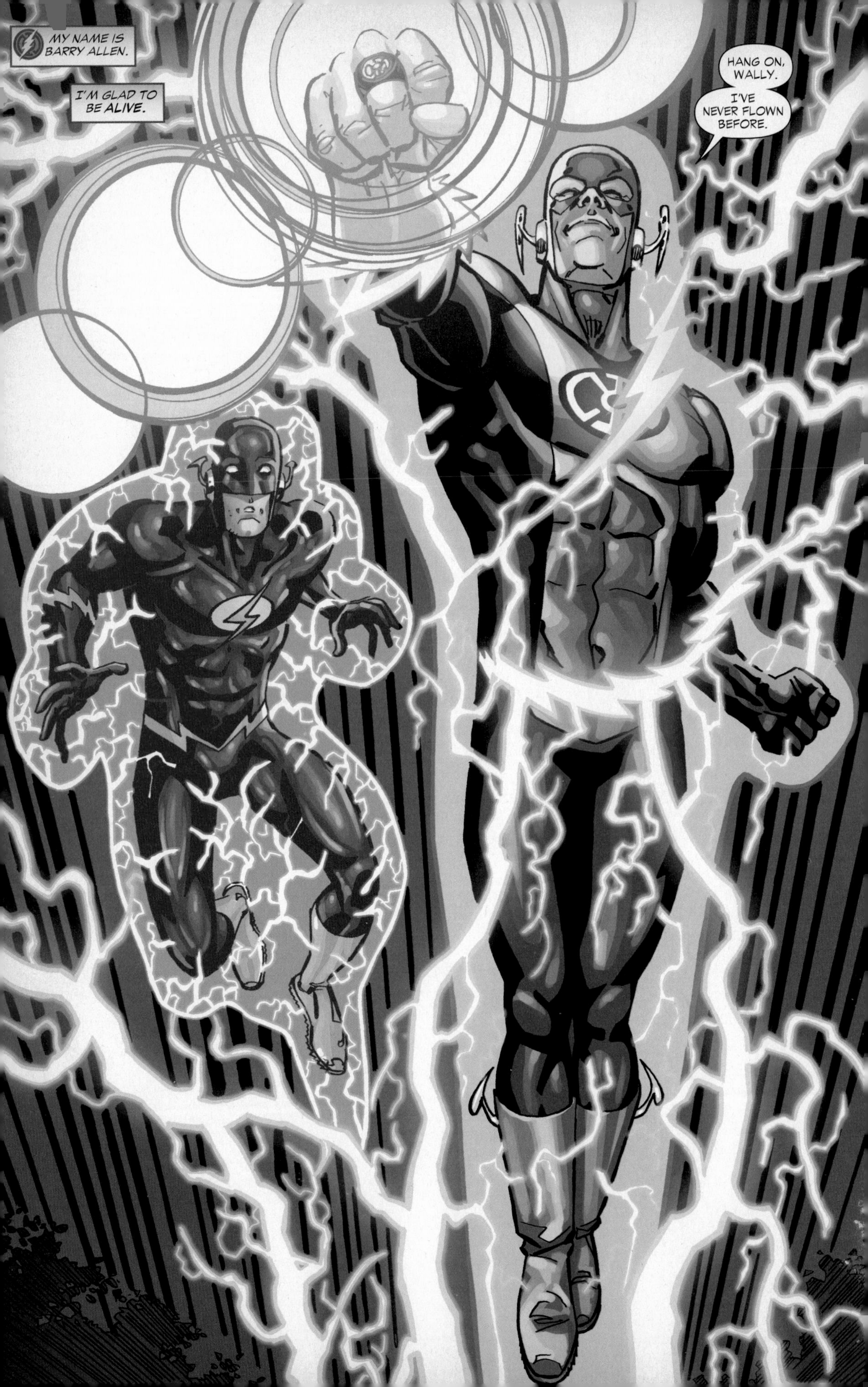

MY NAME IS BARRY ALLEN.
I'M GLAD TO BE ALIVE.
HANG ON, WALLY.
I'VE NEVER FLOWN BEFORE.

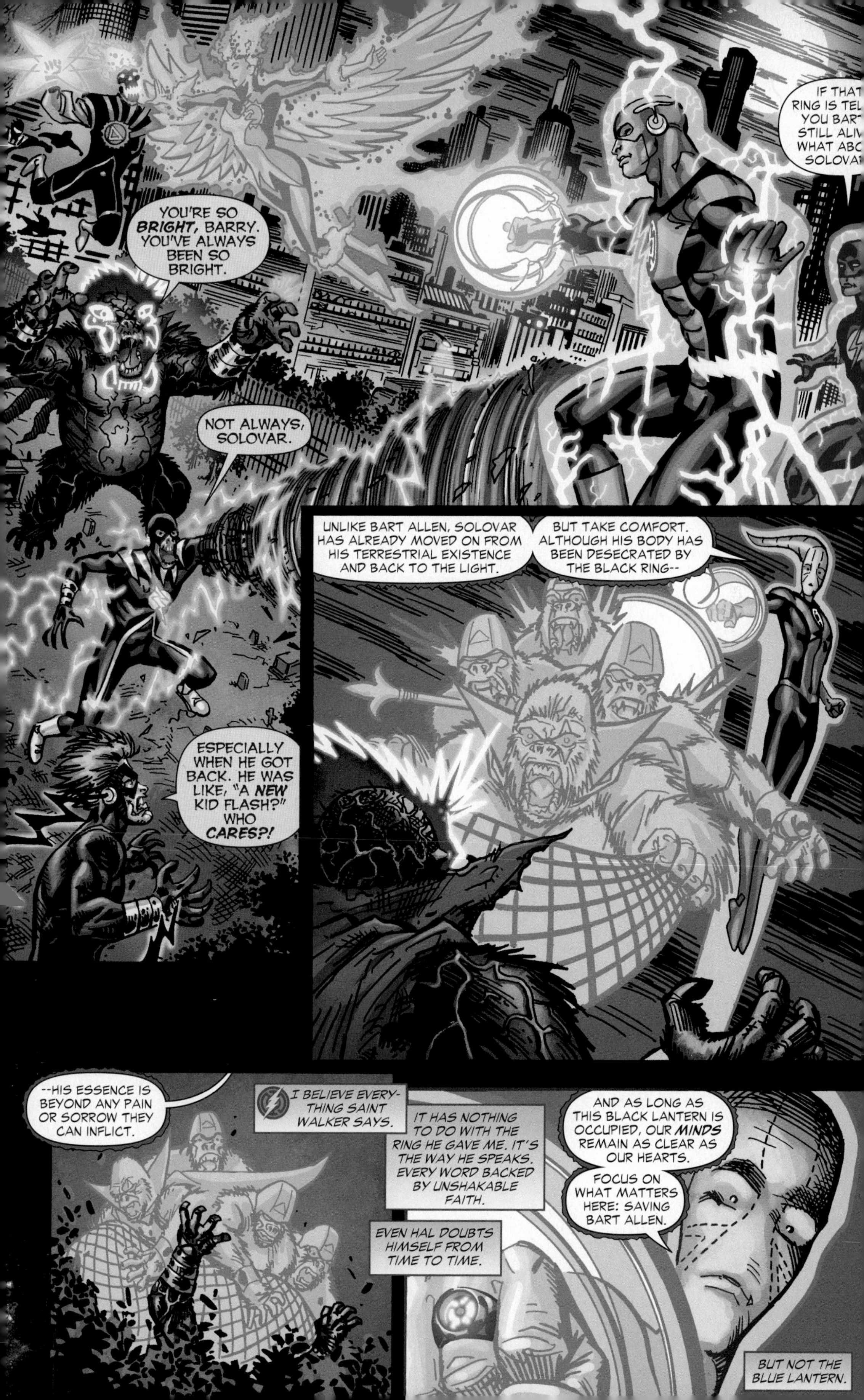
YOU'RE SO BRIGHT, BARRY. YOU'VE ALWAYS BEEN SO BRIGHT.
IF THAT RING IS TEL YOU BART STILL ALIV WHAT ABO SOLOVAR
NOT ALWAYS, SOLOVAR.
ESPECIALLY WHEN HE GOT BACK. HE WAS LIKE, "A NEW KID FLASH?" WHO CARES?!
UNLIKE BART ALLEN, SOLOVAR HAS ALREADY MOVED ON FROM HIS TERRESTRIAL EXISTENCE AND BACK TO THE LIGHT.
BUT TAKE COMFORT. ALTHOUGH HIS BODY HAS BEEN DESECRATED BY THE BLACK RING--
--HIS ESSENCE IS BEYOND ANY PAIN OR SORROW THEY CAN INFLICT.
I BELIEVE EVERYTHING SAINT WALKER SAYS.
IT HAS NOTHING TO DO WITH THE RING HE GAVE ME. IT'S THE WAY HE SPEAKS. EVERY WORD BACKED BY UNSHAKABLE FAITH.
EVEN HAL DOUBTS HIMSELF FROM TIME TO TIME.
AND AS LONG AS THIS BLACK LANTERN IS OCCUPIED, OUR MINDS REMAIN AS CLEAR AS OUR HEARTS.
FOCUS ON WHAT MATTERS HERE: SAVING BART ALLEN.
BUT NOT THE BLUE LANTERN.

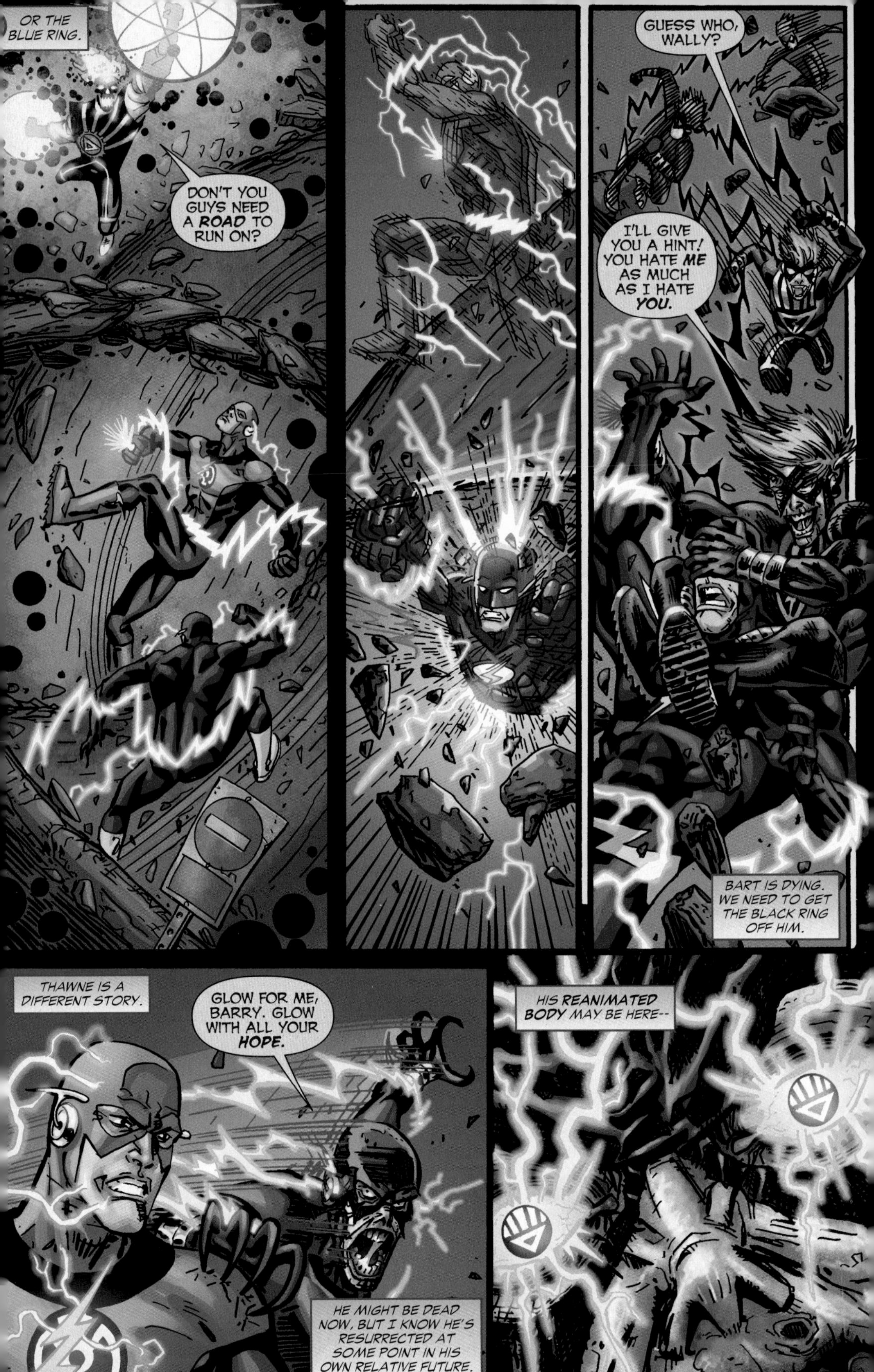

OR THE BLUE RING.
DON'T YOU GUYS NEED A ROAD TO RUN ON?
GUESS WHO, WALLY?
I'LL GIVE YOU A HINT! YOU HATE ME AS MUCH AS I HATE YOU.
BART IS DYING. WE NEED TO GET THE BLACK RING OFF HIM.
THAWNE IS A DIFFERENT STORY.
GLOW FOR ME, BARRY. GLOW WITH ALL YOUR HOPE.
HE MIGHT BE DEAD NOW, BUT I KNOW HE'S RESURRECTED AT SOME POINT IN HIS OWN RELATIVE FUTURE.
HIS REANIMATED BODY MAY BE HERE--

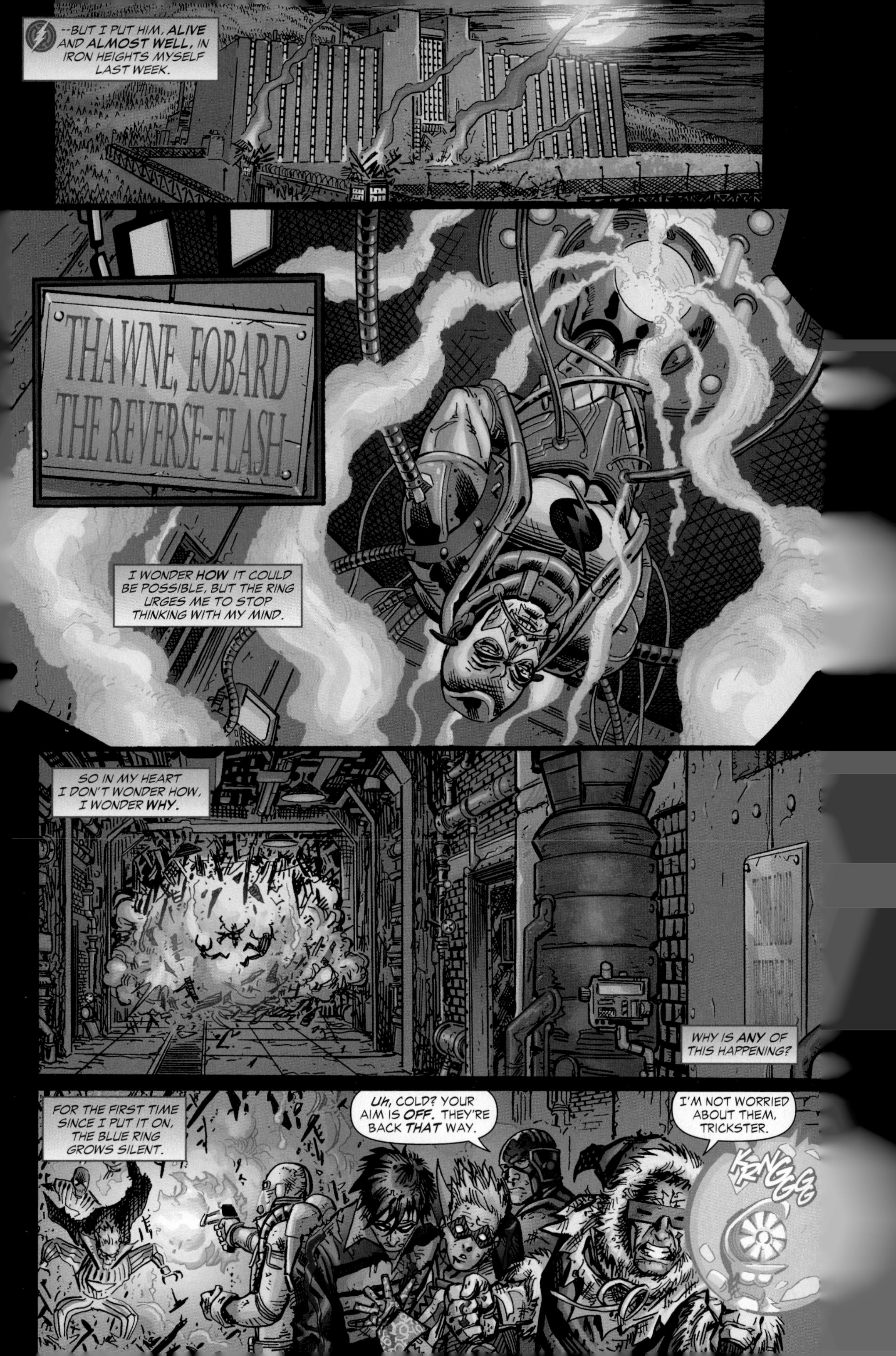
--BUT I PUT HIM, ALIVE AND ALMOST WELL, IN IRON HEIGHTS MYSELF LAST WEEK.
THAWNE, EOBARD
THE REVERSE-FLASH
I WONDER HOW IT COULD BE POSSIBLE, BUT THE RING URGES ME TO STOP THINKING WITH MY MIND.
SO IN MY HEART I DON'T WONDER HOW, I WONDER WHY.
WHY IS ANY OF THIS HAPPENING?
FOR THE FIRST TIME SINCE I PUT IT ON, THE BLUE RING GROWS SILENT.
Uh, COLD? YOUR AIM IS OFF. THEY'RE BACK THAT WAY.
I'M NOT WORRIED ABOUT THEM, TRICKSTER.
KRNGGG

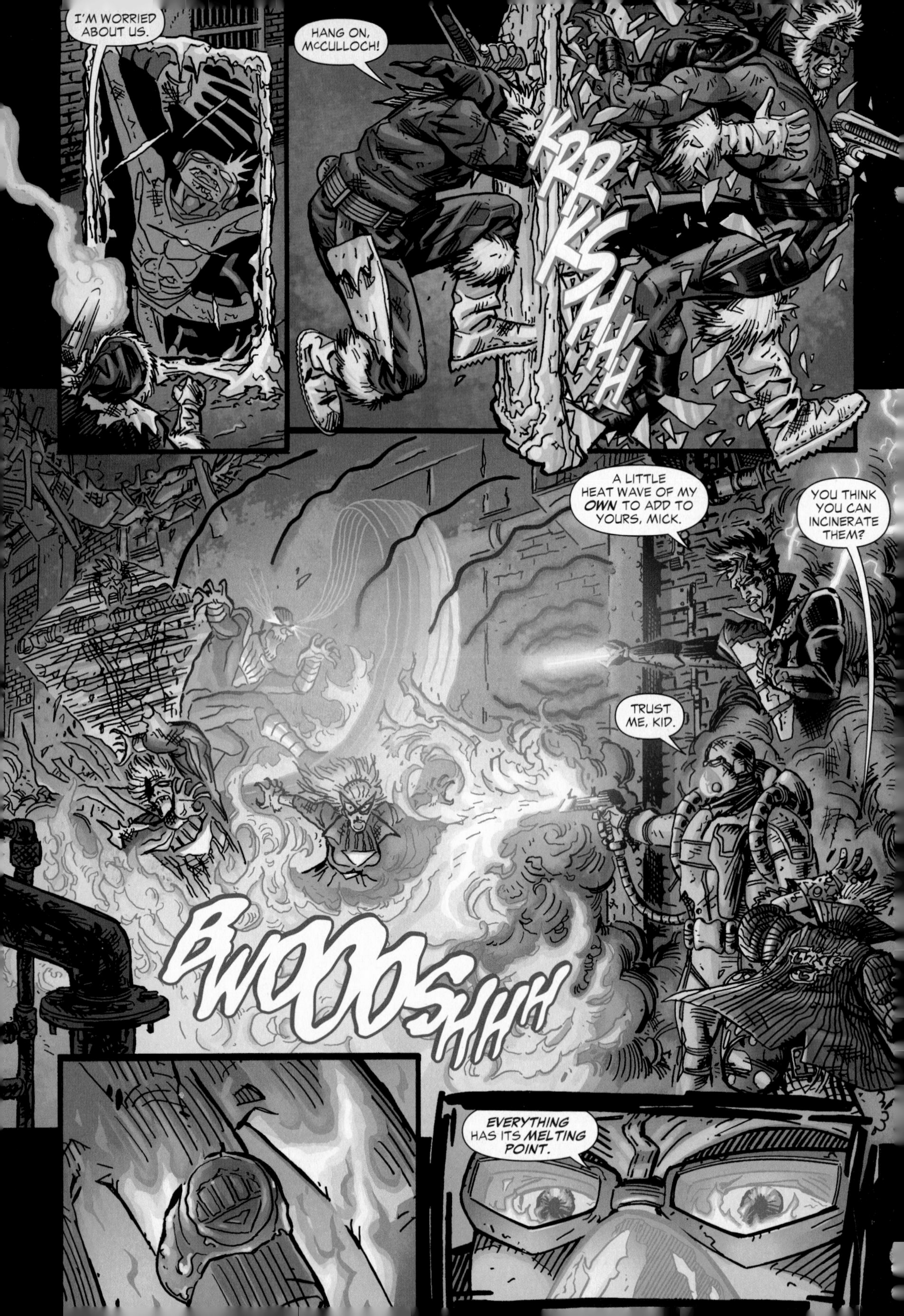
I'M WORRIED ABOUT US.
HANG ON, McCULLOCH!
KRRKKSHHHH
A LITTLE HEAT WAVE OF MY *OWN* TO ADD TO YOURS, MICK.
YOU THINK YOU CAN INCINERATE THEM?
TRUST ME, KID.
BWOOOSHHH
EVERYTHING HAS ITS *MELTING POINT.*

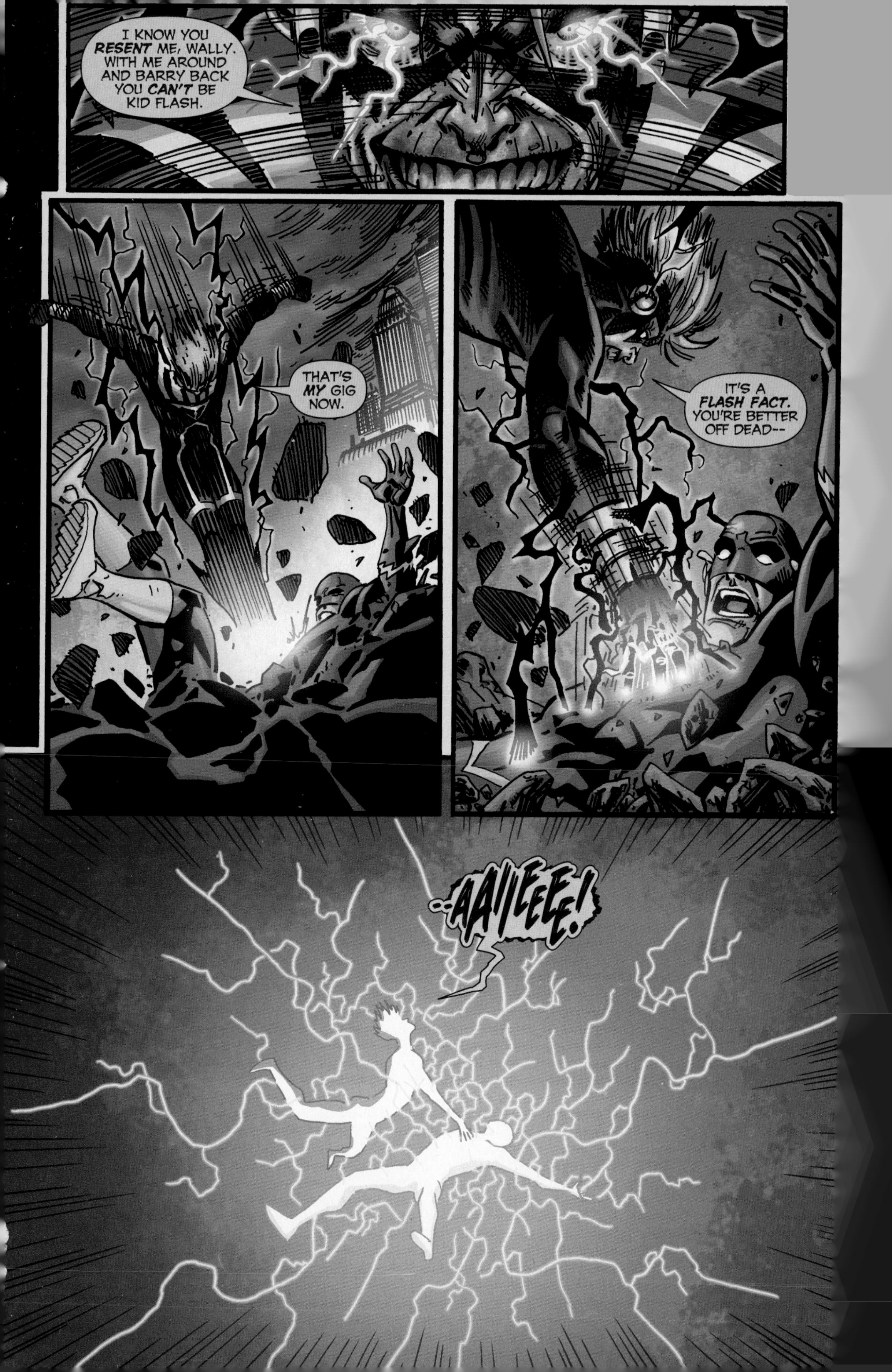

I KNOW YOU RESENT ME, WALLY. WITH ME AROUND AND BARRY BACK YOU CAN'T BE KID FLASH.
THAT'S MY GIG NOW.
IT'S A FLASH FACT. YOU'RE BETTER OFF DEAD--
--AAIIEEE!

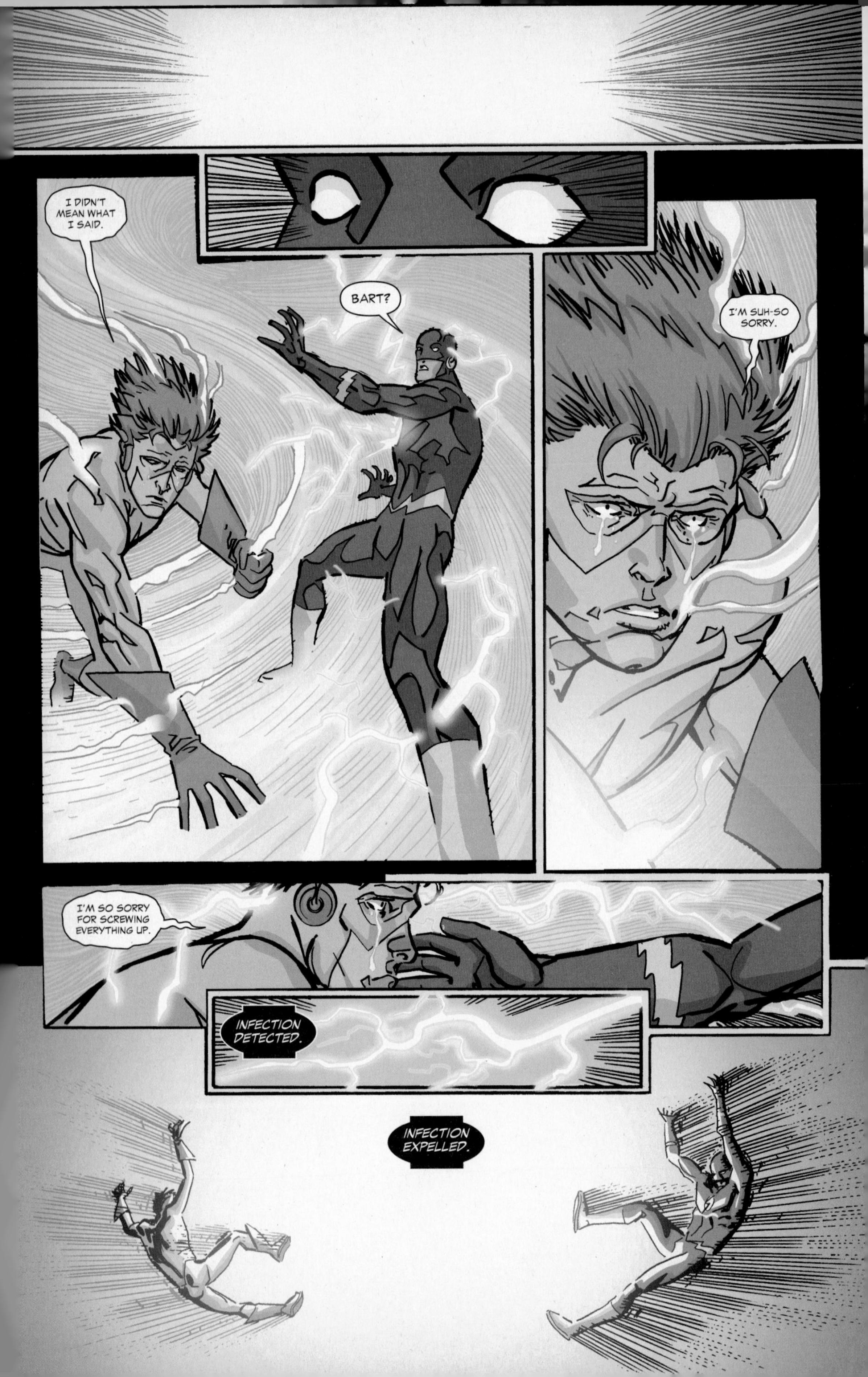
I DIDN'T MEAN WHAT I SAID.
BART?
I'M SUH-SO SORRY.
I'M SO SORRY FOR SCREWING EVERYTHING UP.
INFECTION DETECTED.
INFECTION EXPELLED.

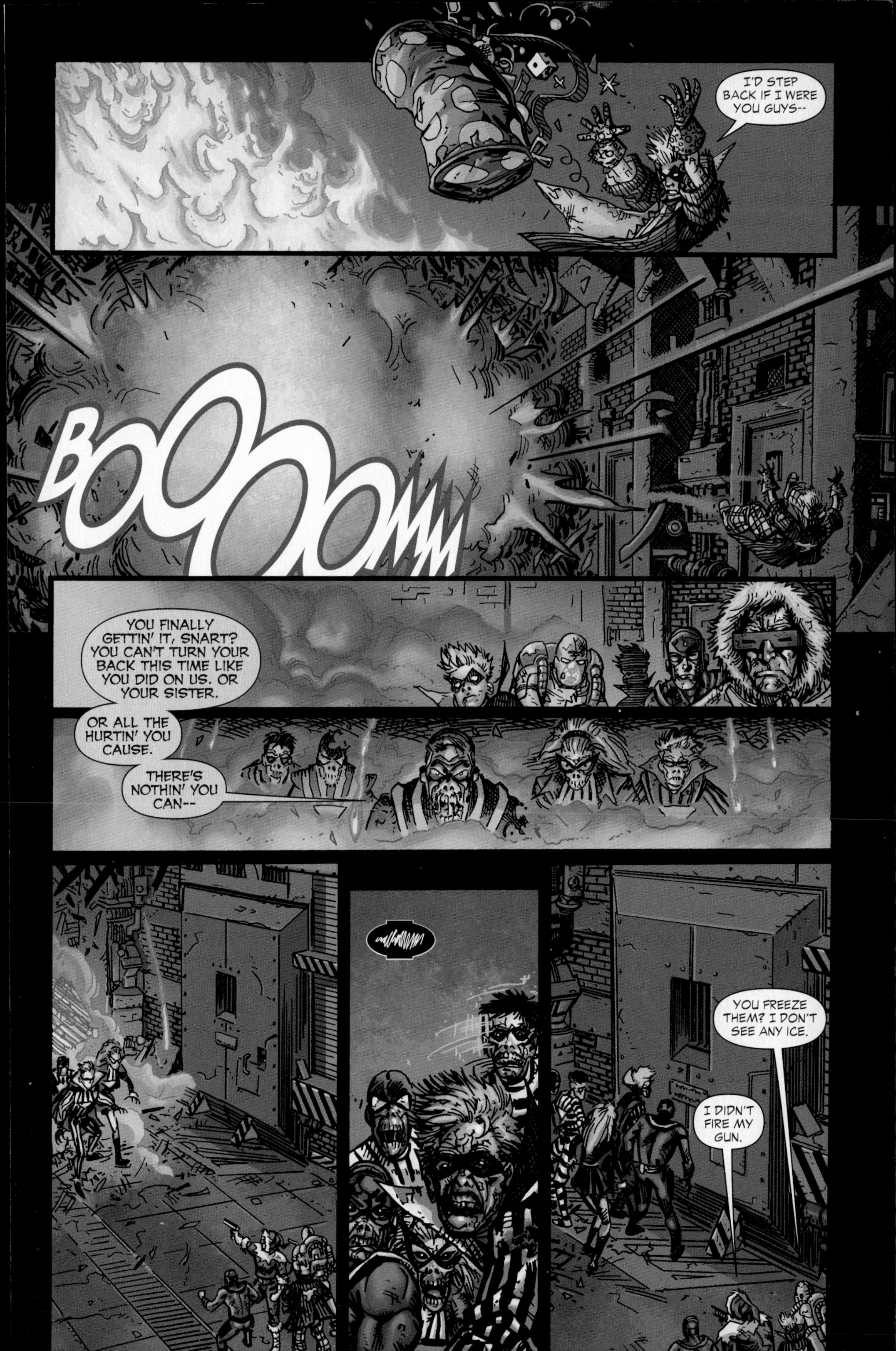
I'D STEP BACK IF I WERE YOU GUYS--
BOOOOM
YOU FINALLY GETTIN' IT, SNART? YOU CAN'T TURN YOUR BACK THIS TIME LIKE YOU DID ON US. OR YOUR SISTER.
OR ALL THE HURTIN' YOU CAUSE.
THERE'S NOTHIN' YOU CAN--
YOU FREEZE THEM? I DON'T SEE ANY ICE.
I DIDN'T FIRE MY GUN.

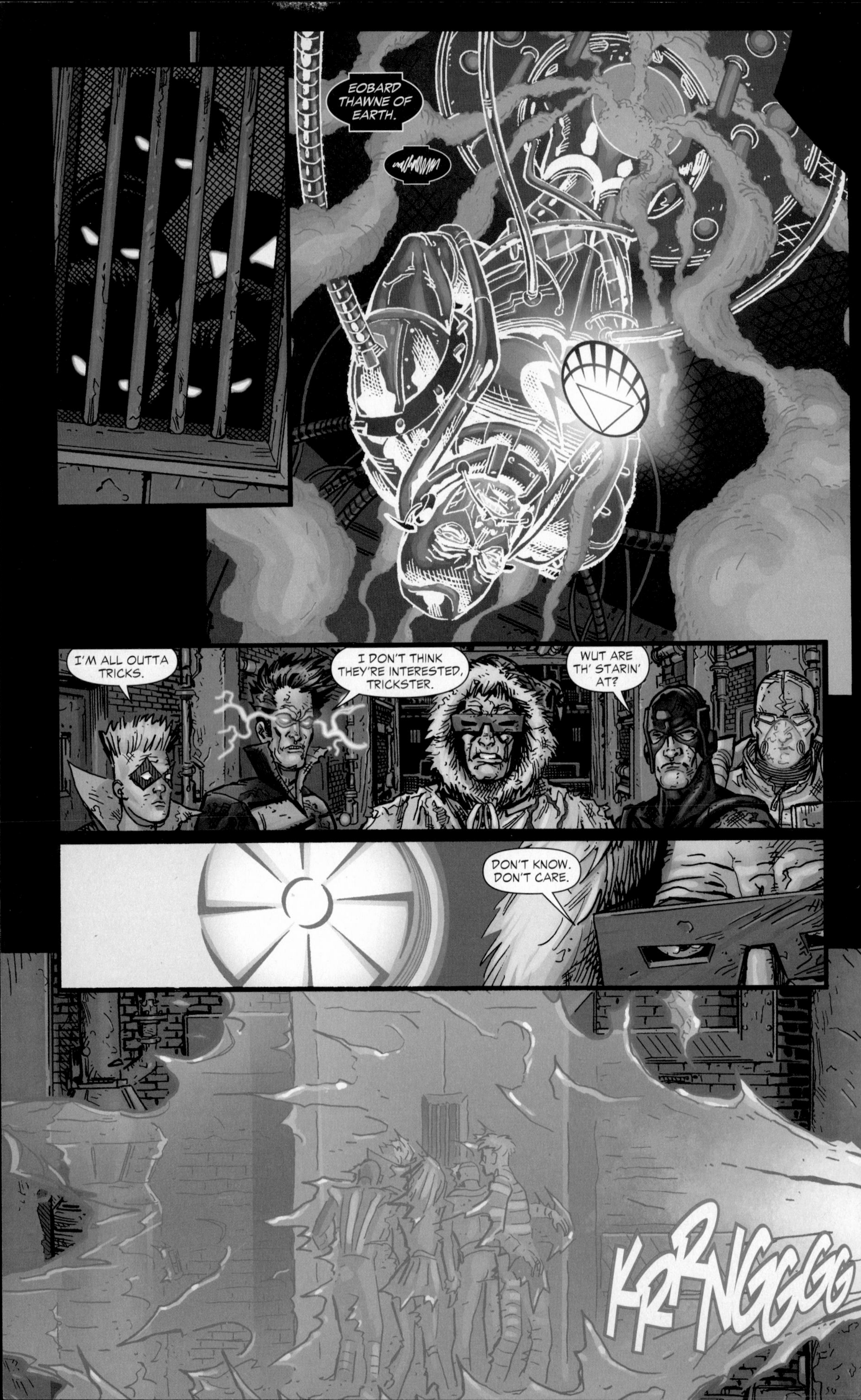
EOBARD THAWNE OF EARTH.
I'M ALL OUTTA TRICKS.
I DON'T THINK THEY'RE INTERESTED, TRICKSTER.
WUT ARE TH' STARIN' AT?
DON'T KNOW. DON'T CARE.
KRRNGGGG

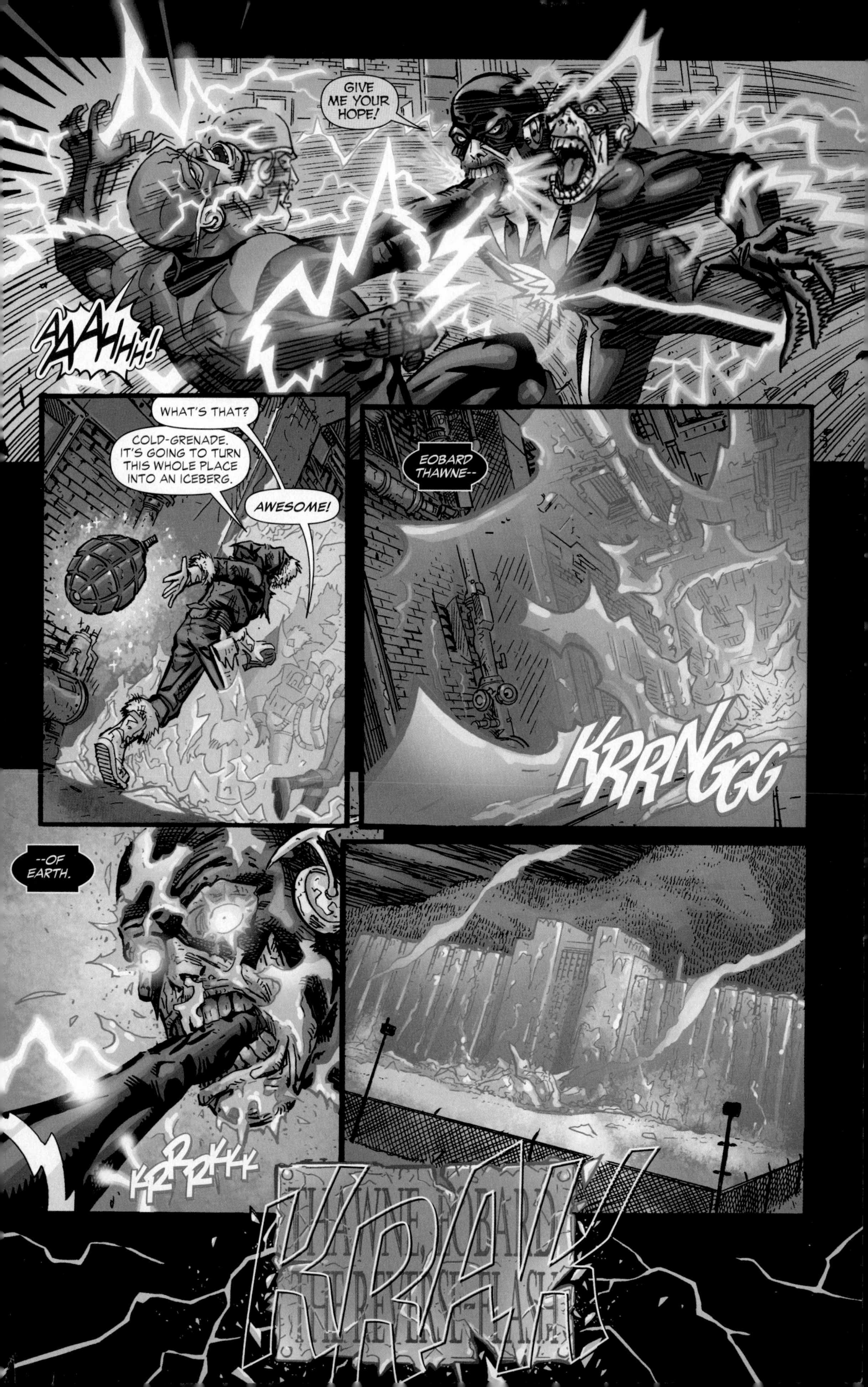
GIVE ME YOUR HOPE!
AAAHHH!
WHAT'S THAT?
COLD-GRENADE. IT'S GOING TO TURN THIS WHOLE PLACE INTO AN ICEBERG.
AWESOME!
EOBARD THAWNE--
KRRNGGG
--OF EARTH.
KRRRKKK
KRAK

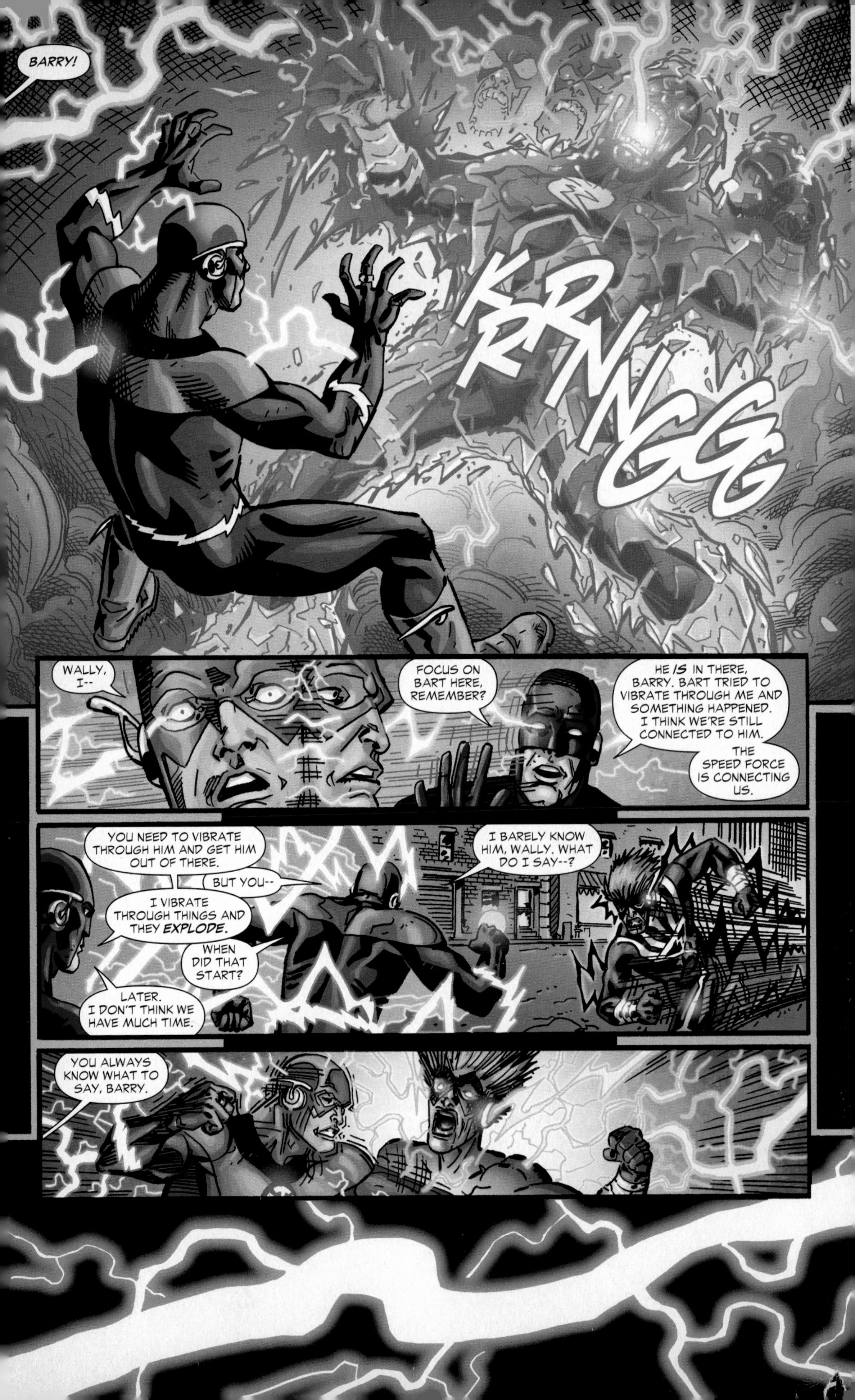
BARRY!
KRRNNGGG
WALLY, I--
FOCUS ON BART HERE, REMEMBER?
HE IS IN THERE, BARRY. BART TRIED TO VIBRATE THROUGH ME AND SOMETHING HAPPENED. I THINK WE'RE STILL CONNECTED TO HIM.
THE SPEED FORCE IS CONNECTING US.
YOU NEED TO VIBRATE THROUGH HIM AND GET HIM OUT OF THERE.
BUT YOU--
I VIBRATE THROUGH THINGS AND THEY EXPLODE.
WHEN DID THAT START?
LATER. I DON'T THINK WE HAVE MUCH TIME.
I BARELY KNOW HIM, WALLY. WHAT DO I SAY--?
YOU ALWAYS KNOW WHAT TO SAY, BARRY.

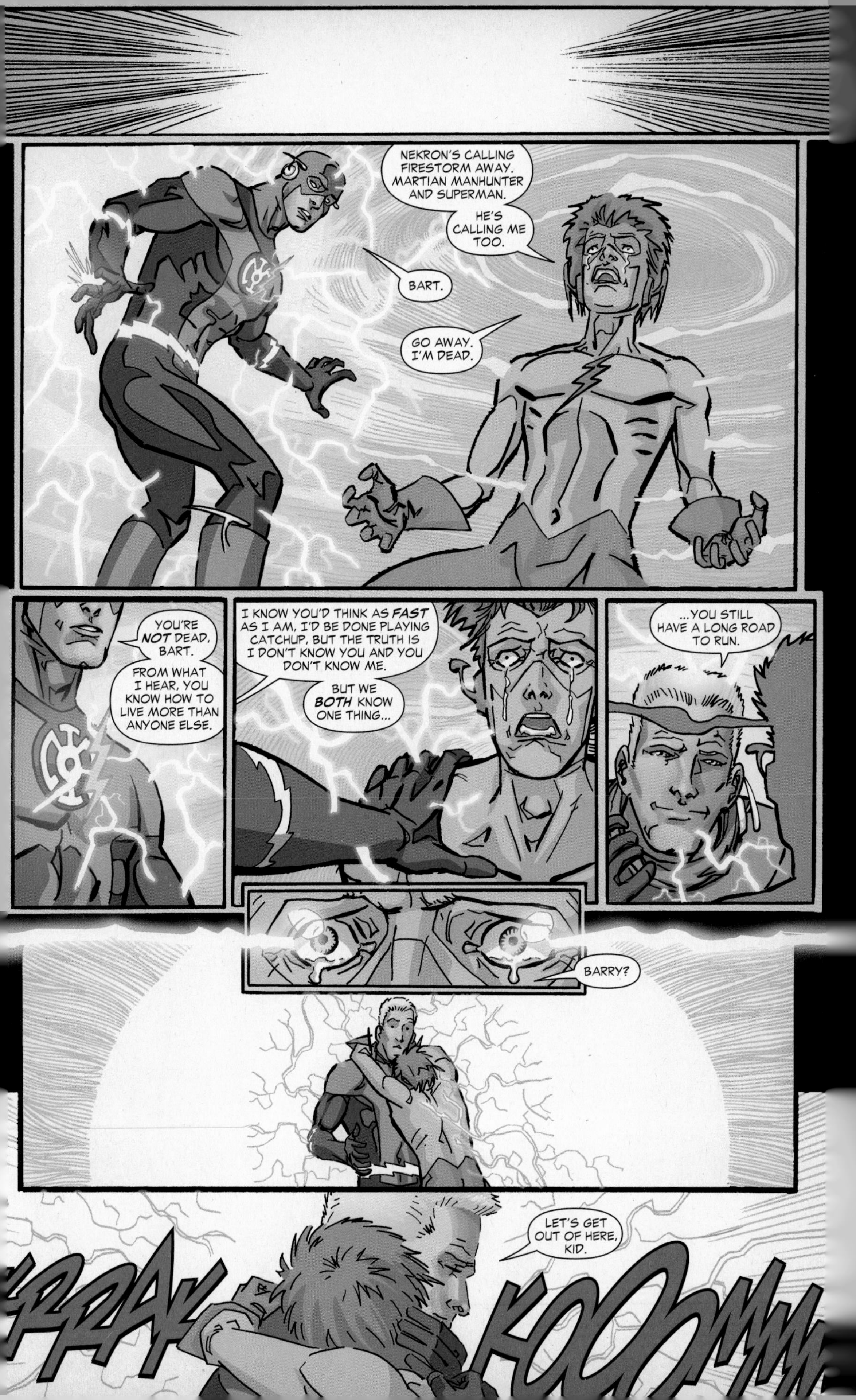
NEKRON'S CALLING FIRESTORM AWAY. MARTIAN MANHUNTER AND SUPERMAN.
HE'S CALLING ME TOO.
BART.
GO AWAY. I'M DEAD.
YOU'RE NOT DEAD, BART.
FROM WHAT I HEAR, YOU KNOW HOW TO LIVE MORE THAN ANYONE ELSE.
I KNOW YOU'D THINK AS FAST AS I AM, I'D BE DONE PLAYING CATCHUP, BUT THE TRUTH IS I DON'T KNOW YOU AND YOU DON'T KNOW ME.
BUT WE BOTH KNOW ONE THING...
...YOU STILL HAVE A LONG ROAD TO RUN.
BARRY?
LET'S GET OUT OF HERE, KID.
KRRAK
KOOOMM

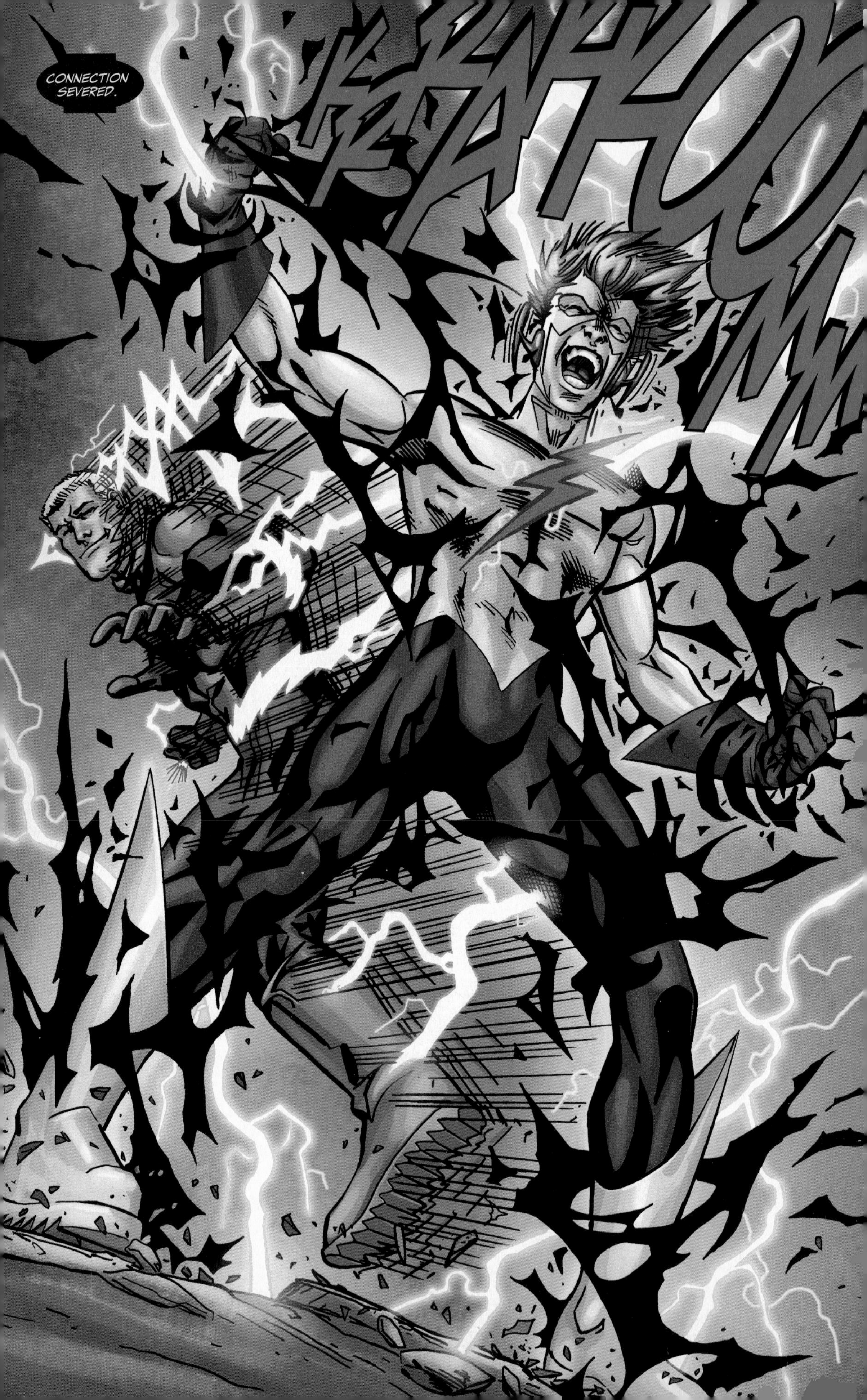
CONNECTION SEVERED.

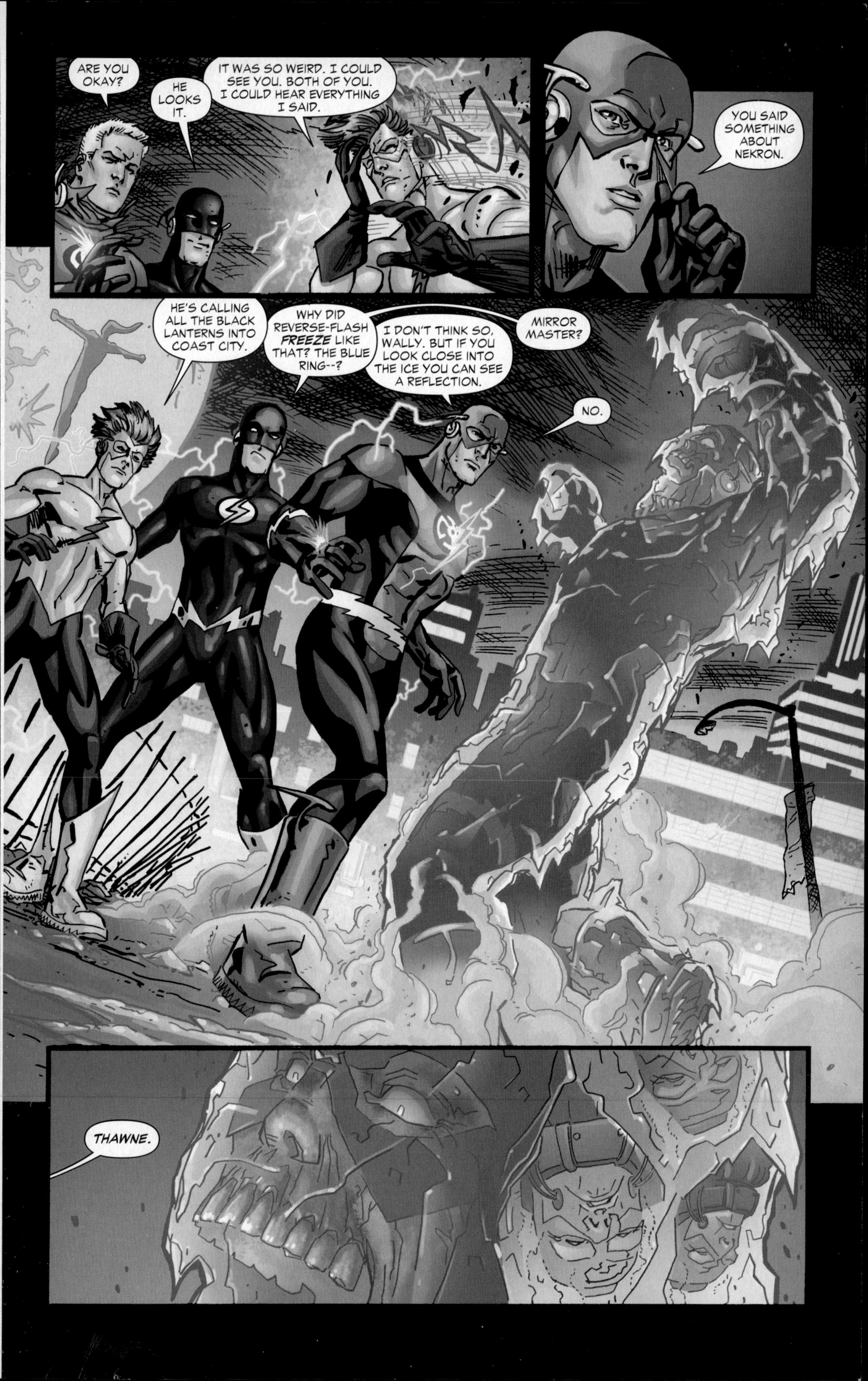

ARE YOU OKAY?
HE LOOKS IT.
IT WAS SO WEIRD. I COULD SEE YOU. BOTH OF YOU. I COULD HEAR EVERYTHING I SAID.
YOU SAID SOMETHING ABOUT NEKRON.
HE'S CALLING ALL THE BLACK LANTERNS INTO COAST CITY.
WHY DID REVERSE-FLASH FREEZE LIKE THAT? THE BLUE RING--?
MIRROR MASTER?
I DON'T THINK SO, WALLY. BUT IF YOU LOOK CLOSE INTO THE ICE YOU CAN SEE A REFLECTION.
NO.
THAWNE.

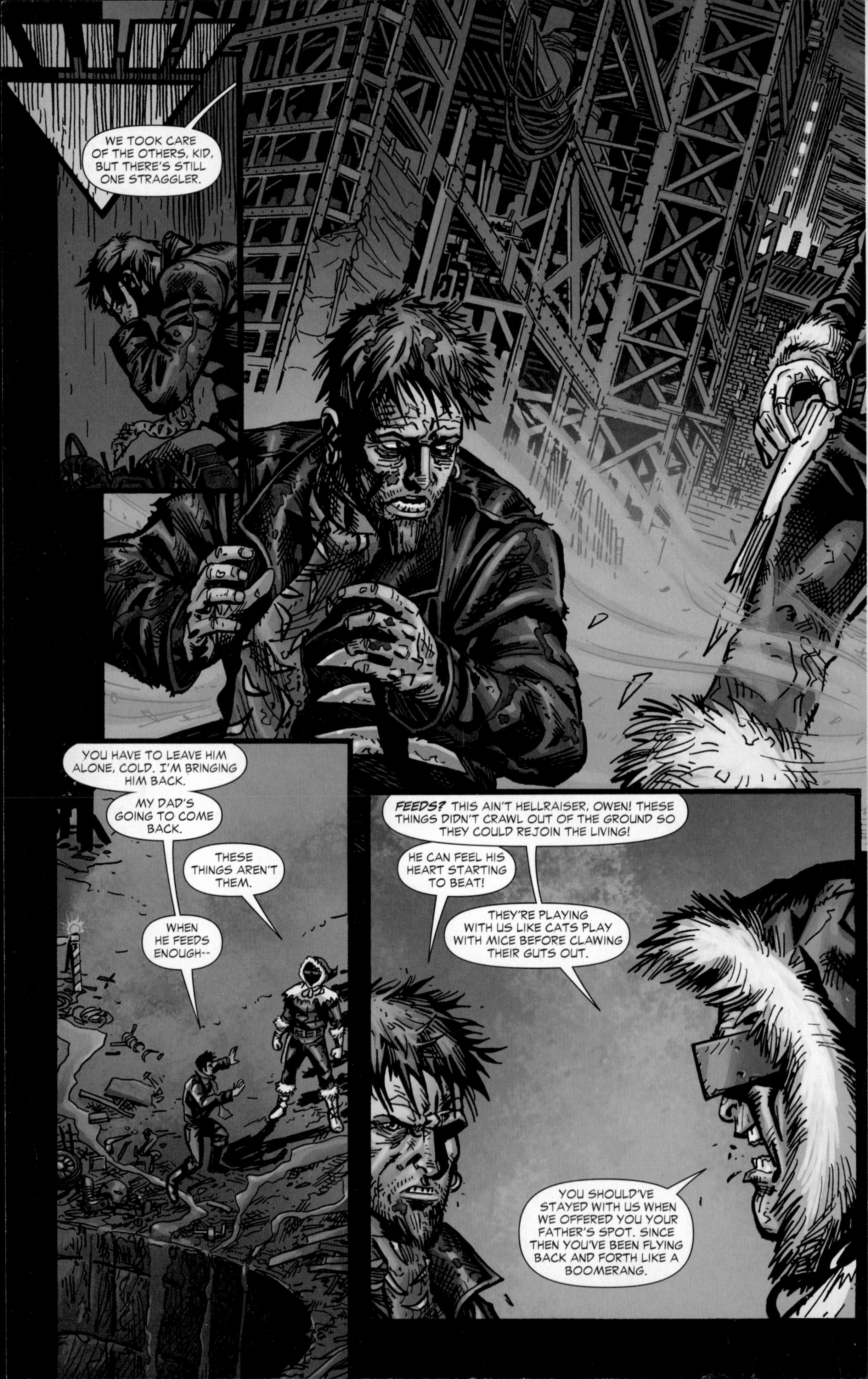
WE TOOK CARE OF THE OTHERS, KID, BUT THERE'S STILL ONE STRAGGLER.
YOU HAVE TO LEAVE HIM ALONE, COLD. I'M BRINGING HIM BACK.
MY DAD'S GOING TO COME BACK.
THESE THINGS AREN'T THEM.
WHEN HE FEEDS ENOUGH--
FEEDS? THIS AIN'T HELLRAISER, OWEN! THESE THINGS DIDN'T CRAWL OUT OF THE GROUND SO THEY COULD REJOIN THE LIVING!
HE CAN FEEL HIS HEART STARTING TO BEAT!
THEY'RE PLAYING WITH US LIKE CATS PLAY WITH MICE BEFORE CLAWING THEIR GUTS OUT.
YOU SHOULD'VE STAYED WITH US WHEN WE OFFERED YOU YOUR FATHER'S SPOT. SINCE THEN YOU'VE BEEN FLYING BACK AND FORTH LIKE A BOOMERANG.

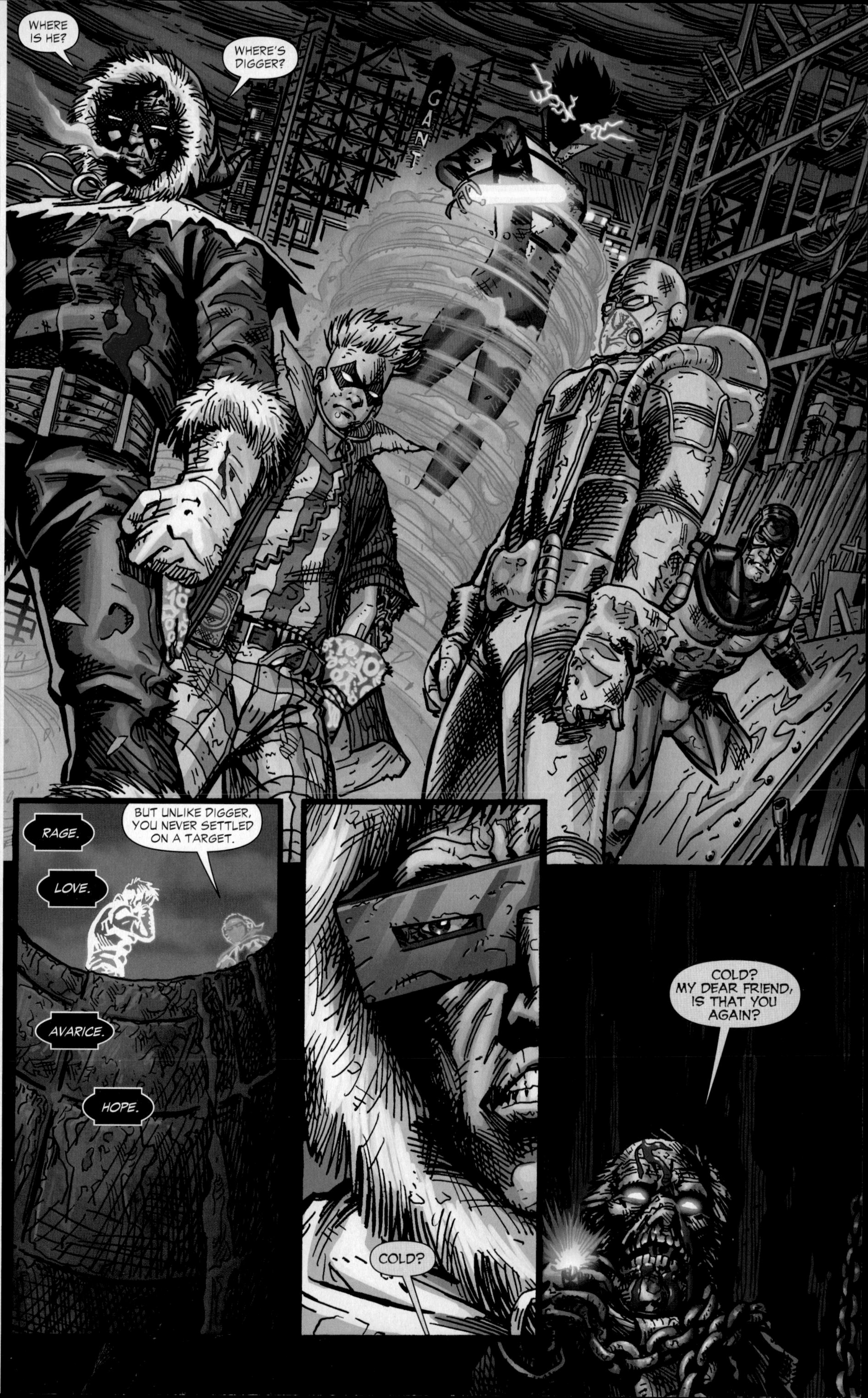
WHERE IS HE?
WHERE'S DIGGER?
GANT
RAGE.
BUT UNLIKE DIGGER, YOU NEVER SETTLED ON A TARGET.
LOVE.
AVARICE.
HOPE.
COLD?
COLD? MY DEAR FRIEND, IS THAT YOU AGAIN?

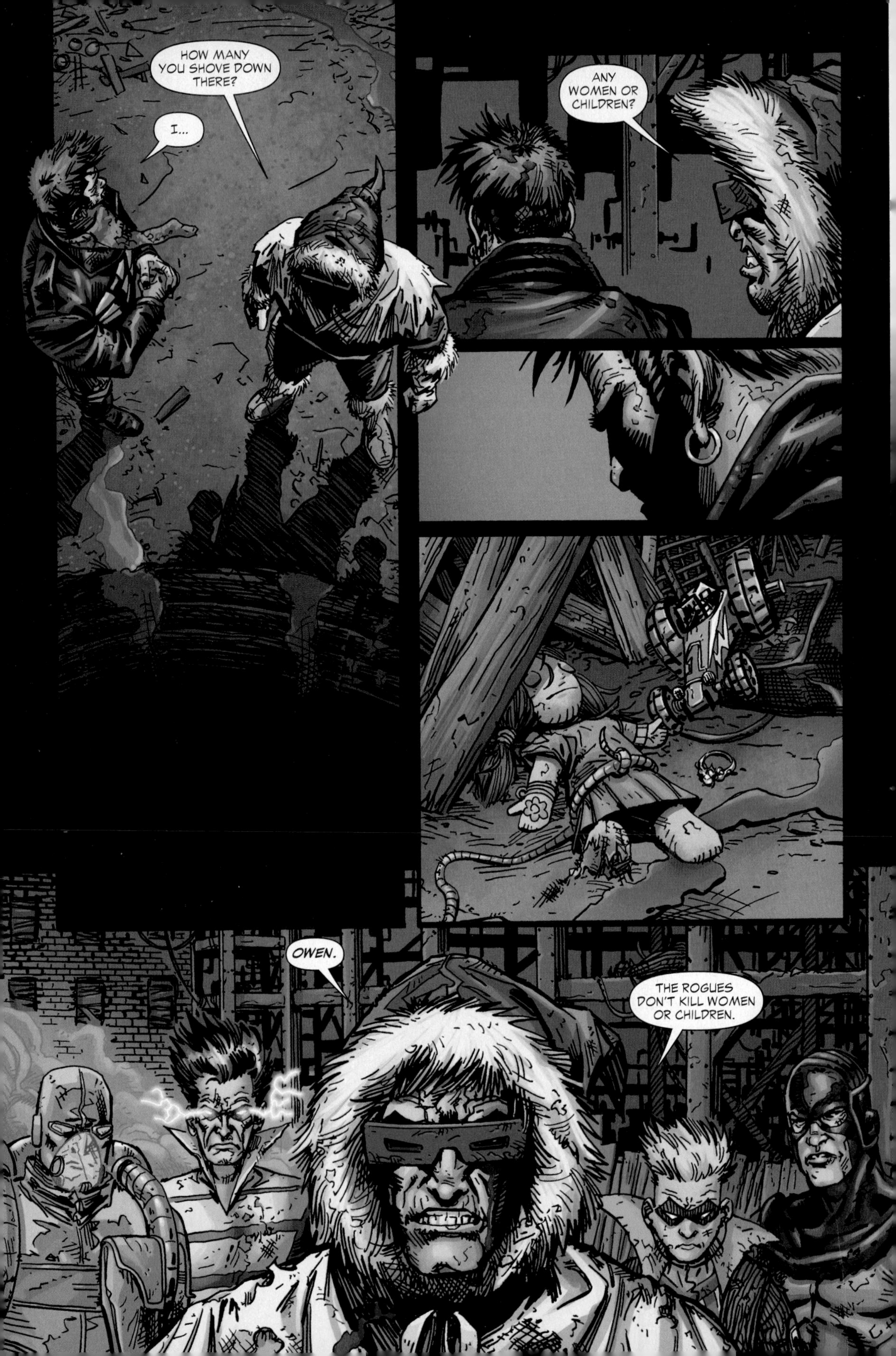
HOW MANY YOU SHOVE DOWN THERE?
I...
ANY WOMEN OR CHILDREN?
OWEN.
THE ROGUES DON'T KILL WOMEN OR CHILDREN.

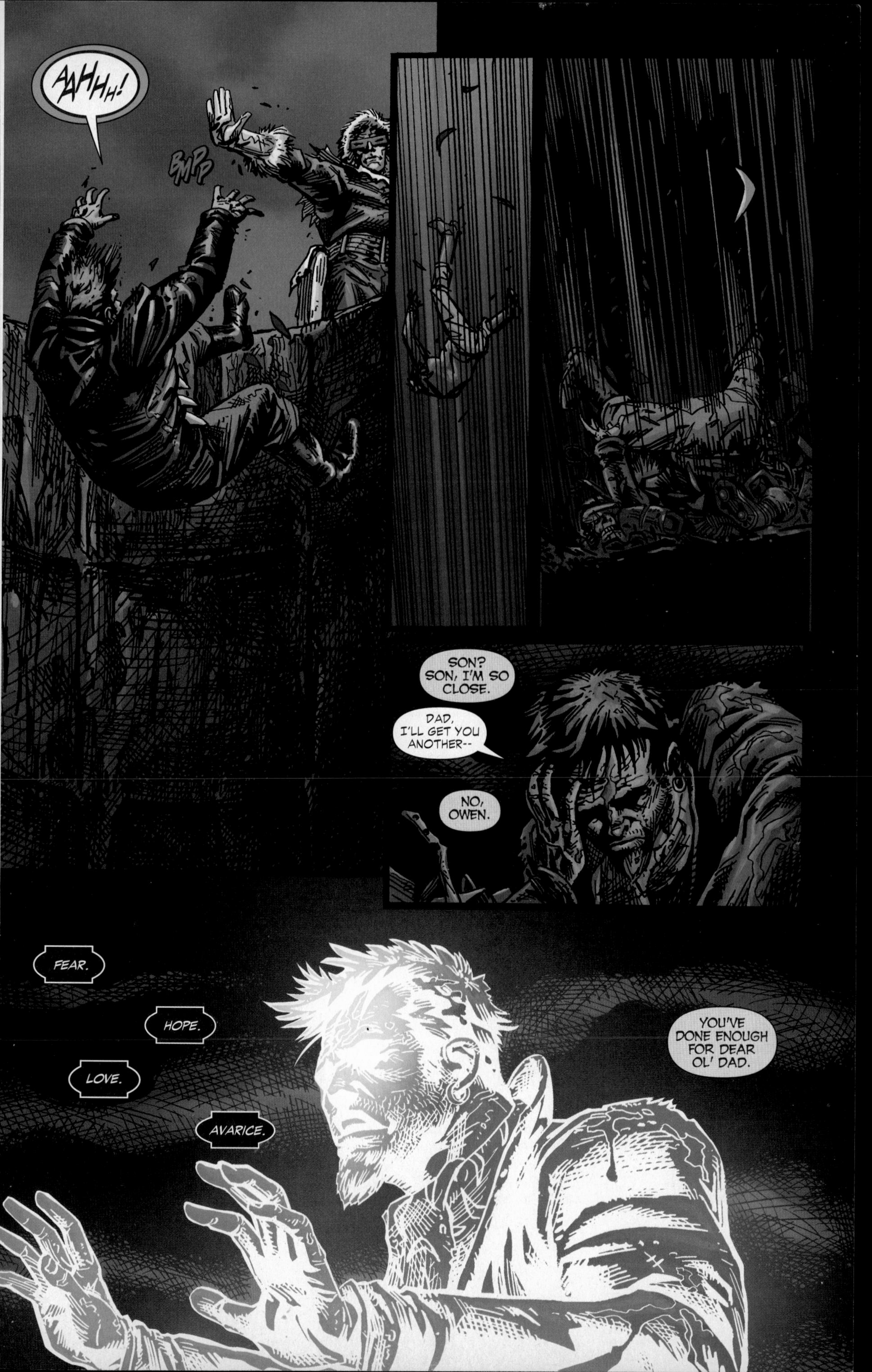
AAHHH!
BMPP
SON? SON, I'M SO CLOSE.
DAD, I'LL GET YOU ANOTHER--
NO, OWEN.
FEAR.
HOPE.
LOVE.
AVARICE.
YOU'VE DONE ENOUGH FOR DEAR OL' DAD.

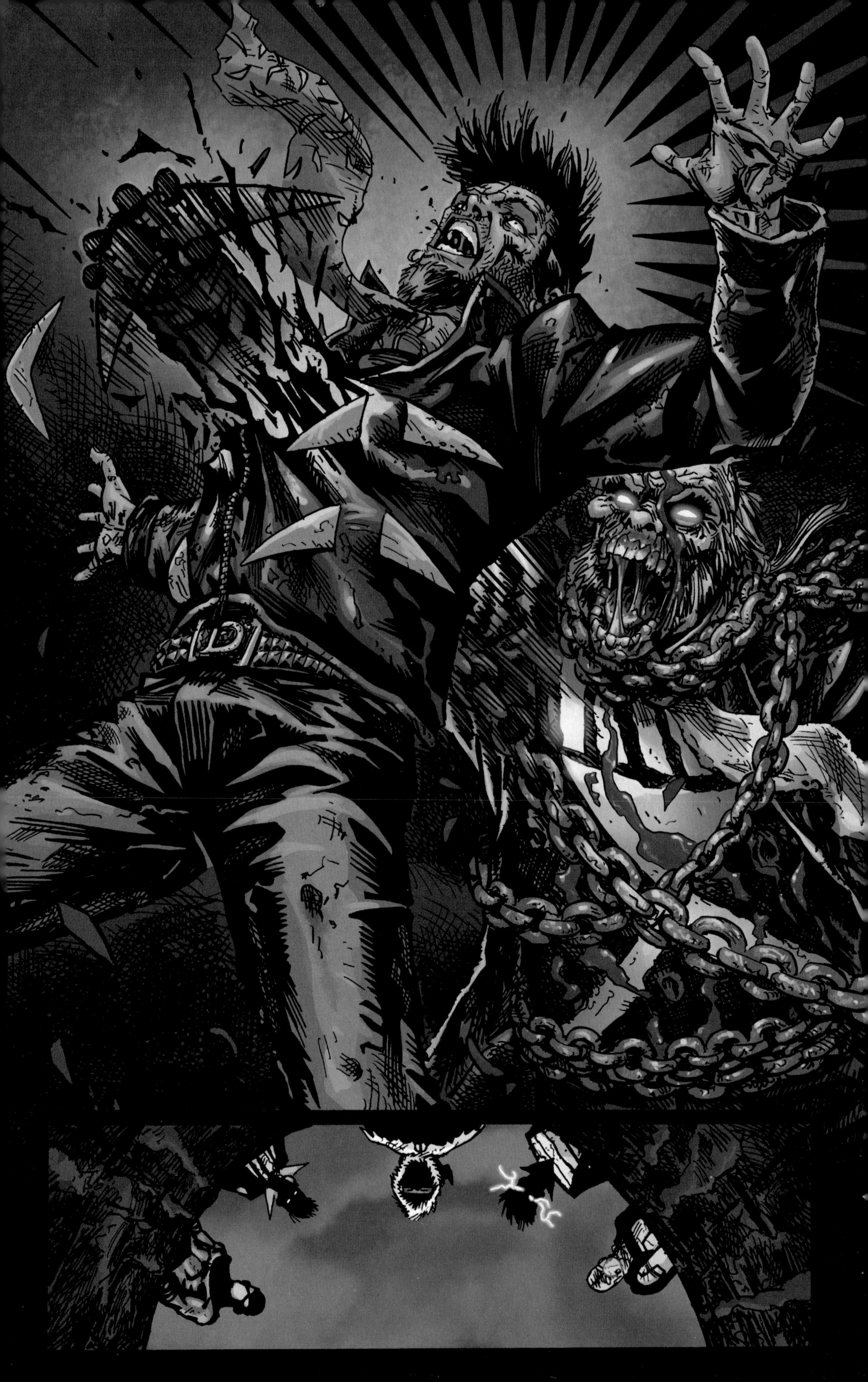

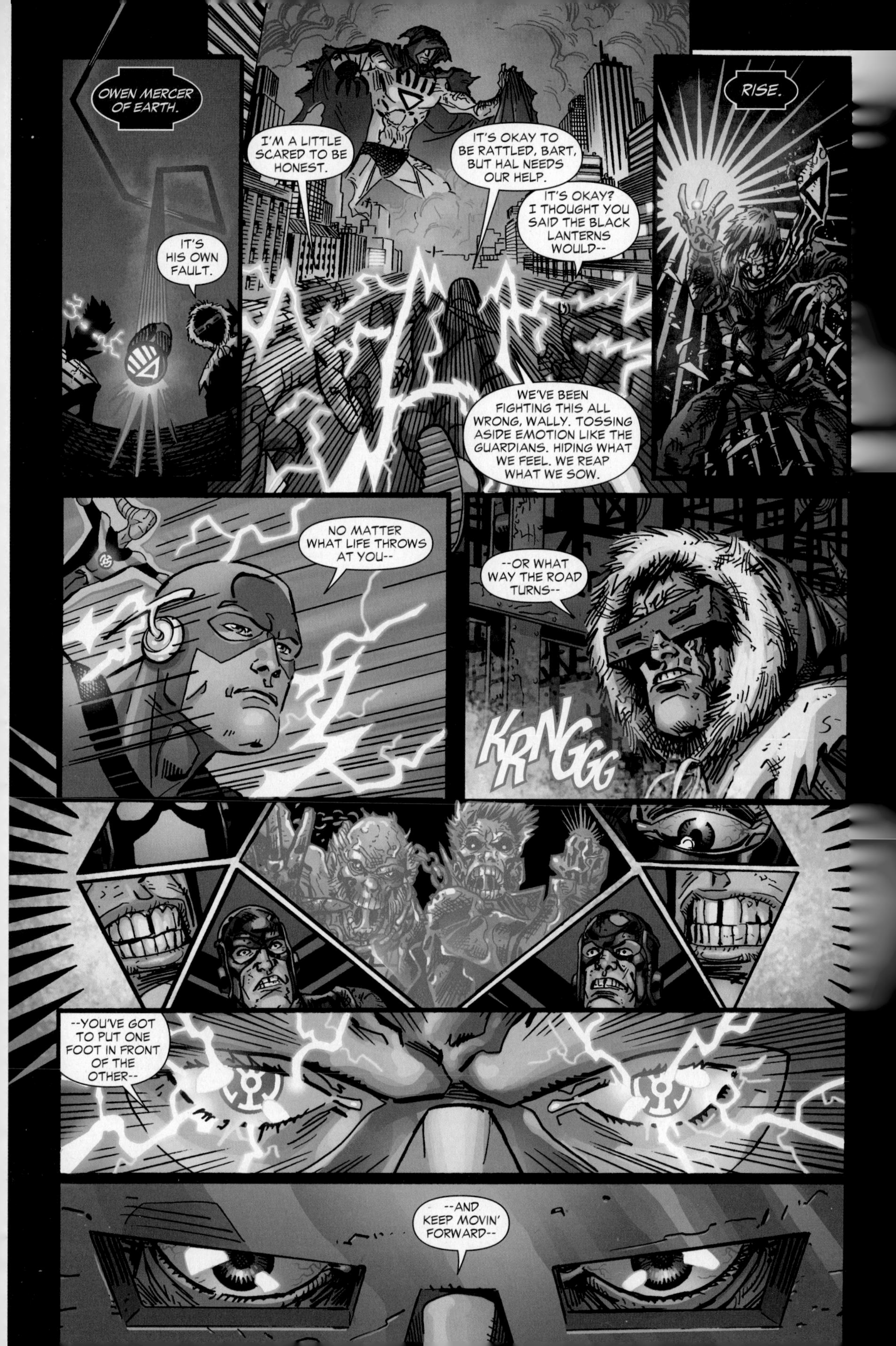
OWEN MERCER OF EARTH.
IT'S HIS OWN FAULT.
I'M A LITTLE SCARED TO BE HONEST.
IT'S OKAY TO BE RATTLED, BART, BUT HAL NEEDS OUR HELP.
IT'S OKAY? I THOUGHT YOU SAID THE BLACK LANTERNS WOULD--
WE'VE BEEN FIGHTING THIS ALL WRONG, WALLY. TOSSING ASIDE EMOTION LIKE THE GUARDIANS. HIDING WHAT WE FEEL. WE REAP WHAT WE SOW.
RISE.
NO MATTER WHAT LIFE THROWS AT YOU--
--OR WHAT WAY THE ROAD TURNS--
KRRNGGG
--YOU'VE GOT TO PUT ONE FOOT IN FRONT OF THE OTHER--
--AND KEEP MOVIN' FORWARD--

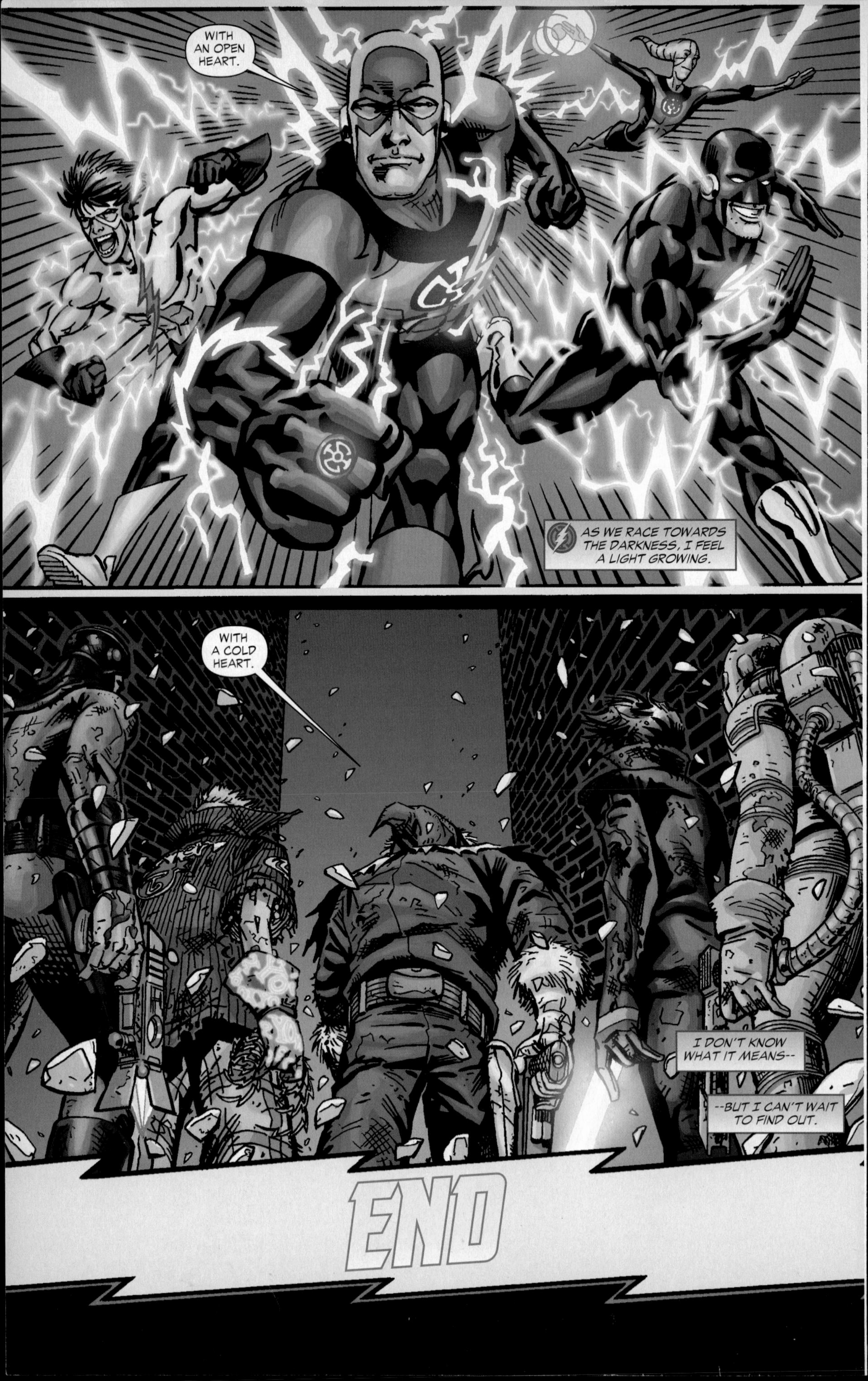
WITH AN OPEN HEART.
AS WE RACE TOWARDS THE DARKNESS, I FEEL A LIGHT GROWING.
WITH A COLD HEART.
I DON'T KNOW WHAT IT MEANS--
--BUT I CAN'T WAIT TO FIND OUT.
END

BLACKEST NIGHT: JSA 1
Cover by Gene Ha

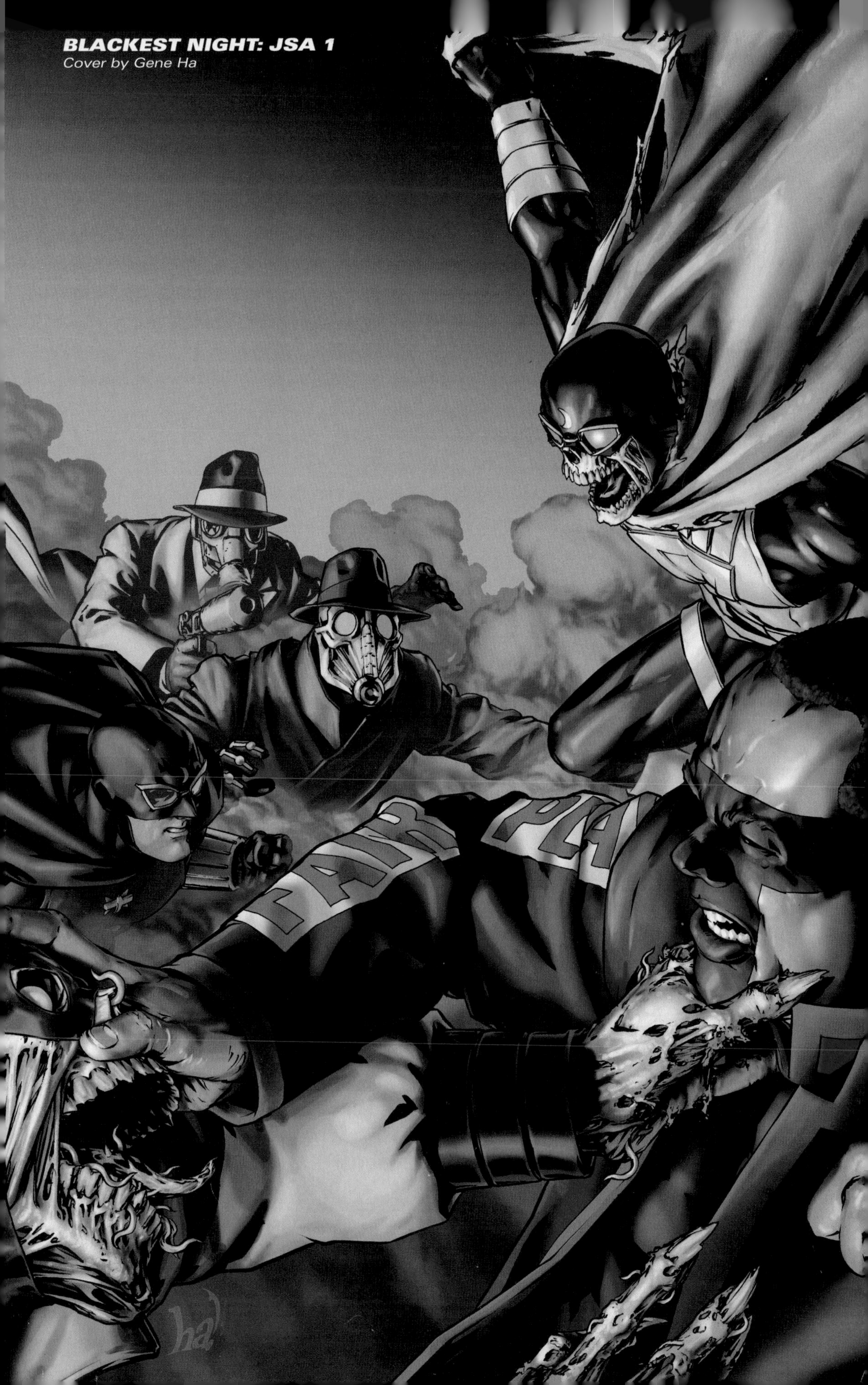

LOST SOULS

JAMES ROBINSON
WRITER

EDDY BARROWS
MARCOS MARZ
PENCILS

JULIO FERREIRA
LUCIANA DEL NEGRO
RUY JOSÉ
INKS

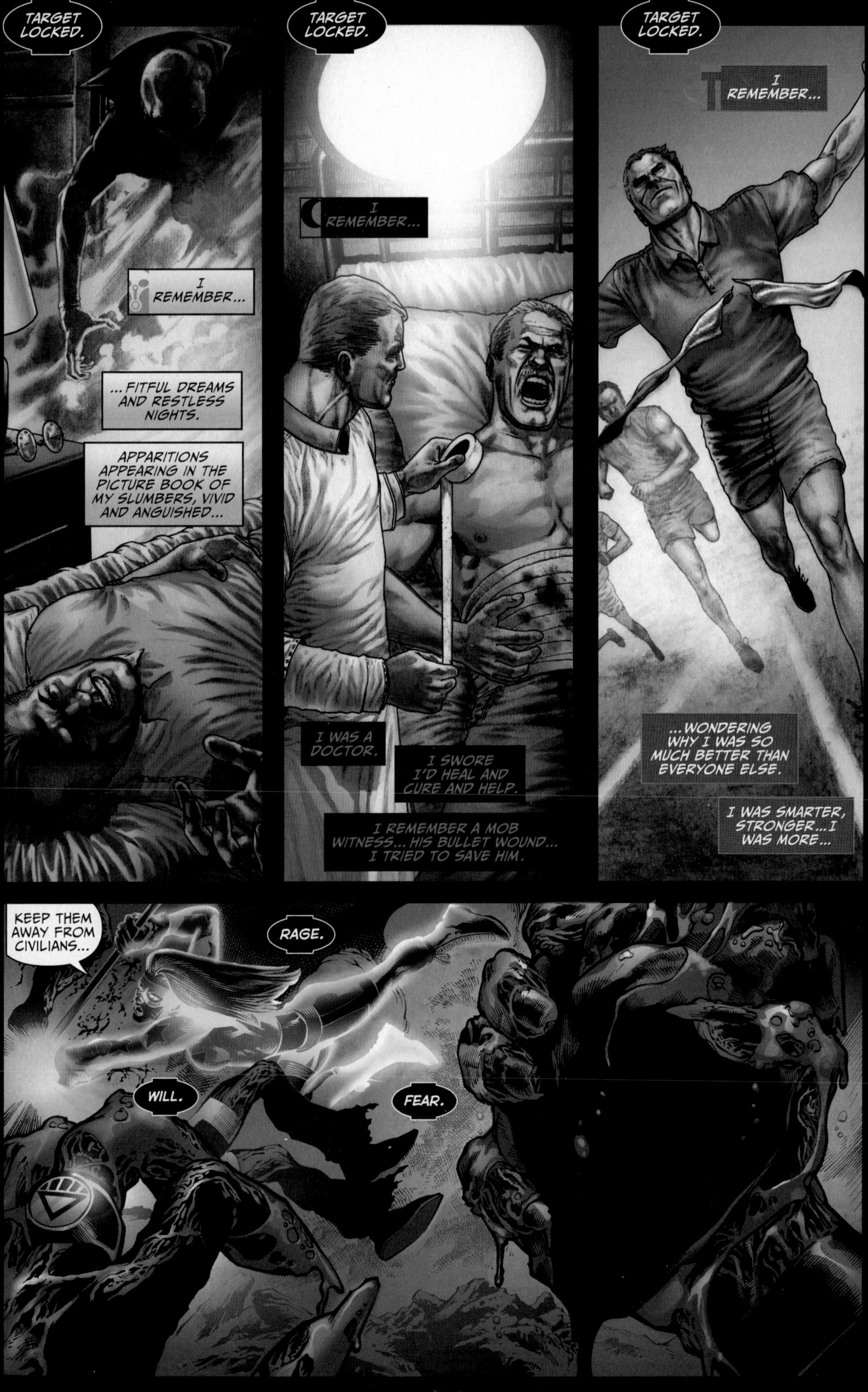
TARGET LOCKED.
I REMEMBER...
...FITFUL DREAMS AND RESTLESS NIGHTS.
APPARITIONS APPEARING IN THE PICTURE BOOK OF MY SLUMBERS, VIVID AND ANGUISHED...
TARGET LOCKED.
I REMEMBER...
I WAS A DOCTOR.
I SWORE I'D HEAL AND CURE AND HELP.
I REMEMBER A MOB WITNESS... HIS BULLET WOUND... I TRIED TO SAVE HIM.
TARGET LOCKED.
I REMEMBER...
...WONDERING WHY I WAS SO MUCH BETTER THAN EVERYONE ELSE.
I WAS SMARTER, STRONGER...I WAS MORE...
KEEP THEM AWAY FROM CIVILIANS...
RAGE.
WILL.
FEAR.

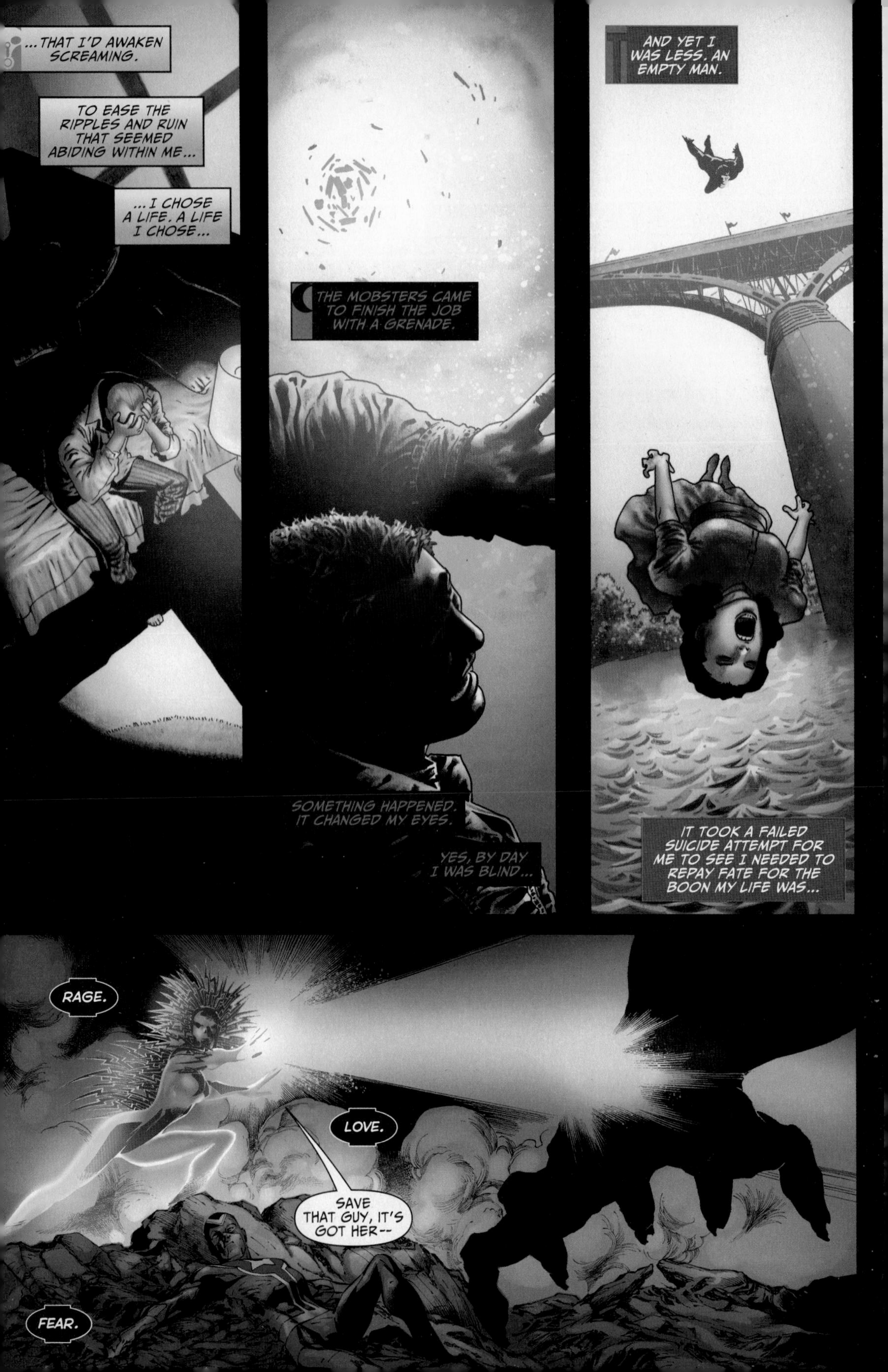
...THAT I'D AWAKEN SCREAMING.
TO EASE THE RIPPLES AND RUIN THAT SEEMED ABIDING WITHIN ME...
...I CHOSE A LIFE. A LIFE I CHOSE...
THE MOBSTERS CAME TO FINISH THE JOB WITH A GRENADE.
SOMETHING HAPPENED. IT CHANGED MY EYES.
YES, BY DAY I WAS BLIND...
AND YET I WAS LESS. AN EMPTY MAN.
IT TOOK A FAILED SUICIDE ATTEMPT FOR ME TO SEE I NEEDED TO REPAY FATE FOR THE BOON MY LIFE WAS...
RAGE.
LOVE.
SAVE THAT GUY, IT'S GOT HER--
FEAR.

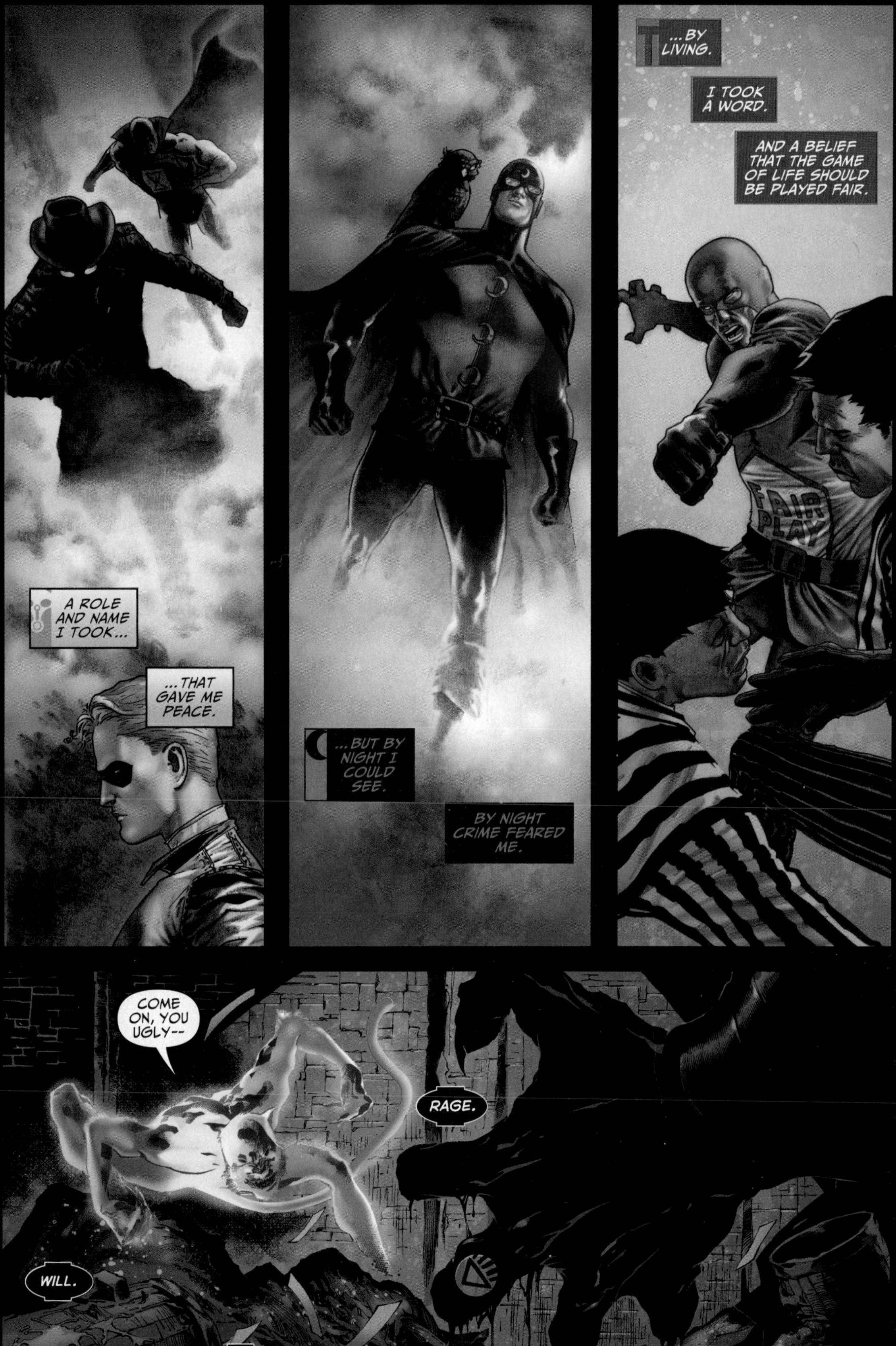
A ROLE AND NAME I TOOK...
...THAT GAVE ME PEACE.
...BUT BY NIGHT I COULD SEE.
BY NIGHT CRIME FEARED ME.
...BY LIVING.
I TOOK A WORD.
AND A BELIEF THAT THE GAME OF LIFE SHOULD BE PLAYED FAIR.
FAIR PLAY
COME ON, YOU UGLY--
RAGE.
WILL.
FEAR.

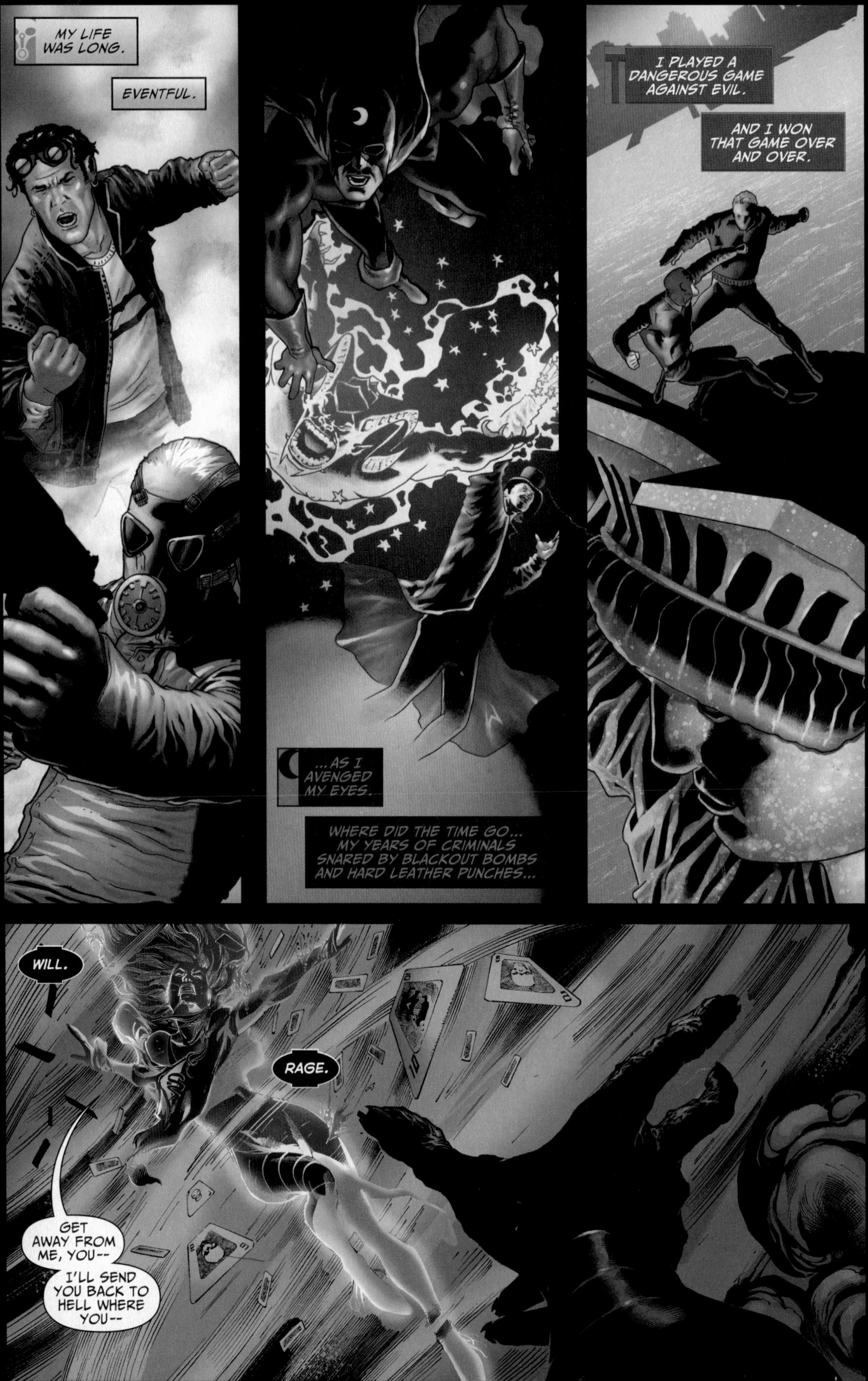
MY LIFE WAS LONG.
EVENTFUL.
...AS I AVENGED MY EYES.
WHERE DID THE TIME GO... MY YEARS OF CRIMINALS SNARED BY BLACKOUT BOMBS AND HARD LEATHER PUNCHES...
I PLAYED A DANGEROUS GAME AGAINST EVIL.
AND I WON THAT GAME OVER AND OVER.
WILL.
RAGE.
GET AWAY FROM ME, YOU--
I'LL SEND YOU BACK TO HELL WHERE YOU--

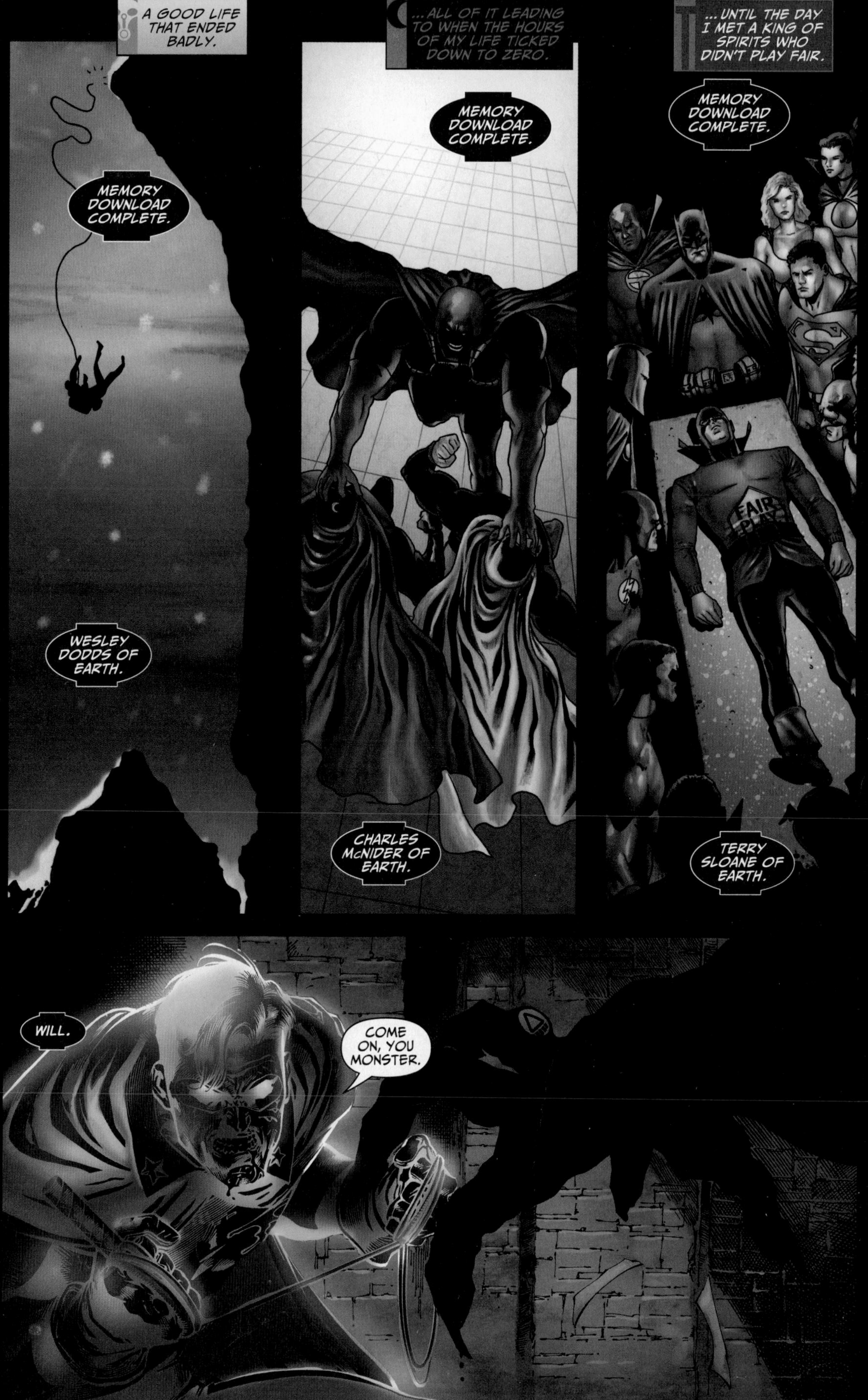
A GOOD LIFE THAT ENDED BADLY.
MEMORY DOWNLOAD COMPLETE.
WESLEY DODDS OF EARTH.
...ALL OF IT LEADING TO WHEN THE HOURS OF MY LIFE TICKED DOWN TO ZERO.
MEMORY DOWNLOAD COMPLETE.
CHARLES McNIDER OF EARTH.
...UNTIL THE DAY I MET A KING OF SPIRITS WHO DIDN'T PLAY FAIR.
MEMORY DOWNLOAD COMPLETE.
FAIR PLAY
TERRY SLOANE OF EARTH.
WILL.
COME ON, YOU MONSTER.

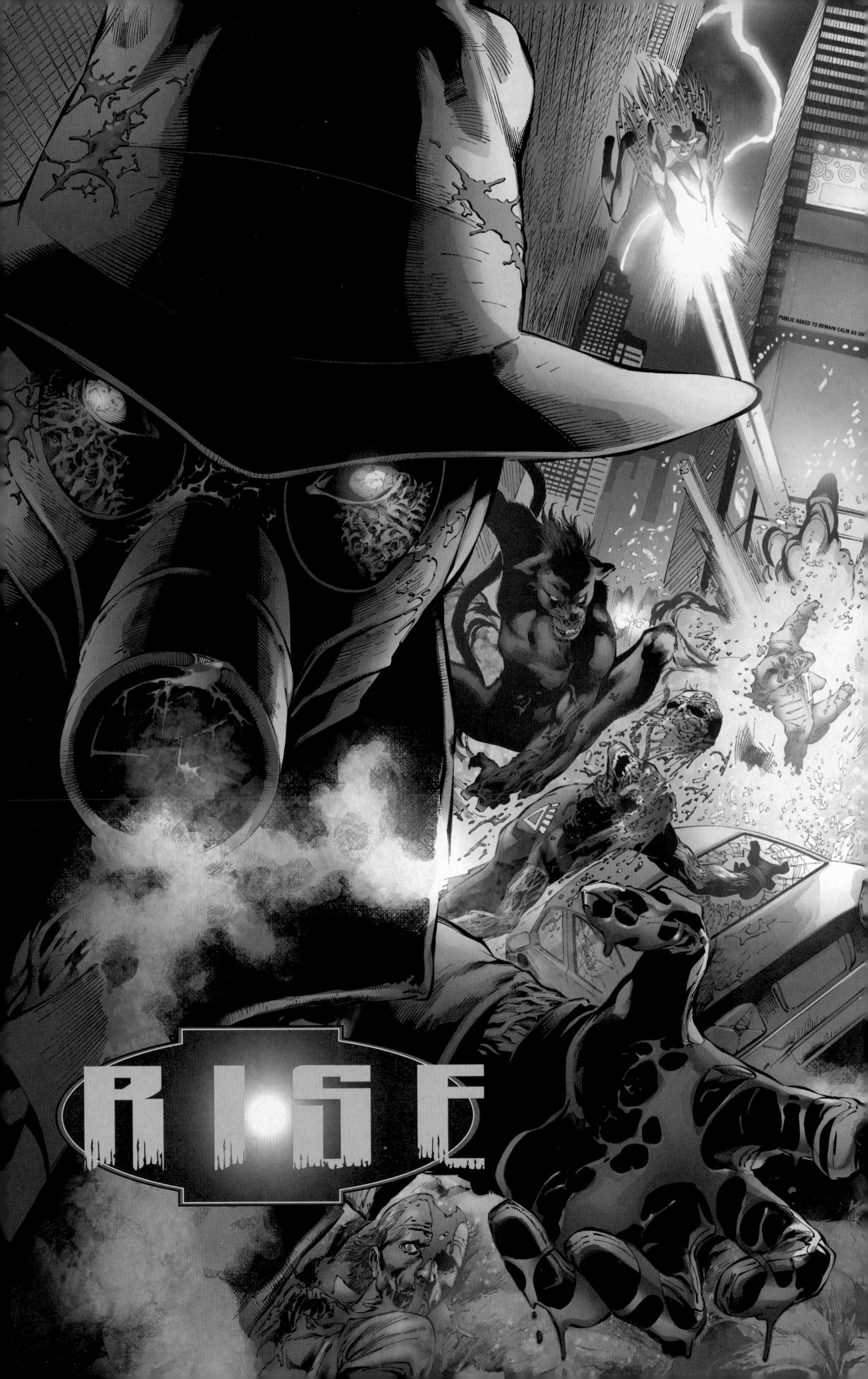
PUBLIC ASKED TO REMAIN CALM AS UN
RISE

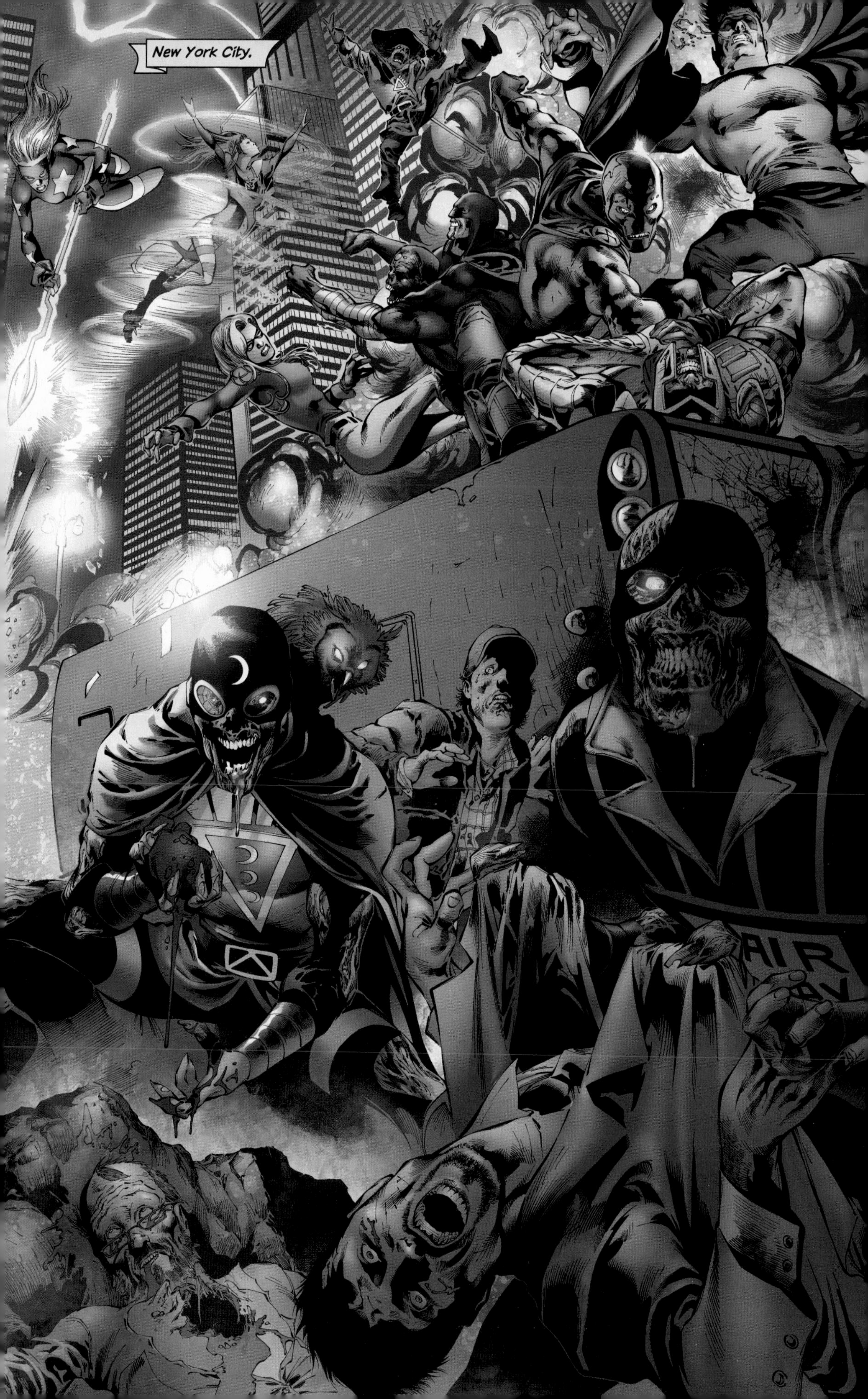
New York City.

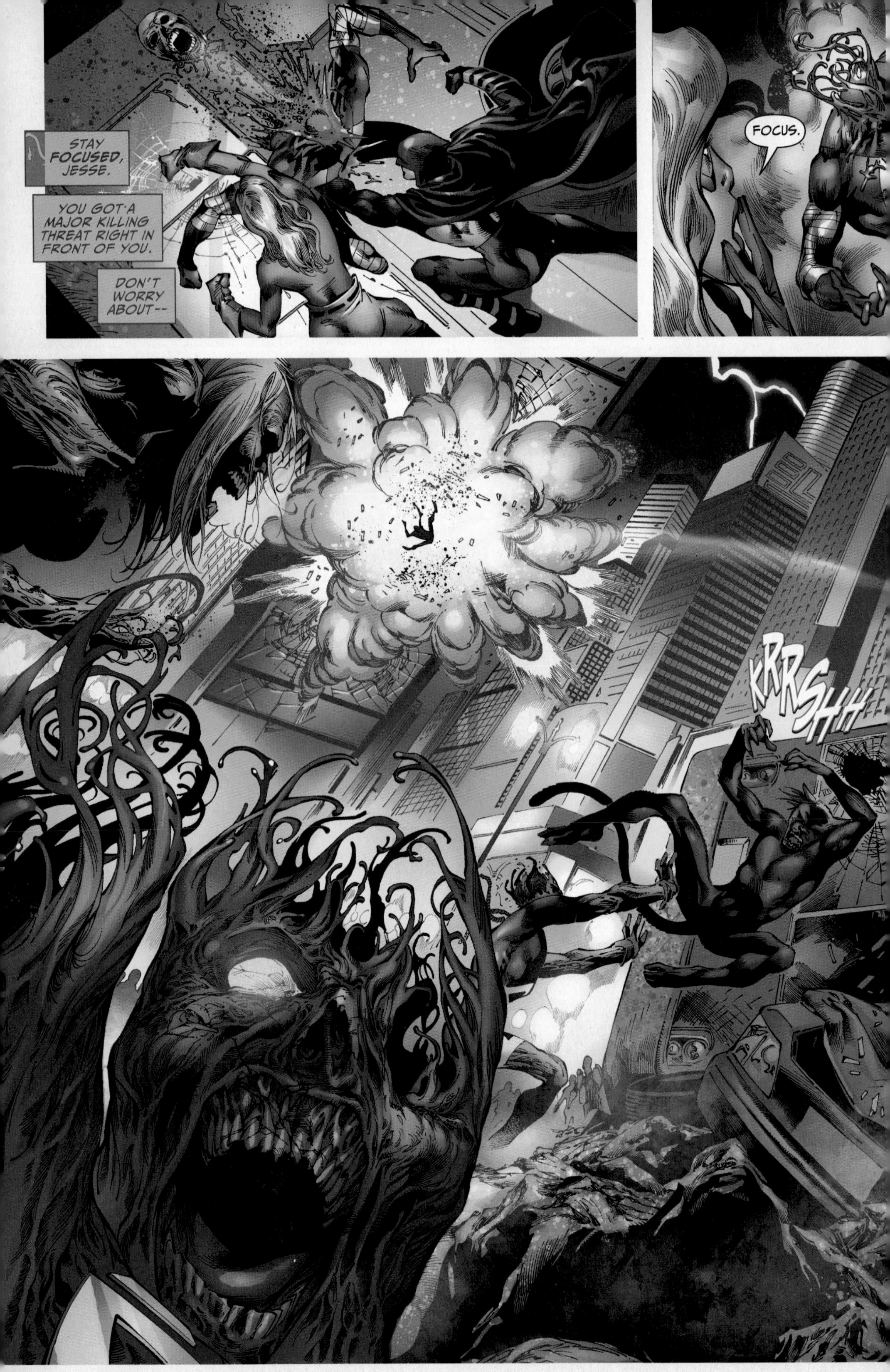
STAY FOCUSED, JESSE.
YOU GOT A MAJOR KILLING THREAT RIGHT IN FRONT OF YOU.
DON'T WORRY ABOUT--
FOCUS.
KRRSHH

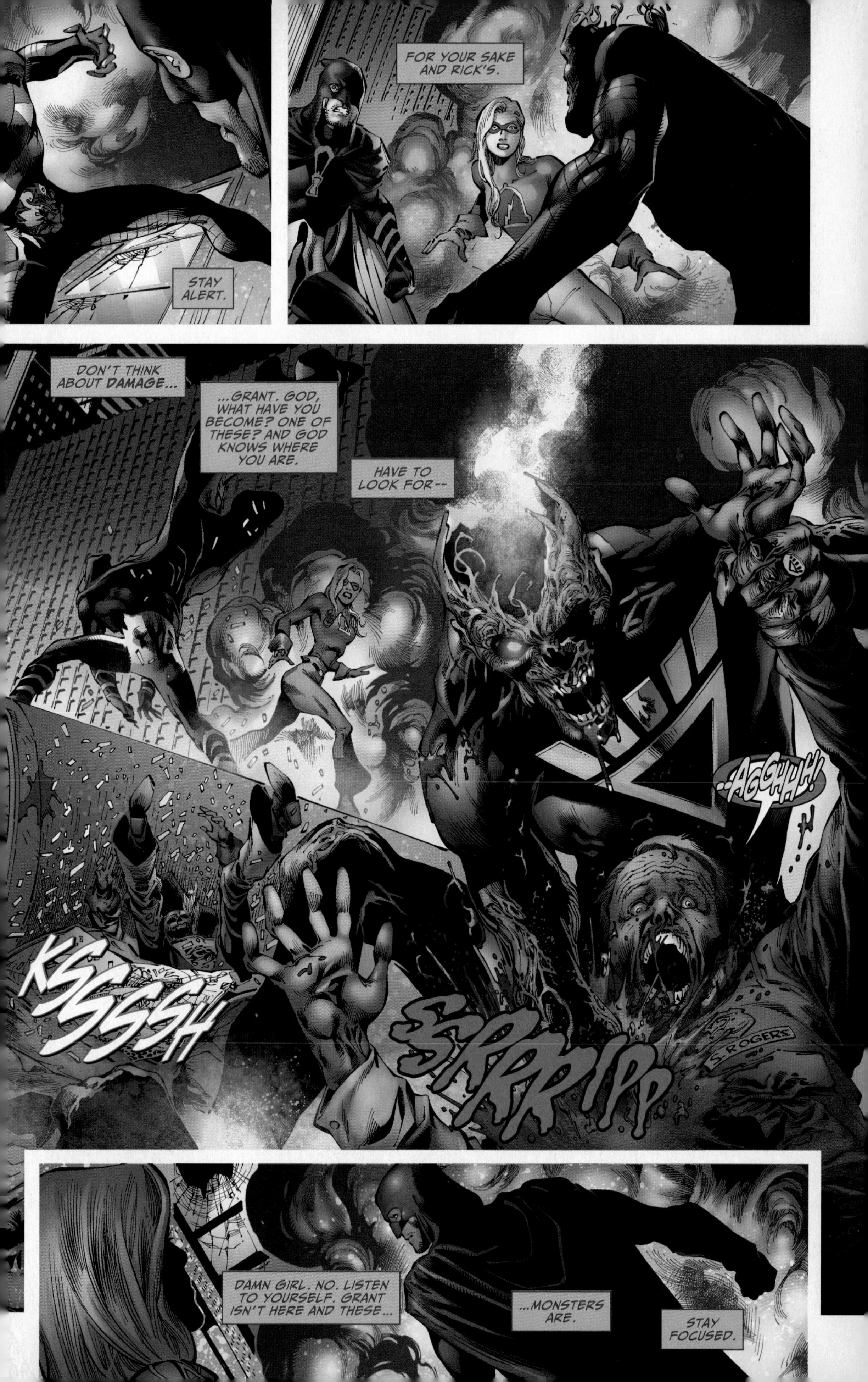
STAY ALERT.
FOR YOUR SAKE AND RICK'S.
DON'T THINK ABOUT DAMAGE...
...GRANT. GOD, WHAT HAVE YOU BECOME? ONE OF THESE? AND GOD KNOWS WHERE YOU ARE.
HAVE TO LOOK FOR--
..AGGHHH!
KSSSSH
SKRRIPP
S. ROGERS
DAMN GIRL. NO. LISTEN TO YOURSELF. GRANT ISN'T HERE AND THESE...
...MONSTERS ARE.
STAY FOCUSED.

HOW YOU KIDS HOLDING UP?

FINE, FLASH.

JAY... HAVE... HAVE YOU SEEN DAMAGE?

GRANT'S *GONE*, JESSE. THE DARKNESS GOT HIM.

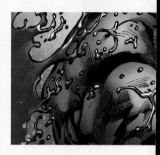

I CONVINCED HIM TO COME BACK TO ALL THIS, ALAN. I CONVINCED HIM TO JOIN THE JSA.

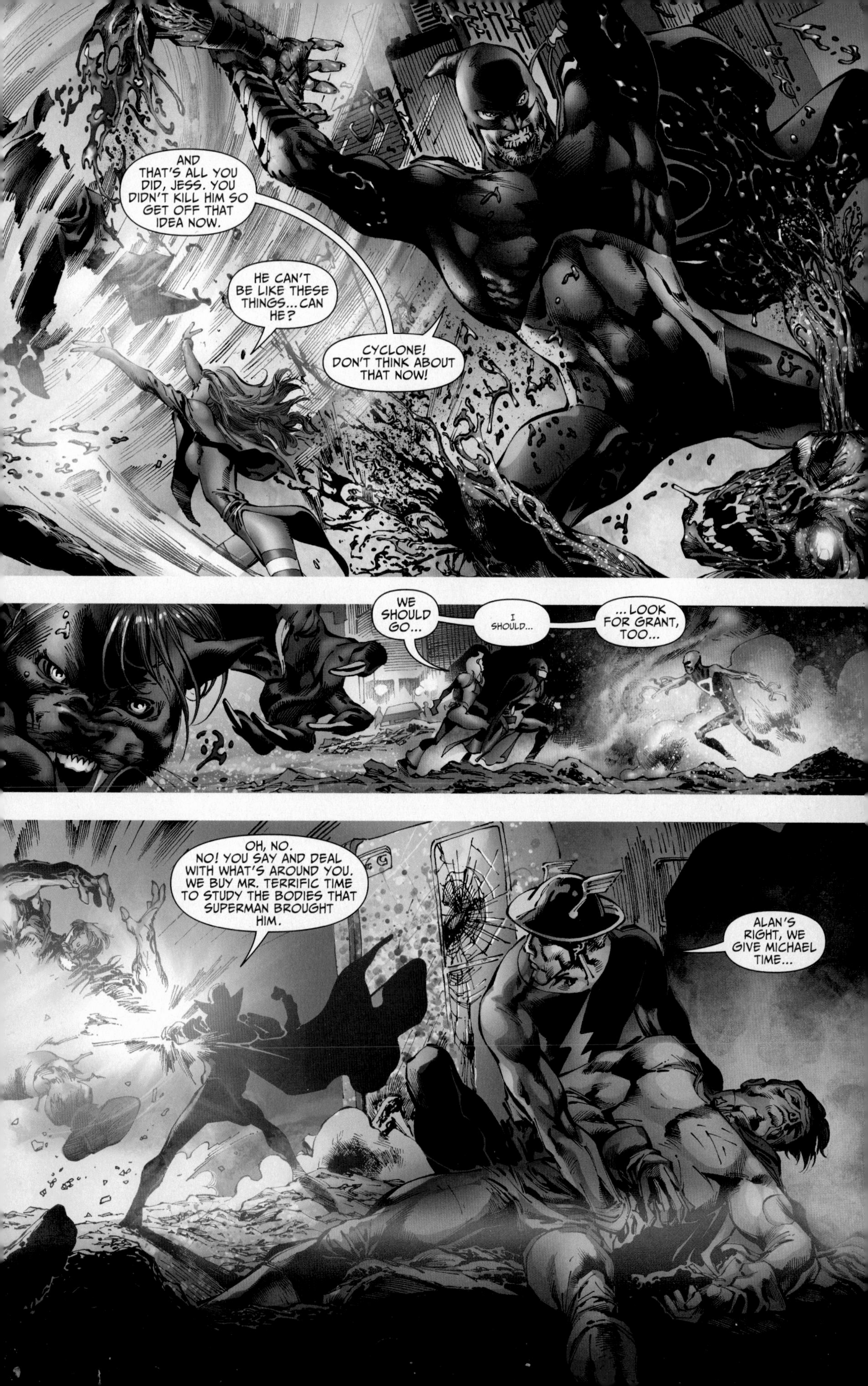
AND THAT'S ALL YOU DID, JESS. YOU DIDN'T KILL HIM SO GET OFF THAT IDEA NOW.
HE CAN'T BE LIKE THESE THINGS...CAN HE?
CYCLONE! DON'T THINK ABOUT THAT NOW!
WE SHOULD GO...
I SHOULD...
...LOOK FOR GRANT, TOO...
OH, NO. NO! YOU SAY AND DEAL WITH WHAT'S AROUND YOU. WE BUY MR. TERRIFIC TIME TO STUDY THE BODIES THAT SUPERMAN BROUGHT HIM.
ALAN'S RIGHT, WE GIVE MICHAEL TIME...

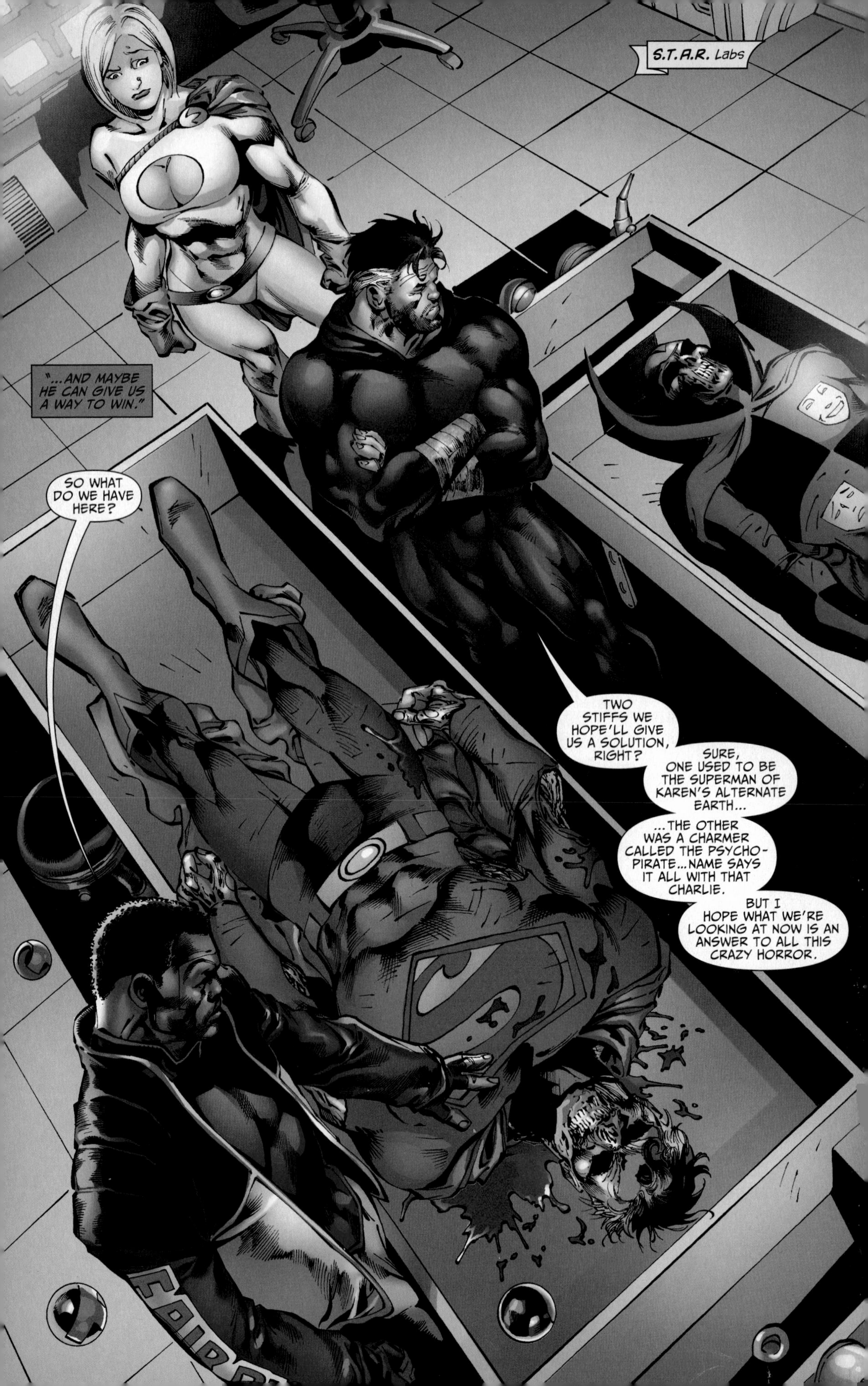
S.T.A.R. Labs
"...AND MAYBE HE CAN GIVE US A WAY TO WIN."
SO WHAT DO WE HAVE HERE?
TWO STIFFS WE HOPE'LL GIVE US A SOLUTION, RIGHT?
SURE, ONE USED TO BE THE SUPERMAN OF KAREN'S ALTERNATE EARTH...
...THE OTHER WAS A CHARMER CALLED THE PSYCHO-PIRATE...NAME SAYS IT ALL WITH THAT CHARLIE.
BUT I HOPE WHAT WE'RE LOOKING AT NOW IS AN ANSWER TO ALL THIS CRAZY HORROR.

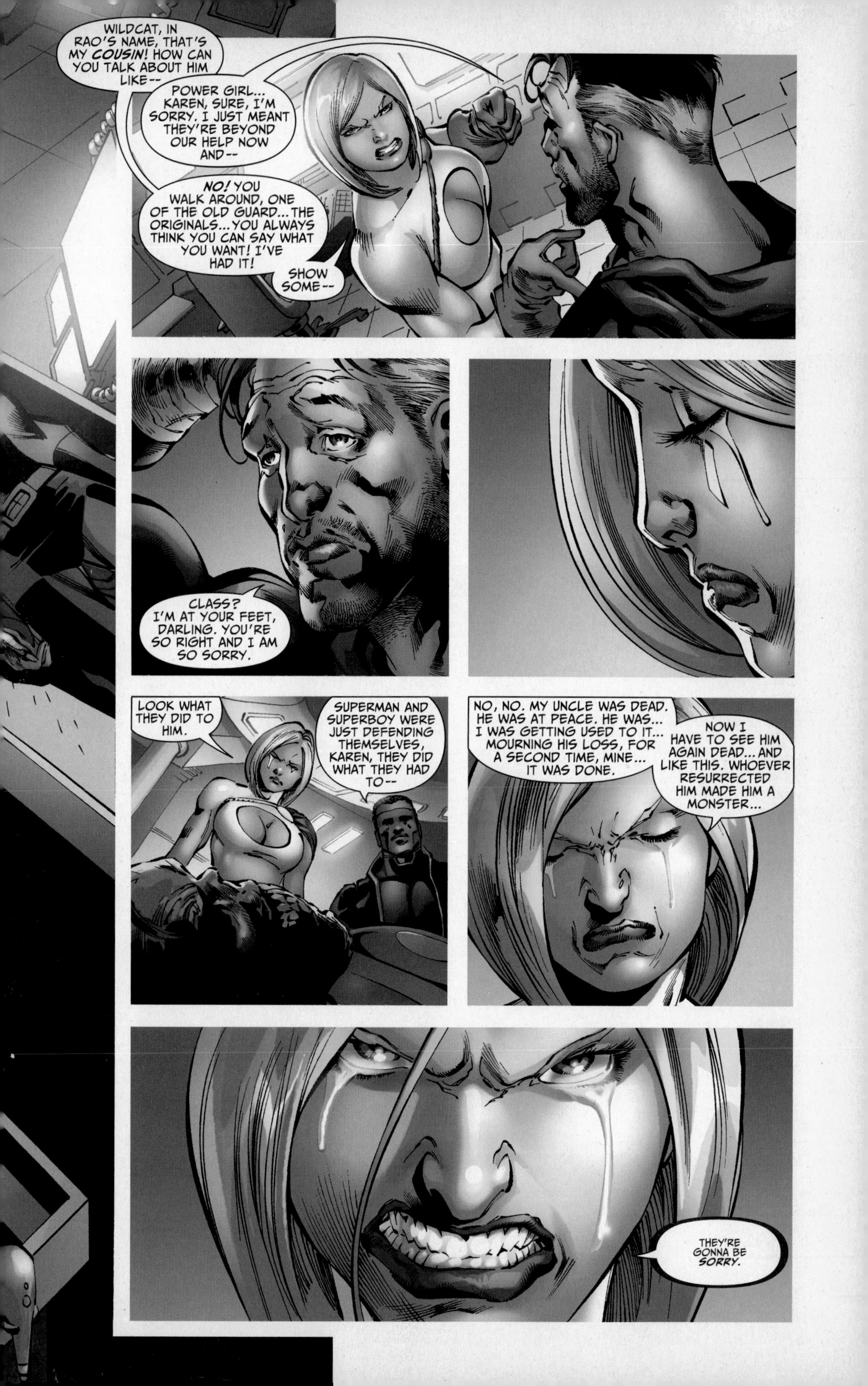
WILDCAT, IN RAO'S NAME, THAT'S MY COUSIN! HOW CAN YOU TALK ABOUT HIM LIKE--
POWER GIRL... KAREN, SURE, I'M SORRY. I JUST MEANT THEY'RE BEYOND OUR HELP NOW AND--
NO! YOU WALK AROUND, ONE OF THE OLD GUARD... THE ORIGINALS... YOU ALWAYS THINK YOU CAN SAY WHAT YOU WANT! I'VE HAD IT!
SHOW SOME--
CLASS? I'M AT YOUR FEET, DARLING. YOU'RE SO RIGHT AND I AM SO SORRY.
LOOK WHAT THEY DID TO HIM.
SUPERMAN AND SUPERBOY WERE JUST DEFENDING THEMSELVES, KAREN, THEY DID WHAT THEY HAD TO--
NO, NO. MY UNCLE WAS DEAD. HE WAS AT PEACE. HE WAS... I WAS GETTING USED TO IT... MOURNING HIS LOSS, FOR A SECOND TIME, MINE... IT WAS DONE.
NOW I HAVE TO SEE HIM AGAIN DEAD... AND LIKE THIS. WHOEVER RESURRECTED HIM MADE HIM A MONSTER...
THEY'RE GONNA BE SORRY.

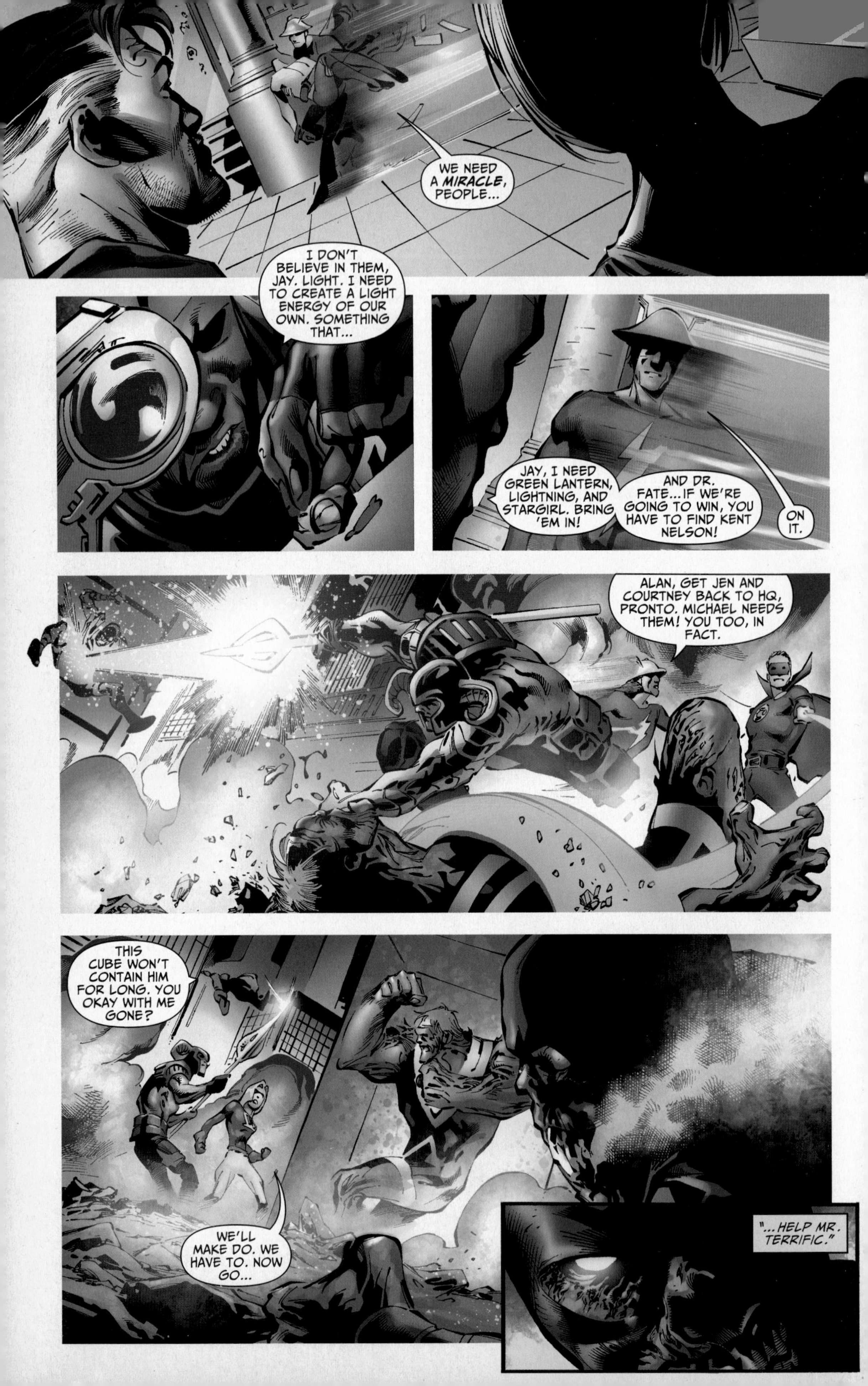
WE NEED A *MIRACLE*, PEOPLE...
I DON'T BELIEVE IN THEM, JAY. LIGHT. I NEED TO CREATE A LIGHT ENERGY OF OUR OWN. SOMETHING THAT...
JAY, I NEED GREEN LANTERN, LIGHTNING, AND STARGIRL. BRING 'EM IN!
AND DR. FATE...IF WE'RE GOING TO WIN, YOU HAVE TO FIND KENT NELSON!
ON IT.
ALAN, GET JEN AND COURTNEY BACK TO HQ, PRONTO. MICHAEL NEEDS THEM! YOU TOO, IN FACT.
THIS CUBE WON'T CONTAIN HIM FOR LONG. YOU OKAY WITH ME GONE?
WE'LL MAKE DO. WE HAVE TO. NOW GO...
"...HELP MR. TERRIFIC."

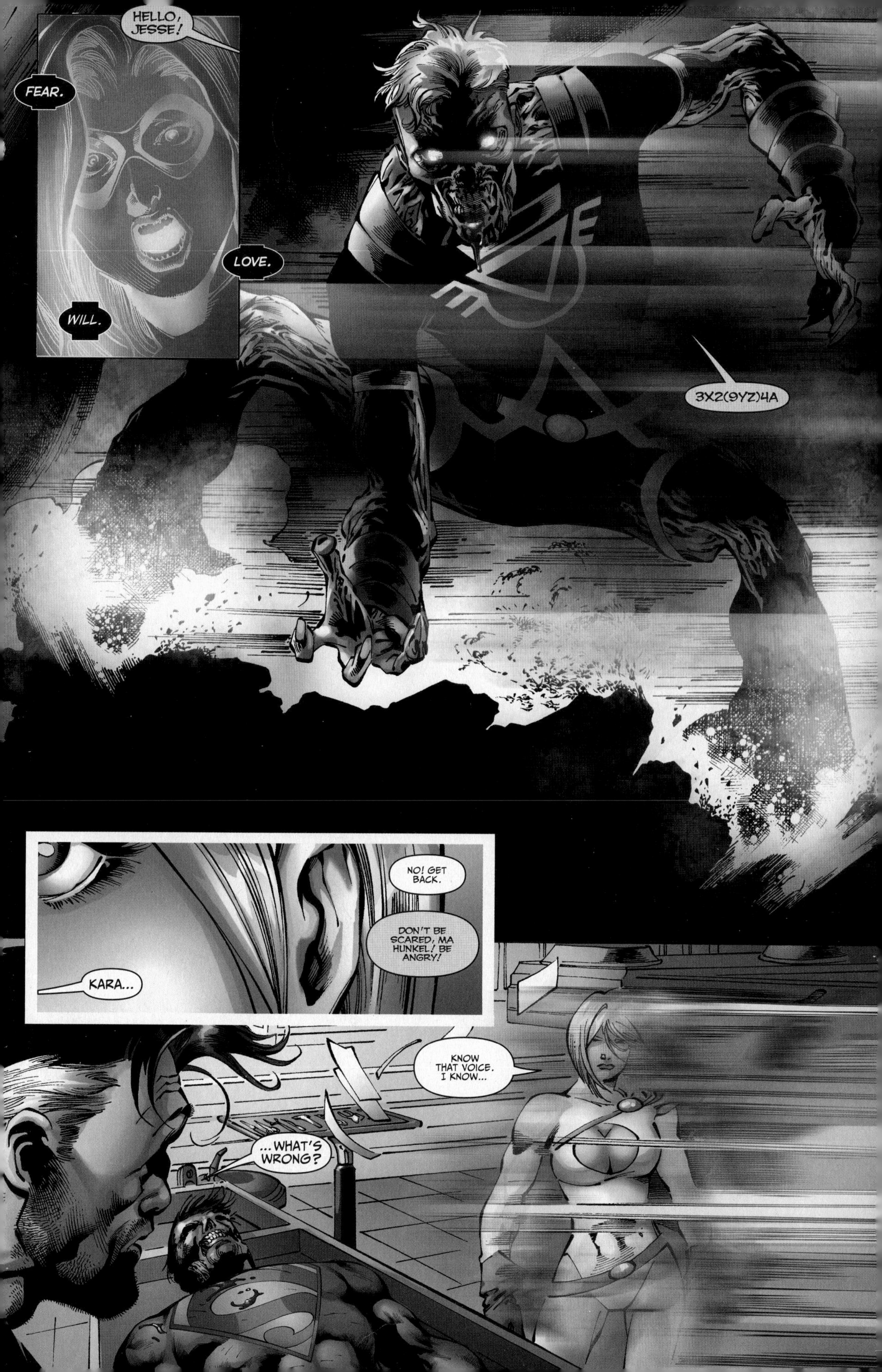

HELLO, JESSE!
FEAR.
LOVE.
WILL.
3X2(9YZ)4A
NO! GET BACK.
DON'T BE SCARED, MA HUNKEL! BE ANGRY!
KARA...
KNOW THAT VOICE. I KNOW...
...WHAT'S WRONG?

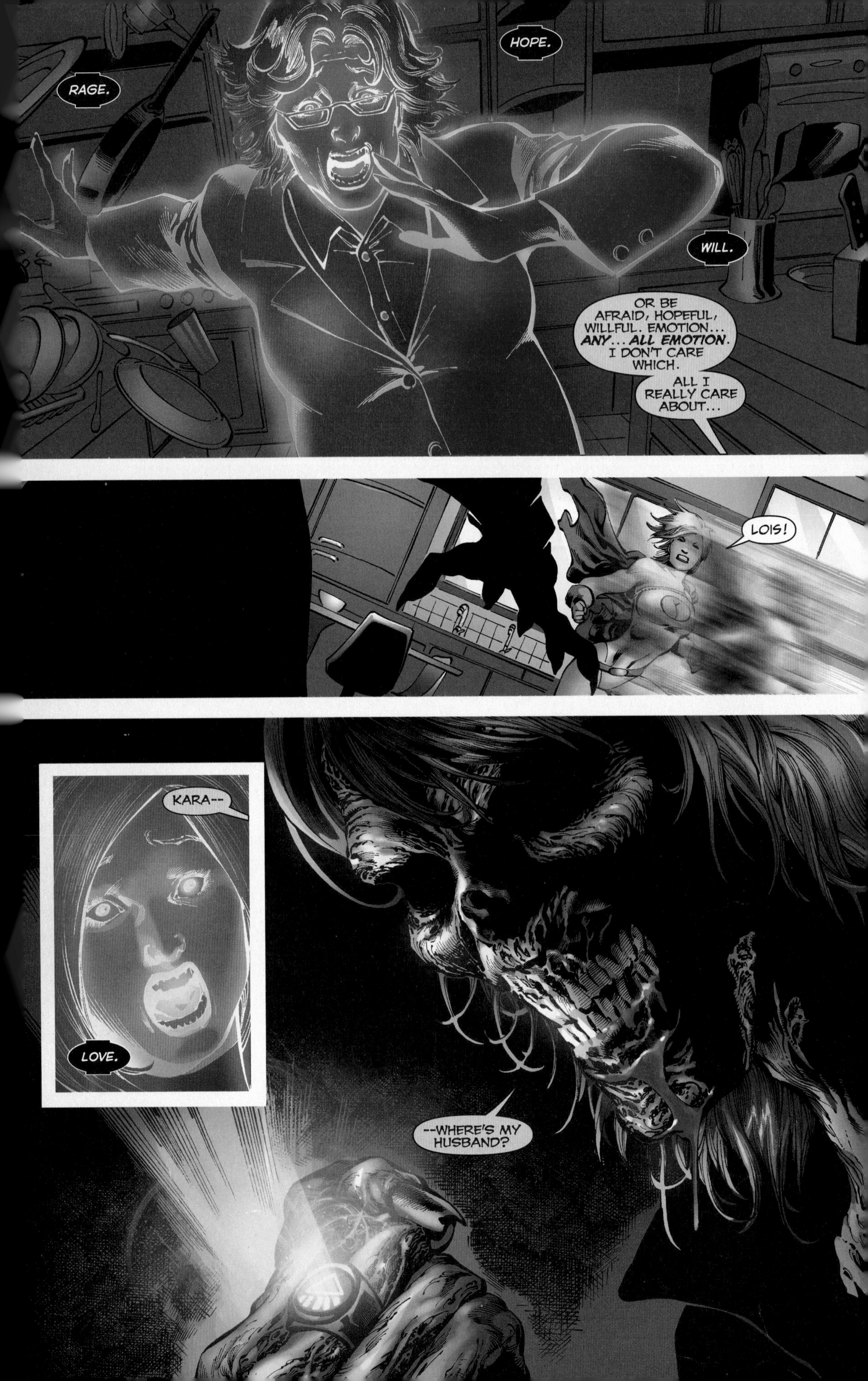
RAGE.
HOPE.
WILL.
OR BE AFRAID, HOPEFUL, WILLFUL. EMOTION... ANY... ALL EMOTION. I DON'T CARE WHICH.
ALL I REALLY CARE ABOUT...
LOIS!
KARA--
LOVE.
--WHERE'S MY HUSBAND?

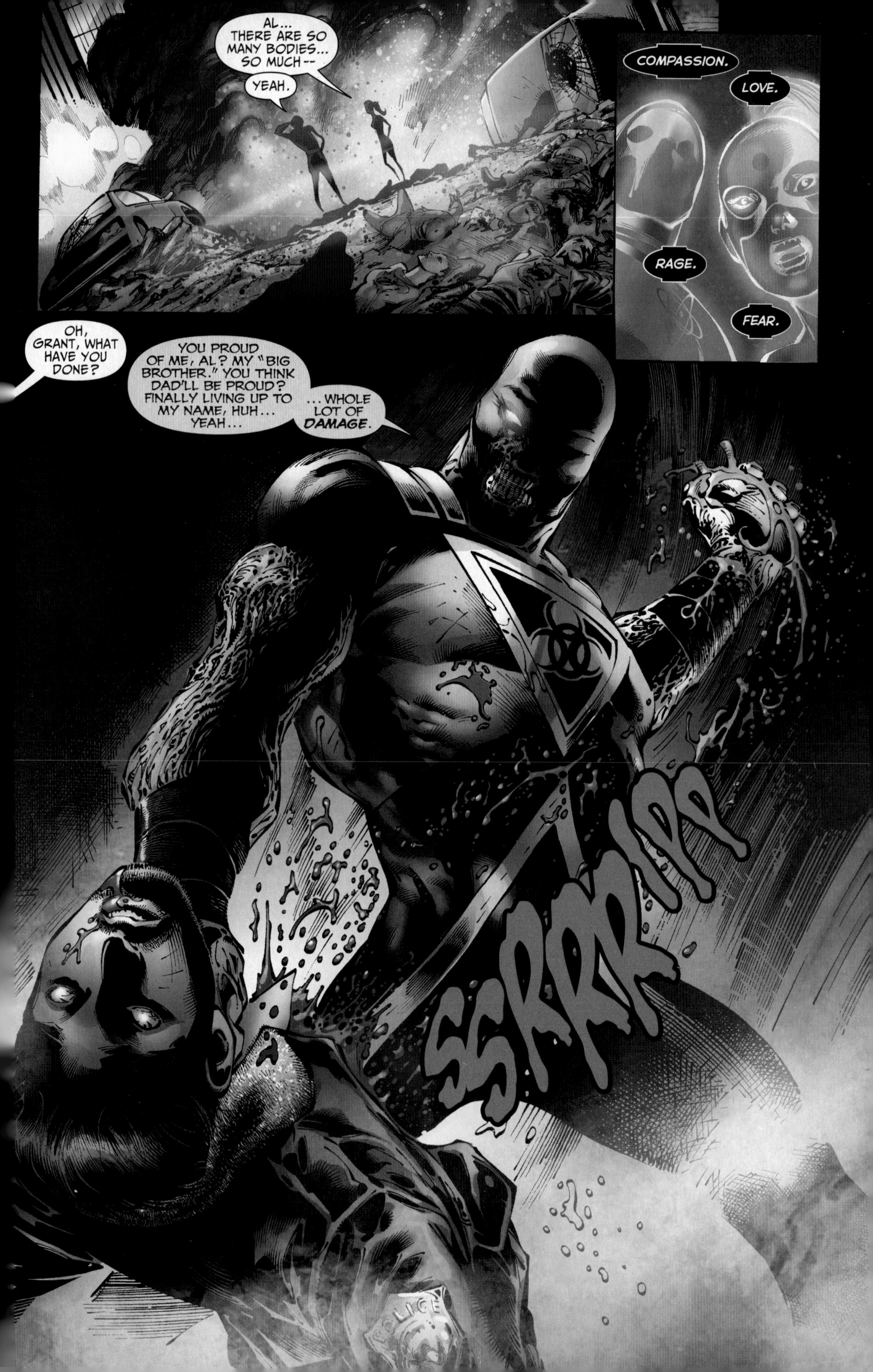
AL... THERE ARE SO MANY BODIES... SO MUCH--
YEAH.
COMPASSION.
LOVE.
RAGE.
FEAR.
OH, GRANT, WHAT HAVE YOU DONE?
YOU PROUD OF ME, AL? MY "BIG BROTHER." YOU THINK DAD'LL BE PROUD? FINALLY LIVING UP TO MY NAME, HUH... YEAH...
...WHOLE LOT OF DAMAGE.
SSRRIPP
POLICE

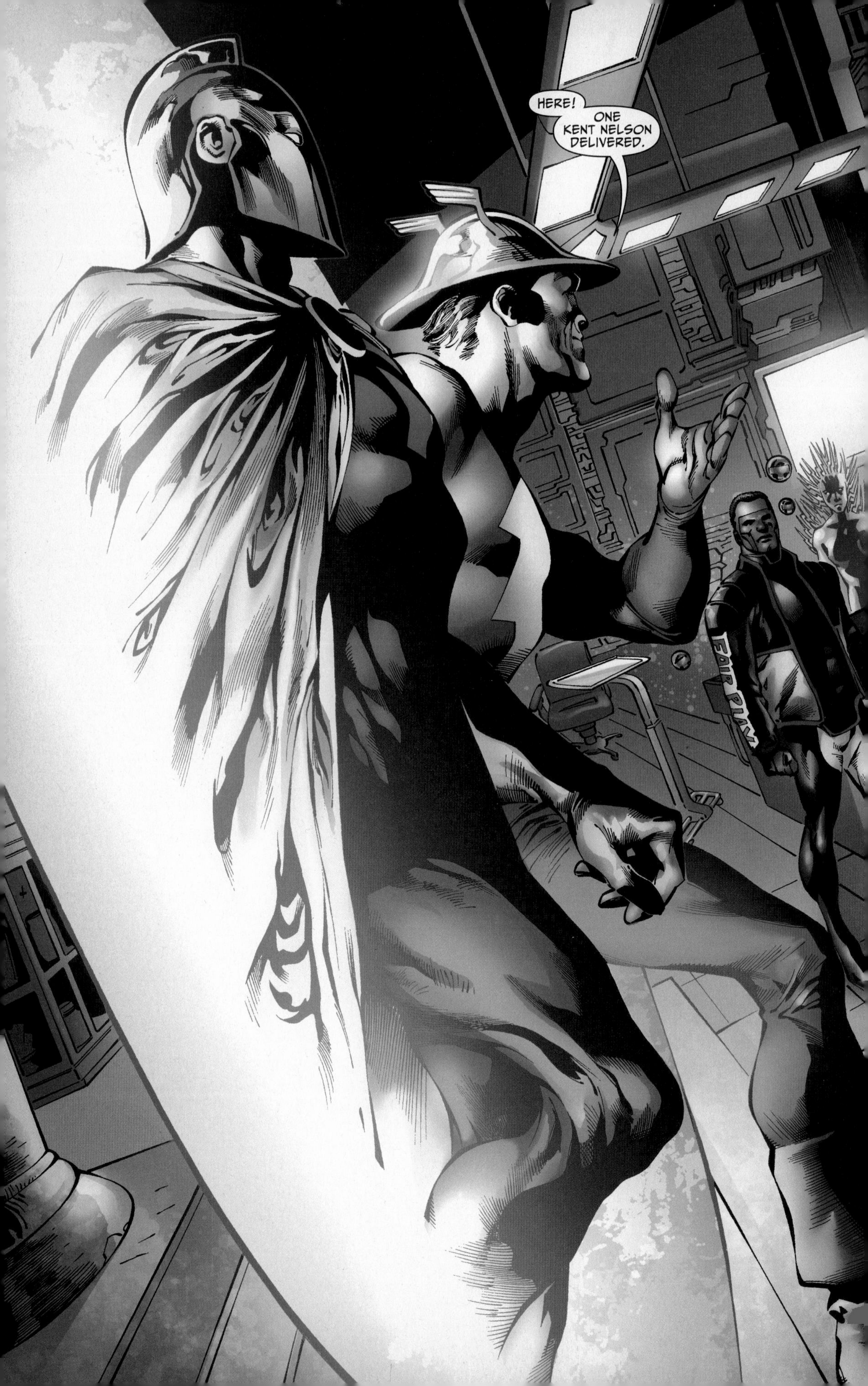
HERE!
ONE KENT NELSON DELIVERED.
FAIR PLAY

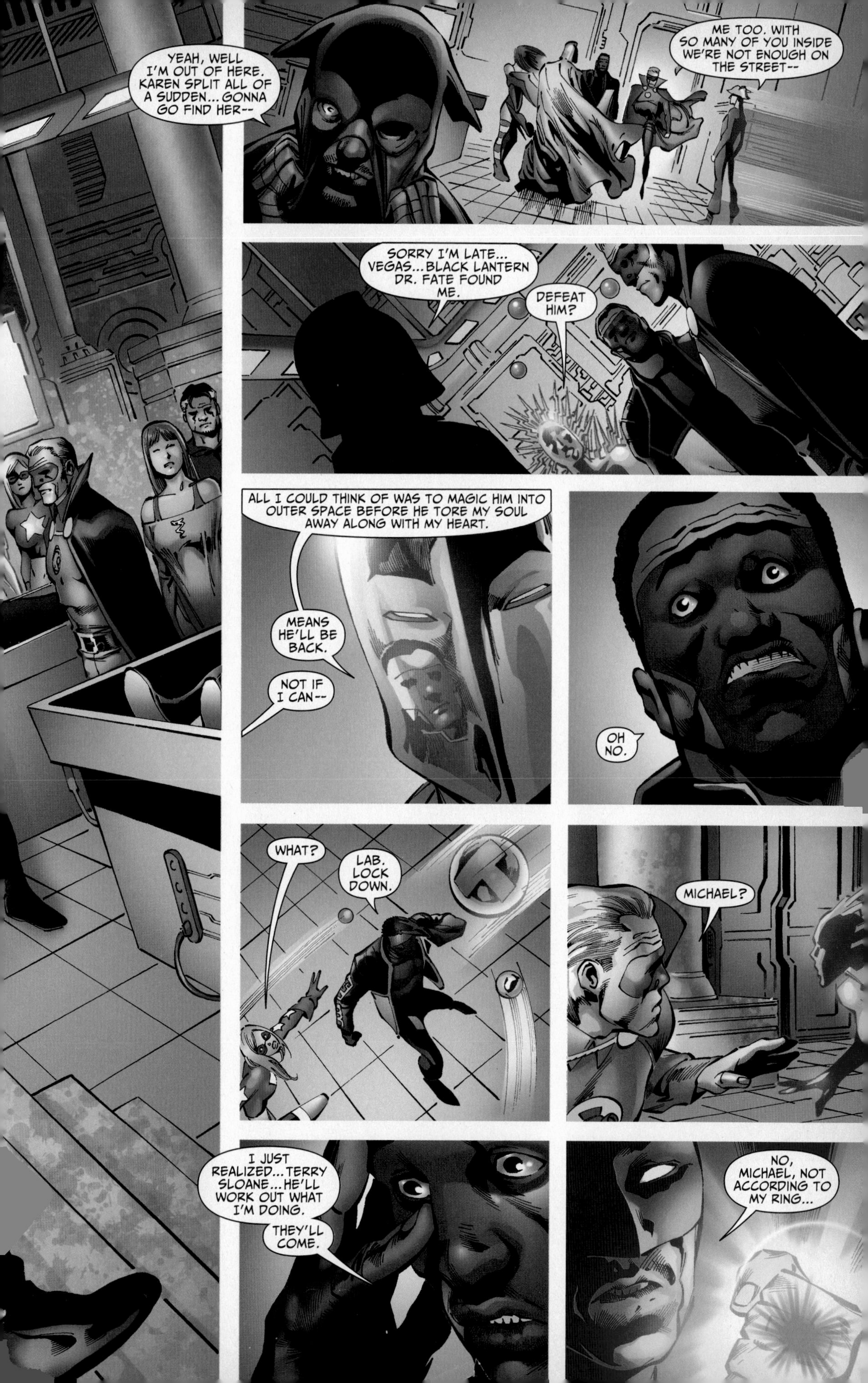
YEAH, WELL I'M OUT OF HERE. KAREN SPLIT ALL OF A SUDDEN... GONNA GO FIND HER--
ME TOO. WITH SO MANY OF YOU INSIDE WE'RE NOT ENOUGH ON THE STREET--
SORRY I'M LATE... VEGAS... BLACK LANTERN DR. FATE FOUND ME.
DEFEAT HIM?
ALL I COULD THINK OF WAS TO MAGIC HIM INTO OUTER SPACE BEFORE HE TORE MY SOUL AWAY ALONG WITH MY HEART.
MEANS HE'LL BE BACK.
NOT IF I CAN--
OH NO.
WHAT?
LAB. LOCK DOWN.
MICHAEL?
I JUST REALIZED... TERRY SLOANE... HE'LL WORK OUT WHAT I'M DOING.
THEY'LL COME.
NO, MICHAEL, NOT ACCORDING TO MY RING...

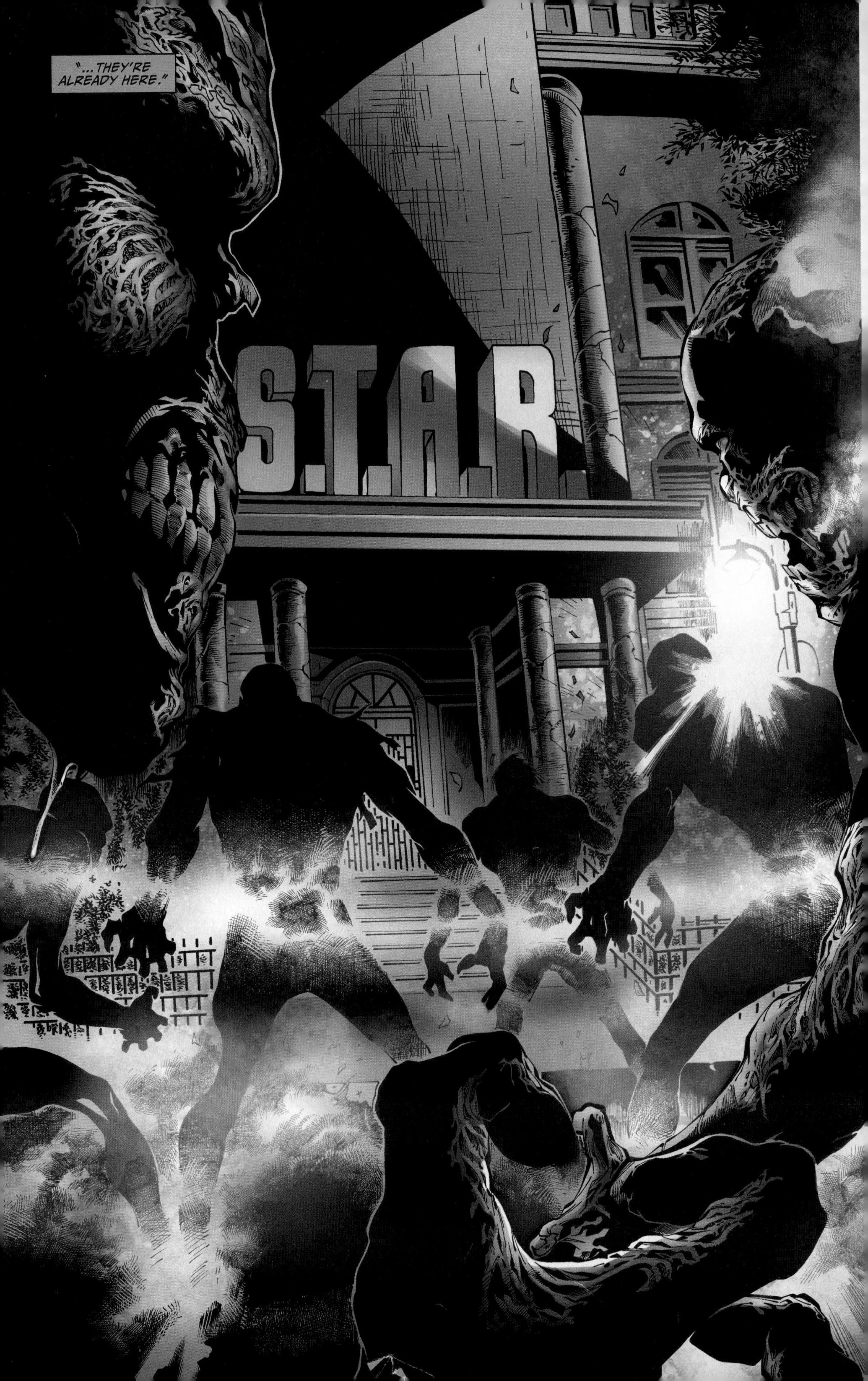
"...THEY'RE ALREADY HERE."
S.T.A.R.

BLACKEST NIGHT: JSA 2
Cover by Gene Ha

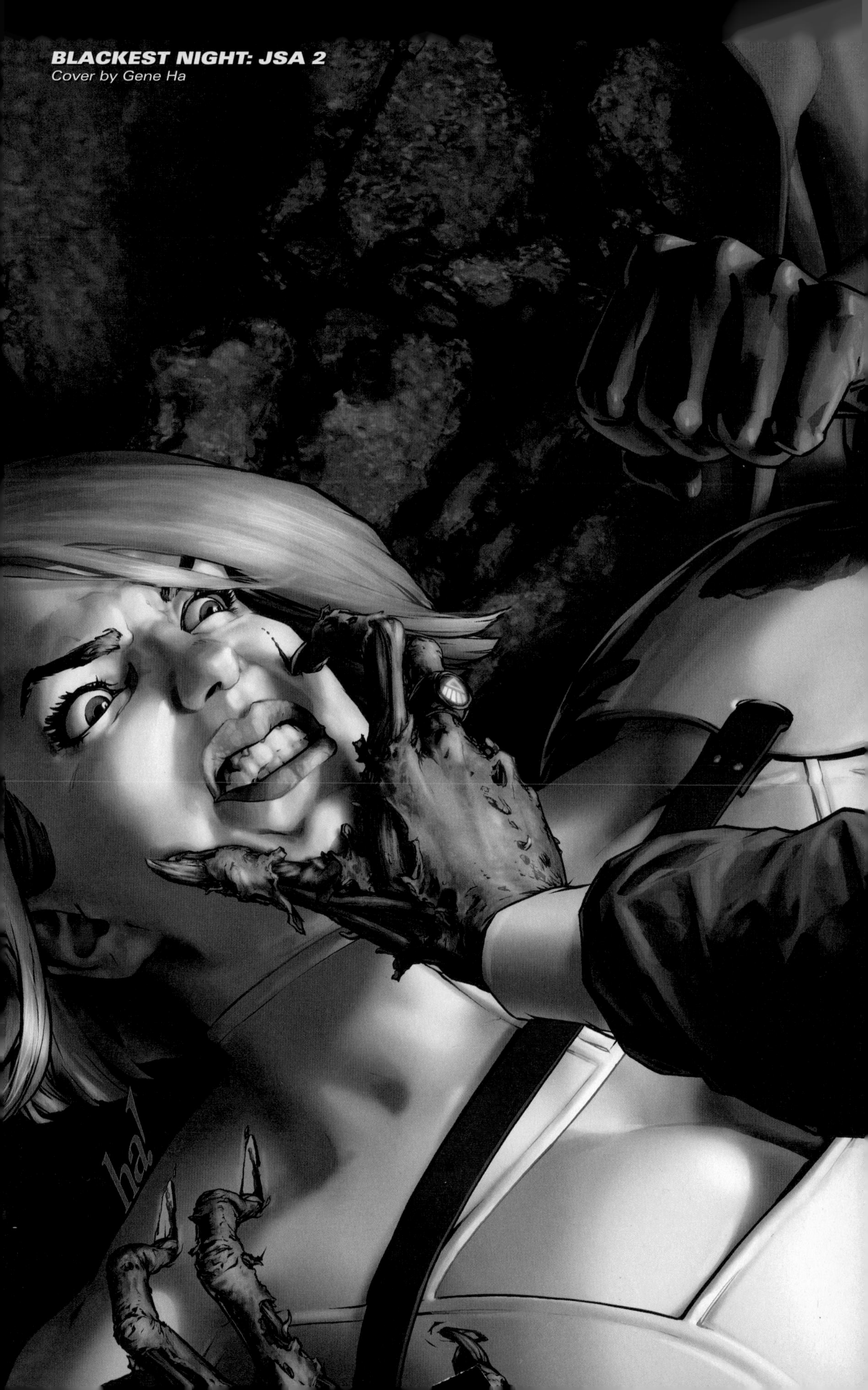

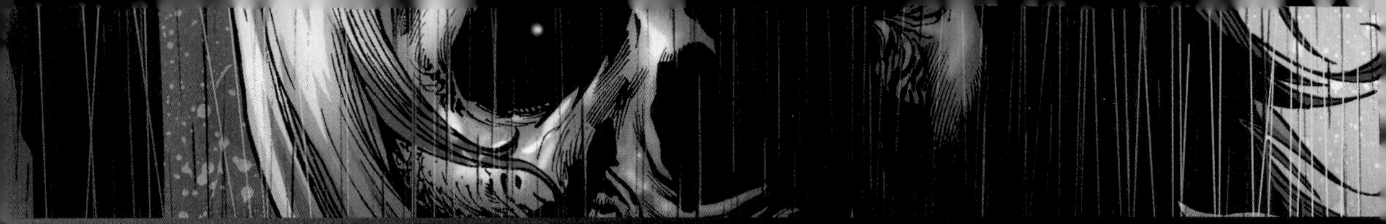

TROUBLED SOULS

JAMES ROBINSON
TONY BEDARD
WRITERS

EDDY BARROWS
MARCOS MARZ
PENCILS

JULIO FERREIRA
EBER FERREIRA
LUCIANA DEL NEGRO
INKS

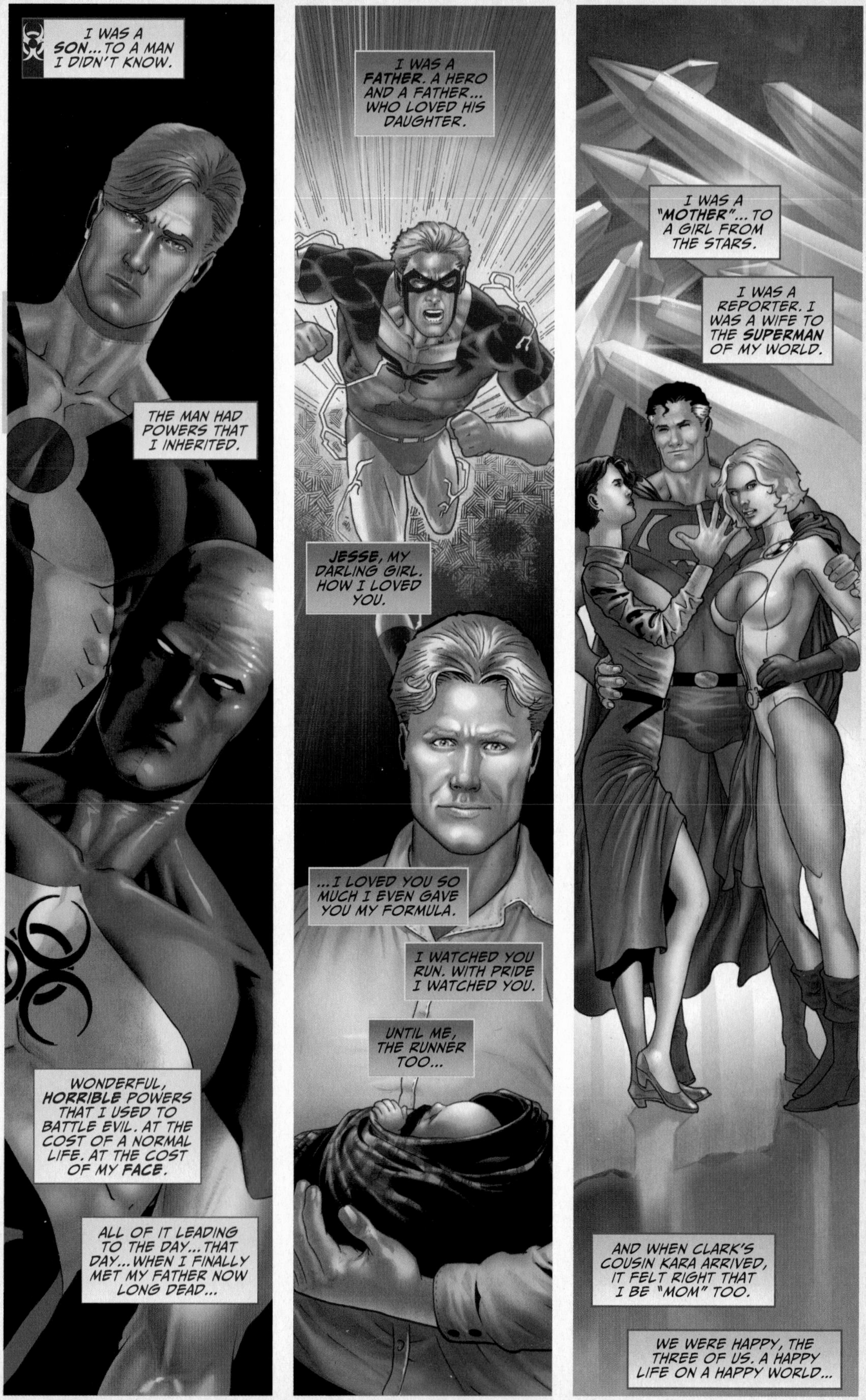
I WAS A SON...TO A MAN I DIDN'T KNOW.
THE MAN HAD POWERS THAT I INHERITED.
WONDERFUL, HORRIBLE POWERS THAT I USED TO BATTLE EVIL. AT THE COST OF A NORMAL LIFE. AT THE COST OF MY FACE.
ALL OF IT LEADING TO THE DAY...THAT DAY...WHEN I FINALLY MET MY FATHER NOW LONG DEAD...
I WAS A FATHER. A HERO AND A FATHER... WHO LOVED HIS DAUGHTER.
JESSE, MY DARLING GIRL. HOW I LOVED YOU.
...I LOVED YOU SO MUCH I EVEN GAVE YOU MY FORMULA.
I WATCHED YOU RUN. WITH PRIDE I WATCHED YOU.
UNTIL ME, THE RUNNER TOO...
I WAS A "MOTHER"...TO A GIRL FROM THE STARS.
I WAS A REPORTER. I WAS A WIFE TO THE SUPERMAN OF MY WORLD.
AND WHEN CLARK'S COUSIN KARA ARRIVED, IT FELT RIGHT THAT I BE "MOM" TOO.
WE WERE HAPPY, THE THREE OF US. A HAPPY LIFE ON A HAPPY WORLD...

...AND JOINED HIM.

...CAME TO THE END OF THE ROAD.

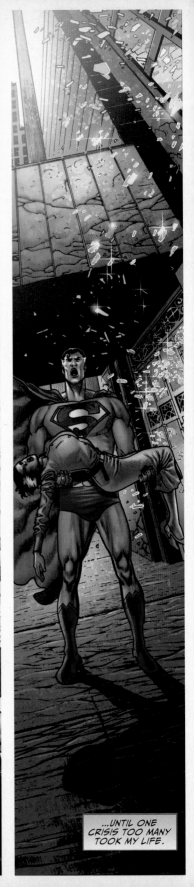

...UNTIL ONE CRISIS TOO MANY TOOK MY LIFE.

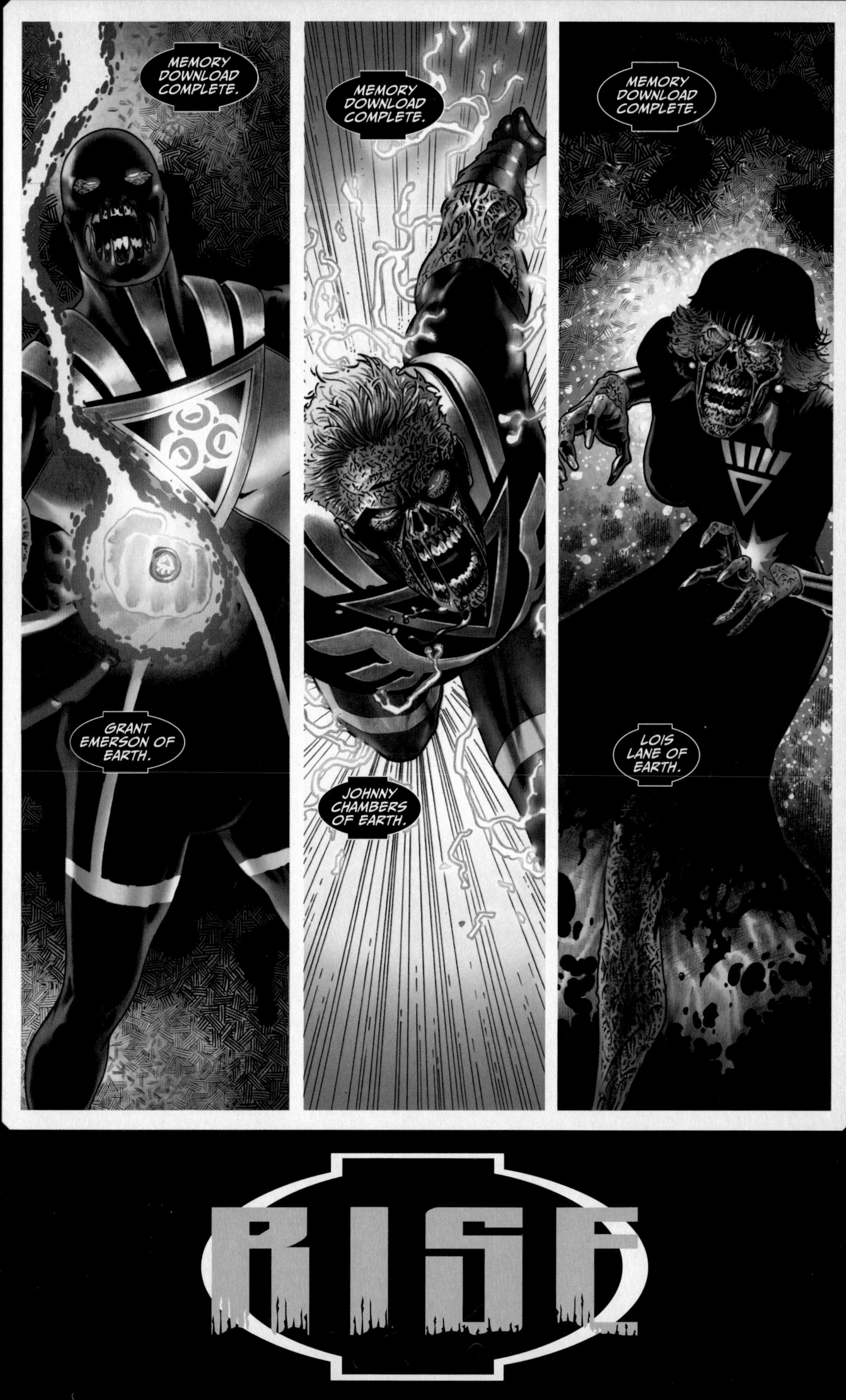
MEMORY DOWNLOAD COMPLETE.
GRANT EMERSON OF EARTH.
MEMORY DOWNLOAD COMPLETE.
JOHNNY CHAMBERS OF EARTH.
MEMORY DOWNLOAD COMPLETE.
LOIS LANE OF EARTH.
RISE

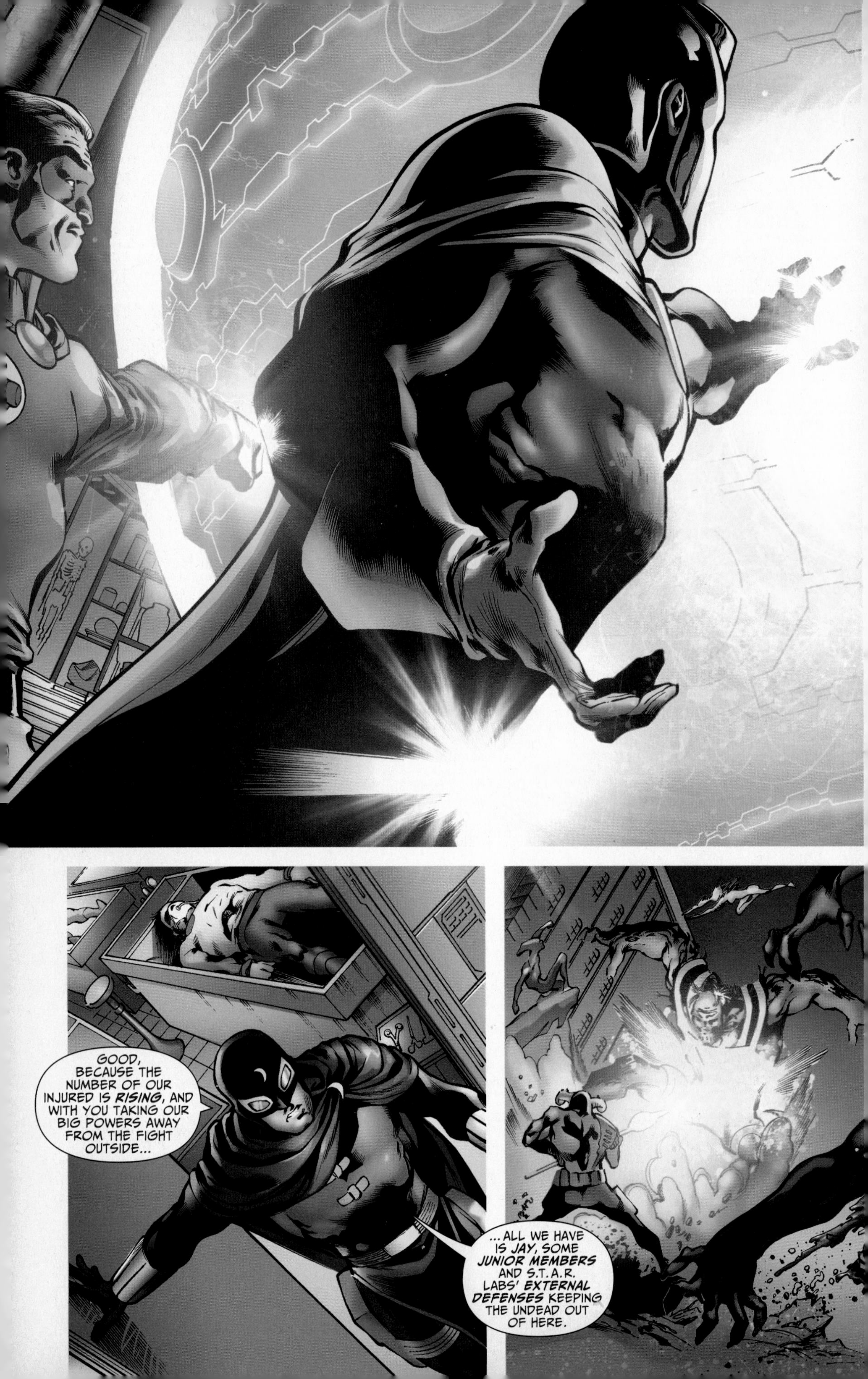
GOOD, BECAUSE THE NUMBER OF OUR INJURED IS *RISING*, AND WITH YOU TAKING OUR BIG POWERS AWAY FROM THE FIGHT OUTSIDE...
...ALL WE HAVE IS *JAY*, SOME *JUNIOR MEMBERS* AND S.T.A.R. LABS' *EXTERNAL DEFENSES* KEEPING THE UNDEAD OUT OF HERE.

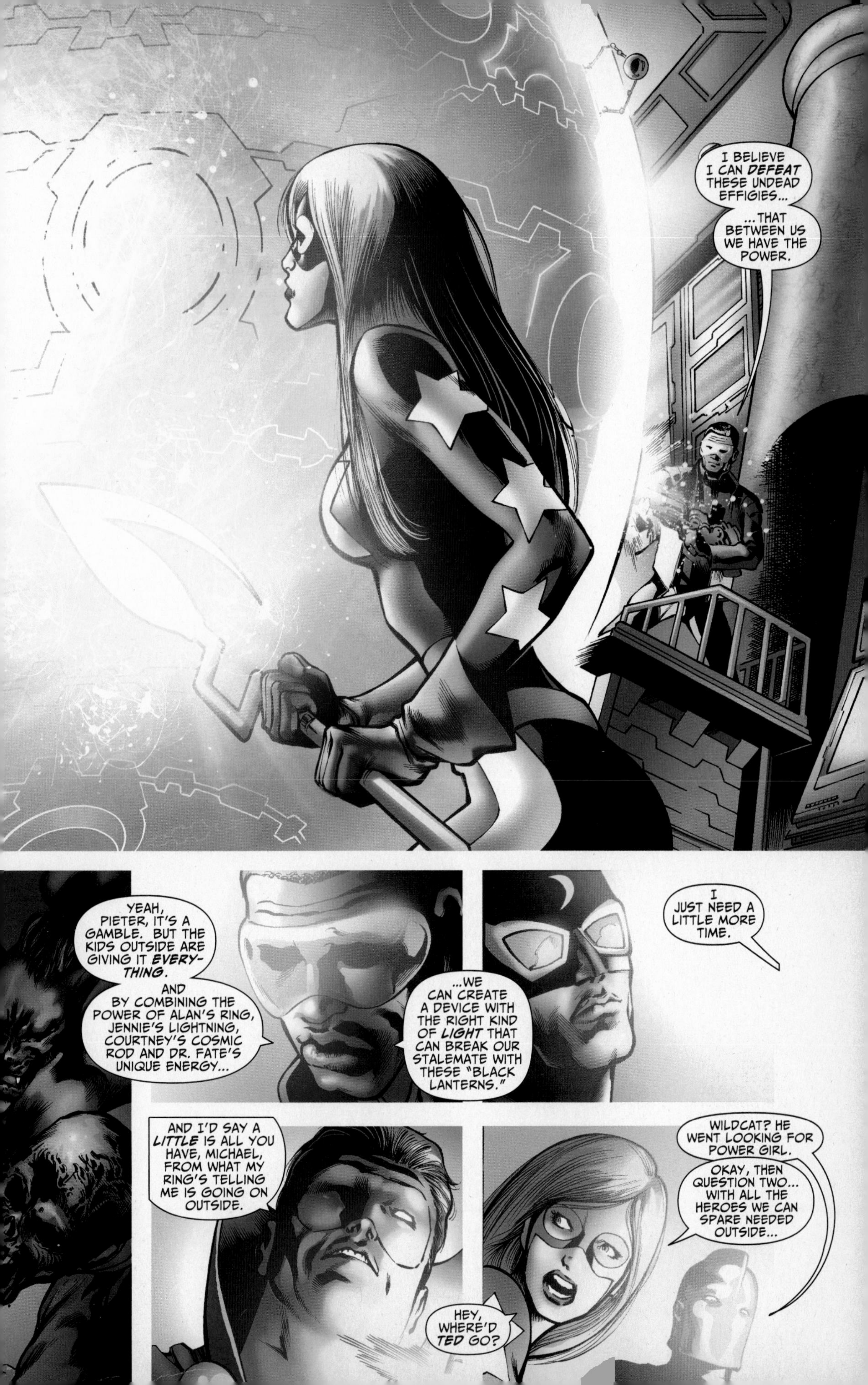
I BELIEVE I CAN DEFEAT THESE UNDEAD EFFIGIES...
...THAT BETWEEN US WE HAVE THE POWER.
YEAH, PIETER, IT'S A GAMBLE. BUT THE KIDS OUTSIDE ARE GIVING IT EVERY-THING.
AND BY COMBINING THE POWER OF ALAN'S RING, JENNIE'S LIGHTNING, COURTNEY'S COSMIC ROD AND DR. FATE'S UNIQUE ENERGY...
...WE CAN CREATE A DEVICE WITH THE RIGHT KIND OF LIGHT THAT CAN BREAK OUR STALEMATE WITH THESE "BLACK LANTERNS."
I JUST NEED A LITTLE MORE TIME.
AND I'D SAY A LITTLE IS ALL YOU HAVE, MICHAEL, FROM WHAT MY RING'S TELLING ME IS GOING ON OUTSIDE.
HEY, WHERE'D TED GO?
WILDCAT? HE WENT LOOKING FOR POWER GIRL.
OKAY, THEN QUESTION TWO... WITH ALL THE HEROES WE CAN SPARE NEEDED OUTSIDE...

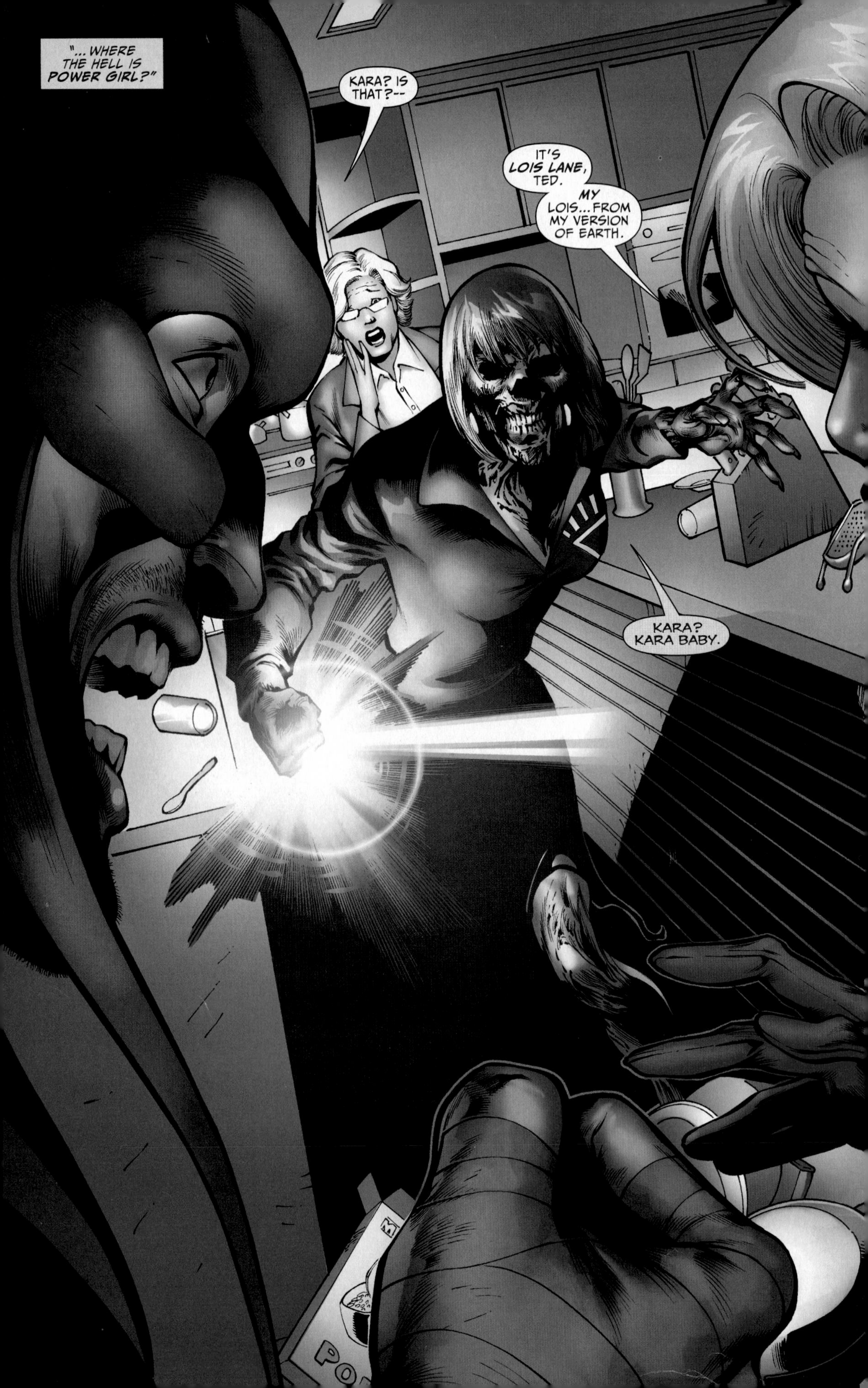
"...WHERE THE HELL IS POWER GIRL?"
KARA? IS THAT?--
IT'S LOIS LANE, TED. MY LOIS...FROM MY VERSION OF EARTH.
KARA? KARA BABY.

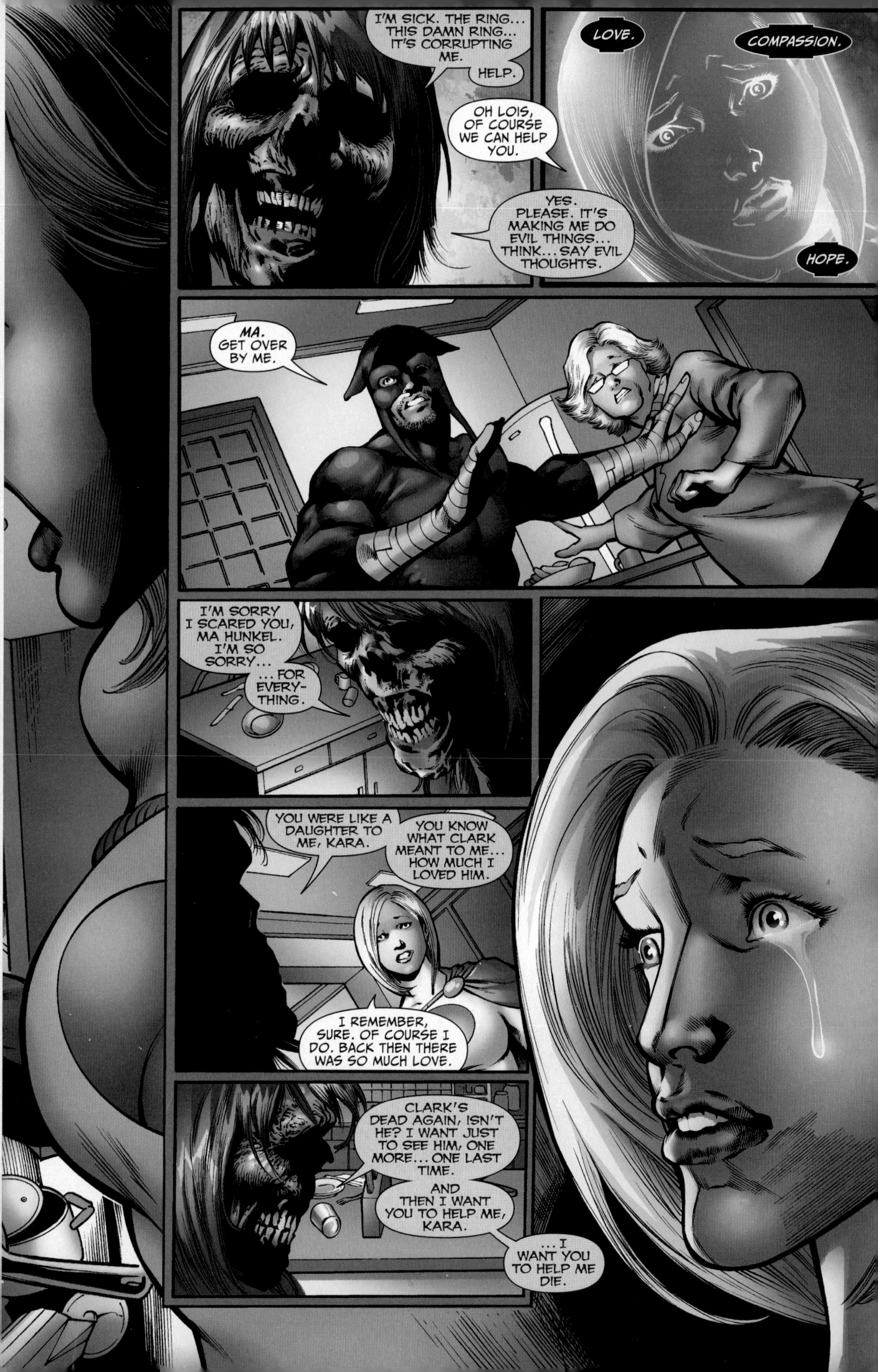
I'M SICK. THE RING... THIS DAMN RING... IT'S CORRUPTING ME.
HELP.
LOVE.
COMPASSION.
OH LOIS, OF COURSE WE CAN HELP YOU.
YES. PLEASE. IT'S MAKING ME DO EVIL THINGS... THINK... SAY EVIL THOUGHTS.
HOPE.
MA. GET OVER BY ME.
I'M SORRY I SCARED YOU, MA HUNKEL. I'M SO SORRY...
...FOR EVERY-THING.
YOU WERE LIKE A DAUGHTER TO ME, KARA.
YOU KNOW WHAT CLARK MEANT TO ME... HOW MUCH I LOVED HIM.
I REMEMBER, SURE. OF COURSE I DO. BACK THEN THERE WAS SO MUCH LOVE.
CLARK'S DEAD AGAIN, ISN'T HE? I WANT JUST TO SEE HIM, ONE MORE... ONE LAST TIME.
AND THEN I WANT YOU TO HELP ME, KARA.
...I WANT YOU TO HELP ME DIE.

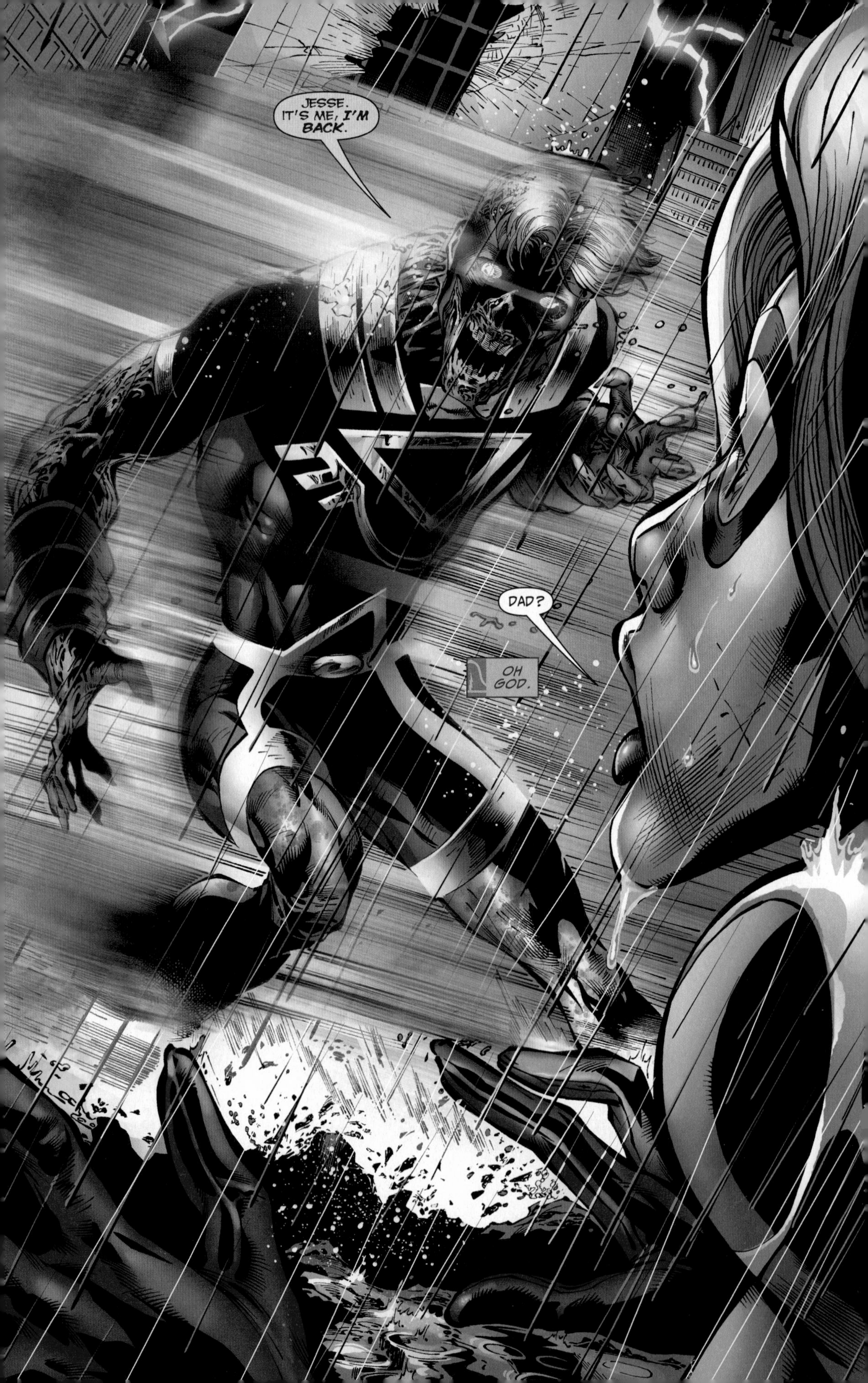
JESSE. IT'S ME, I'M BACK.
DAD?
OH GOD.

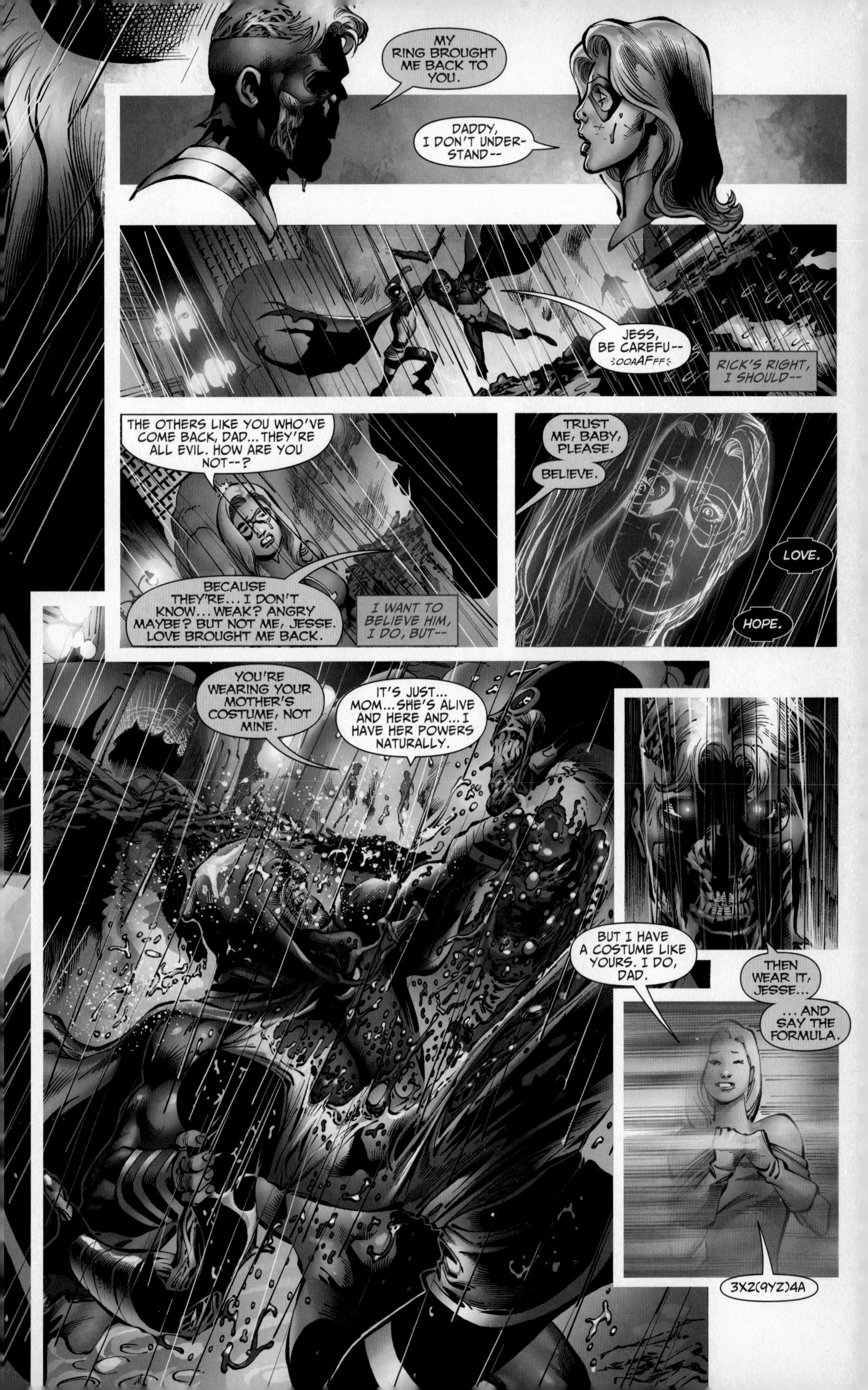
MY RING BROUGHT ME BACK TO YOU.
DADDY, I DON'T UNDER-STAND--
JESS, BE CAREFU--
OOAAFFF
RICK'S RIGHT, I SHOULD--
THE OTHERS LIKE YOU WHO'VE COME BACK, DAD... THEY'RE ALL EVIL. HOW ARE YOU NOT--?
BECAUSE THEY'RE... I DON'T KNOW... WEAK? ANGRY MAYBE? BUT NOT ME, JESSE. LOVE BROUGHT ME BACK.
I WANT TO BELIEVE HIM, I DO, BUT--
TRUST ME, BABY, PLEASE.
BELIEVE.
LOVE.
HOPE.
YOU'RE WEARING YOUR MOTHER'S COSTUME, NOT MINE.
IT'S JUST... MOM... SHE'S ALIVE AND HERE AND... I HAVE HER POWERS NATURALLY.
BUT I HAVE A COSTUME LIKE YOURS. I DO, DAD.
THEN WEAR IT, JESSE...
...AND SAY THE FORMULA.
3X2(9YZ)4A

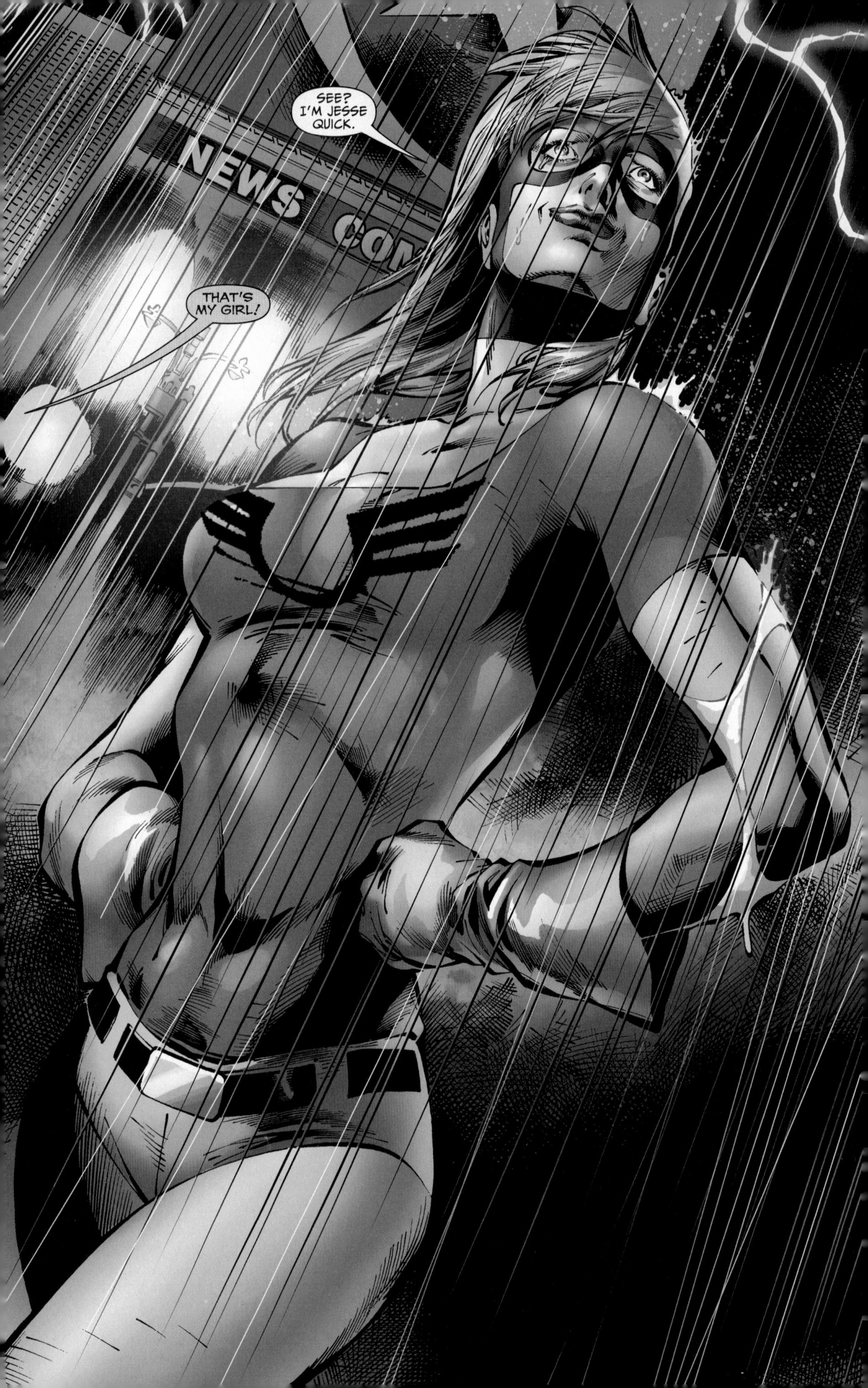
SEE? I'M JESSE QUICK.
THAT'S MY GIRL!
NEWS

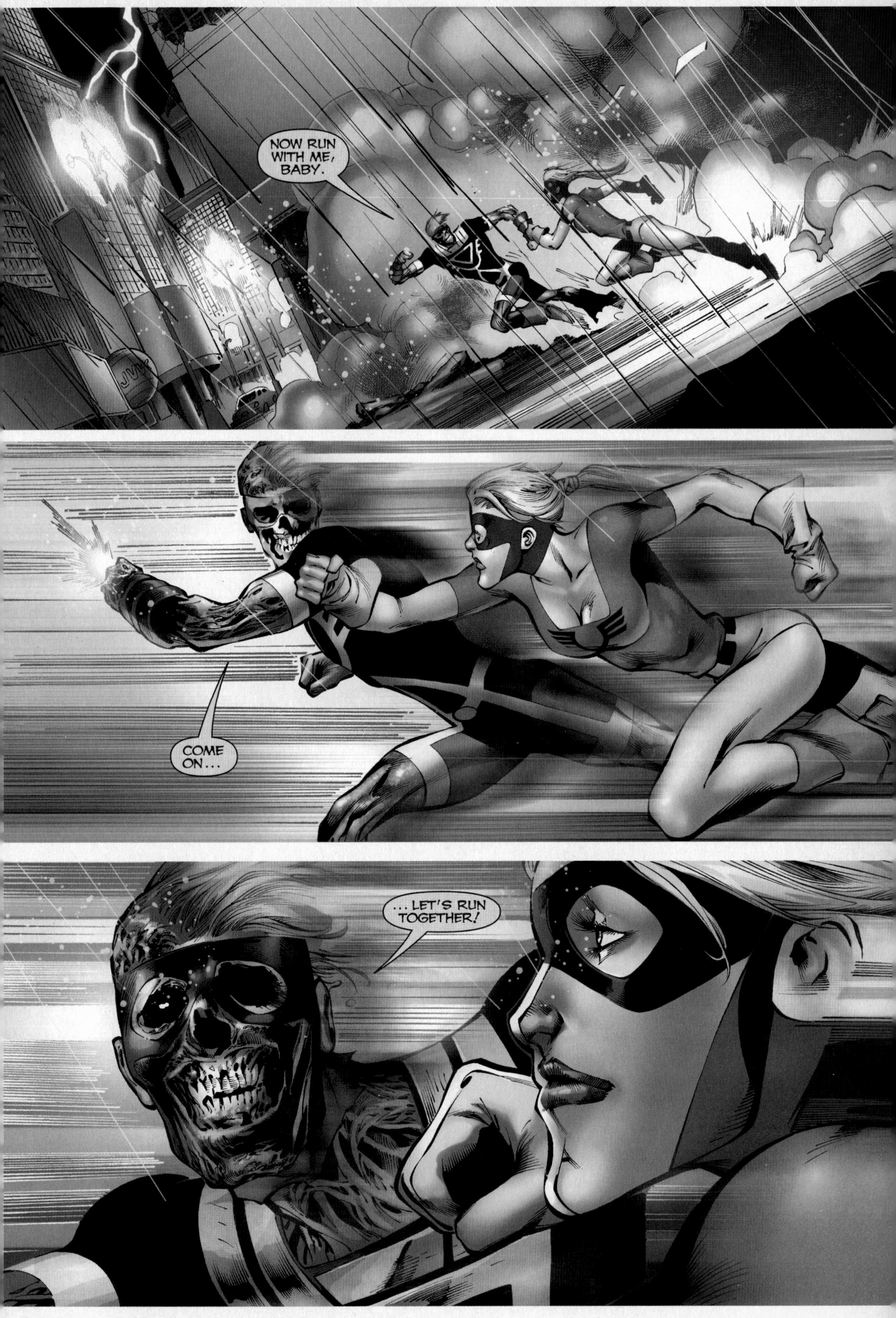
NOW RUN WITH ME, BABY.
COME ON...
...LET'S RUN TOGETHER!

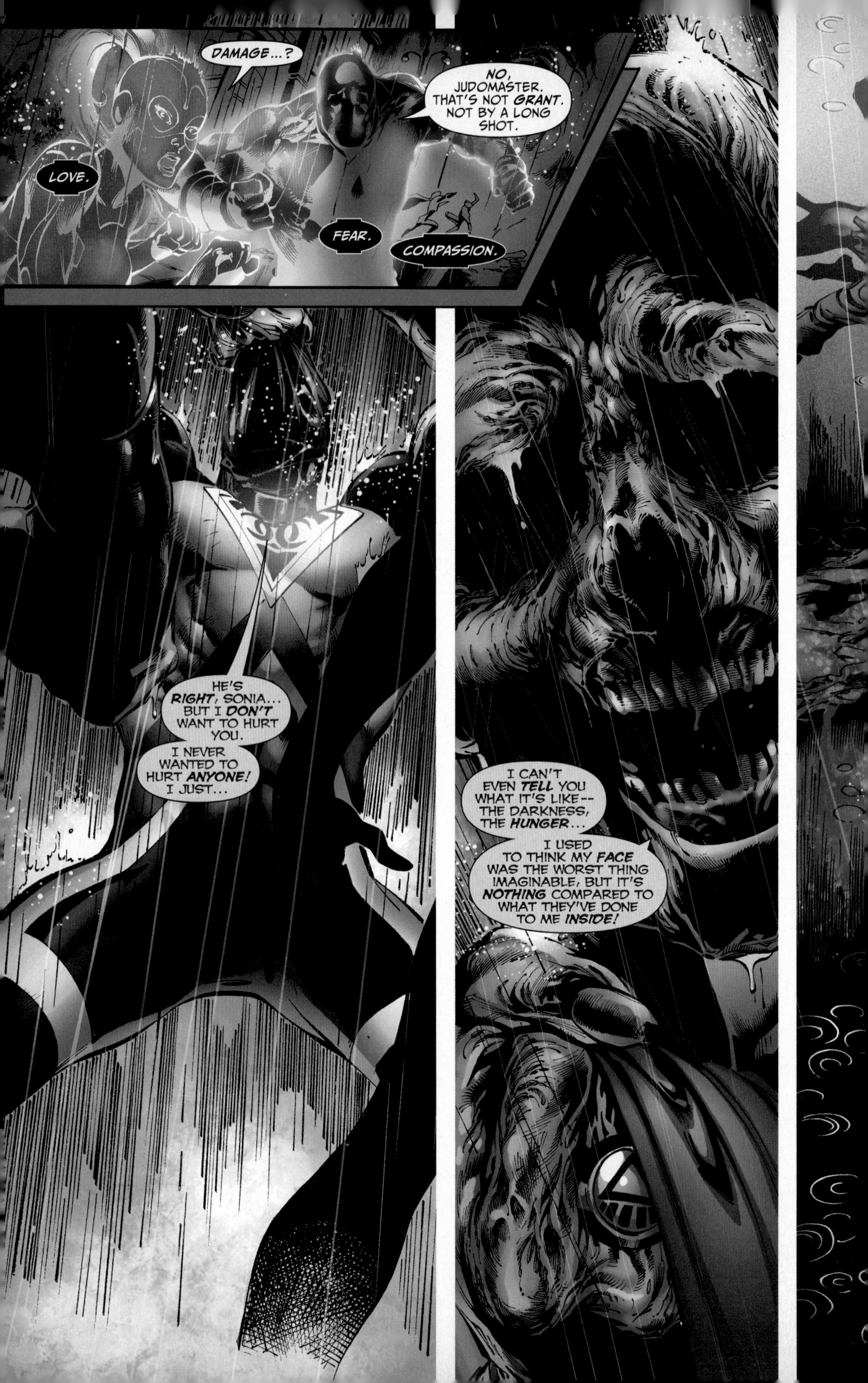
DAMAGE...?
NO, JUDOMASTER. THAT'S NOT GRANT. NOT BY A LONG SHOT.
LOVE.
FEAR.
COMPASSION.
HE'S RIGHT, SONIA... BUT I DON'T WANT TO HURT YOU.
I NEVER WANTED TO HURT ANYONE! I JUST...
I CAN'T EVEN TELL YOU WHAT IT'S LIKE-- THE DARKNESS, THE HUNGER...
I USED TO THINK MY FACE WAS THE WORST THING IMAGINABLE, BUT IT'S NOTHING COMPARED TO WHAT THEY'VE DONE TO ME INSIDE!

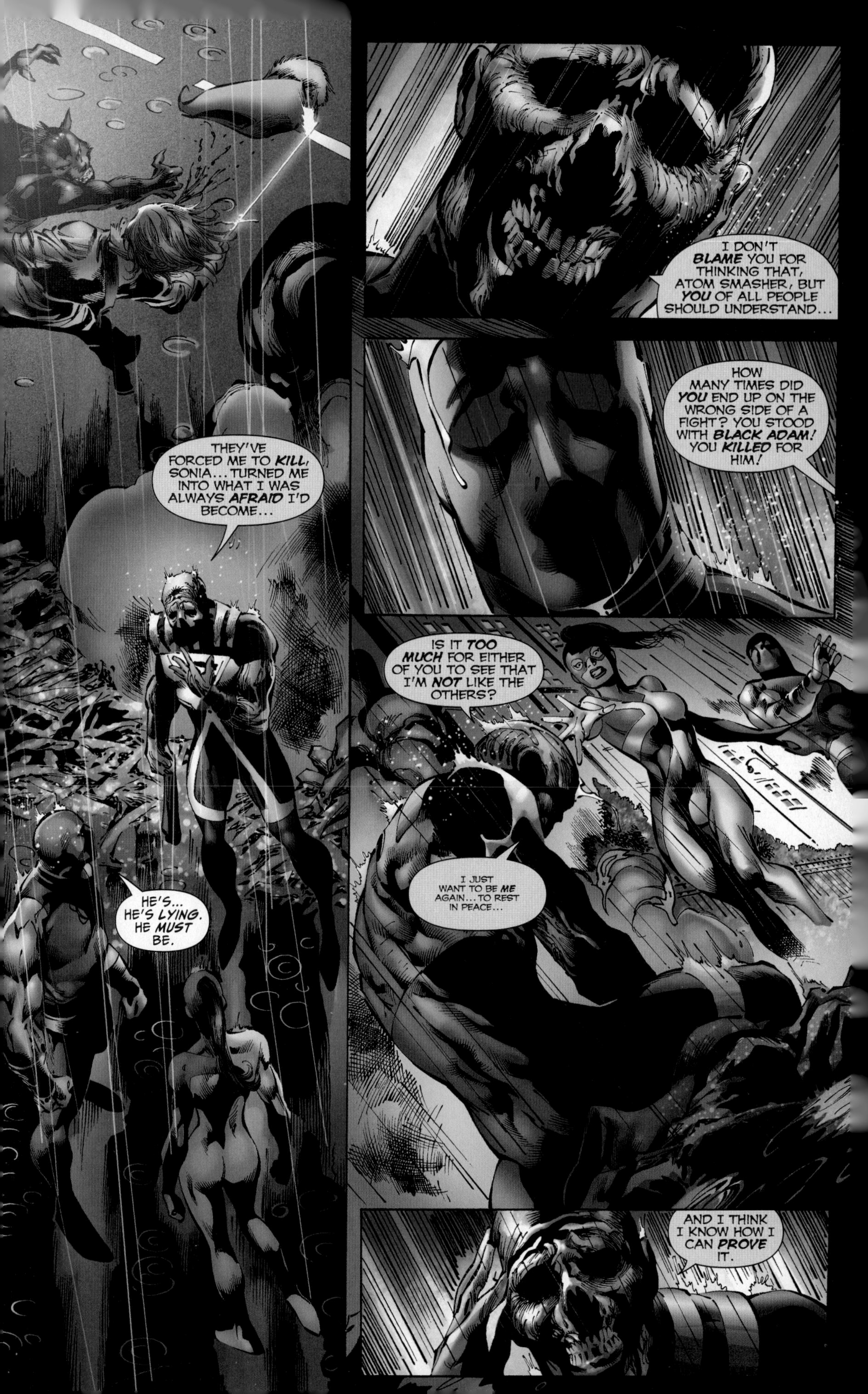
THEY'VE FORCED ME TO KILL, SONIA... TURNED ME INTO WHAT I WAS ALWAYS AFRAID I'D BECOME...
HE'S... HE'S LYING. HE MUST BE.
I DON'T BLAME YOU FOR THINKING THAT, ATOM SMASHER, BUT YOU OF ALL PEOPLE SHOULD UNDERSTAND...
HOW MANY TIMES DID YOU END UP ON THE WRONG SIDE OF A FIGHT? YOU STOOD WITH BLACK ADAM! YOU KILLED FOR HIM!
IS IT TOO MUCH FOR EITHER OF YOU TO SEE THAT I'M NOT LIKE THE OTHERS?
I JUST WANT TO BE ME AGAIN... TO REST IN PEACE...
AND I THINK I KNOW HOW I CAN PROVE IT.

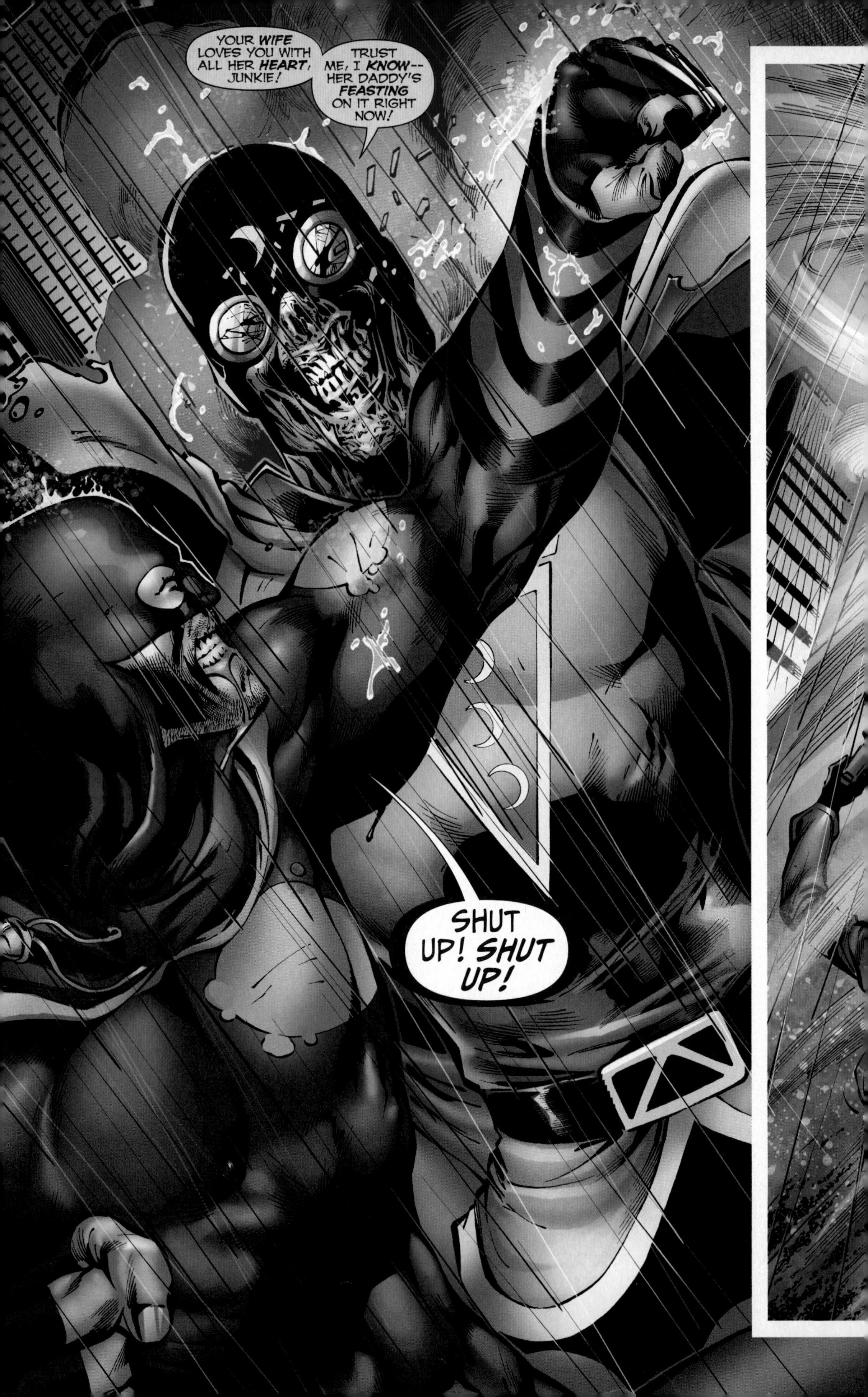
YOUR WIFE LOVES YOU WITH ALL HER HEART, JUNKIE!
TRUST ME, I KNOW-- HER DADDY'S FEASTING ON IT RIGHT NOW!
SHUT UP! SHUT UP!

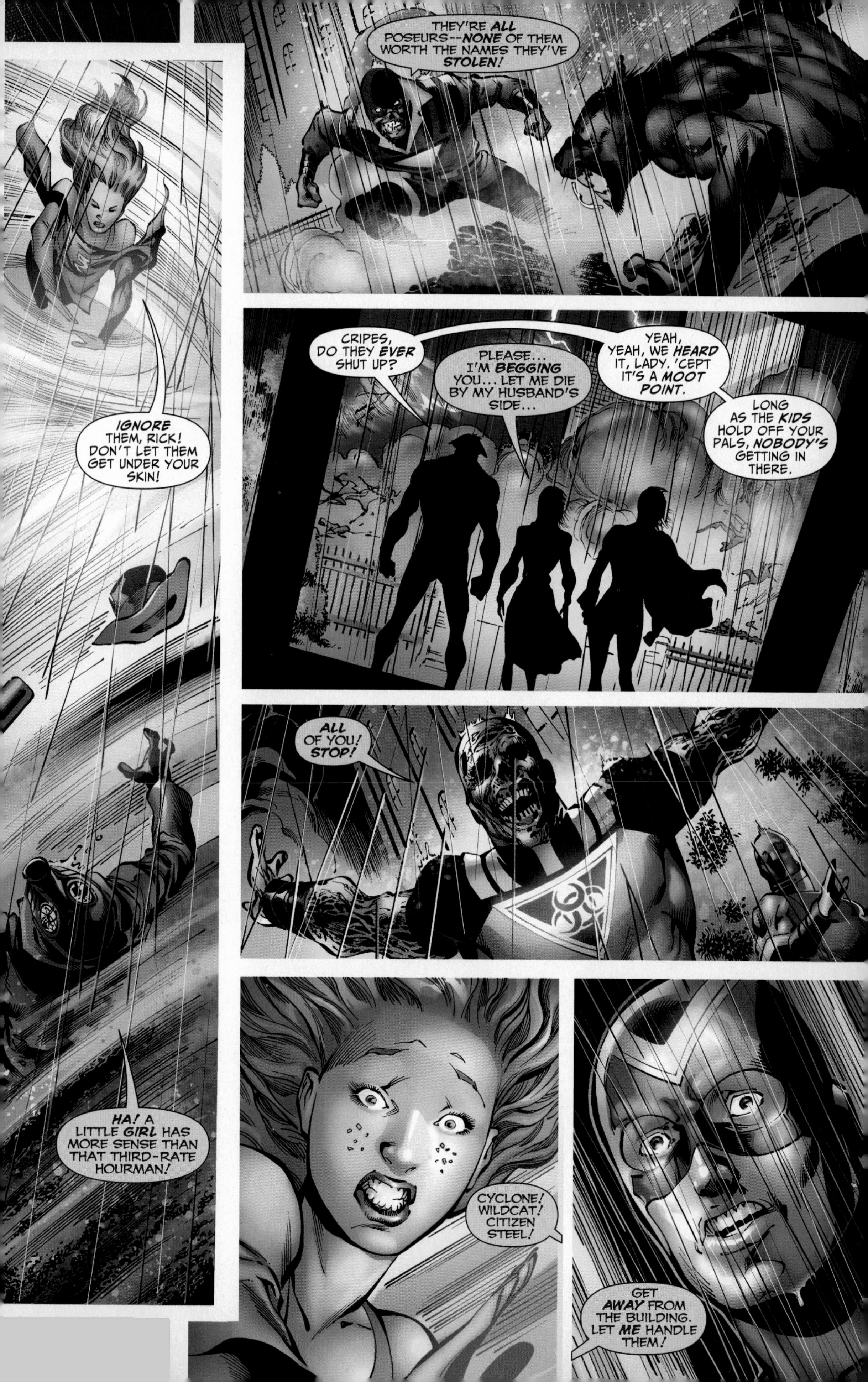
THEY'RE ALL POSEURS--NONE OF THEM WORTH THE NAMES THEY'VE STOLEN!
IGNORE THEM, RICK! DON'T LET THEM GET UNDER YOUR SKIN!
HA! A LITTLE GIRL HAS MORE SENSE THAN THAT THIRD-RATE HOURMAN!
CRIPES, DO THEY EVER SHUT UP?
PLEASE... I'M BEGGING YOU... LET ME DIE BY MY HUSBAND'S SIDE...
YEAH, YEAH, WE HEARD IT, LADY. 'CEPT IT'S A MOOT POINT.
LONG AS THE KIDS HOLD OFF YOUR PALS, NOBODY'S GETTING IN THERE.
ALL OF YOU! STOP!
CYCLONE! WILDCAT! CITIZEN STEEL!
GET AWAY FROM THE BUILDING. LET ME HANDLE THEM!

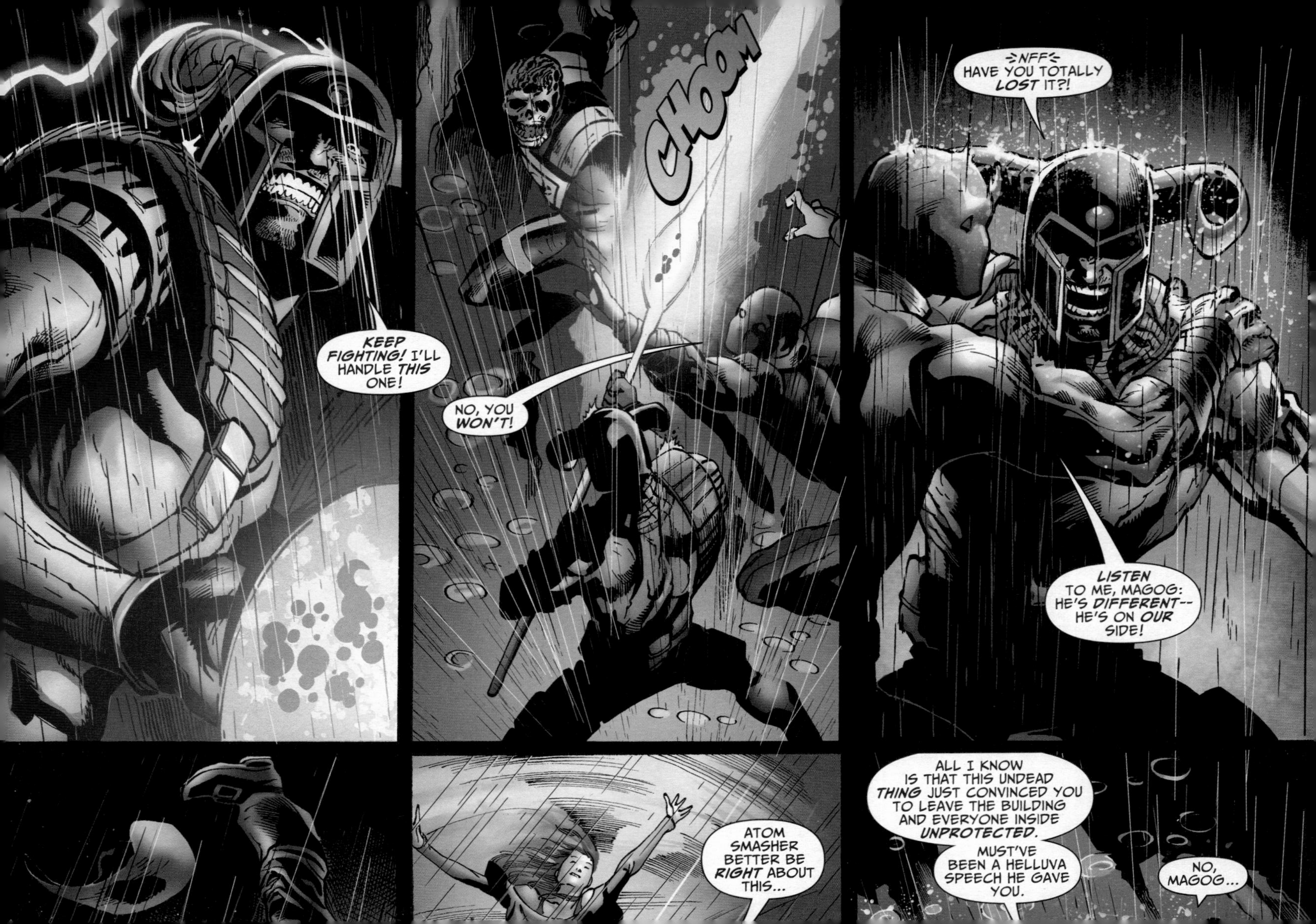
KEEP FIGHTING! I'LL HANDLE THIS ONE!
NO, YOU WON'T!
CHOOM
=NFF= HAVE YOU TOTALLY LOST IT?!
LISTEN TO ME, MAGOG: HE'S DIFFERENT-- HE'S ON OUR SIDE!
ATOM SMASHER BETTER BE RIGHT ABOUT THIS...
ALL I KNOW IS THAT THIS UNDEAD THING JUST CONVINCED YOU TO LEAVE THE BUILDING AND EVERYONE INSIDE UNPROTECTED.
MUST'VE BEEN A HELLUVA SPEECH HE GAVE YOU.
NO, MAGOG...

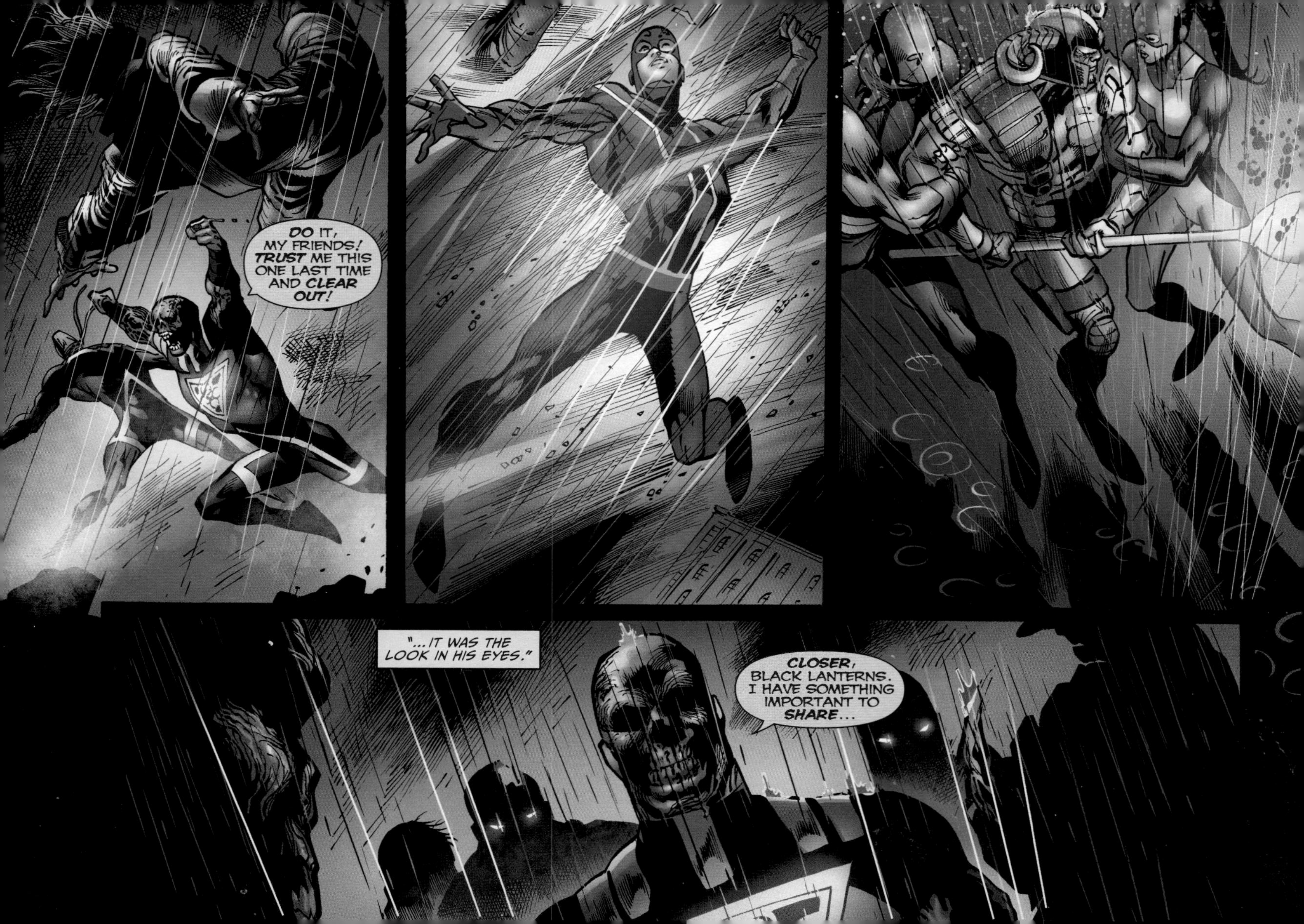
DO IT, MY FRIENDS! TRUST ME THIS ONE LAST TIME AND CLEAR OUT!
"...IT WAS THE LOOK IN HIS EYES."
CLOSER, BLACK LANTERNS. I HAVE SOMETHING IMPORTANT TO SHARE...

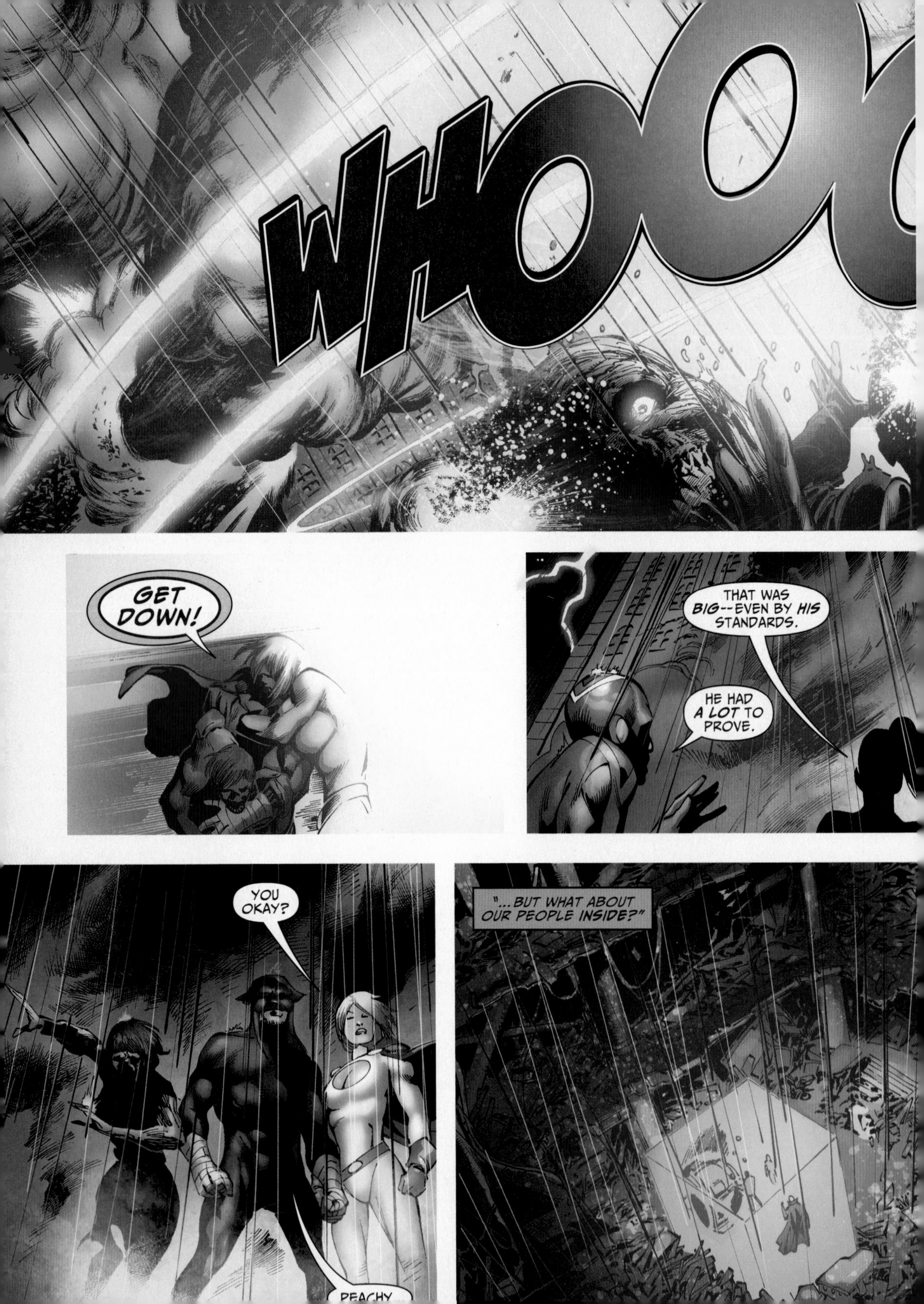
WHOO
GET DOWN!
THAT WAS BIG--EVEN BY HIS STANDARDS.
HE HAD A LOT TO PROVE.
YOU OKAY?
PEACHY
"...BUT WHAT ABOUT OUR PEOPLE INSIDE?"

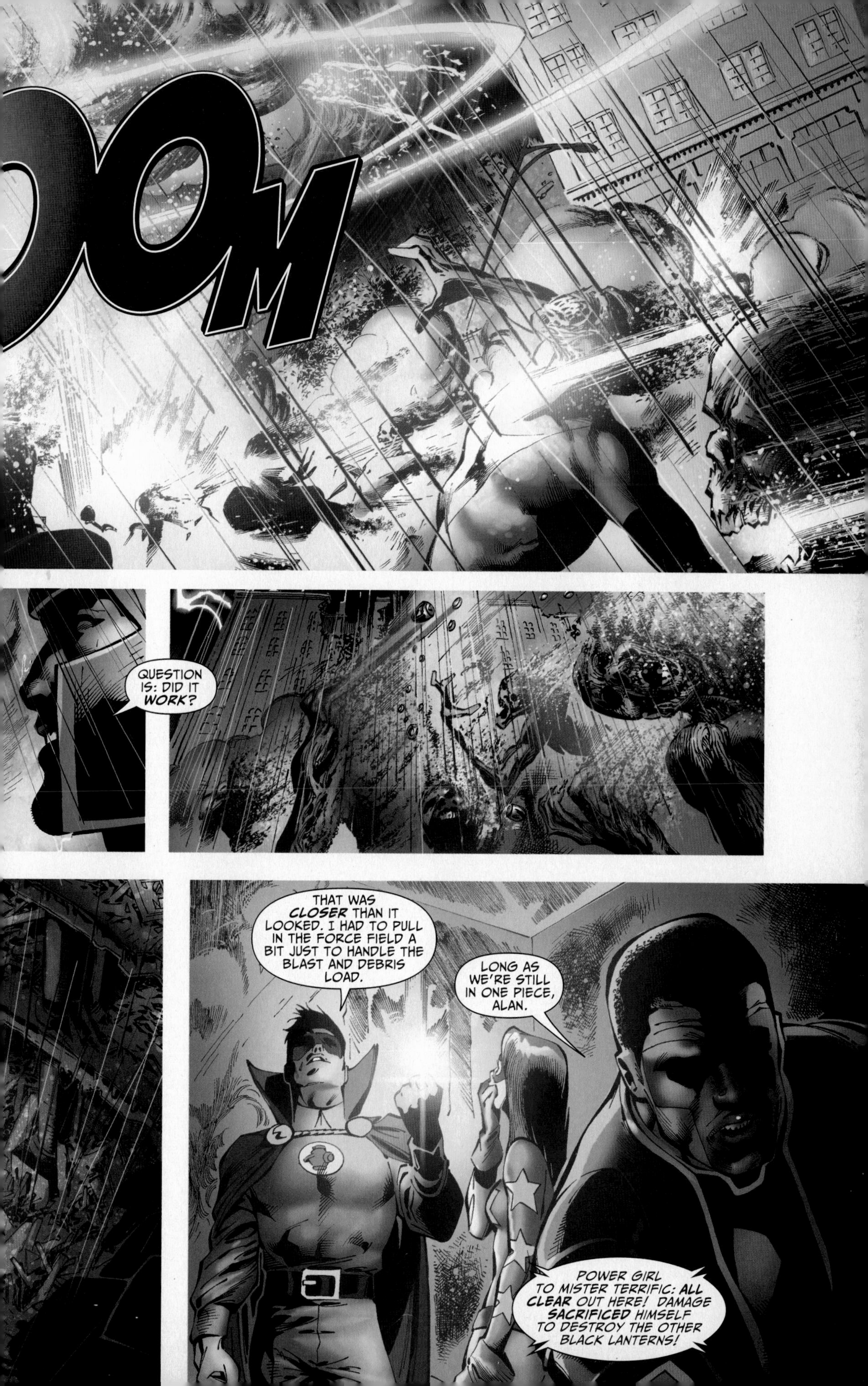

OOM
QUESTION IS: DID IT WORK?
THAT WAS CLOSER THAN IT LOOKED. I HAD TO PULL IN THE FORCE FIELD A BIT JUST TO HANDLE THE BLAST AND DEBRIS LOAD.
LONG AS WE'RE STILL IN ONE PIECE, ALAN.
POWER GIRL TO MISTER TERRIFIC: ALL CLEAR OUT HERE! DAMAGE SACRIFICED HIMSELF TO DESTROY THE OTHER BLACK LANTERNS!

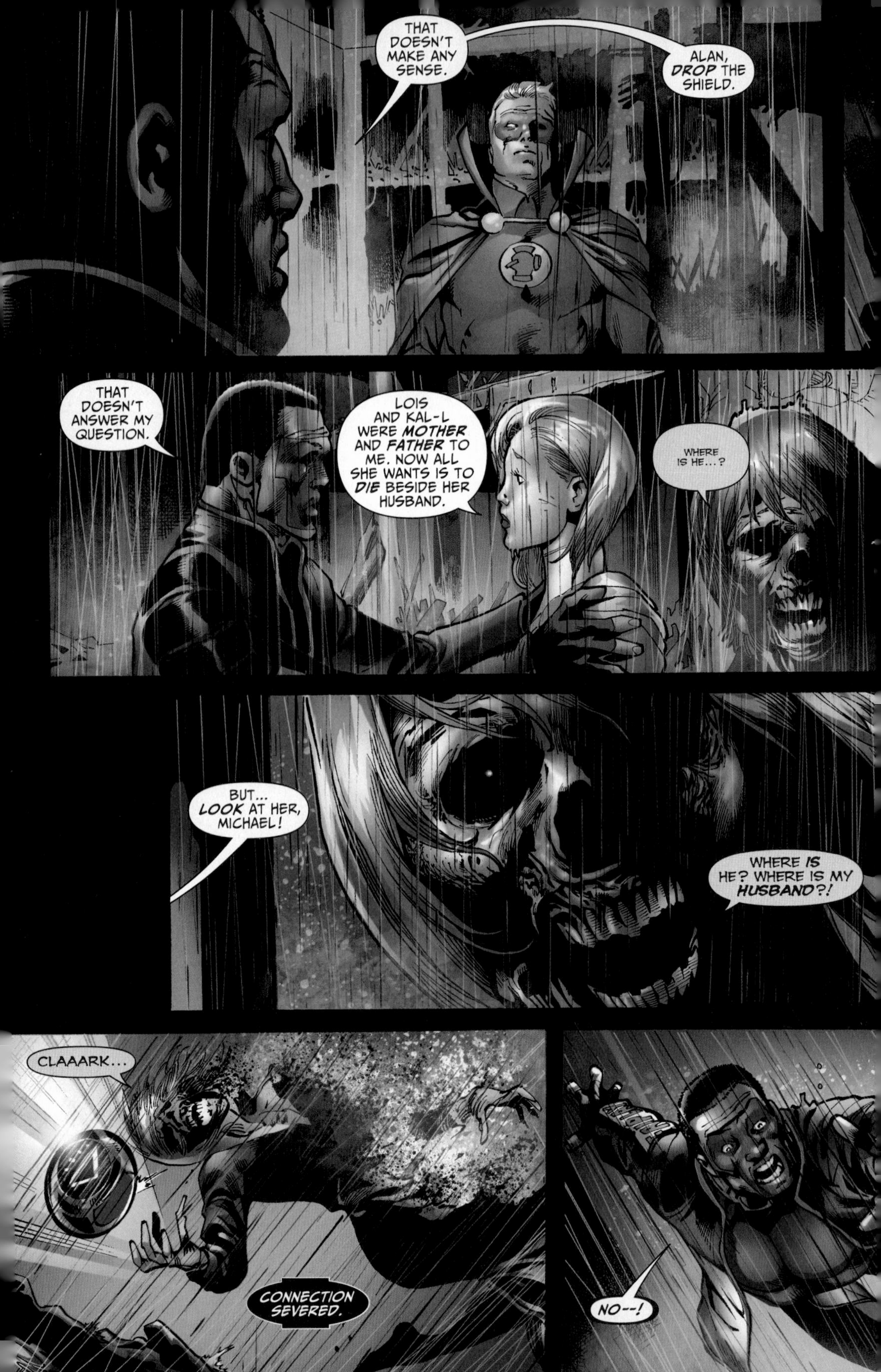
THAT DOESN'T MAKE ANY SENSE.
ALAN, DROP THE SHIELD.
THAT DOESN'T ANSWER MY QUESTION.
LOIS AND KAL-L WERE MOTHER AND FATHER TO ME. NOW ALL SHE WANTS IS TO DIE BESIDE HER HUSBAND.
WHERE IS HE...?
BUT... LOOK AT HER, MICHAEL!
WHERE IS HE? WHERE IS MY HUSBAND?!
CLAAARK...
CONNECTION SEVERED.
NO--!

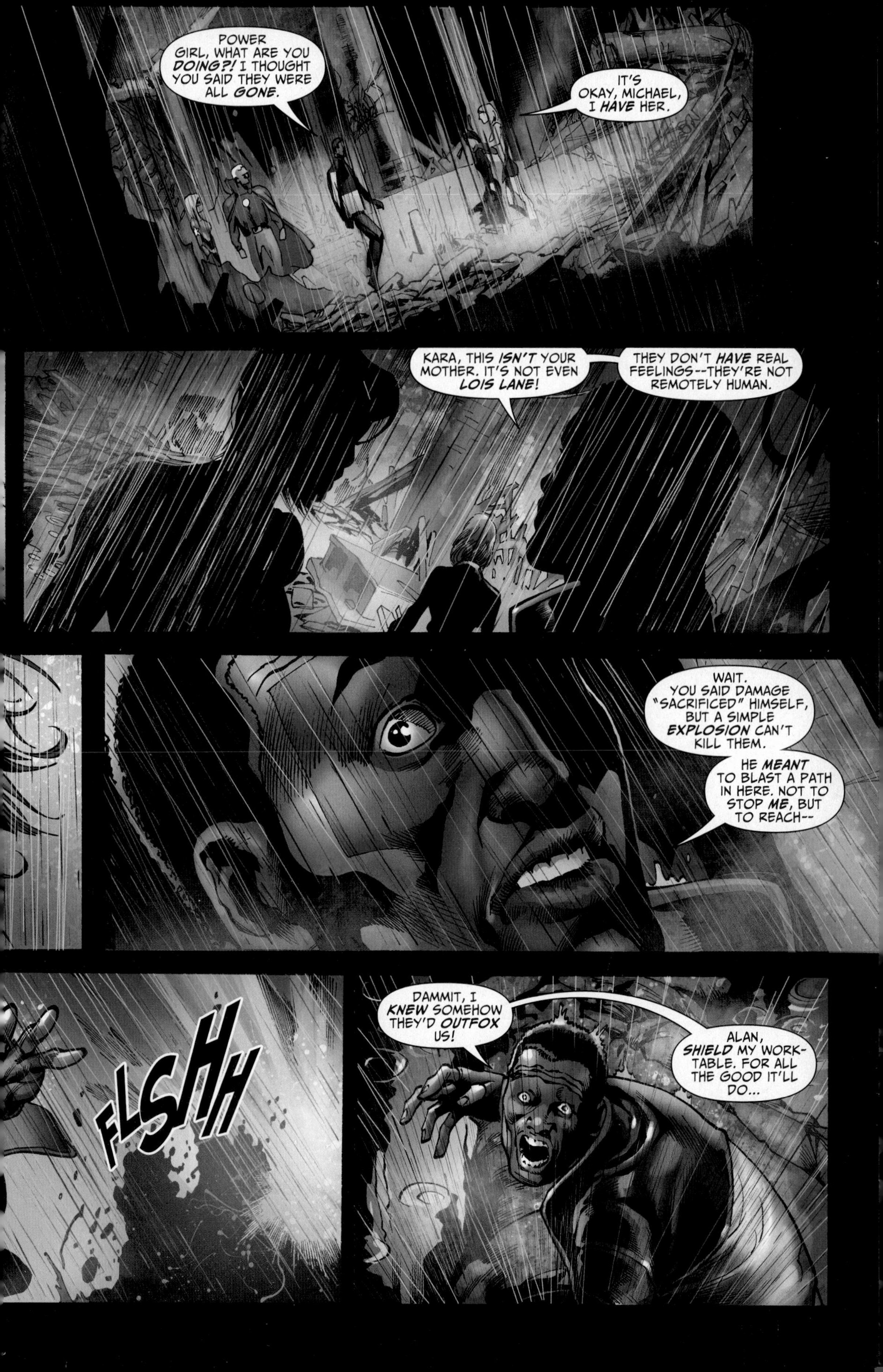
POWER GIRL, WHAT ARE YOU DOING?! I THOUGHT YOU SAID THEY WERE ALL GONE.
IT'S OKAY, MICHAEL, I HAVE HER.
KARA, THIS ISN'T YOUR MOTHER. IT'S NOT EVEN LOIS LANE!
THEY DON'T HAVE REAL FEELINGS--THEY'RE NOT REMOTELY HUMAN.
WAIT. YOU SAID DAMAGE "SACRIFICED" HIMSELF, BUT A SIMPLE EXPLOSION CAN'T KILL THEM.
HE MEANT TO BLAST A PATH IN HERE. NOT TO STOP ME, BUT TO REACH--
FLSHH
DAMMIT, I KNEW SOMEHOW THEY'D OUTFOX US!
ALAN, SHIELD MY WORK-TABLE. FOR ALL THE GOOD IT'LL DO...

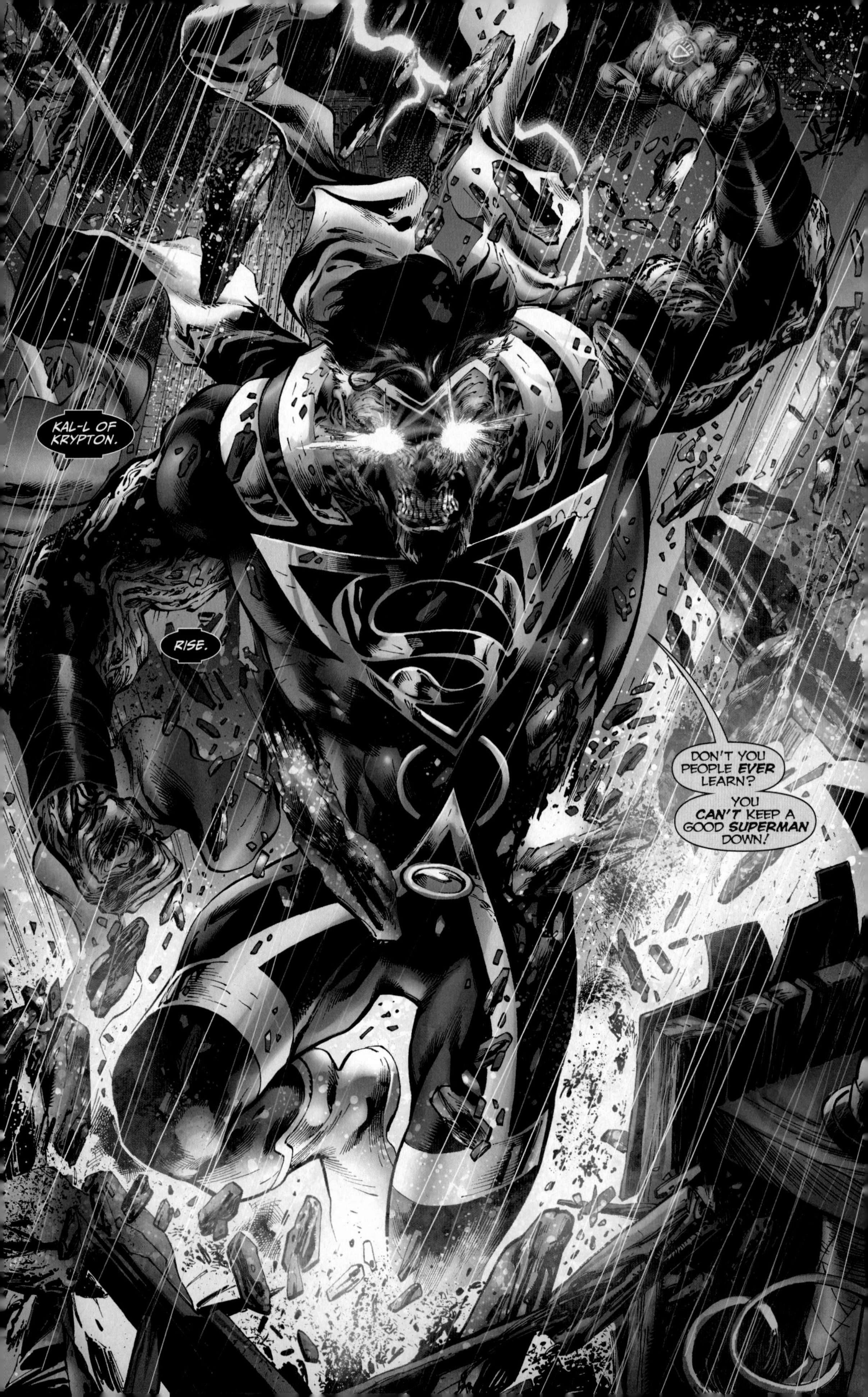
KAL-L OF KRYPTON.
RISE.
DON'T YOU PEOPLE EVER LEARN?
YOU CAN'T KEEP A GOOD SUPERMAN DOWN!

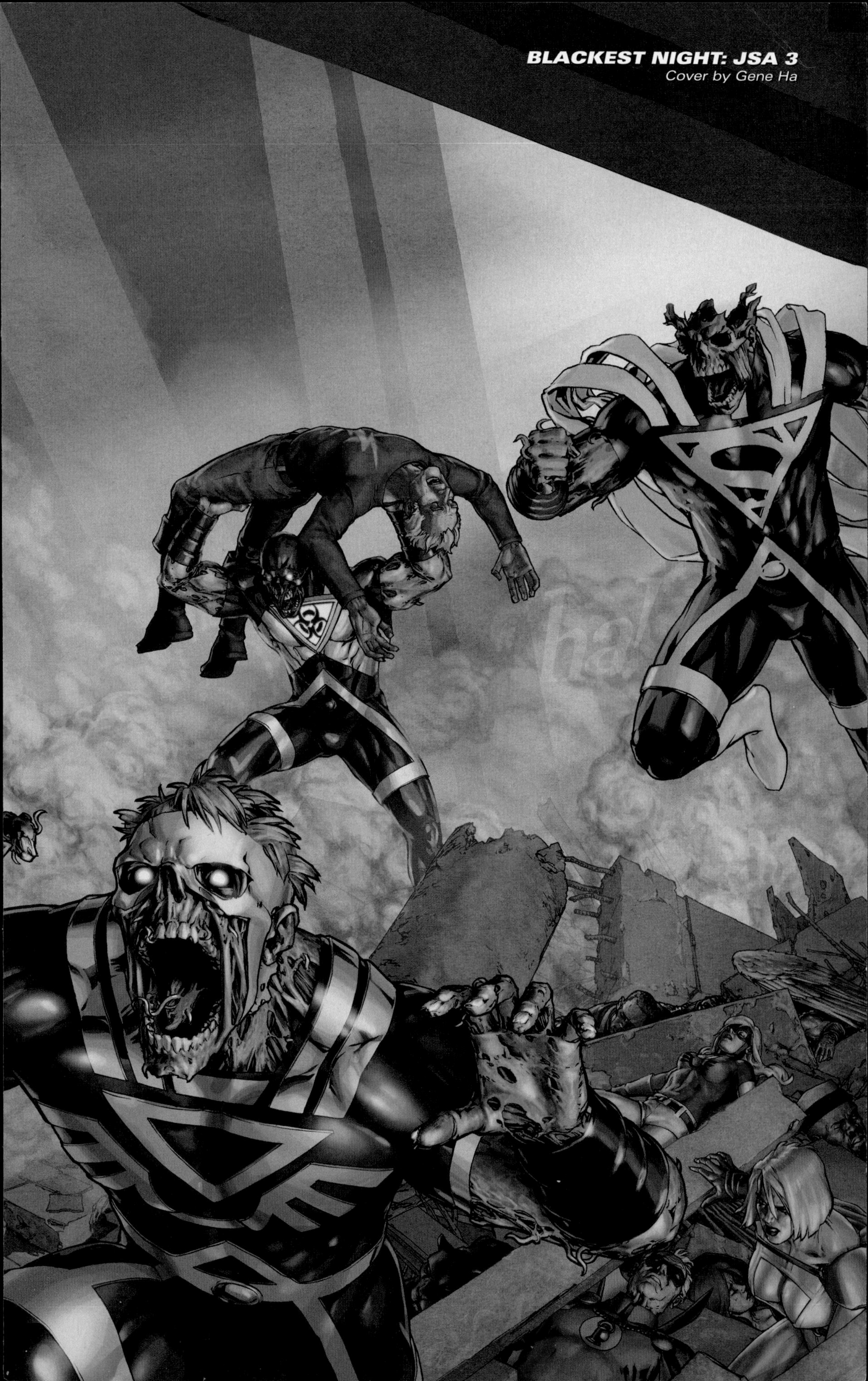

BLACKEST NIGHT: JSA 3
Cover by Gene Ha

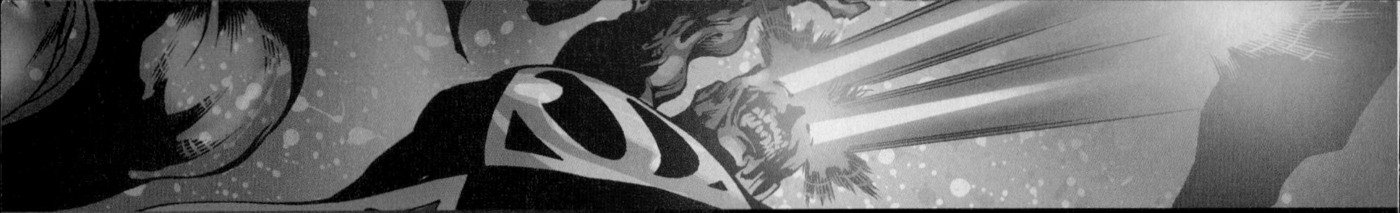

WHITE LIGHTNING

TONY BEDARD
JAMES ROBINSON
WRITERS

EDDY BARROWS
MARCOS MARZ
EDUARDO PANSICA
PENCILS

EDDY BARROWS
LUCIANA DEL NEGRO
WAYNE FAUCHER
EBER FERREIRA
SANDRO RIBEIRO
INKS

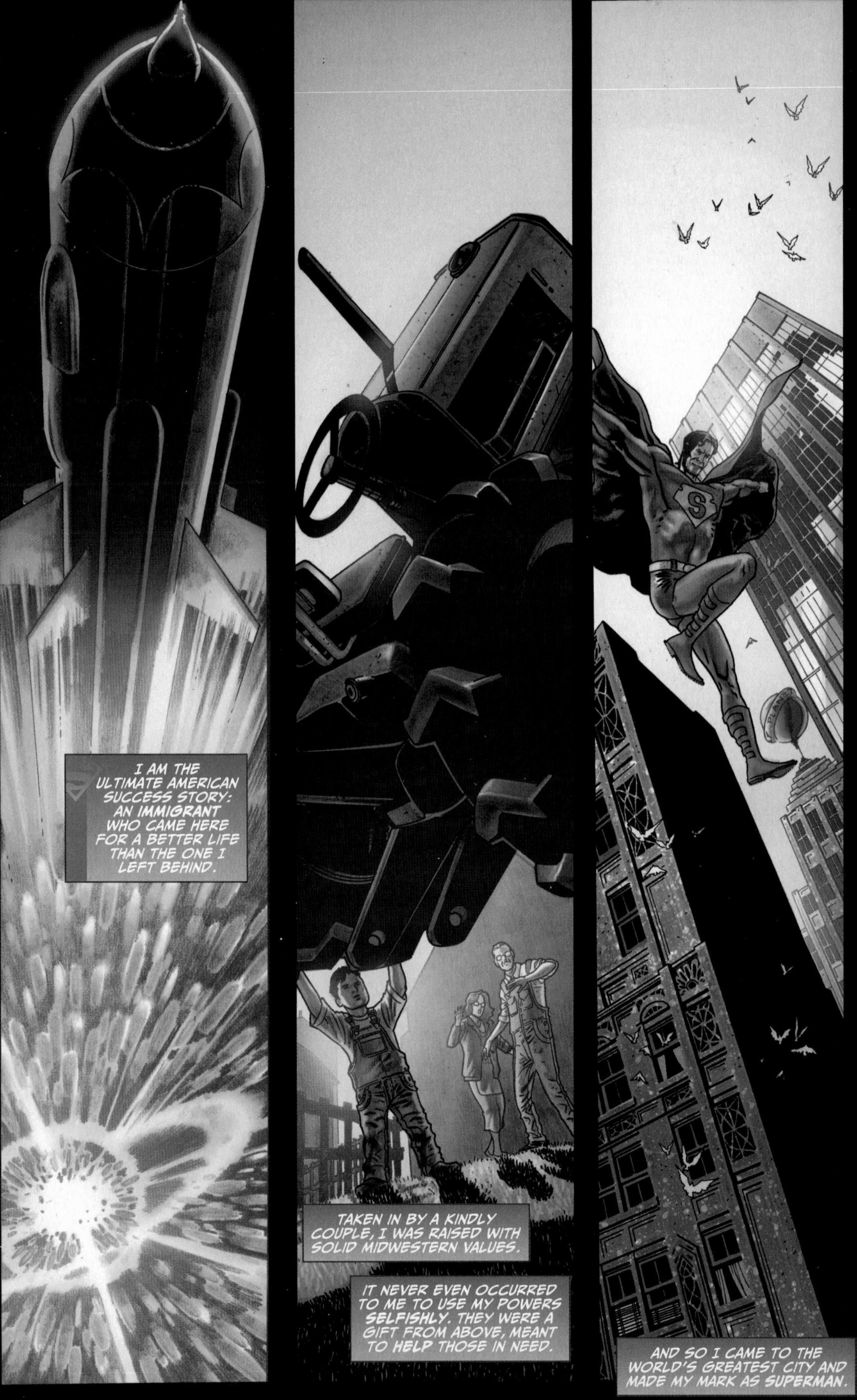
I AM THE ULTIMATE AMERICAN SUCCESS STORY: AN IMMIGRANT WHO CAME HERE FOR A BETTER LIFE THAN THE ONE I LEFT BEHIND.
TAKEN IN BY A KINDLY COUPLE, I WAS RAISED WITH SOLID MIDWESTERN VALUES.
IT NEVER EVEN OCCURRED TO ME TO USE MY POWERS SELFISHLY. THEY WERE A GIFT FROM ABOVE, MEANT TO HELP THOSE IN NEED.
AND SO I CAME TO THE WORLD'S GREATEST CITY AND MADE MY MARK AS SUPERMAN.

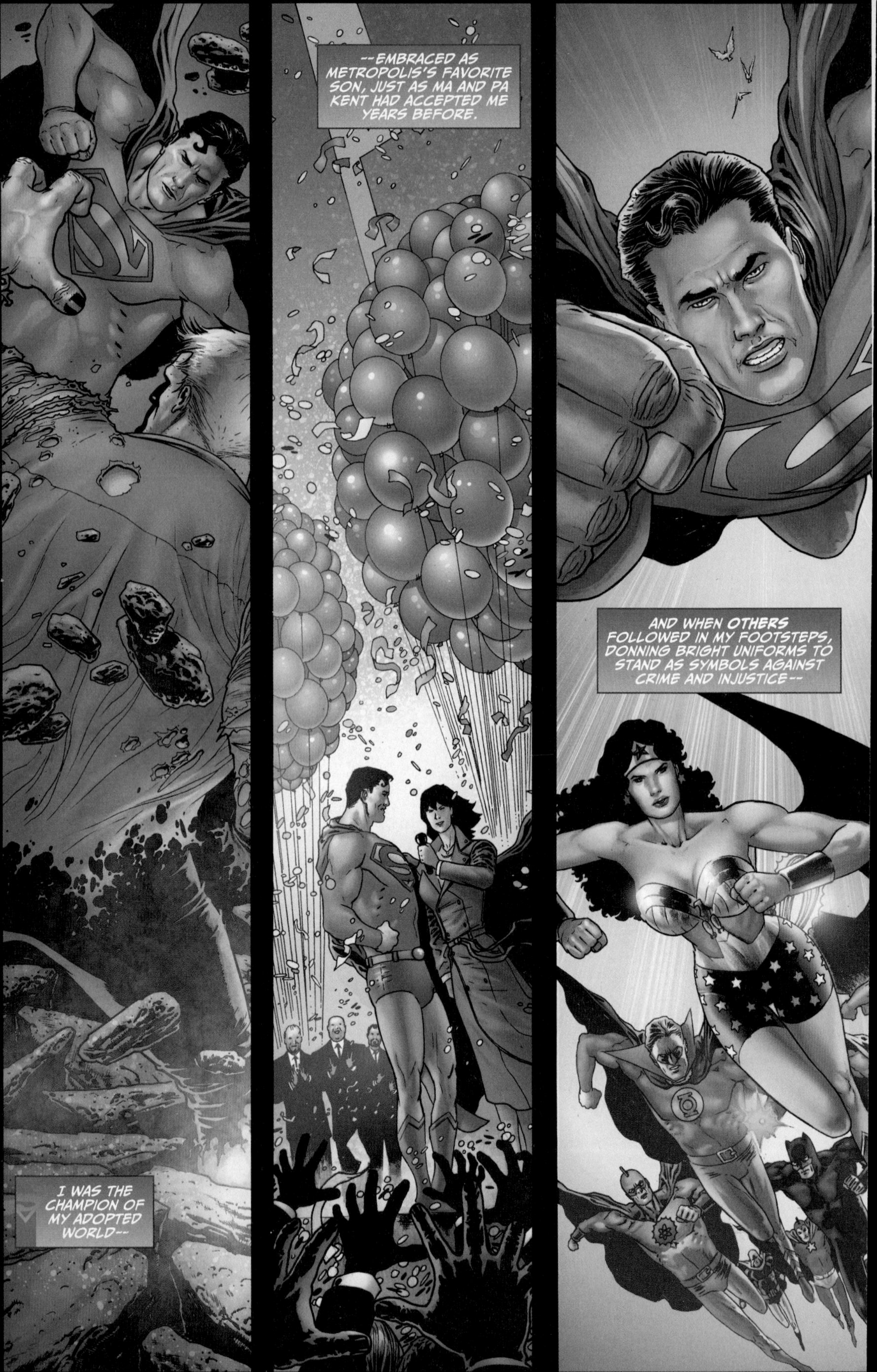
I WAS THE CHAMPION OF MY ADOPTED WORLD--
--EMBRACED AS METROPOLIS'S FAVORITE SON, JUST AS MA AND PA KENT HAD ACCEPTED ME YEARS BEFORE.
AND WHEN OTHERS FOLLOWED IN MY FOOTSTEPS, DONNING BRIGHT UNIFORMS TO STAND AS SYMBOLS AGAINST CRIME AND INJUSTICE--

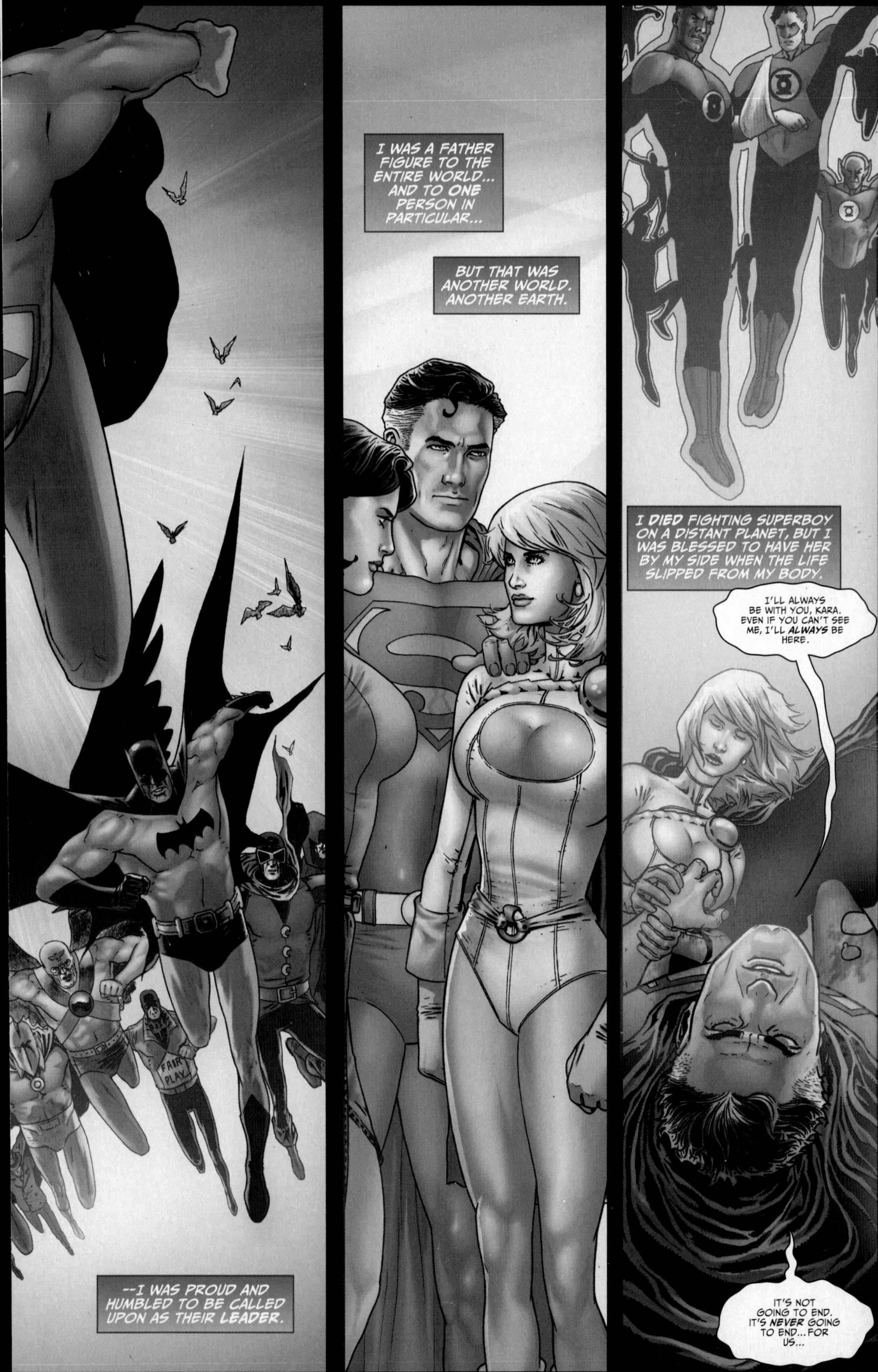
--I WAS PROUD AND HUMBLED TO BE CALLED UPON AS THEIR LEADER.
FAIR PLAY
I WAS A FATHER FIGURE TO THE ENTIRE WORLD... AND TO ONE PERSON IN PARTICULAR...
BUT THAT WAS ANOTHER WORLD. ANOTHER EARTH.
I DIED FIGHTING SUPERBOY ON A DISTANT PLANET, BUT I WAS BLESSED TO HAVE HER BY MY SIDE WHEN THE LIFE SLIPPED FROM MY BODY.
I'LL ALWAYS BE WITH YOU, KARA. EVEN IF YOU CAN'T SEE ME, I'LL ALWAYS BE HERE.
IT'S NOT GOING TO END. IT'S NEVER GOING TO END...FOR US...

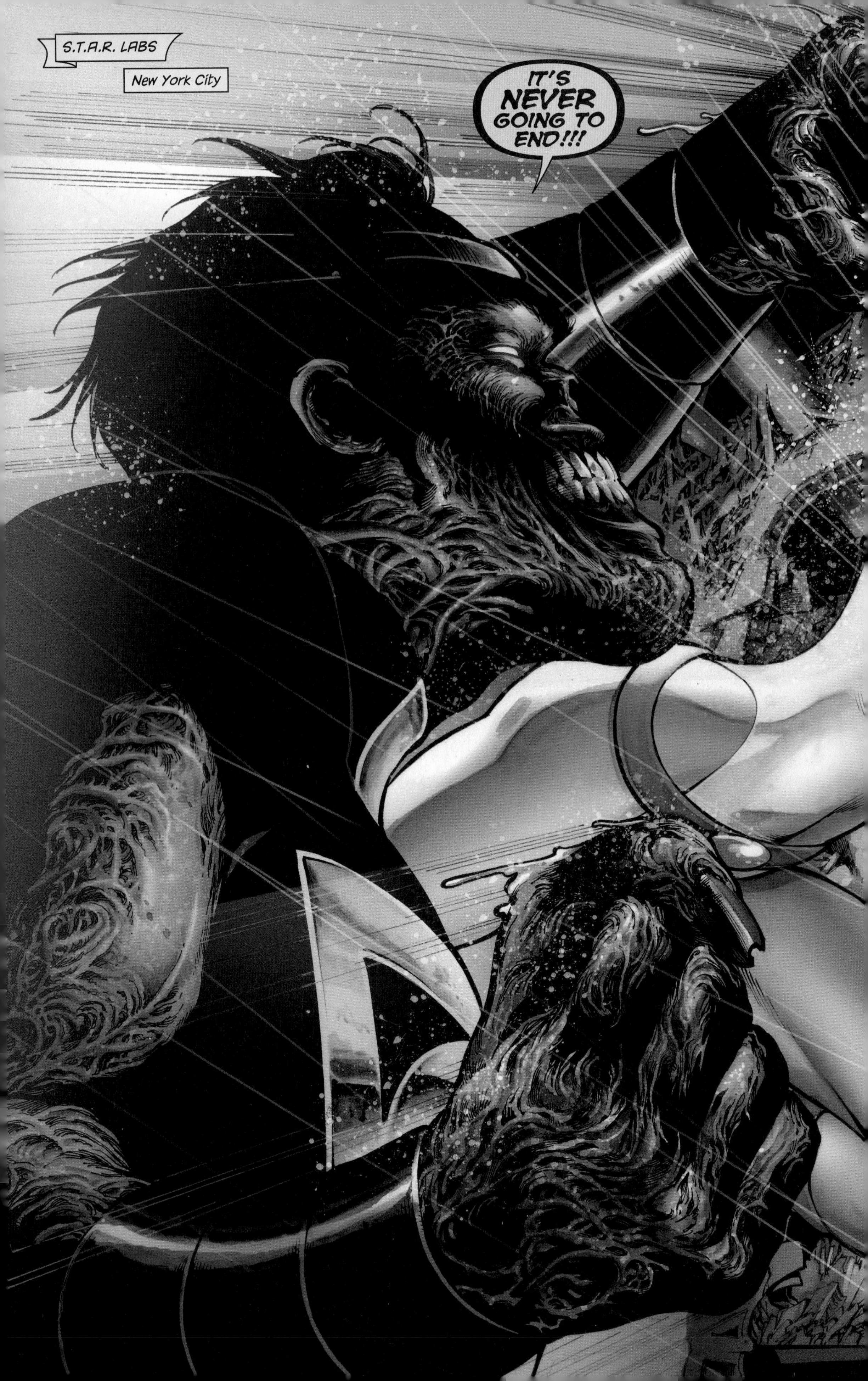
S.T.A.R. LABS
New York City
IT'S NEVER GOING TO END!!!

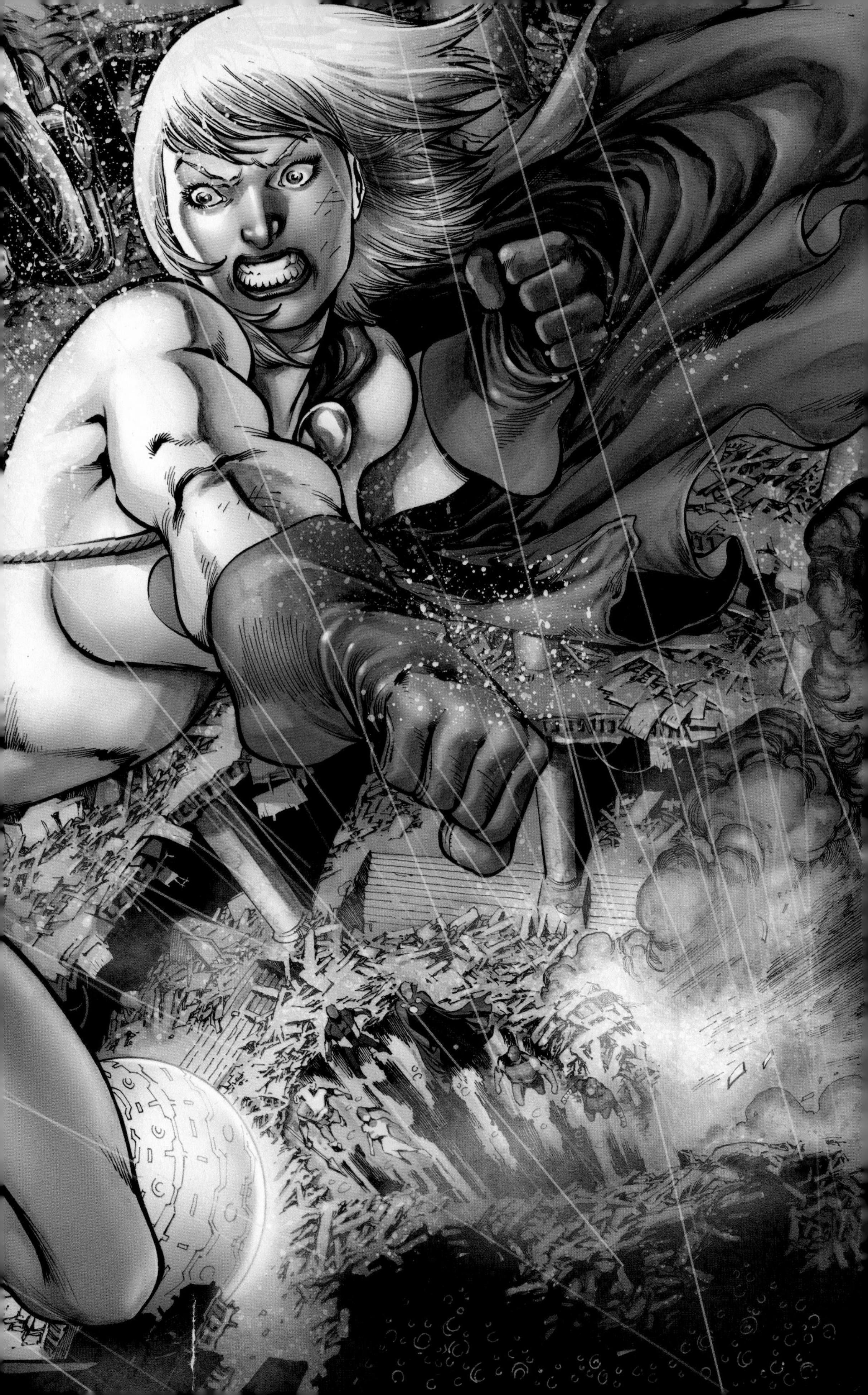

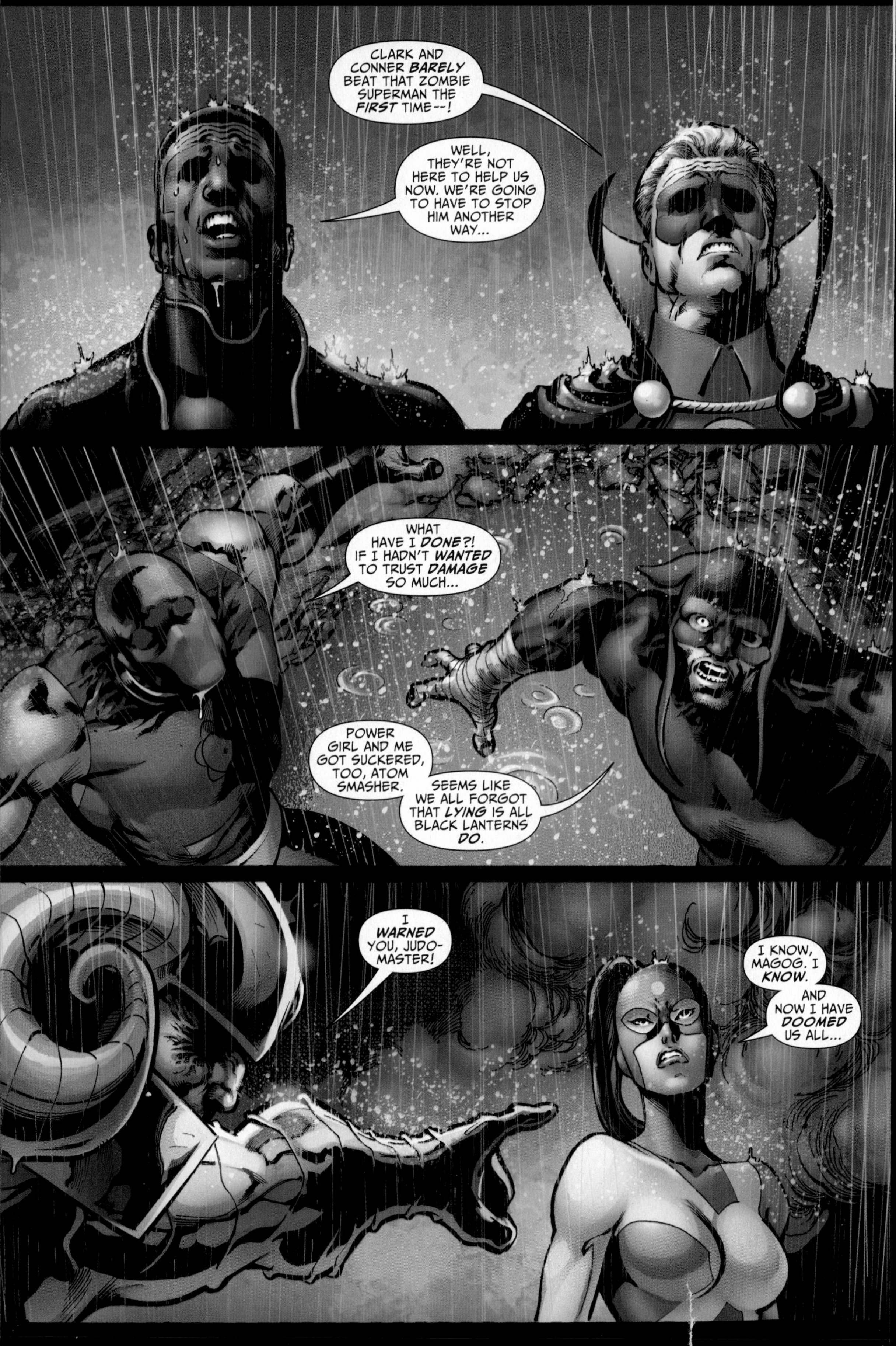
CLARK AND CONNER BARELY BEAT THAT ZOMBIE SUPERMAN THE FIRST TIME--!
WELL, THEY'RE NOT HERE TO HELP US NOW. WE'RE GOING TO HAVE TO STOP HIM ANOTHER WAY...
WHAT HAVE I DONE?! IF I HADN'T WANTED TO TRUST DAMAGE SO MUCH...
POWER GIRL AND ME GOT SUCKERED, TOO, ATOM SMASHER.
SEEMS LIKE WE ALL FORGOT THAT LYING IS ALL BLACK LANTERNS DO.
I WARNED YOU, JUDO-MASTER!
I KNOW, MAGOG. I KNOW.
AND NOW I HAVE DOOMED US ALL...

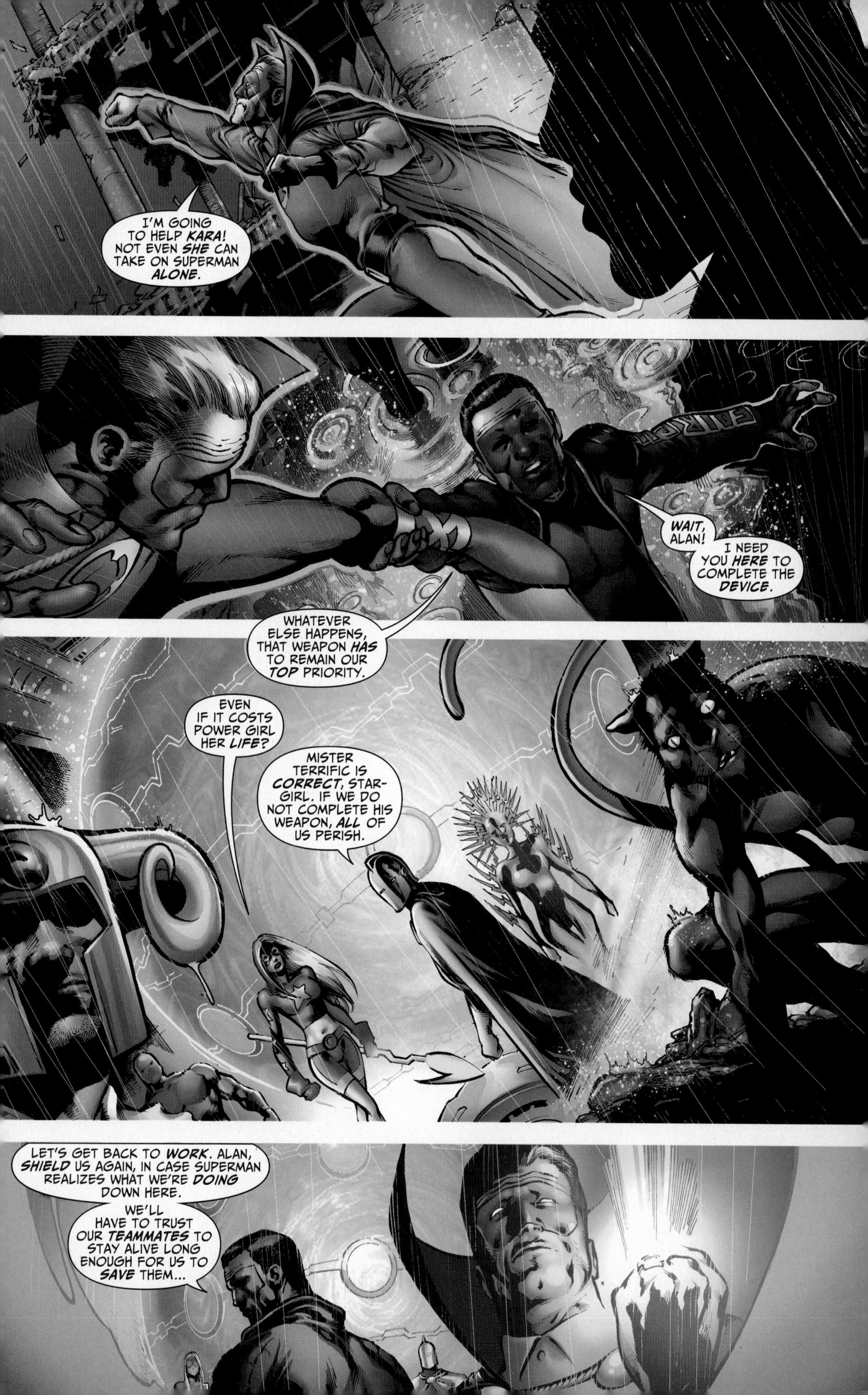
I'M GOING TO HELP KARA! NOT EVEN SHE CAN TAKE ON SUPERMAN ALONE.
WAIT, ALAN!
I NEED YOU HERE TO COMPLETE THE DEVICE.
WHATEVER ELSE HAPPENS, THAT WEAPON HAS TO REMAIN OUR TOP PRIORITY.
EVEN IF IT COSTS POWER GIRL HER LIFE?
MISTER TERRIFIC IS CORRECT, STAR-GIRL. IF WE DO NOT COMPLETE HIS WEAPON, ALL OF US PERISH.
LET'S GET BACK TO WORK. ALAN, SHIELD US AGAIN, IN CASE SUPERMAN REALIZES WHAT WE'RE DOING DOWN HERE.
WE'LL HAVE TO TRUST OUR TEAMMATES TO STAY ALIVE LONG ENOUGH FOR US TO SAVE THEM...

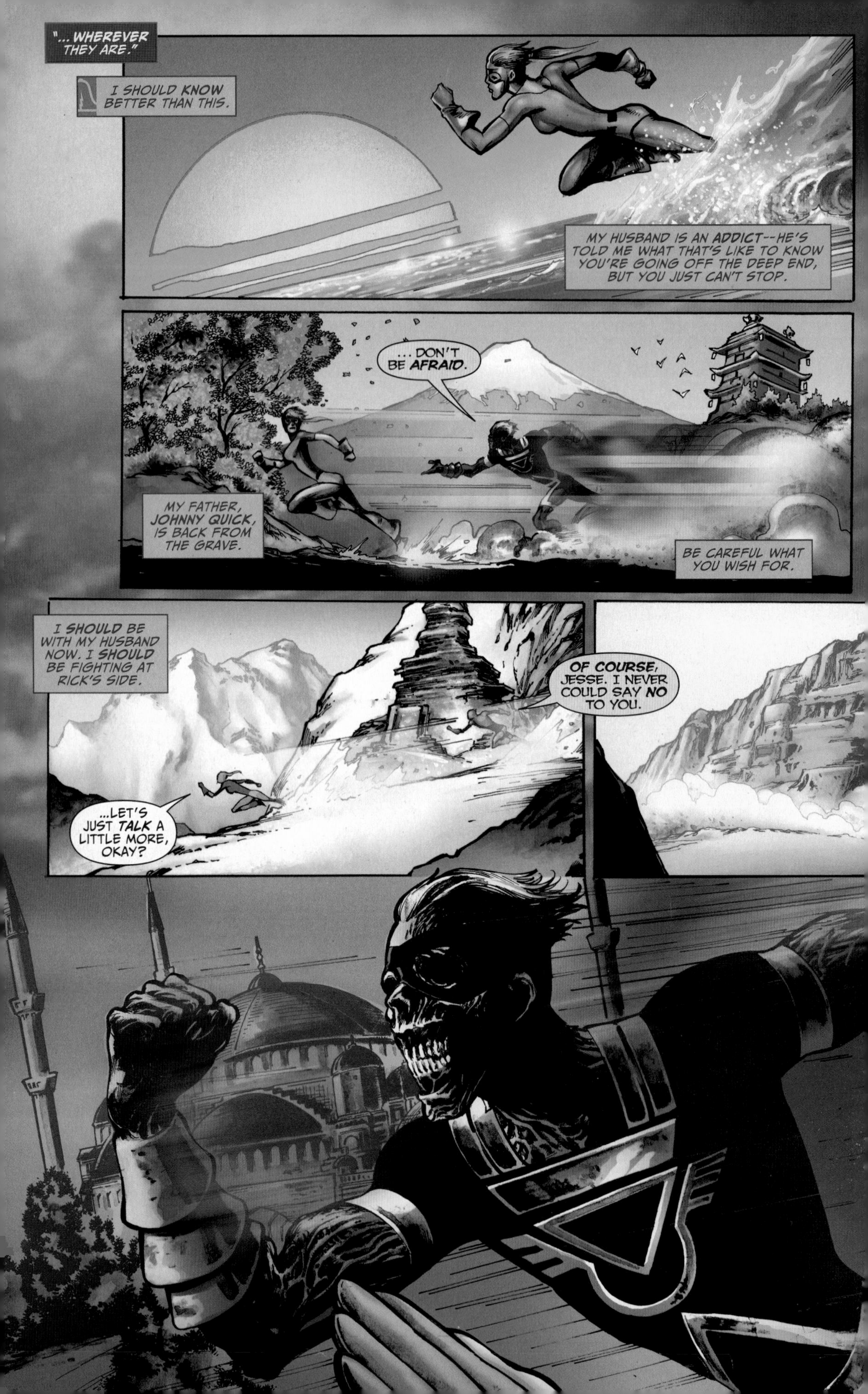
"...WHEREVER THEY ARE."
I SHOULD KNOW BETTER THAN THIS.
MY HUSBAND IS AN ADDICT--HE'S TOLD ME WHAT THAT'S LIKE TO KNOW YOU'RE GOING OFF THE DEEP END, BUT YOU JUST CAN'T STOP.
... DON'T BE AFRAID.
MY FATHER, JOHNNY QUICK, IS BACK FROM THE GRAVE.
BE CAREFUL WHAT YOU WISH FOR.
I SHOULD BE WITH MY HUSBAND NOW. I SHOULD BE FIGHTING AT RICK'S SIDE.
OF COURSE, JESSE. I NEVER COULD SAY NO TO YOU.
...LET'S JUST TALK A LITTLE MORE, OKAY?

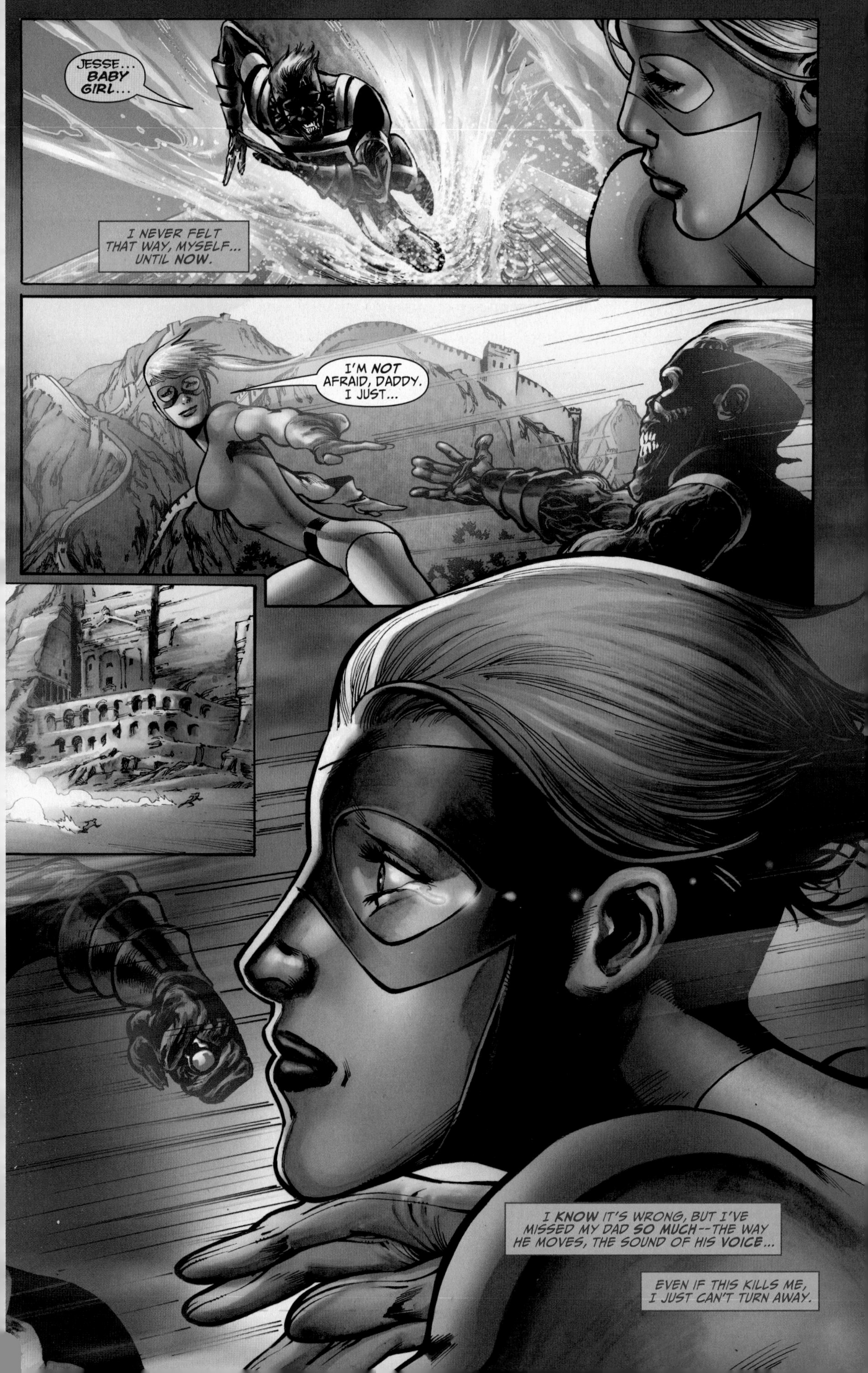
JESSE... BABY GIRL...
I NEVER FELT THAT WAY, MYSELF... UNTIL NOW.
I'M NOT AFRAID, DADDY. I JUST...
I KNOW IT'S WRONG, BUT I'VE MISSED MY DAD SO MUCH--THE WAY HE MOVES, THE SOUND OF HIS VOICE...
EVEN IF THIS KILLS ME, I JUST CAN'T TURN AWAY.

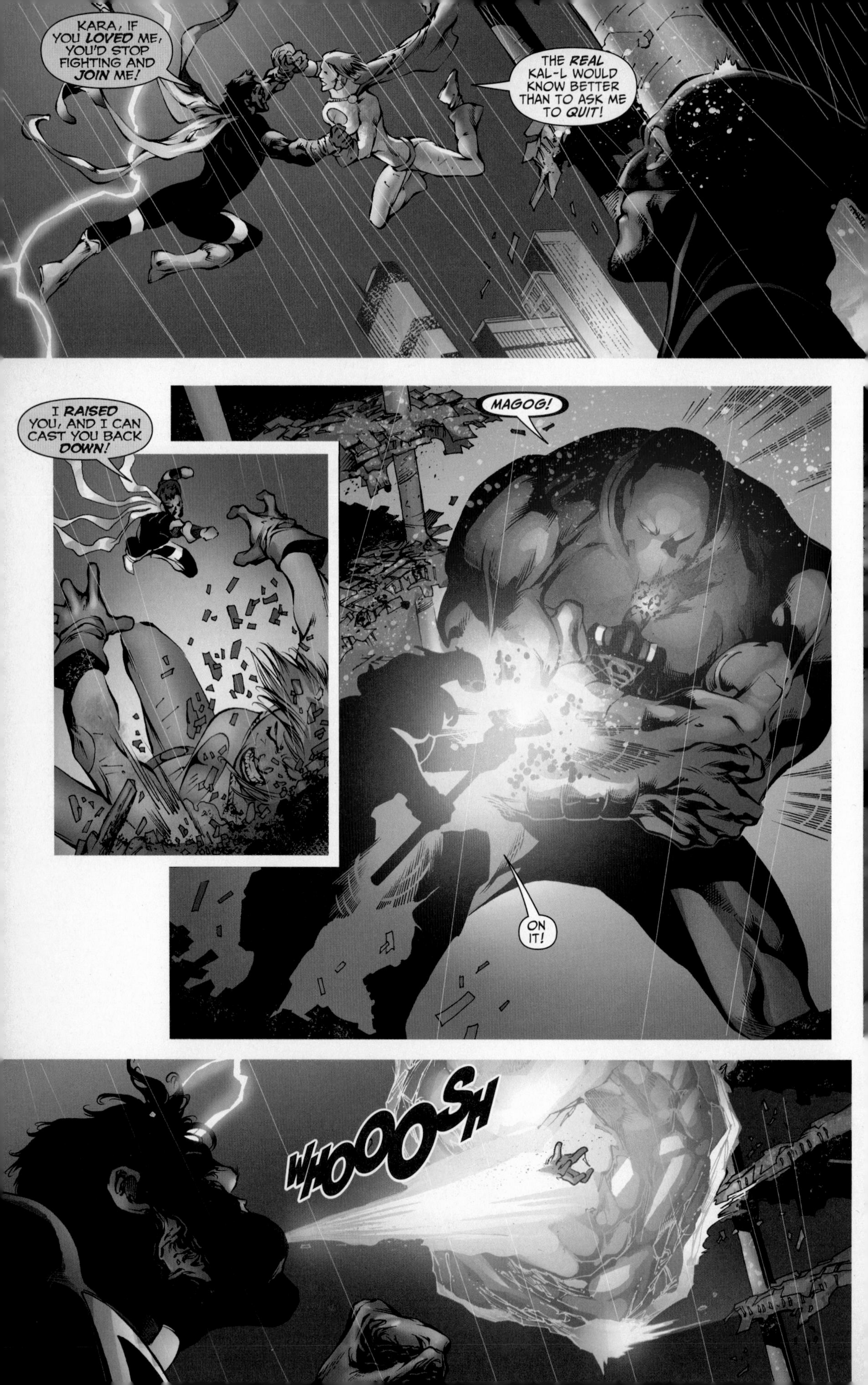
KARA, IF YOU LOVED ME, YOU'D STOP FIGHTING AND JOIN ME!
THE REAL KAL-L WOULD KNOW BETTER THAN TO ASK ME TO QUIT!
I RAISED YOU, AND I CAN CAST YOU BACK DOWN!
MAGOG!
ON IT!
WHOOOOSH

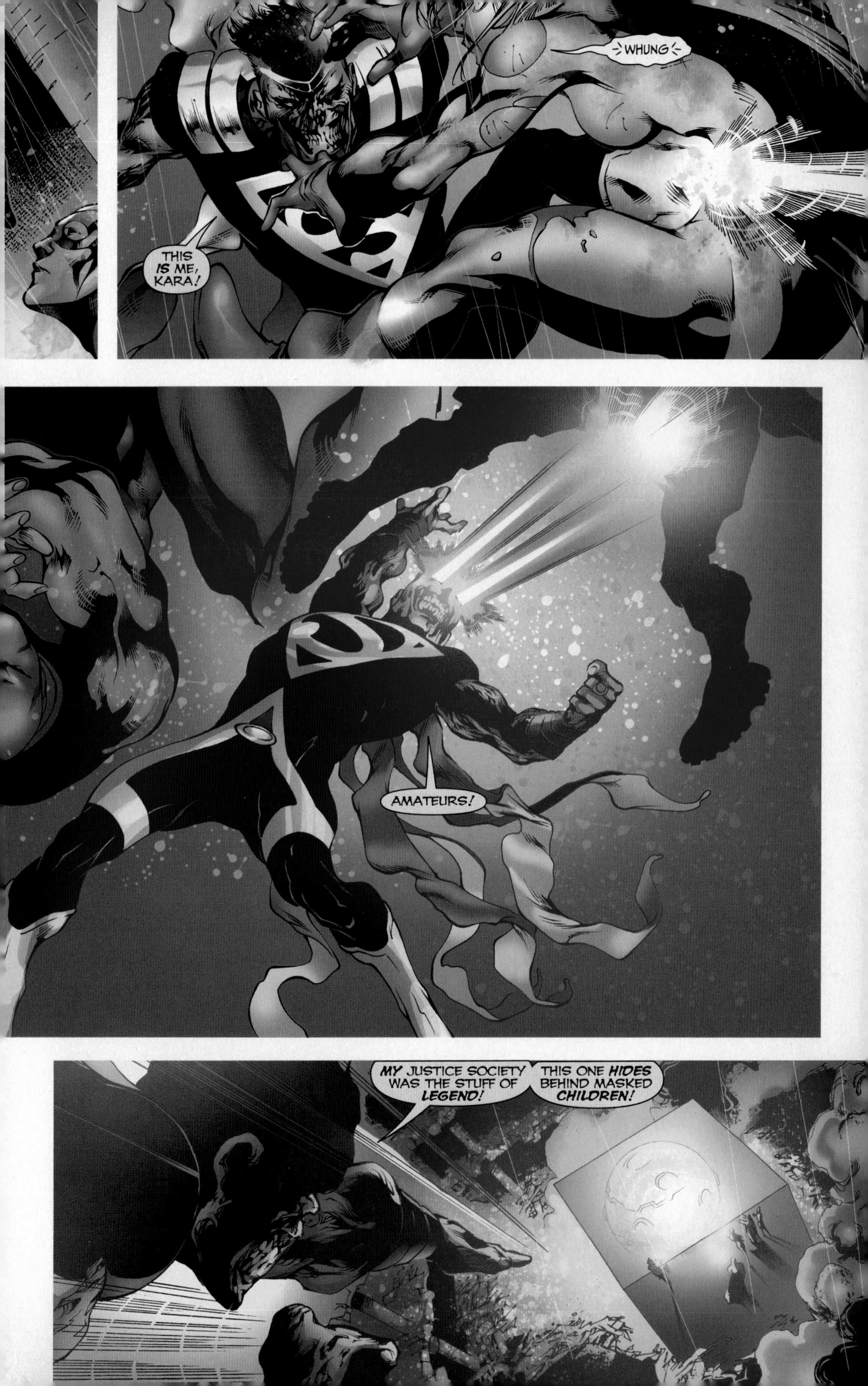
WHUNG
THIS IS ME, KARA!
AMATEURS!
MY JUSTICE SOCIETY WAS THE STUFF OF LEGEND!
THIS ONE HIDES BEHIND MASKED CHILDREN!

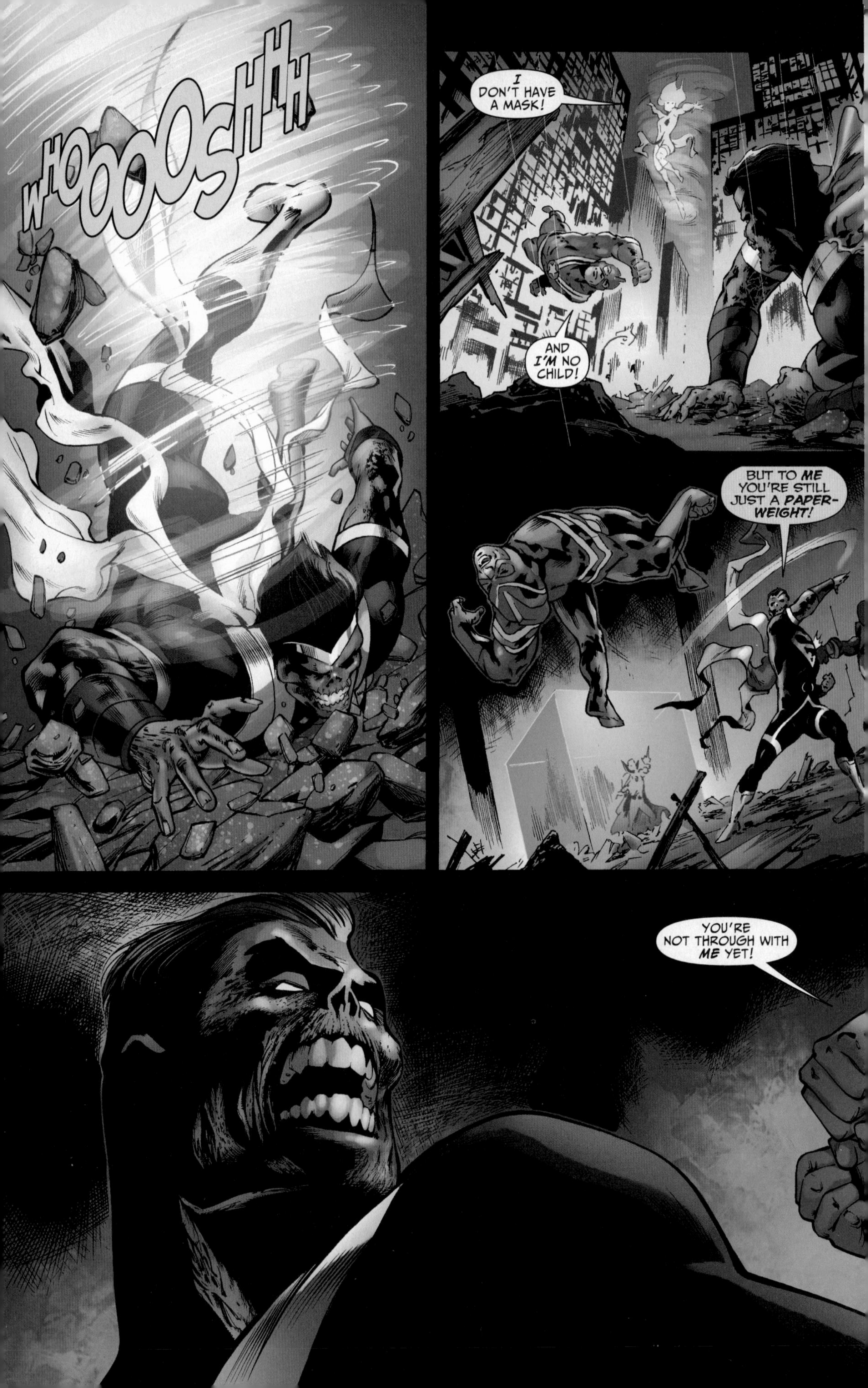
WHOOOOSHHH
I DON'T HAVE A MASK!
AND I'M NO CHILD!
BUT TO ME YOU'RE STILL JUST A PAPER-WEIGHT!
YOU'RE NOT THROUGH WITH ME YET!

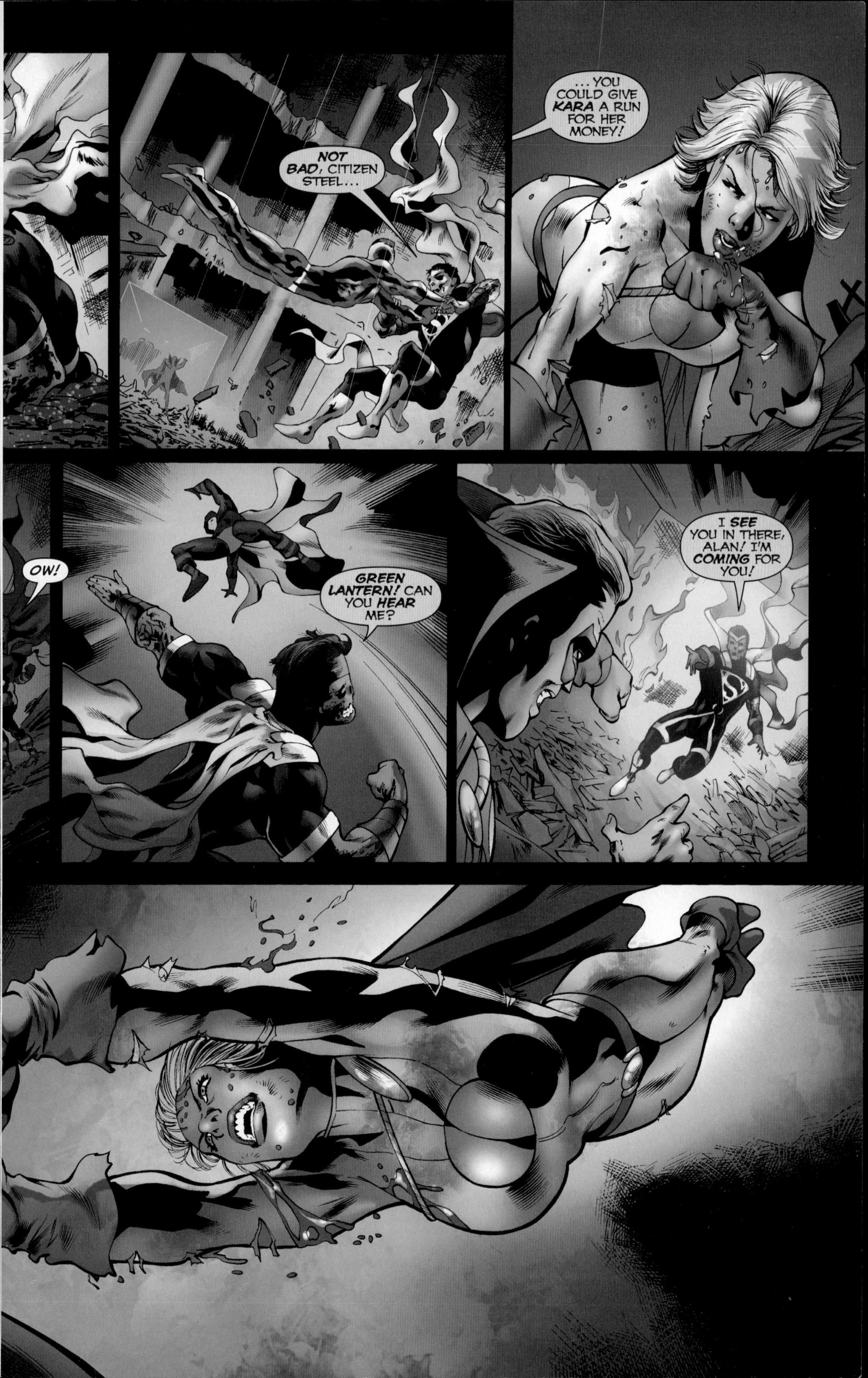
NOT BAD, CITIZEN STEEL...
...YOU COULD GIVE KARA A RUN FOR HER MONEY!
OW!
GREEN LANTERN! CAN YOU HEAR ME?
I SEE YOU IN THERE, ALAN! I'M COMING FOR YOU!

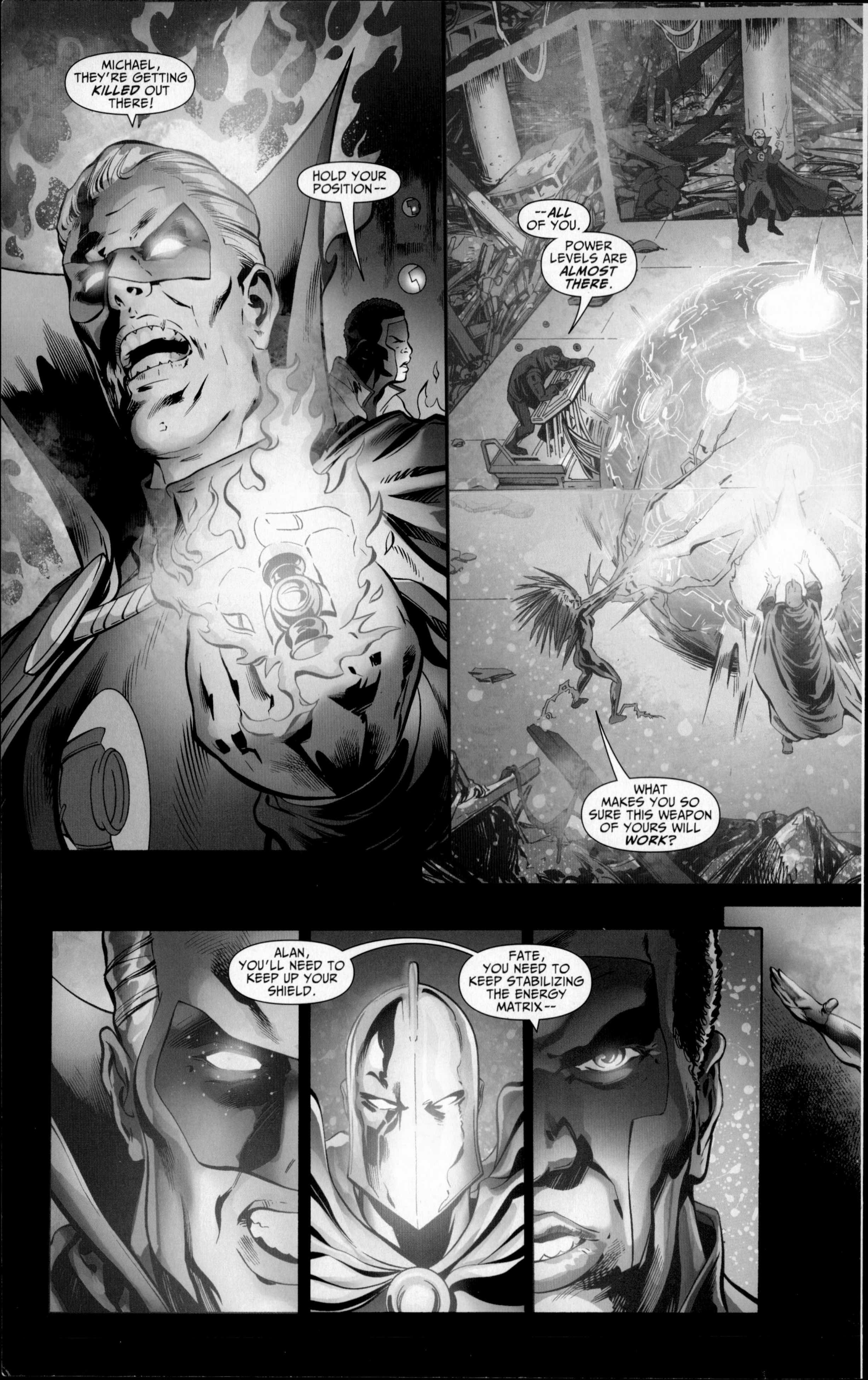
MICHAEL, THEY'RE GETTING KILLED OUT THERE!
HOLD YOUR POSITION--
--ALL OF YOU.
POWER LEVELS ARE ALMOST THERE.
WHAT MAKES YOU SO SURE THIS WEAPON OF YOURS WILL WORK?
ALAN, YOU'LL NEED TO KEEP UP YOUR SHIELD.
FATE, YOU NEED TO KEEP STABILIZING THE ENERGY MATRIX--

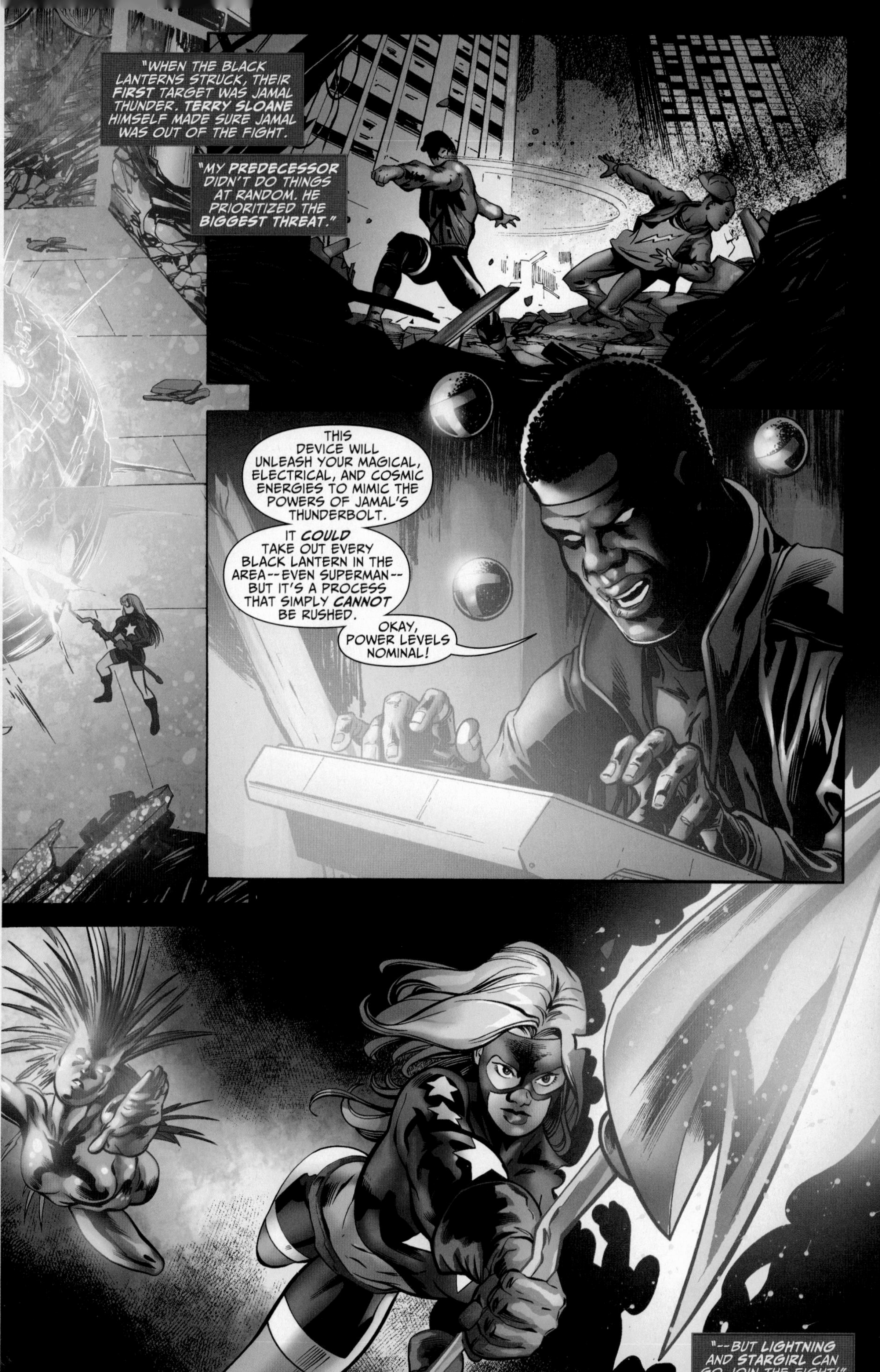
"WHEN THE BLACK LANTERNS STRUCK, THEIR FIRST TARGET WAS JAMAL THUNDER. TERRY SLOANE HIMSELF MADE SURE JAMAL WAS OUT OF THE FIGHT.
"MY PREDECESSOR DIDN'T DO THINGS AT RANDOM. HE PRIORITIZED THE BIGGEST THREAT."
THIS DEVICE WILL UNLEASH YOUR MAGICAL, ELECTRICAL, AND COSMIC ENERGIES TO MIMIC THE POWERS OF JAMAL'S THUNDERBOLT.
IT COULD TAKE OUT EVERY BLACK LANTERN IN THE AREA--EVEN SUPERMAN--BUT IT'S A PROCESS THAT SIMPLY CANNOT BE RUSHED.
OKAY, POWER LEVELS NOMINAL!
"--BUT LIGHTNING AND STARGIRL CAN GO JOIN THE FIGHT!"

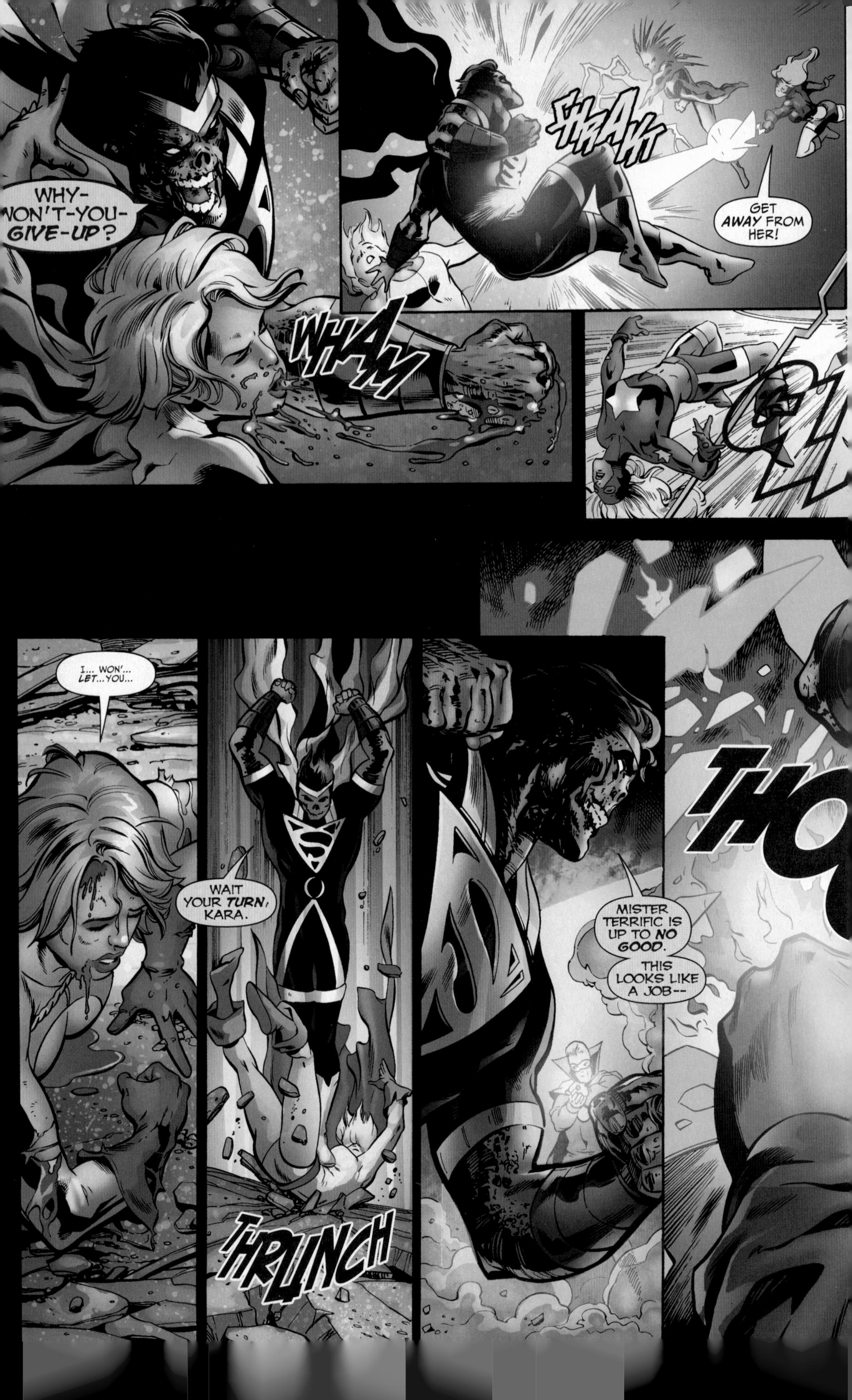
WHY-WON'T-YOU-GIVE-UP?
SHRAKT
GET AWAY FROM HER!
WHAM
I... WON'... LET...YOU...
WAIT YOUR TURN, KARA.
THRUNCH
MISTER TERRIFIC IS UP TO NO GOOD.
THIS LOOKS LIKE A JOB--
THO

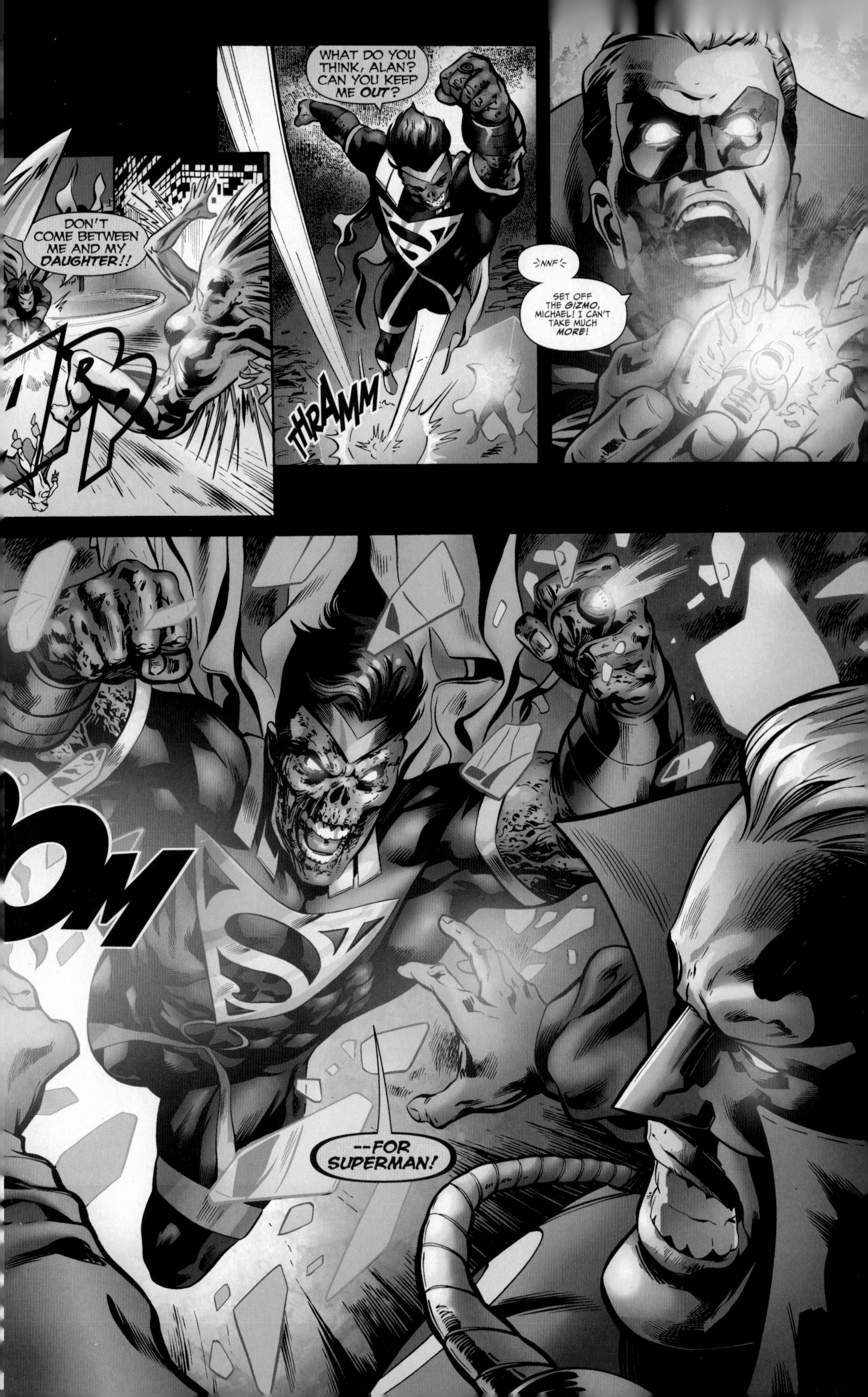
DON'T COME BETWEEN ME AND MY DAUGHTER!!
WHAT DO YOU THINK, ALAN? CAN YOU KEEP ME OUT?
THRAMM
NNF
SET OFF THE GIZMO, MICHAEL! I CAN'T TAKE MUCH MORE!
--FOR SUPERMAN!

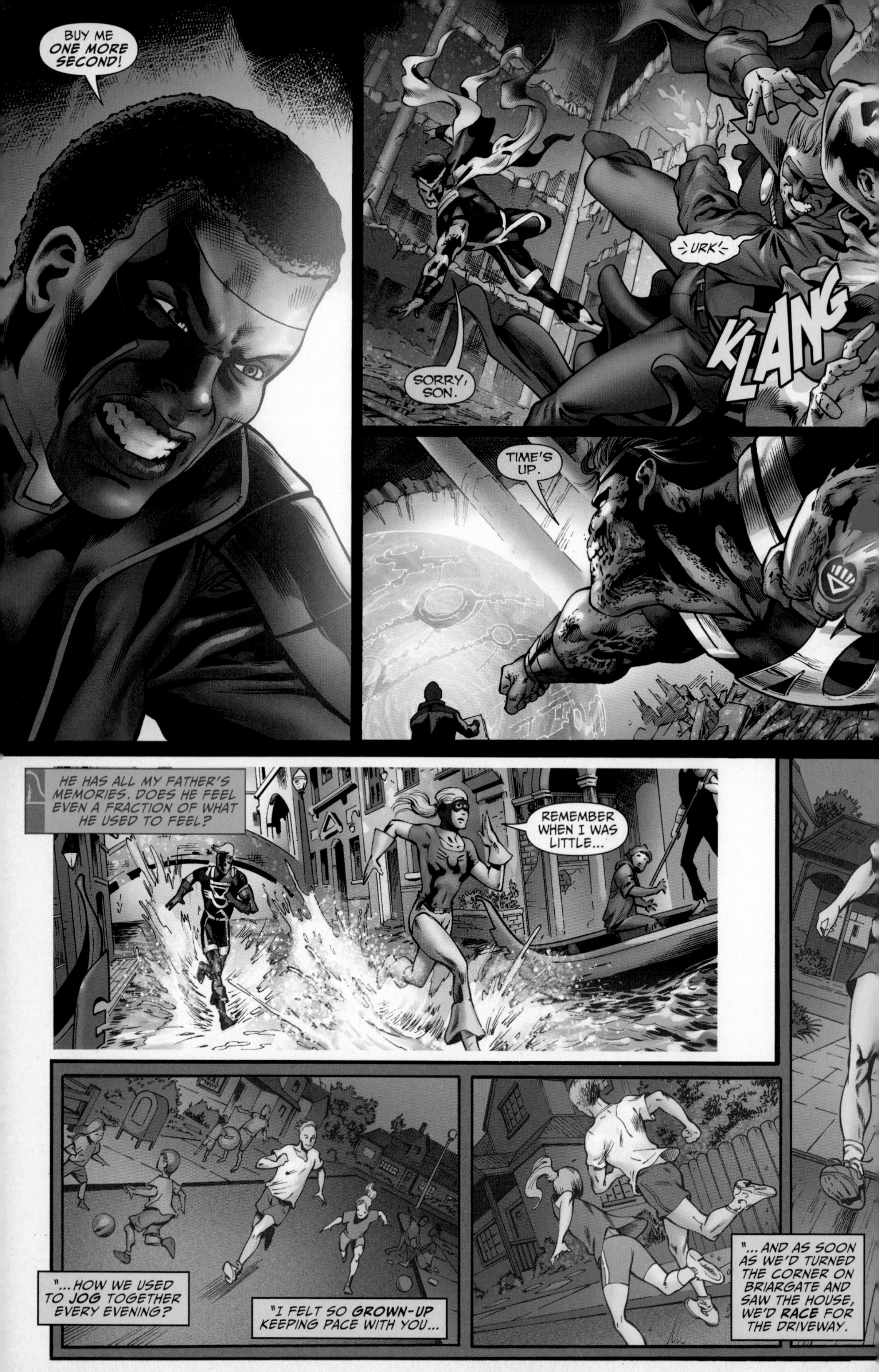
BUY ME ONE MORE SECOND!
URK!
SORRY, SON.
KLANG
TIME'S UP.
HE HAS ALL MY FATHER'S MEMORIES. DOES HE FEEL EVEN A FRACTION OF WHAT HE USED TO FEEL?
REMEMBER WHEN I WAS LITTLE...
"...HOW WE USED TO JOG TOGETHER EVERY EVENING?
"I FELT SO GROWN-UP KEEPING PACE WITH YOU...
"...AND AS SOON AS WE'D TURNED THE CORNER ON BRIARGATE AND SAW THE HOUSE, WE'D RACE FOR THE DRIVEWAY.

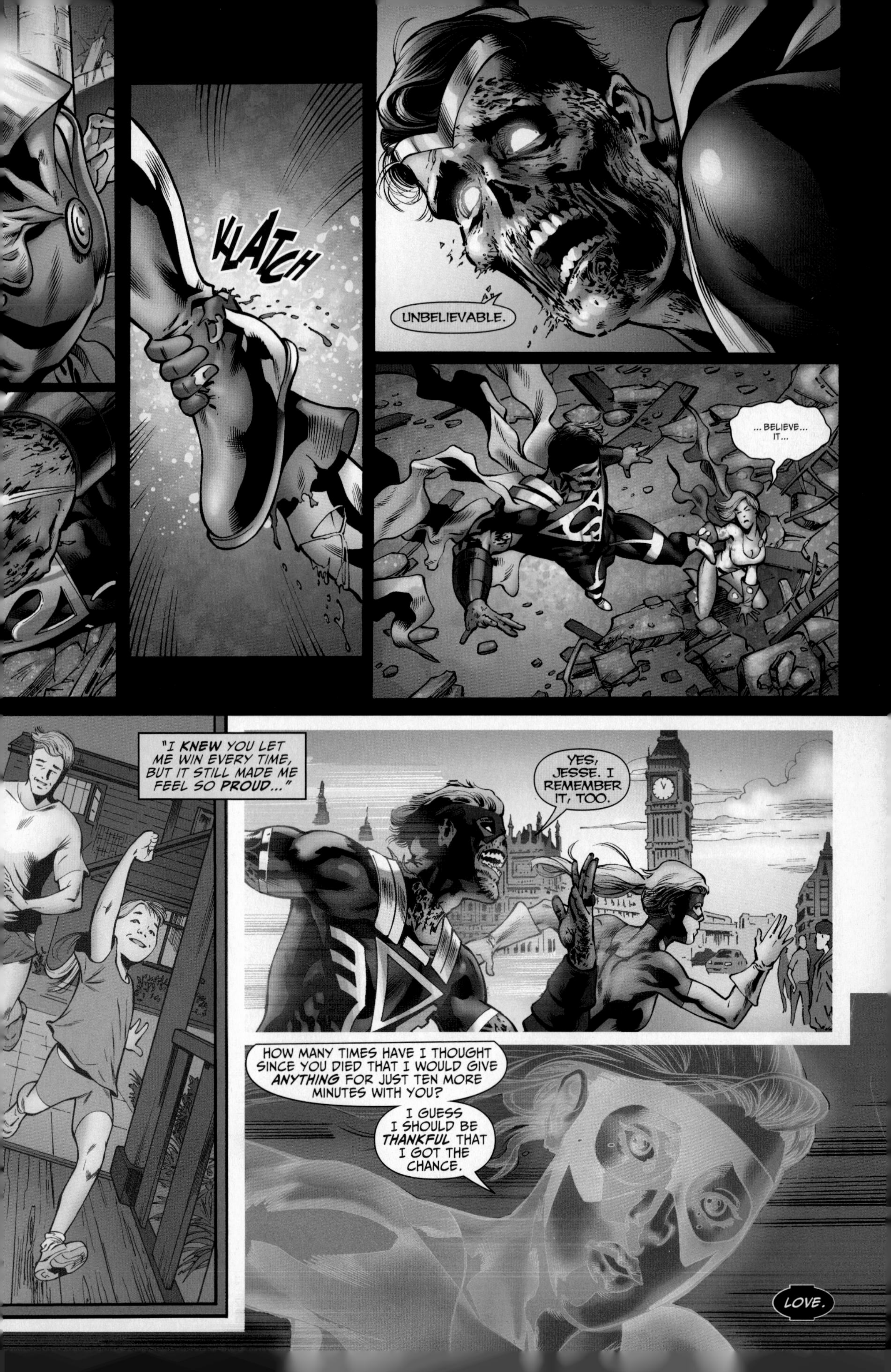
KLATCH
UNBELIEVABLE.
... BELIEVE... IT...
"I KNEW YOU LET ME WIN EVERY TIME, BUT IT STILL MADE ME FEEL SO PROUD..."
YES, JESSE. I REMEMBER IT, TOO.
HOW MANY TIMES HAVE I THOUGHT SINCE YOU DIED THAT I WOULD GIVE ANYTHING FOR JUST TEN MORE MINUTES WITH YOU?
I GUESS I SHOULD BE THANKFUL THAT I GOT THE CHANCE.
LOVE.

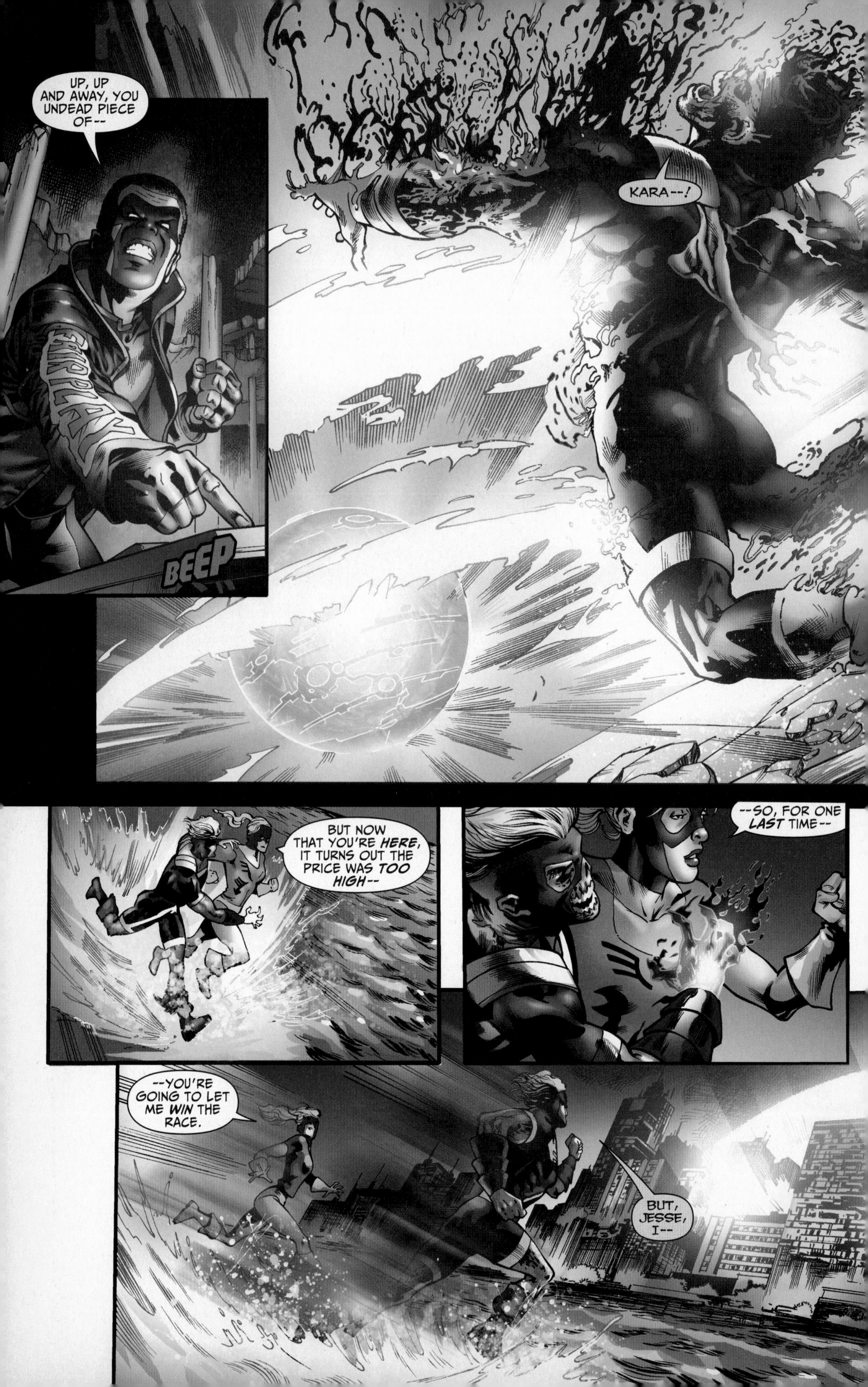
UP, UP AND AWAY, YOU UNDEAD PIECE OF--
EARPLAY
BEEP
KARA--!
BUT NOW THAT YOU'RE *HERE*, IT TURNS OUT THE PRICE WAS *TOO HIGH*--
--SO, FOR ONE *LAST* TIME--
--YOU'RE GOING TO LET ME *WIN* THE RACE.
BUT, JESSE, I--

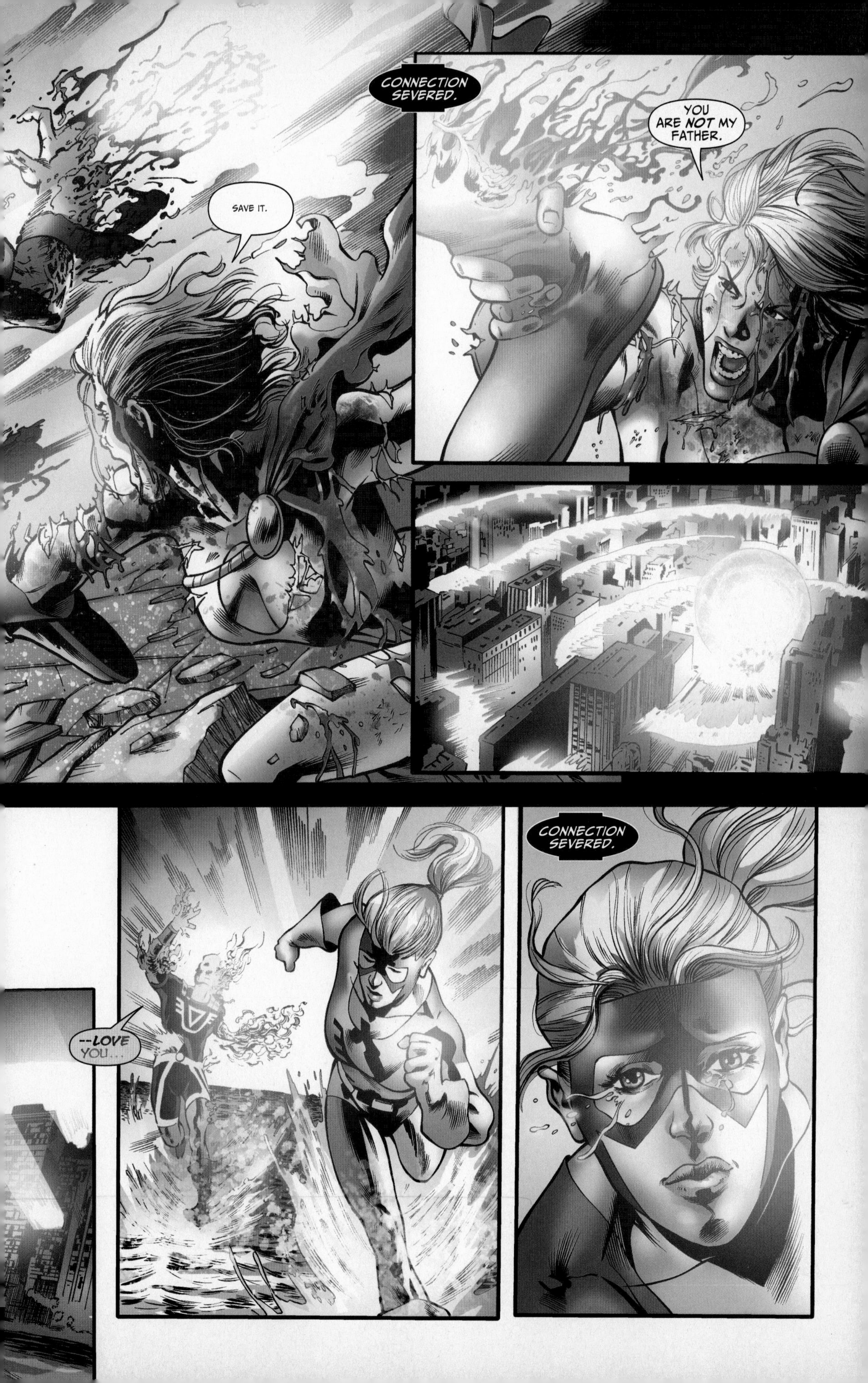
SAVE IT.
CONNECTION SEVERED.
YOU ARE NOT MY FATHER.
--LOVE YOU...
CONNECTION SEVERED.

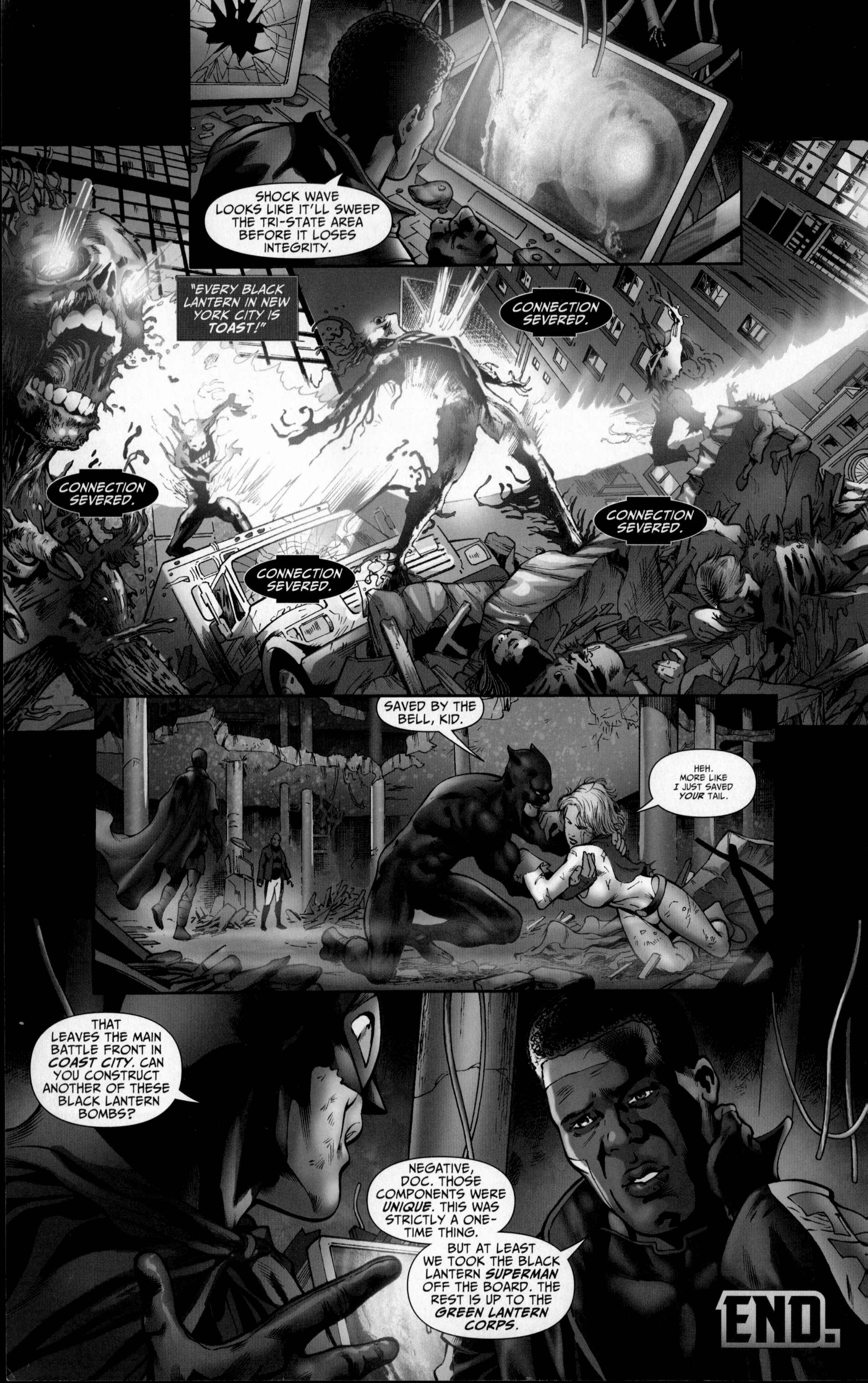
SHOCK WAVE LOOKS LIKE IT'LL SWEEP THE TRI-STATE AREA BEFORE IT LOSES INTEGRITY.
"EVERY BLACK LANTERN IN NEW YORK CITY IS TOAST!"
CONNECTION SEVERED.
CONNECTION SEVERED.
CONNECTION SEVERED.
CONNECTION SEVERED.
SAVED BY THE BELL, KID.
HEH. MORE LIKE I JUST SAVED YOUR TAIL.
THAT LEAVES THE MAIN BATTLE FRONT IN COAST CITY. CAN YOU CONSTRUCT ANOTHER OF THESE BLACK LANTERN BOMBS?
NEGATIVE, DOC. THOSE COMPONENTS WERE UNIQUE. THIS WAS STRICTLY A ONE-TIME THING.
BUT AT LEAST WE TOOK THE BLACK LANTERN SUPERMAN OFF THE BOARD. THE REST IS UP TO THE GREEN LANTERN CORPS.
END.

BLACKEST NIGHT:
WONDER WOMAN 1
Cover by Greg Horn

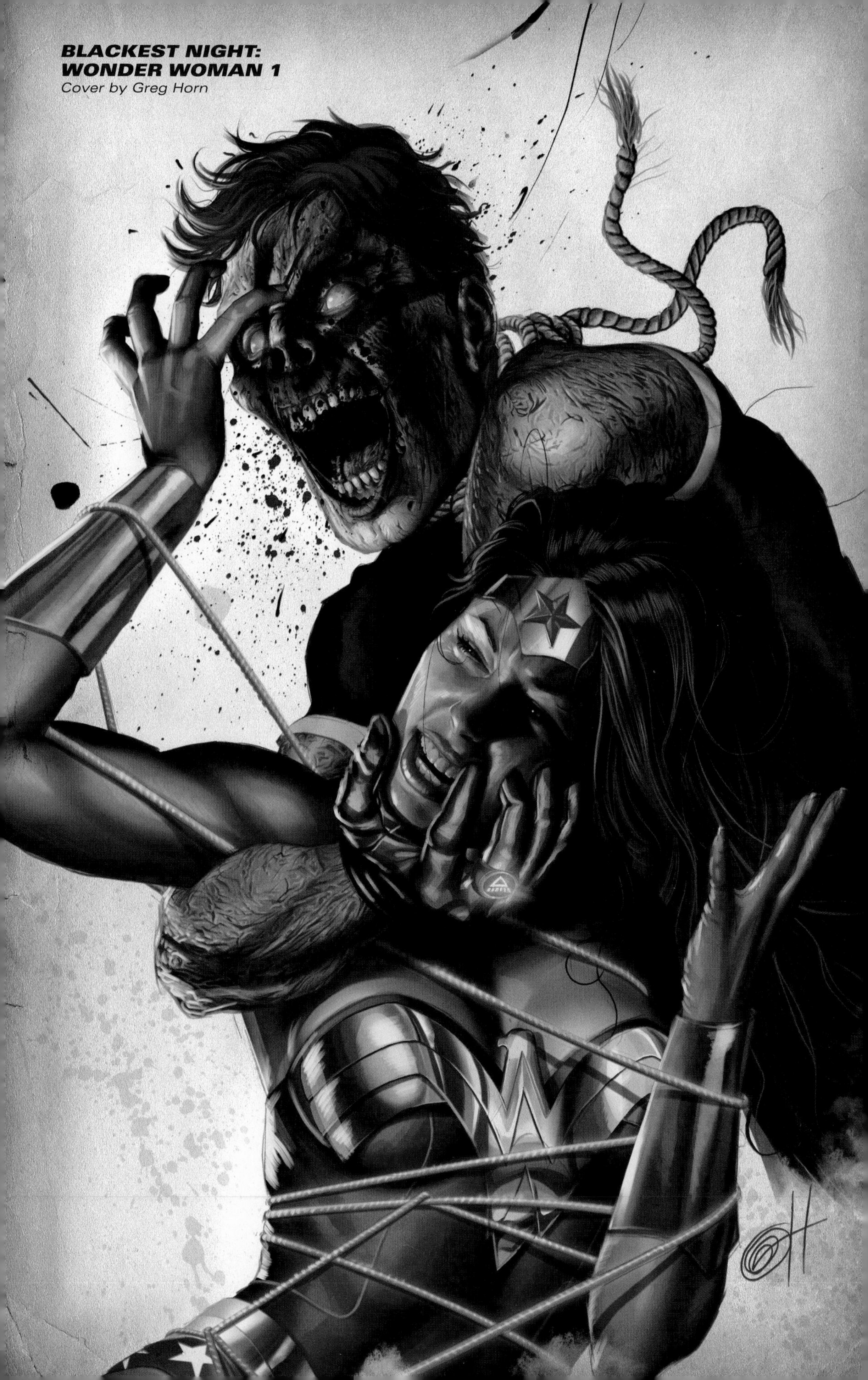

BLACKEST NIGHT: WONDER WOMAN
CHAPTER ONE

GREG RUCKA
WRITER

NICOLA SCOTT
PENCILS

PRENTIS ROLLINS
JONATHAN GLAPION
WALDEN WONG
DREW GERACI
INKS

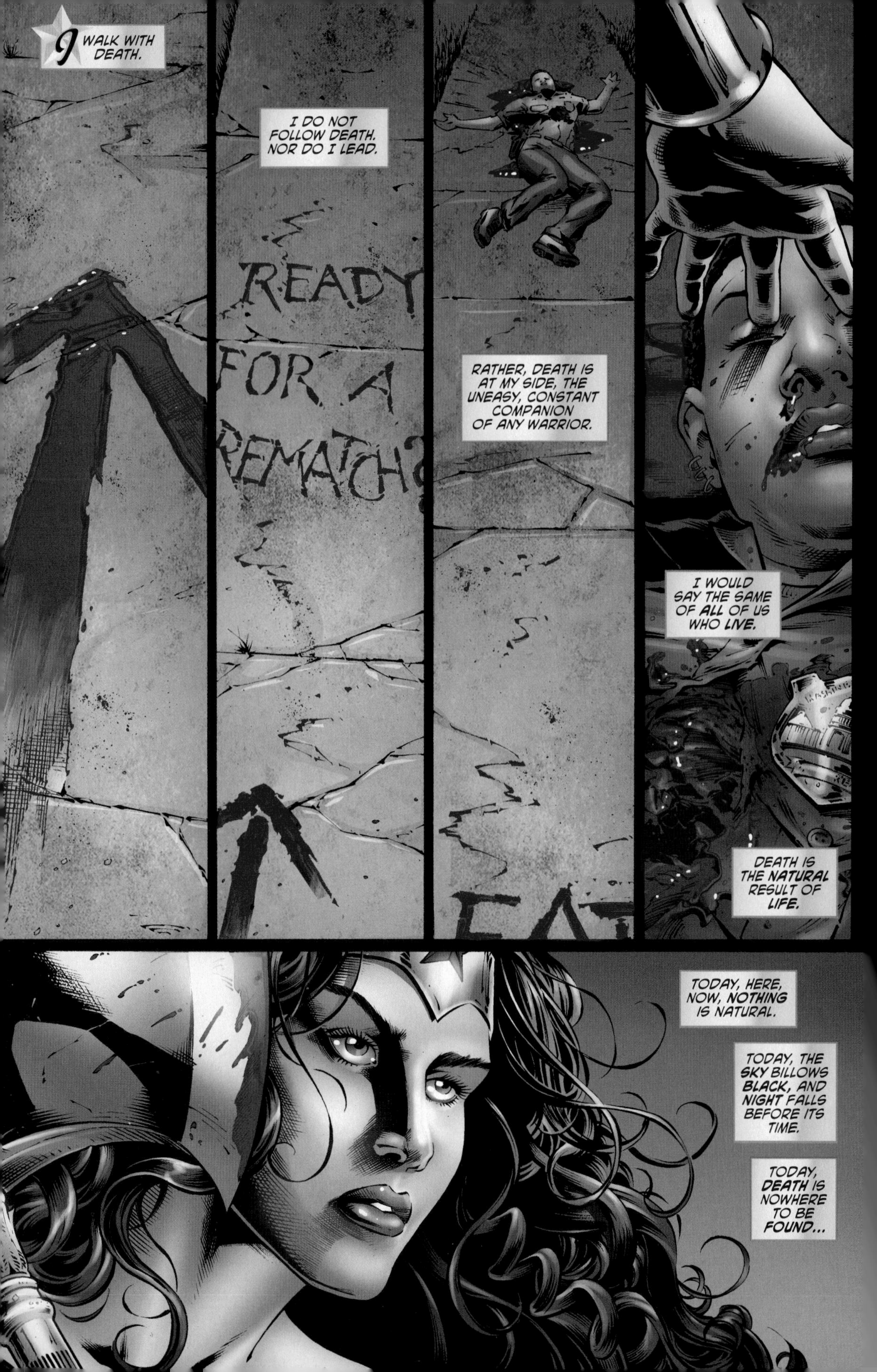

I WALK WITH DEATH.
I DO NOT FOLLOW DEATH. NOR DO I LEAD.
READY FOR A REMATCH?
RATHER, DEATH IS AT MY SIDE, THE UNEASY, CONSTANT COMPANION OF ANY WARRIOR.
I WOULD SAY THE SAME OF ALL OF US WHO LIVE.
DEATH IS THE NATURAL RESULT OF LIFE.
TODAY, HERE, NOW, NOTHING IS NATURAL.
TODAY, THE SKY BILLOWS BLACK, AND NIGHT FALLS BEFORE ITS TIME.
TODAY, DEATH IS NOWHERE TO BE FOUND...

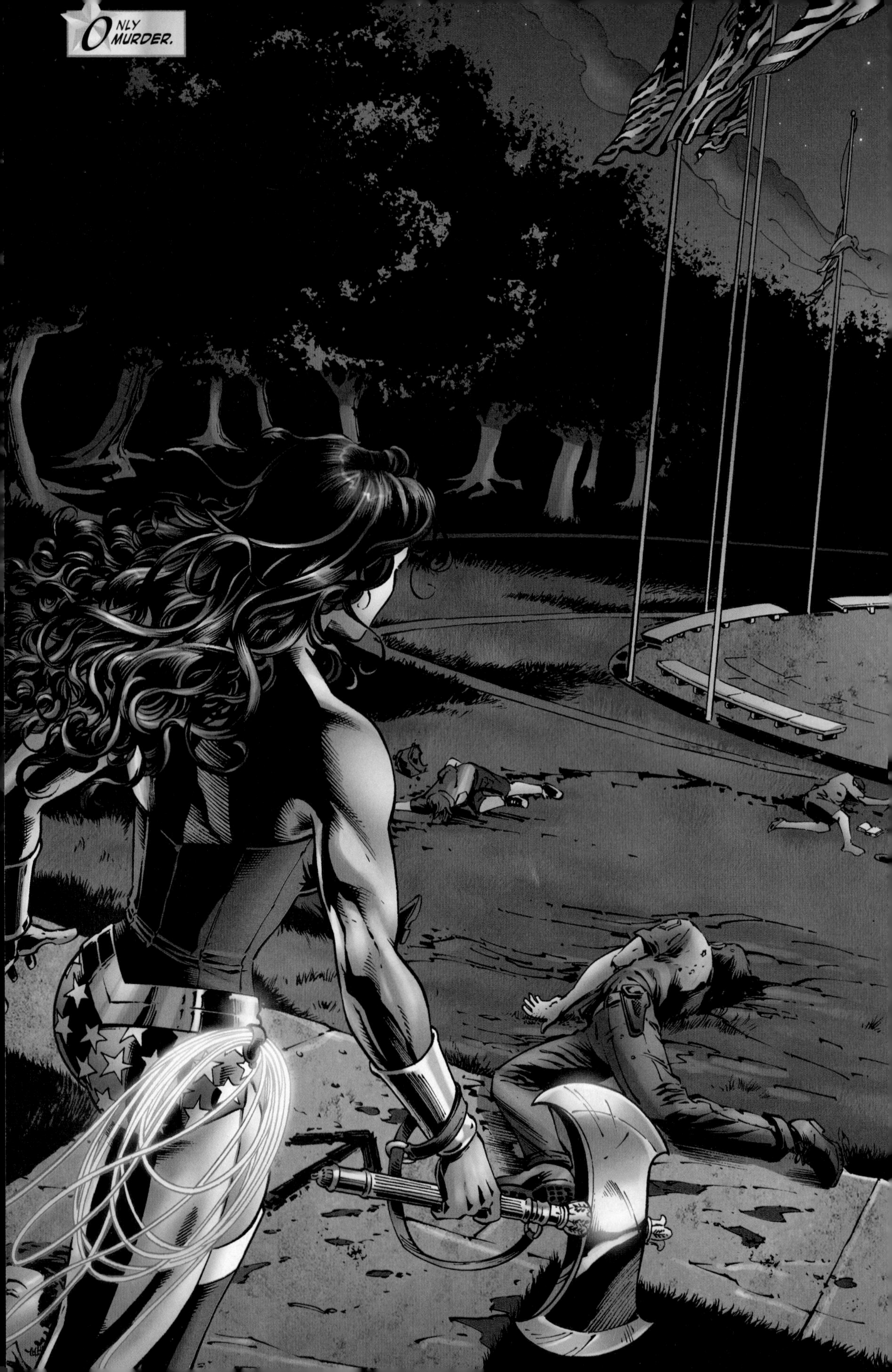
ONLY MURDER.

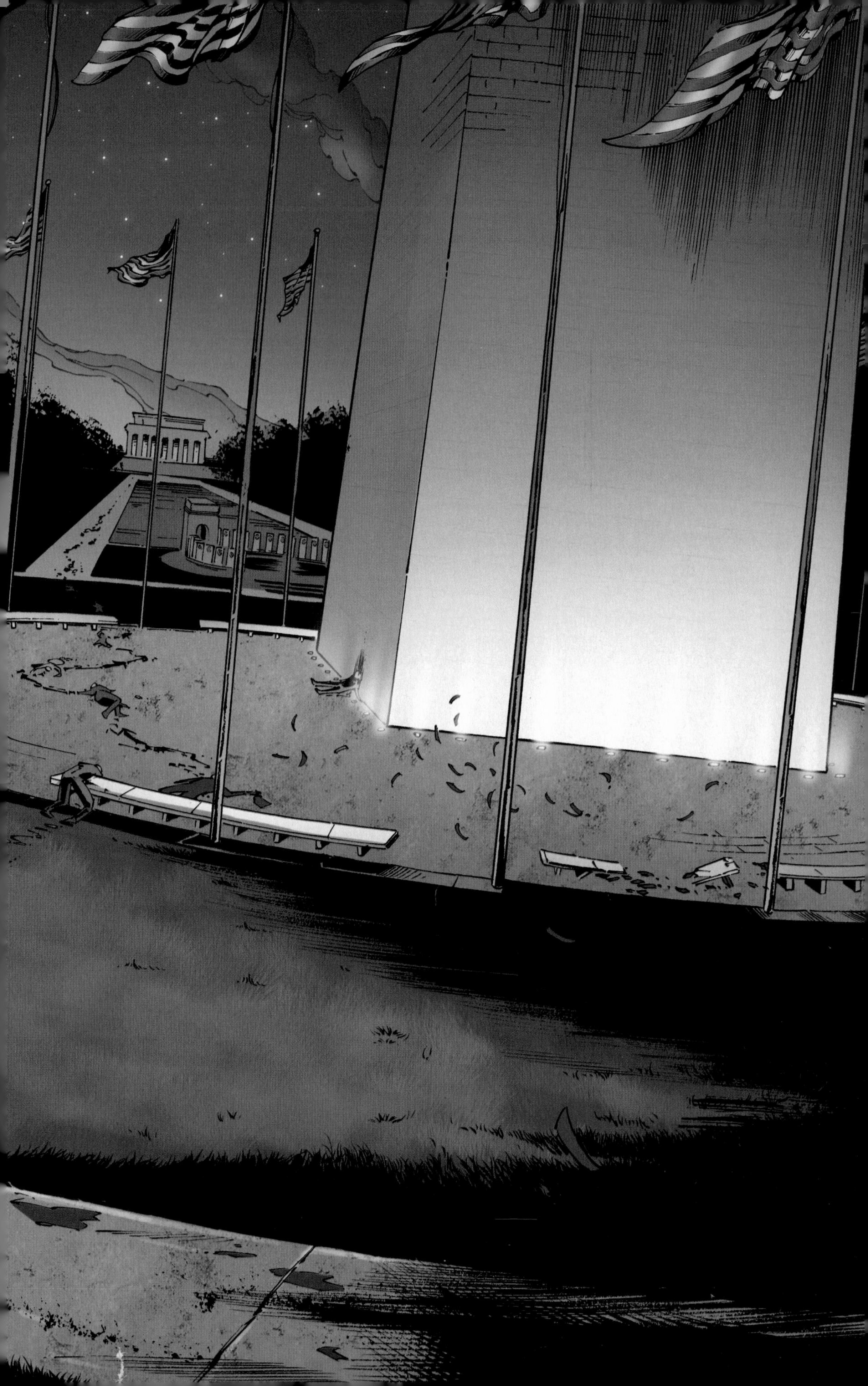

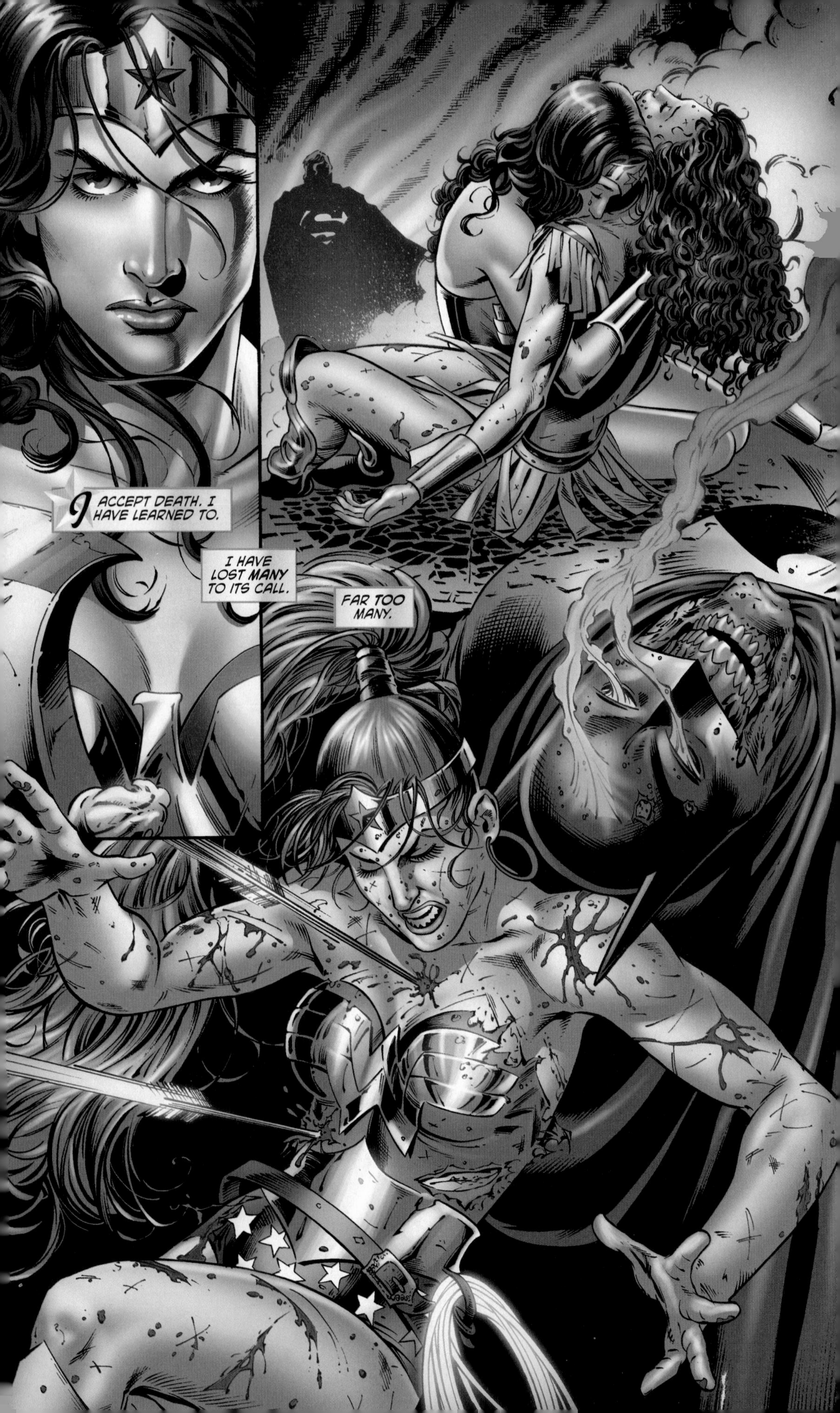
I ACCEPT DEATH. I HAVE LEARNED TO.
I HAVE LOST MANY TO ITS CALL.
FAR TOO MANY.

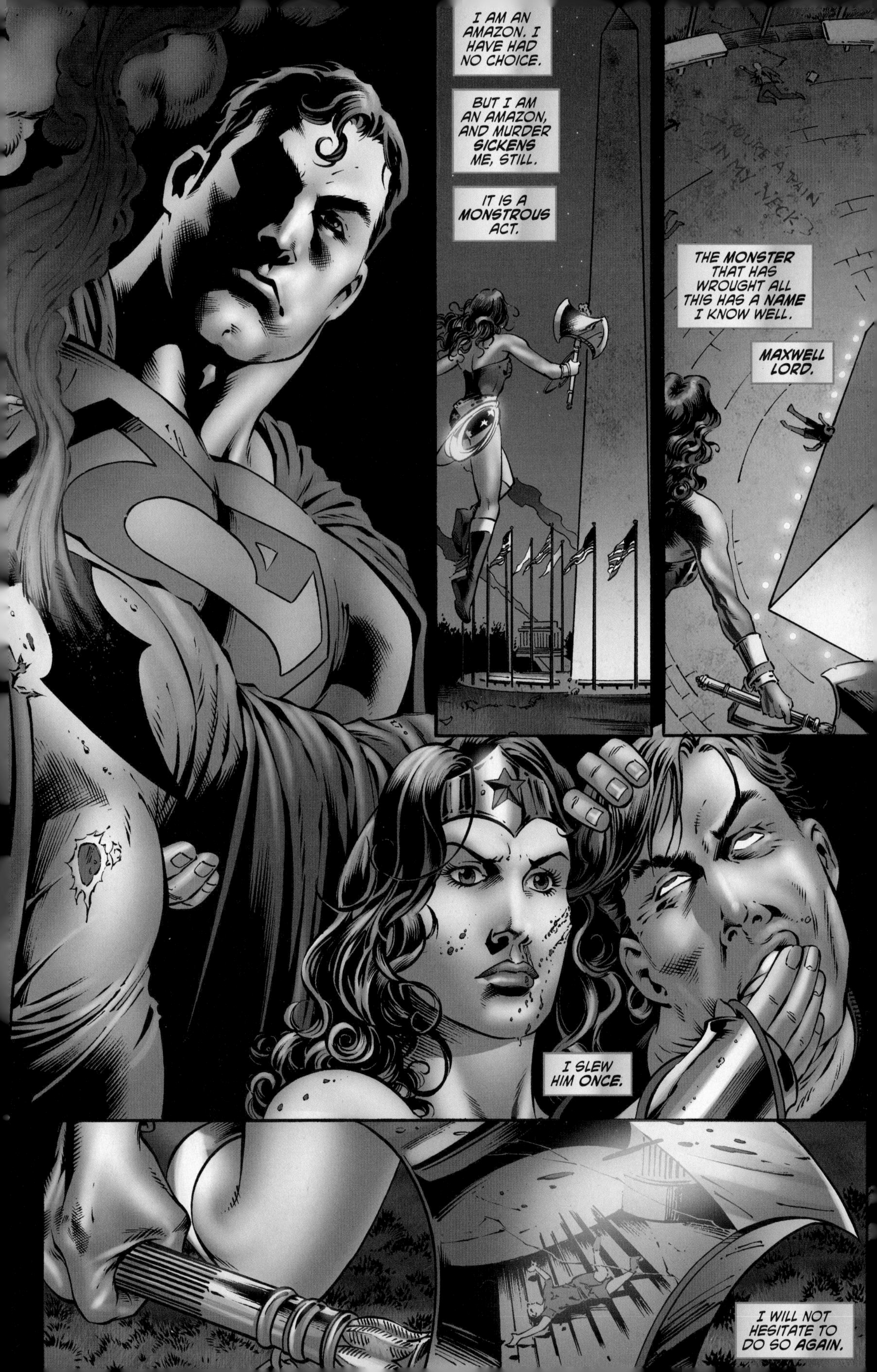
I AM AN AMAZON. I HAVE HAD NO CHOICE.
BUT I AM AN AMAZON, AND MURDER SICKENS ME, STILL.
IT IS A MONSTROUS ACT.
YOU'RE A PAIN IN MY NECK
THE MONSTER THAT HAS WROUGHT ALL THIS HAS A NAME I KNOW WELL.
MAXWELL LORD.
I SLEW HIM ONCE.
I WILL NOT HESITATE TO DO SO AGAIN.

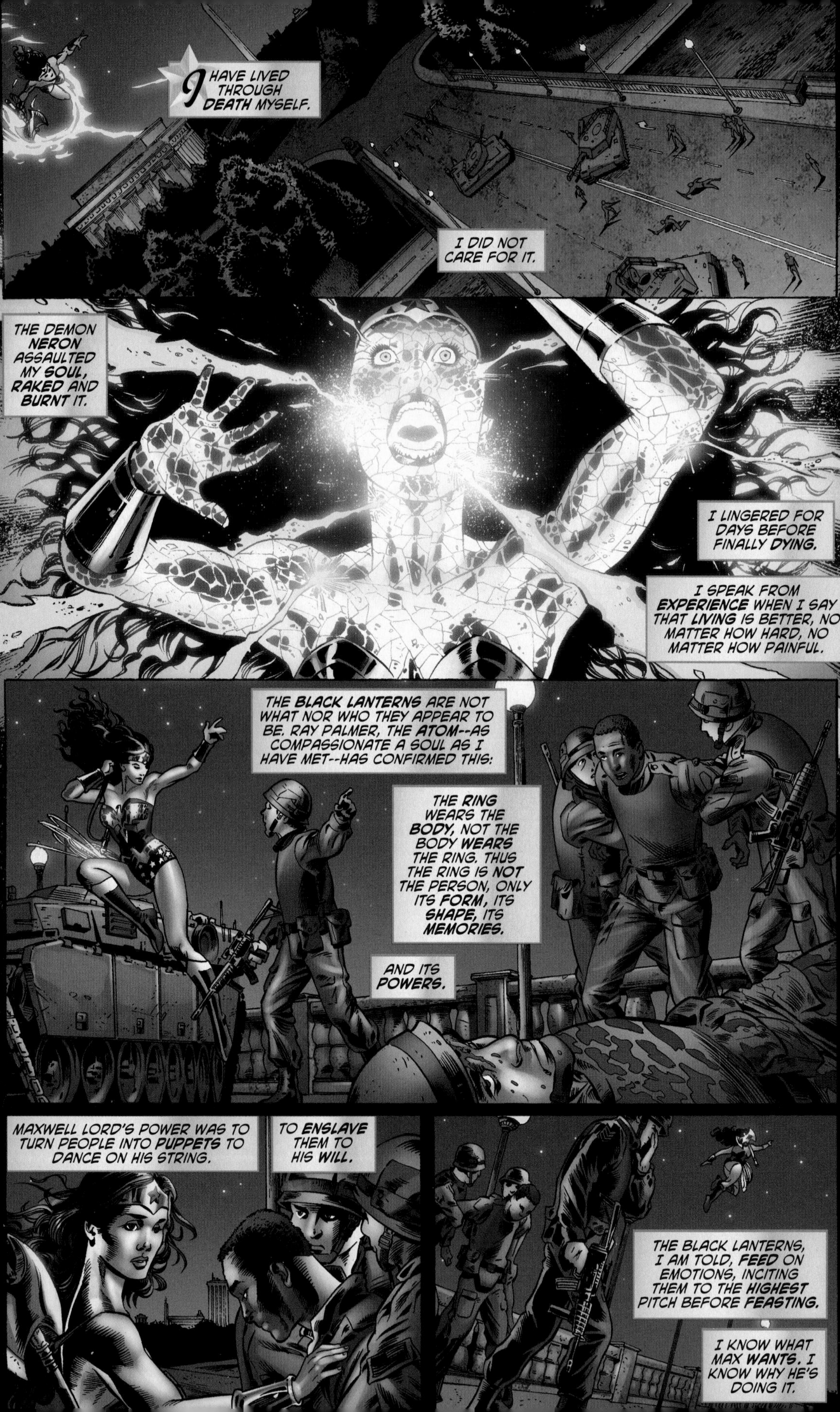
I HAVE LIVED THROUGH DEATH MYSELF.
I DID NOT CARE FOR IT.
THE DEMON NERON ASSAULTED MY SOUL, RAKED AND BURNT IT.
I LINGERED FOR DAYS BEFORE FINALLY DYING.
I SPEAK FROM EXPERIENCE WHEN I SAY THAT LIVING IS BETTER, NO MATTER HOW HARD, NO MATTER HOW PAINFUL.
THE BLACK LANTERNS ARE NOT WHAT NOR WHO THEY APPEAR TO BE. RAY PALMER, THE ATOM--AS COMPASSIONATE A SOUL AS I HAVE MET--HAS CONFIRMED THIS:
THE RING WEARS THE BODY, NOT THE BODY WEARS THE RING. THUS THE RING IS NOT THE PERSON, ONLY ITS FORM, ITS SHAPE, ITS MEMORIES.
AND ITS POWERS.
MAXWELL LORD'S POWER WAS TO TURN PEOPLE INTO PUPPETS TO DANCE ON HIS STRING.
TO ENSLAVE THEM TO HIS WILL.
THE BLACK LANTERNS, I AM TOLD, FEED ON EMOTIONS, INCITING THEM TO THE HIGHEST PITCH BEFORE FEASTING.
I KNOW WHAT MAX WANTS. I KNOW WHY HE'S DOING IT.

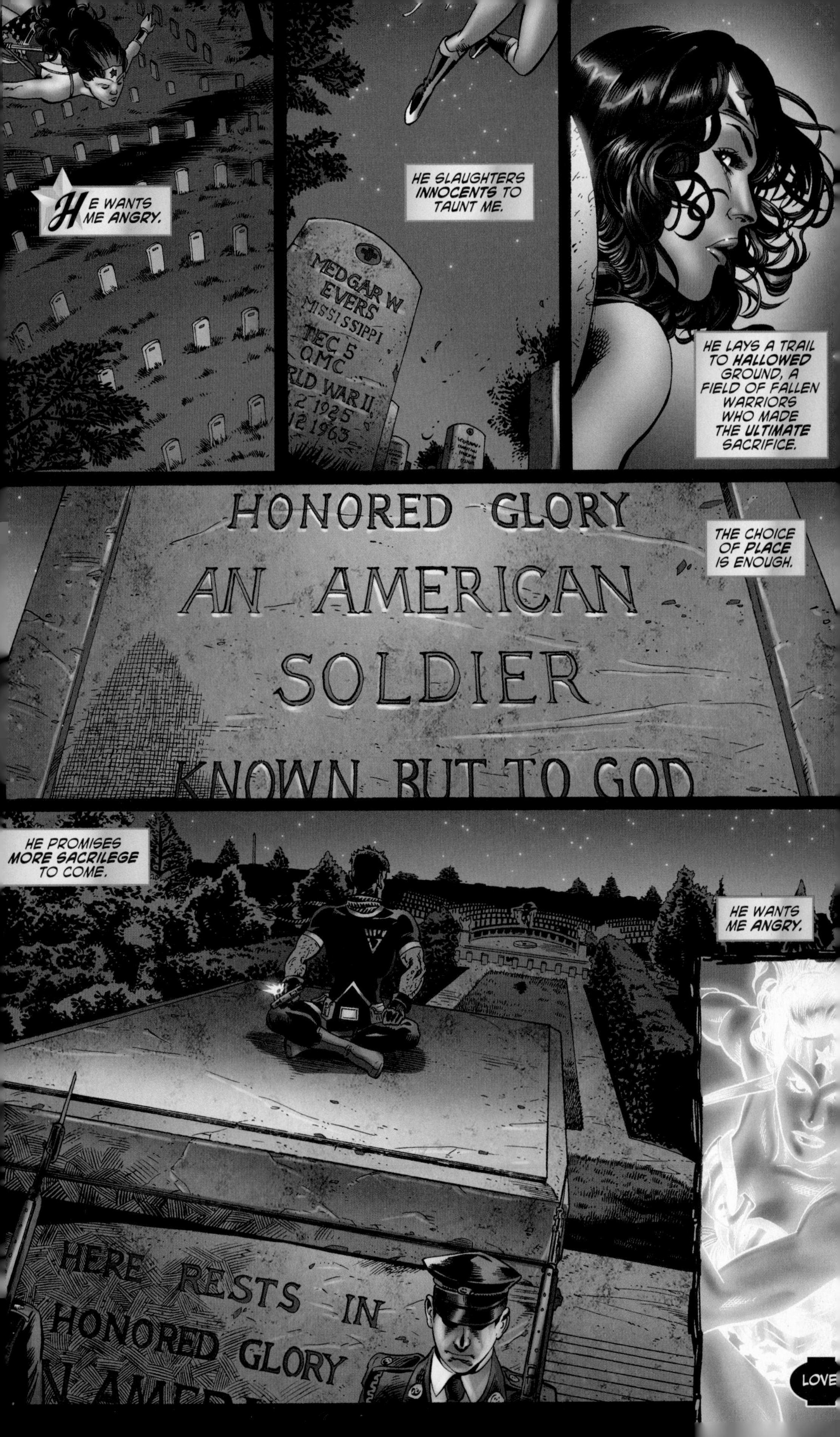
HE WANTS ME ANGRY.
HE SLAUGHTERS INNOCENTS TO TAUNT ME.
MEDGAR W. EVERS
MISSISSIPPI
TEC 5
QMC
RLD WAR II
HE LAYS A TRAIL TO HALLOWED GROUND, A FIELD OF FALLEN WARRIORS WHO MADE THE ULTIMATE SACRIFICE.
HONORED GLORY
AN AMERICAN SOLDIER
KNOWN BUT TO GOD
THE CHOICE OF PLACE IS ENOUGH.
HE PROMISES MORE SACRILEGE TO COME.
HE WANTS ME ANGRY.
HERE RESTS IN
HONORED GLORY
LOVE

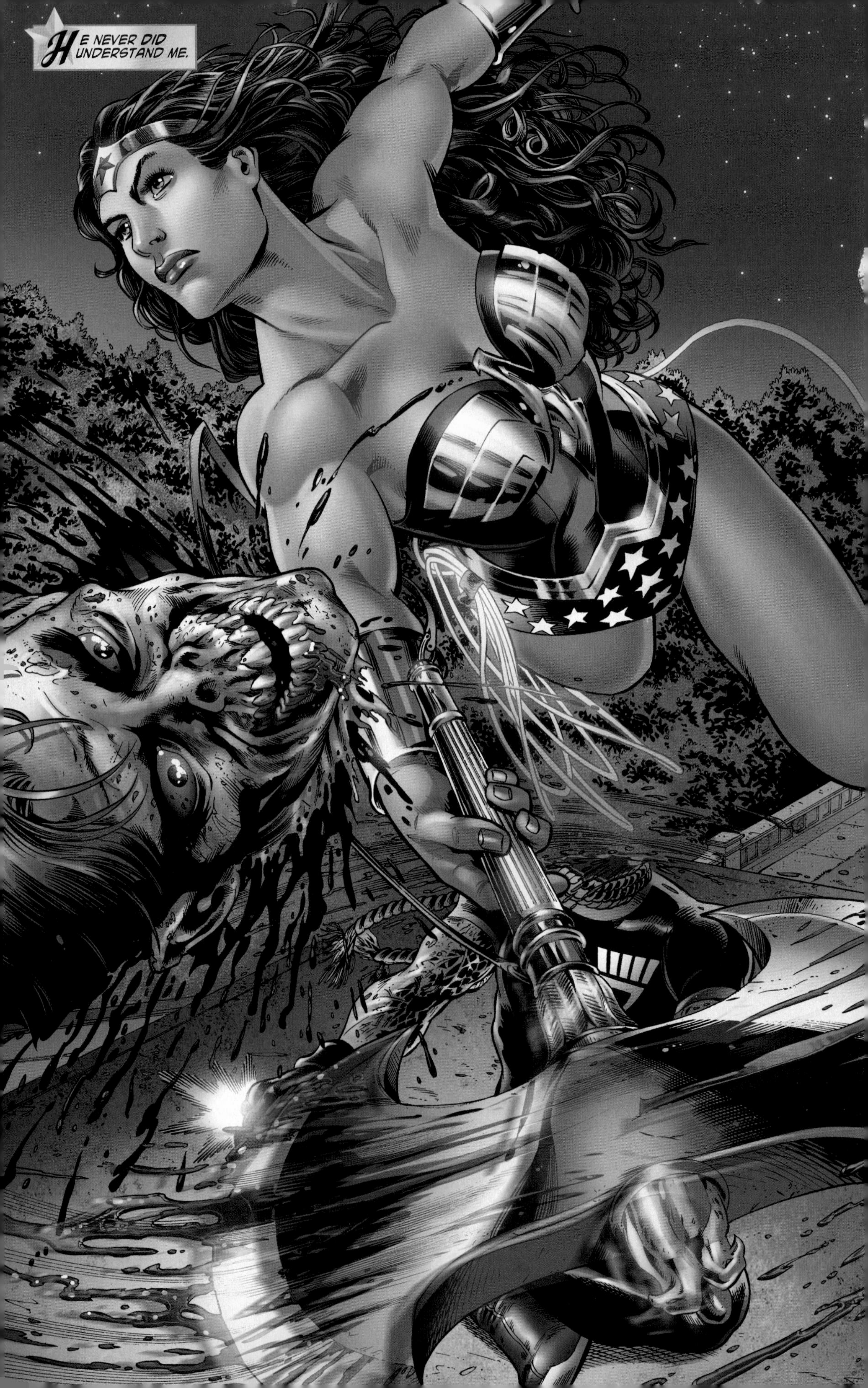
HE NEVER DID UNDERSTAND ME.

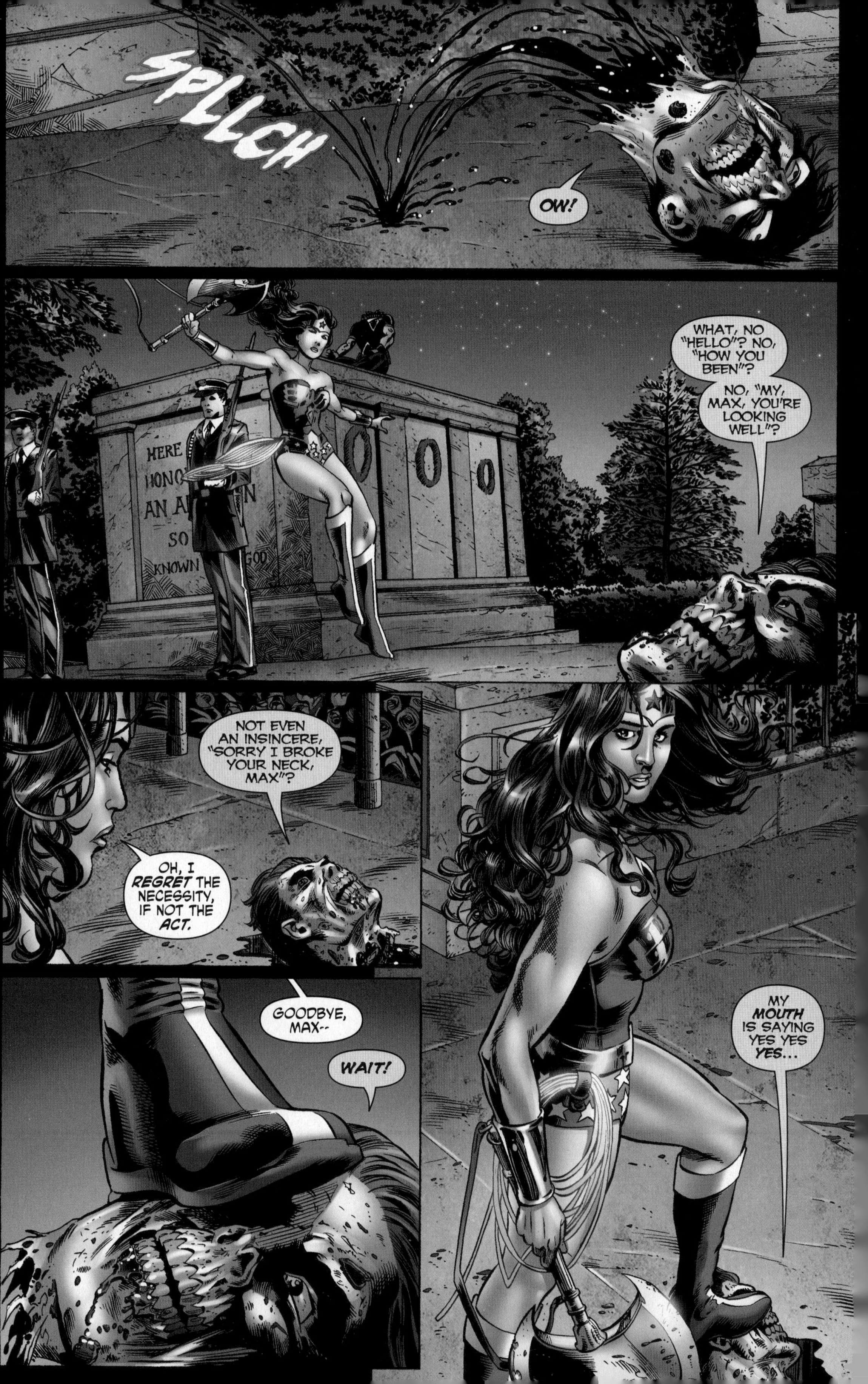
SPLLCH
OW!
WHAT, NO "HELLO"? NO, "HOW YOU BEEN"?
NO, "MY, MAX, YOU'RE LOOKING WELL"?
HERE
HONO
AN A N
SO
KNOWN GOD
NOT EVEN AN INSINCERE, "SORRY I BROKE YOUR NECK, MAX"?
OH, I REGRET THE NECESSITY, IF NOT THE ACT.
GOODBYE, MAX--
WAIT!
MY MOUTH IS SAYING YES YES YES...

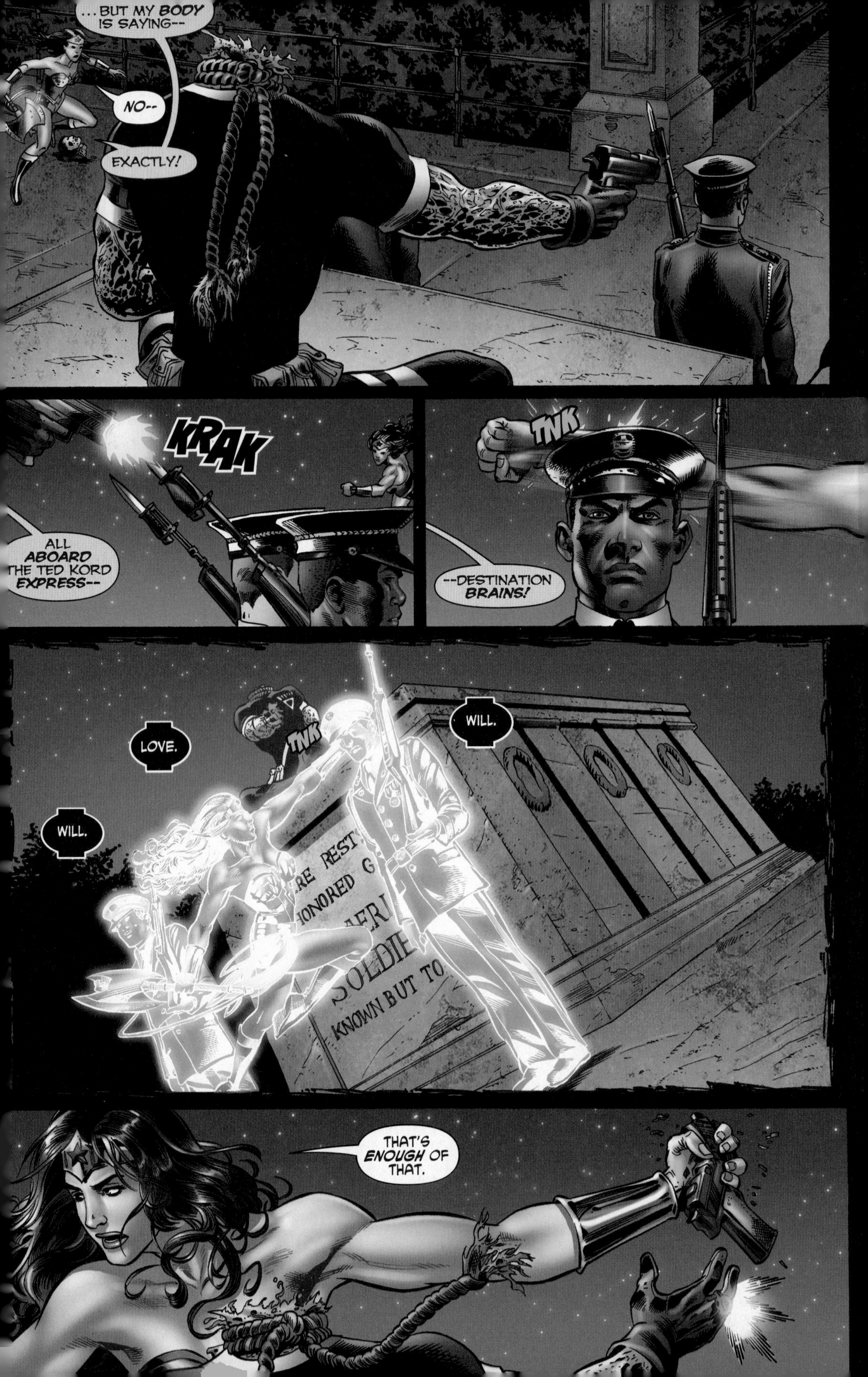
...BUT MY BODY IS SAYING--
NO--
EXACTLY!
KRAK
ALL ABOARD THE TED KORD EXPRESS--
TNK
--DESTINATION BRAINS!
LOVE.
WILL.
WILL.
TNK
...RE REST...
...HONORED G...
...AERI...
SOLDIE...
KNOWN BUT TO...
THAT'S ENOUGH OF THAT.

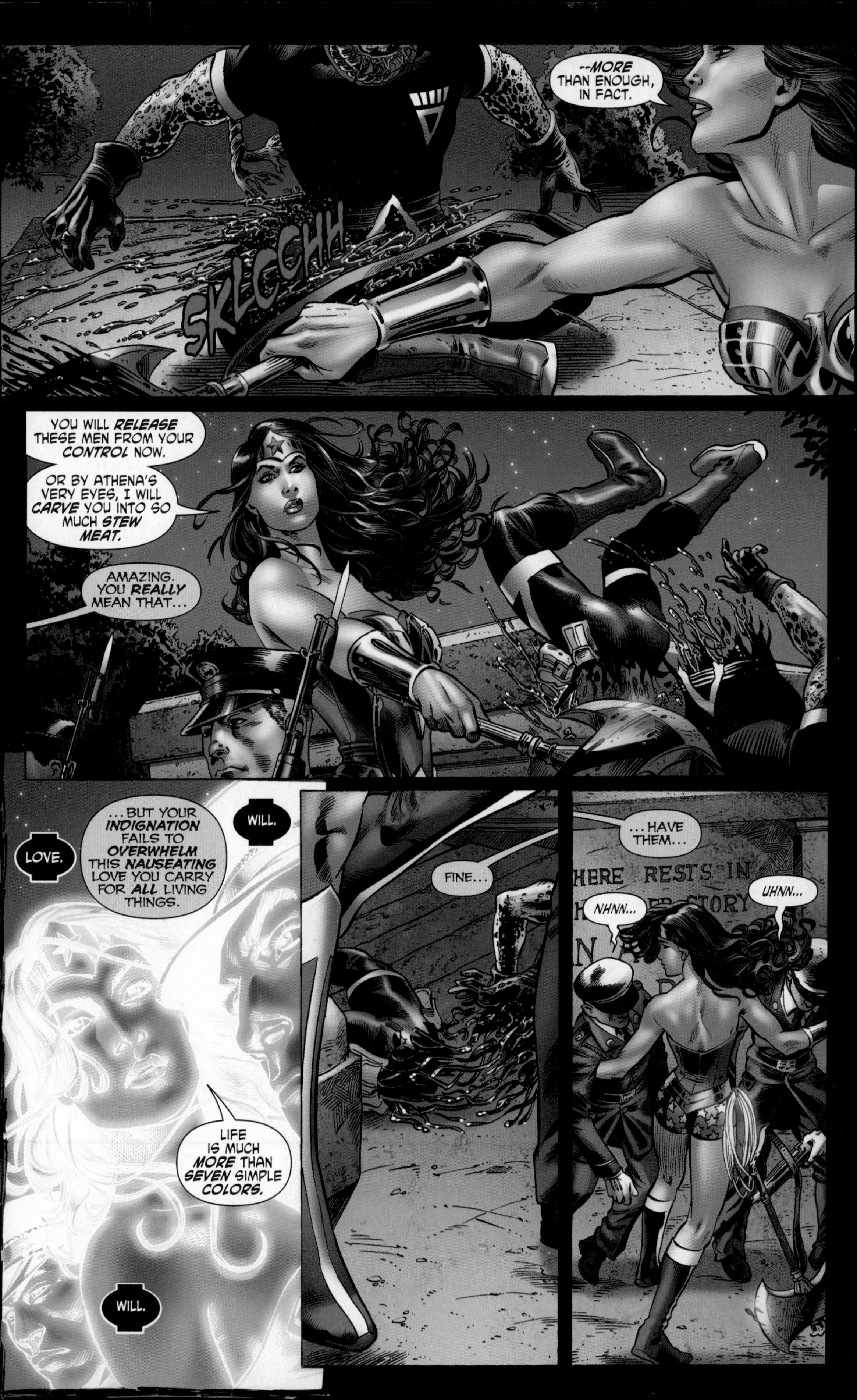
--MORE THAN ENOUGH, IN FACT.
SKLCCHH
YOU WILL RELEASE THESE MEN FROM YOUR CONTROL NOW.
OR BY ATHENA'S VERY EYES, I WILL CARVE YOU INTO SO MUCH STEW MEAT.
AMAZING. YOU REALLY MEAN THAT...
LOVE.
...BUT YOUR INDIGNATION FAILS TO OVERWHELM THIS NAUSEATING LOVE YOU CARRY FOR ALL LIVING THINGS.
WILL.
LIFE IS MUCH MORE THAN SEVEN SIMPLE COLORS.
WILL.
FINE...
...HAVE THEM...
HERE RESTS IN
NHNN...
UHNN...

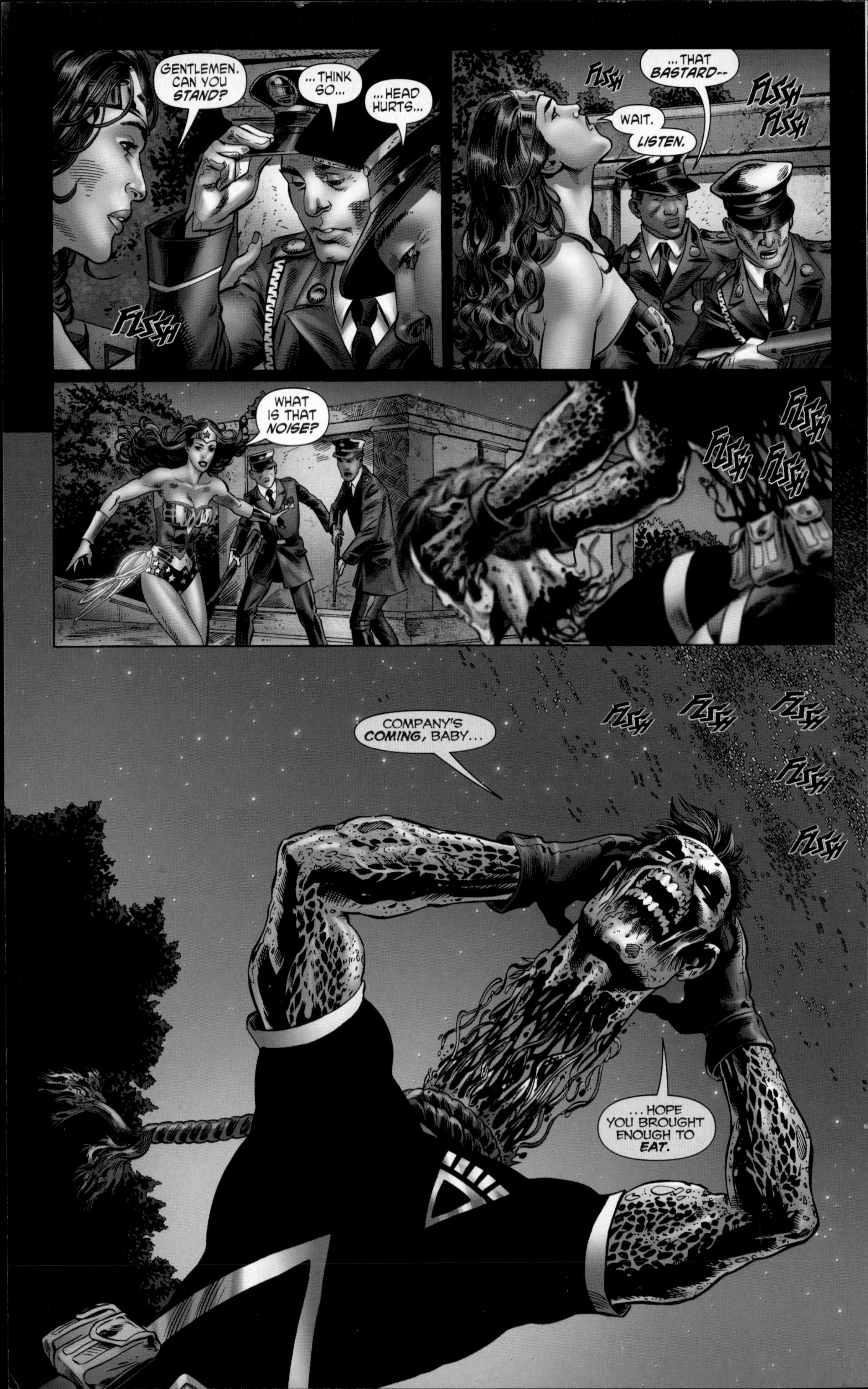
GENTLEMEN. CAN YOU STAND?
...THINK SO...
...HEAD HURTS...
FSSH
FSSH
...THAT BASTARD--
FSSH FSSH
WAIT. LISTEN.
WHAT IS THAT NOISE?
FSSH
FSSH
FSSH
COMPANY'S COMING, BABY...
FSSH
FSSH
FSSH
FSSH
FSSH
...HOPE YOU BROUGHT ENOUGH TO EAT.

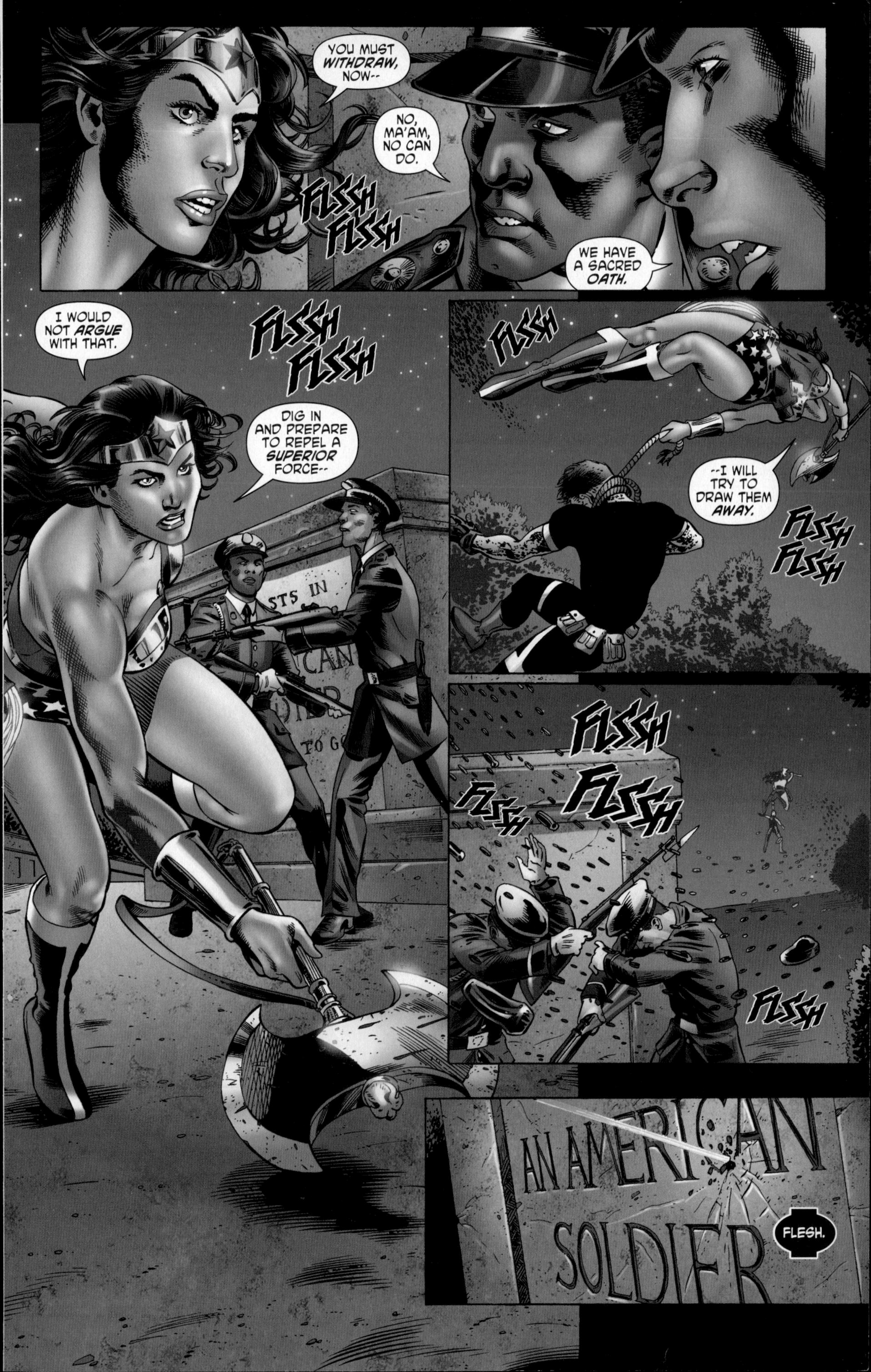
YOU MUST WITHDRAW, NOW--
NO, MA'AM, NO CAN DO.
FLSSH FLSSH
WE HAVE A SACRED OATH.
I WOULD NOT ARGUE WITH THAT.
FLSSH FLSSH
DIG IN AND PREPARE TO REPEL A SUPERIOR FORCE--
STS IN
TO GO
FLSSH
--I WILL TRY TO DRAW THEM AWAY.
FLSSH FLSSH
FLSSH
FLSSH FLSSH
FLSSH
AN AMERICAN SOLDIER
FLESH.

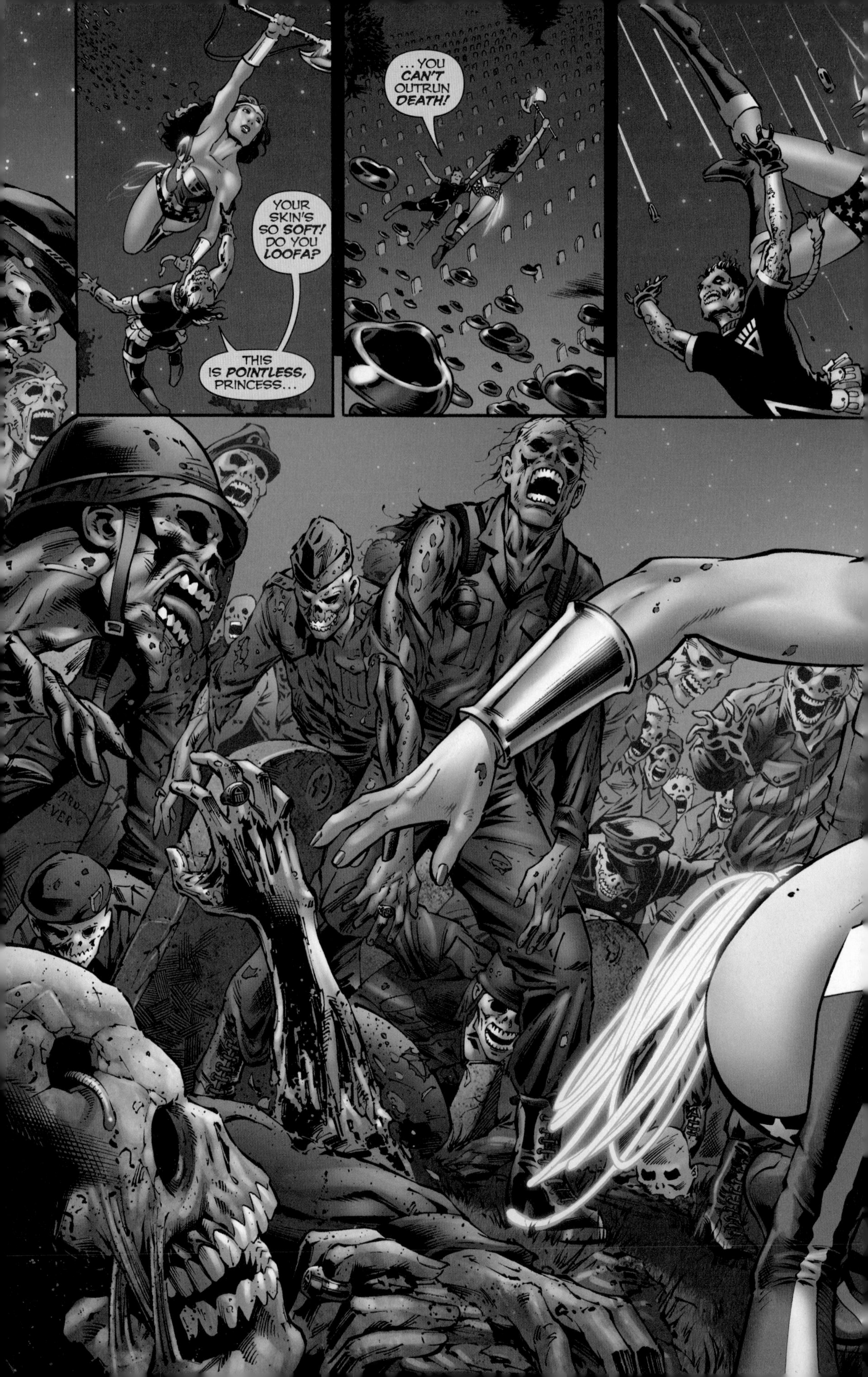
YOUR SKIN'S SO SOFT! DO YOU LOOFA?
THIS IS POINTLESS, PRINCESS...
...YOU CAN'T OUTRUN DEATH!

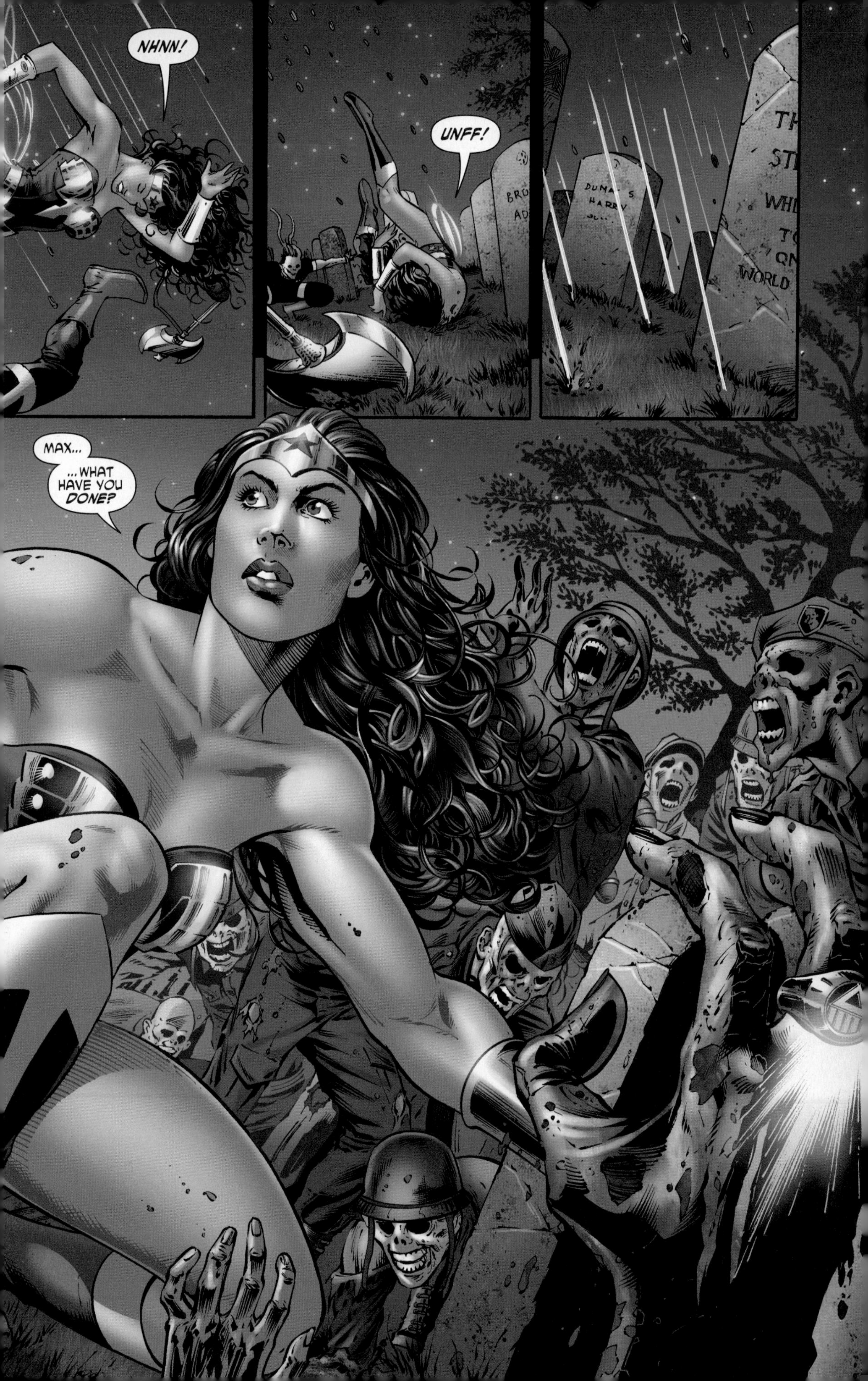
NHNN!
UNFF!
MAX...
...WHAT HAVE YOU DONE?

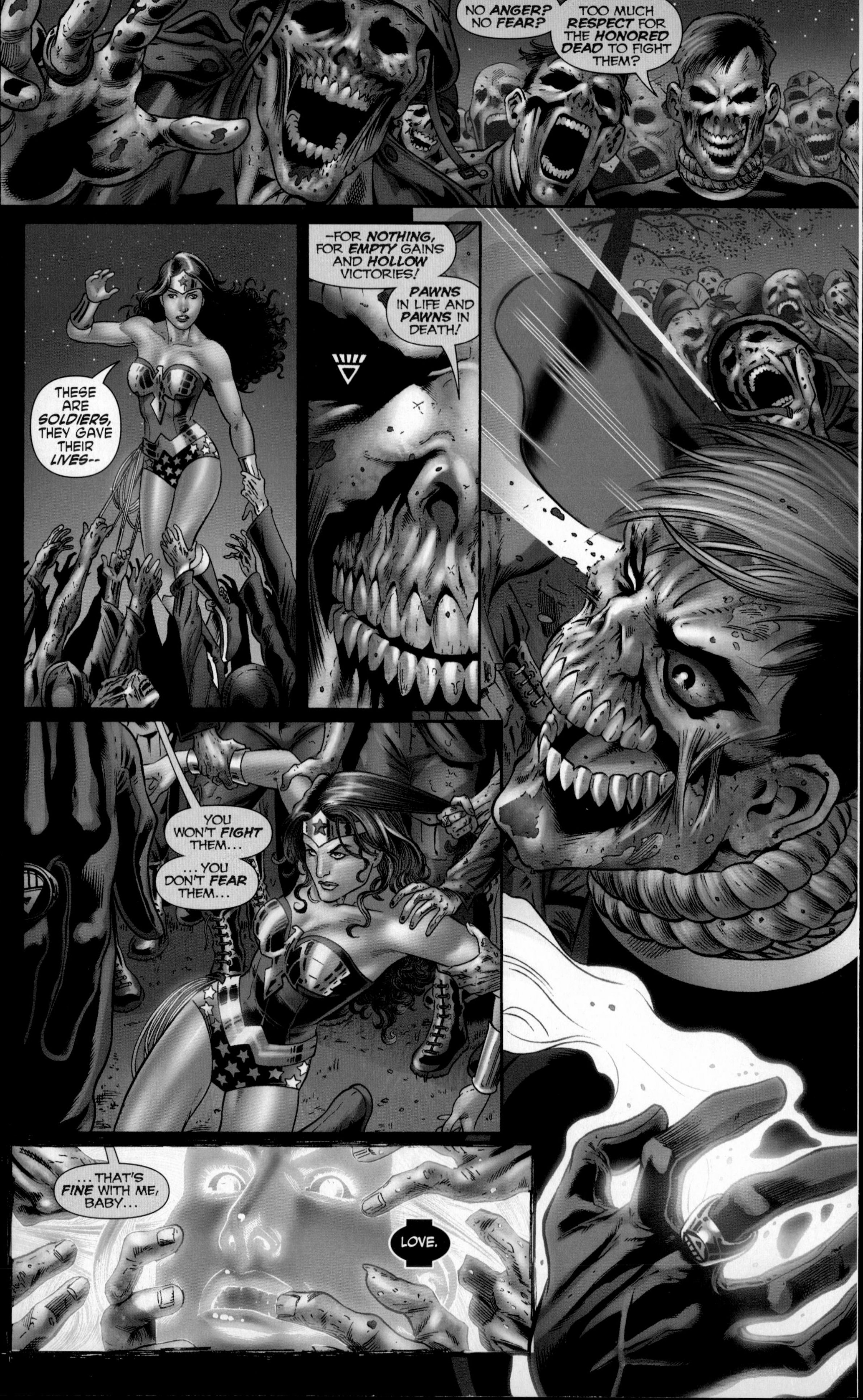
NO ANGER? NO FEAR?
TOO MUCH RESPECT FOR THE HONORED DEAD TO FIGHT THEM?
THESE ARE SOLDIERS, THEY GAVE THEIR LIVES--
--FOR NOTHING, FOR EMPTY GAINS AND HOLLOW VICTORIES!
PAWNS IN LIFE AND PAWNS IN DEATH!
YOU WON'T FIGHT THEM...
...YOU DON'T FEAR THEM...
...THAT'S FINE WITH ME, BABY...
LOVE.

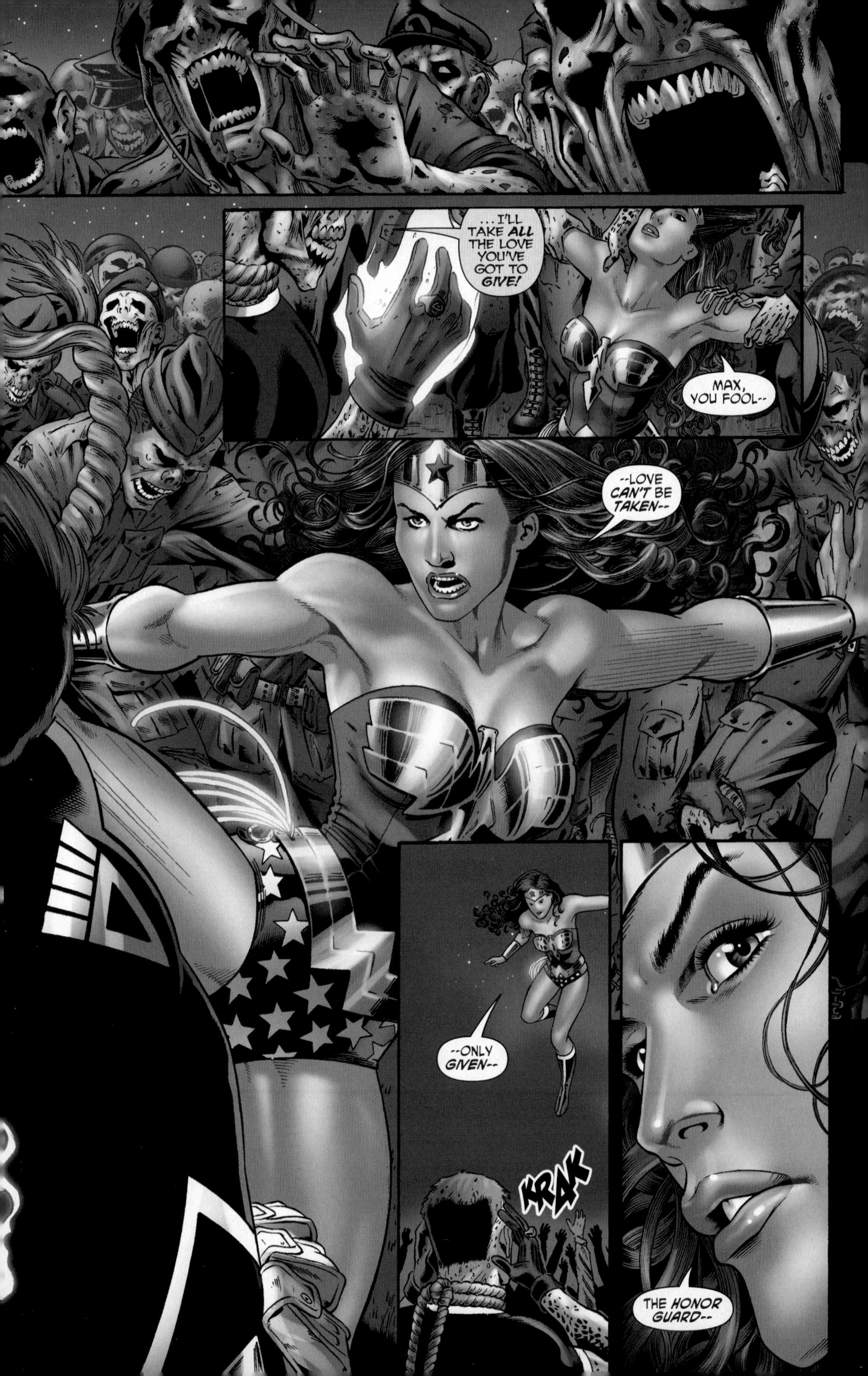
...I'LL TAKE ALL THE LOVE YOU'VE GOT TO GIVE!
MAX, YOU FOOL--
--LOVE CAN'T BE TAKEN--
--ONLY GIVEN--
KRAK
THE HONOR GUARD--

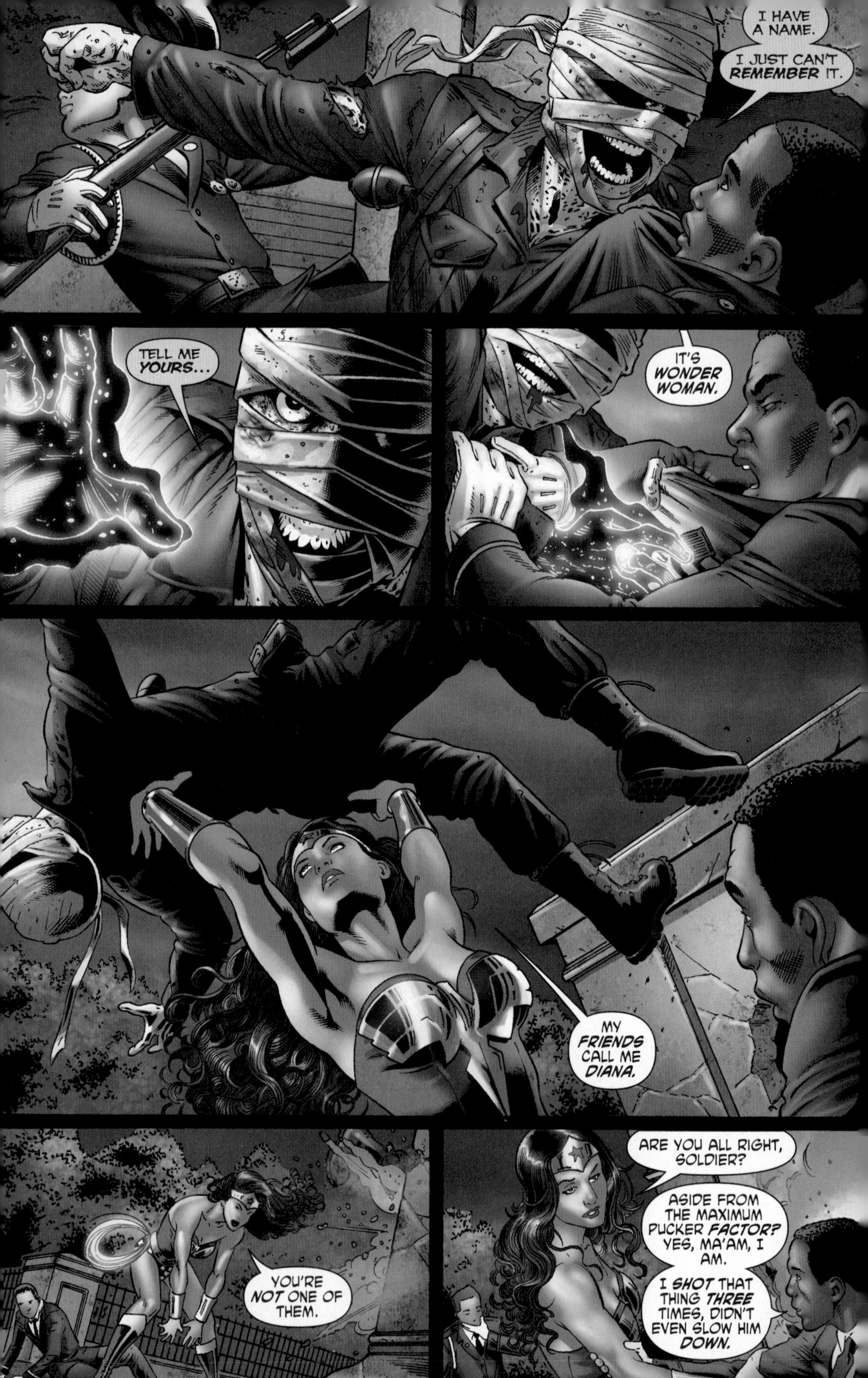
I HAVE A NAME.
I JUST CAN'T REMEMBER IT.
TELL ME YOURS...
IT'S WONDER WOMAN.
MY FRIENDS CALL ME DIANA.
YOU'RE NOT ONE OF THEM.
ARE YOU ALL RIGHT, SOLDIER?
ASIDE FROM THE MAXIMUM PUCKER FACTOR? YES, MA'AM, I AM.
I SHOT THAT THING THREE TIMES, DIDN'T EVEN SLOW HIM DOWN.

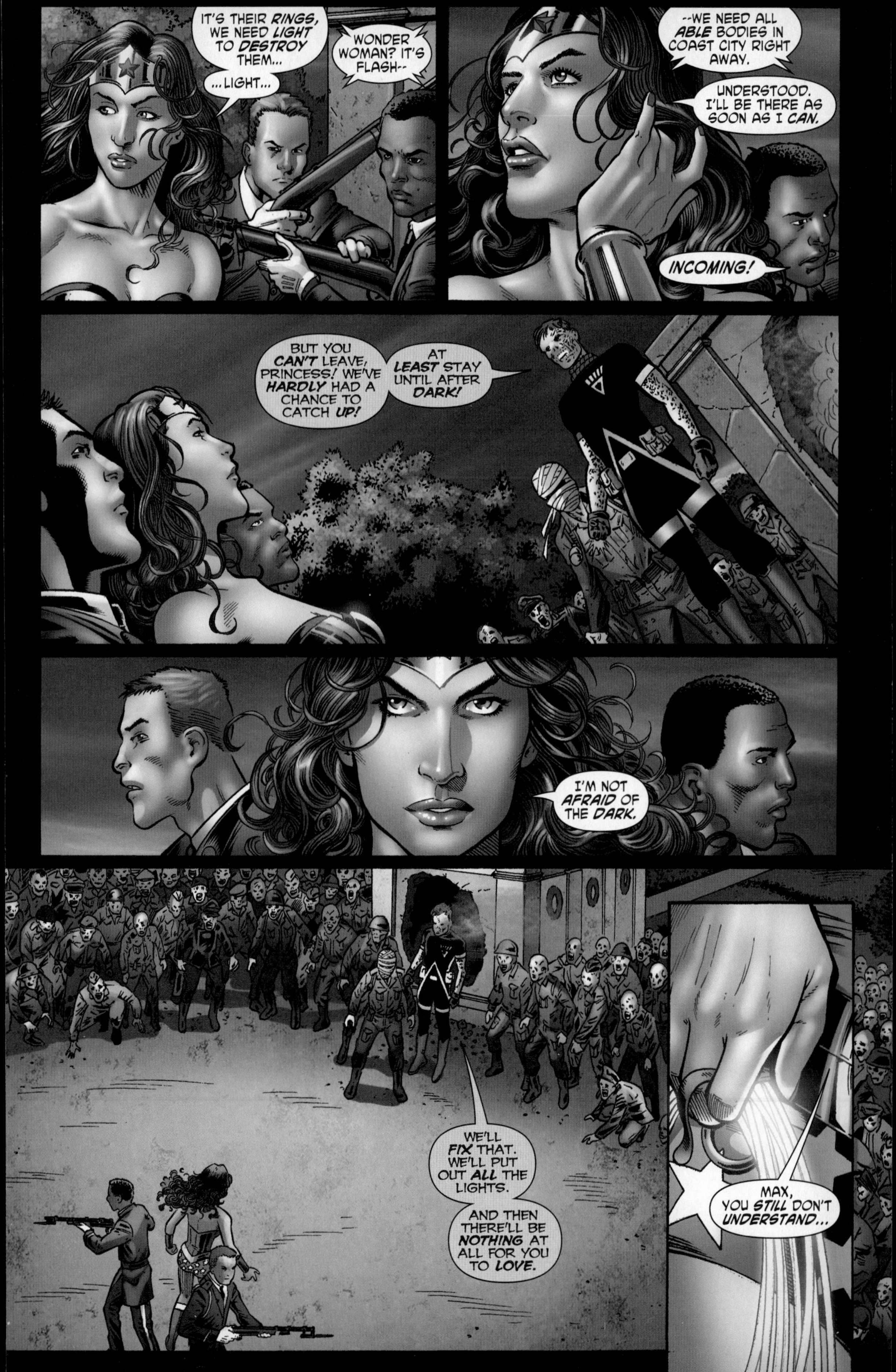
IT'S THEIR RINGS, WE NEED LIGHT TO DESTROY THEM...
...LIGHT...
WONDER WOMAN? IT'S FLASH--
--WE NEED ALL ABLE BODIES IN COAST CITY RIGHT AWAY.
UNDERSTOOD. I'LL BE THERE AS SOON AS I CAN.
INCOMING!
BUT YOU CAN'T LEAVE, PRINCESS! WE'VE HARDLY HAD A CHANCE TO CATCH UP!
AT LEAST STAY UNTIL AFTER DARK!
I'M NOT AFRAID OF THE DARK.
WE'LL FIX THAT. WE'LL PUT OUT ALL THE LIGHTS.
AND THEN THERE'LL BE NOTHING AT ALL FOR YOU TO LOVE.
MAX, YOU STILL DON'T UNDERSTAND...

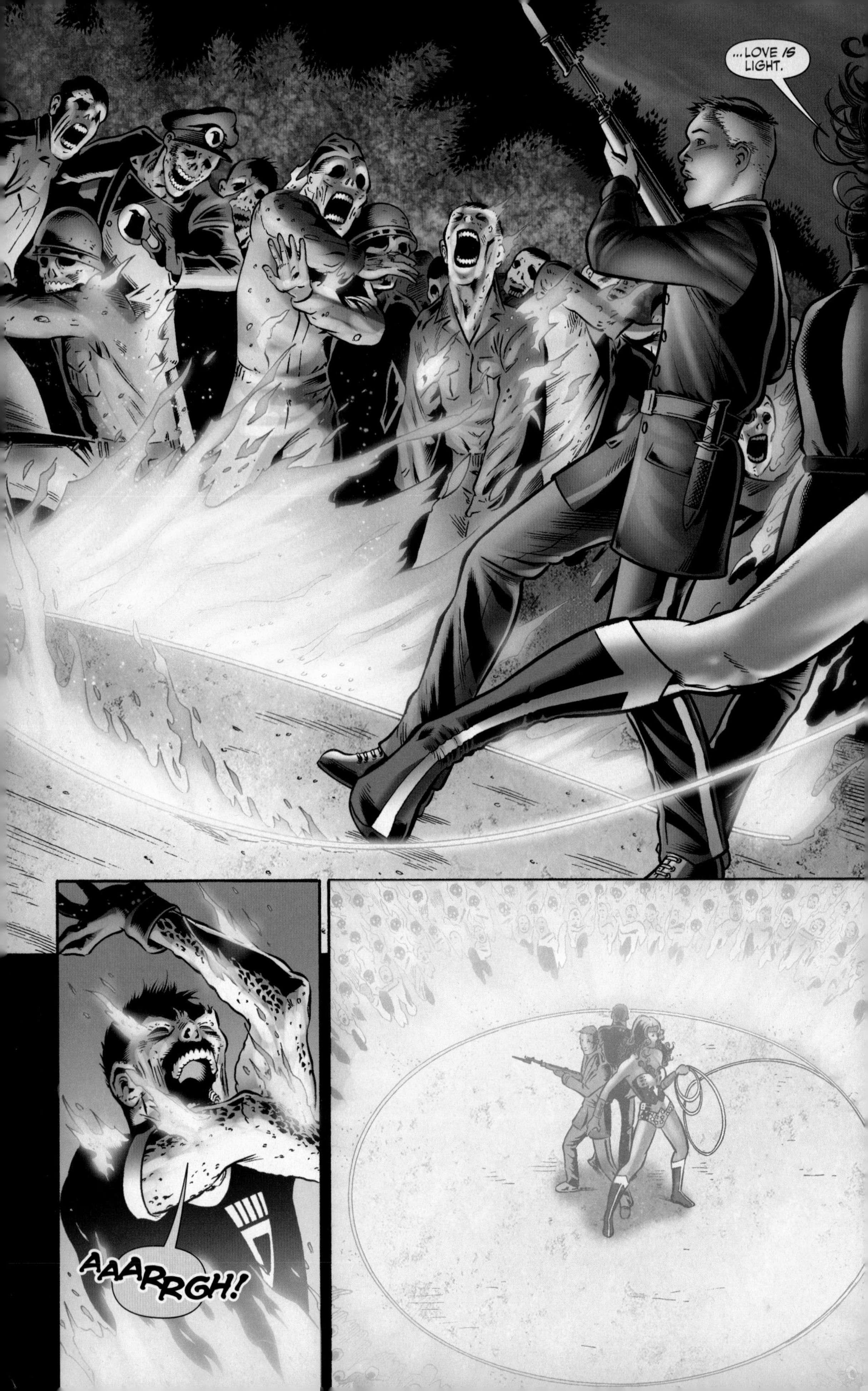
...LOVE IS LIGHT.
AAARRGH!

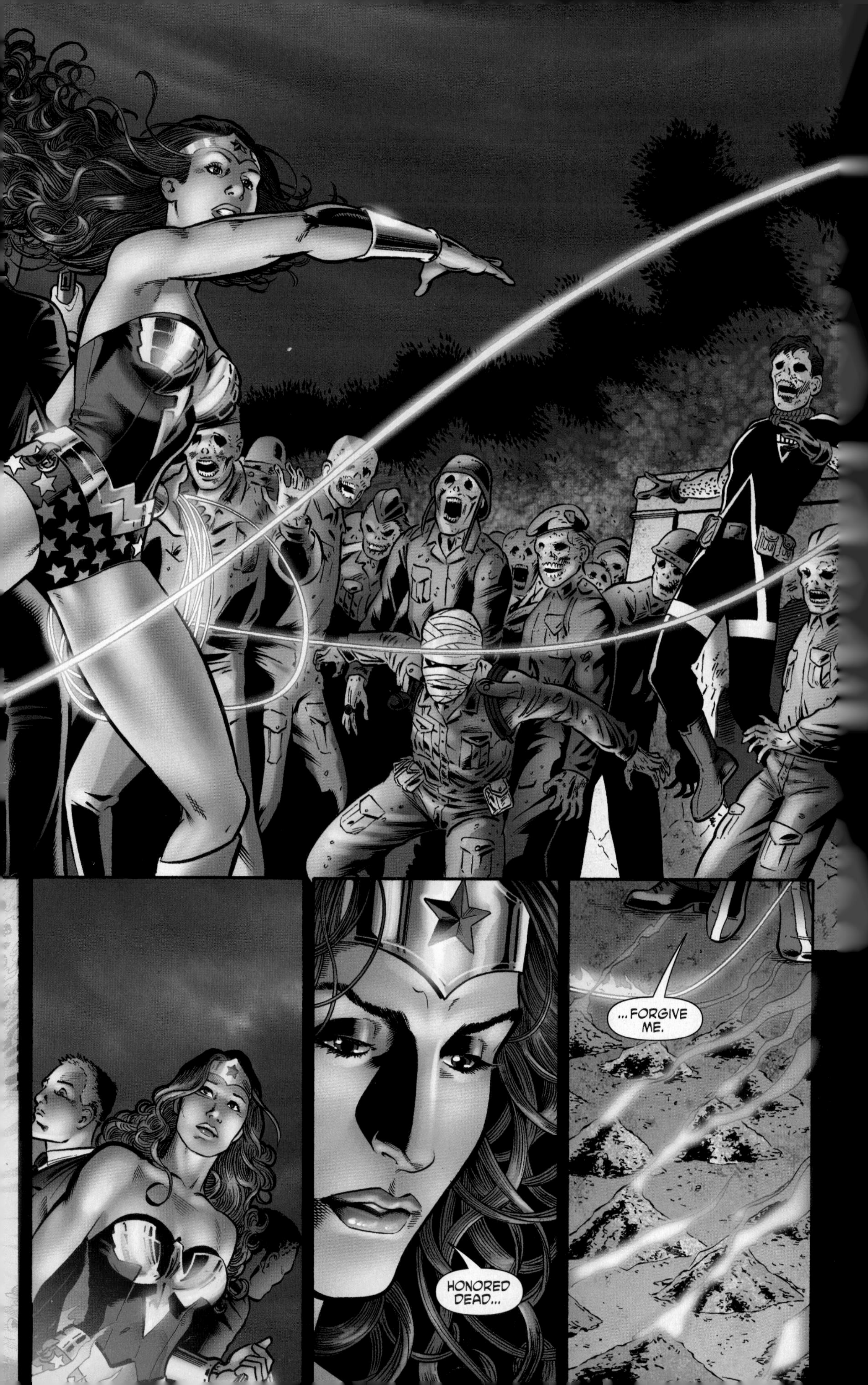
HONORED DEAD...
...FORGIVE ME.

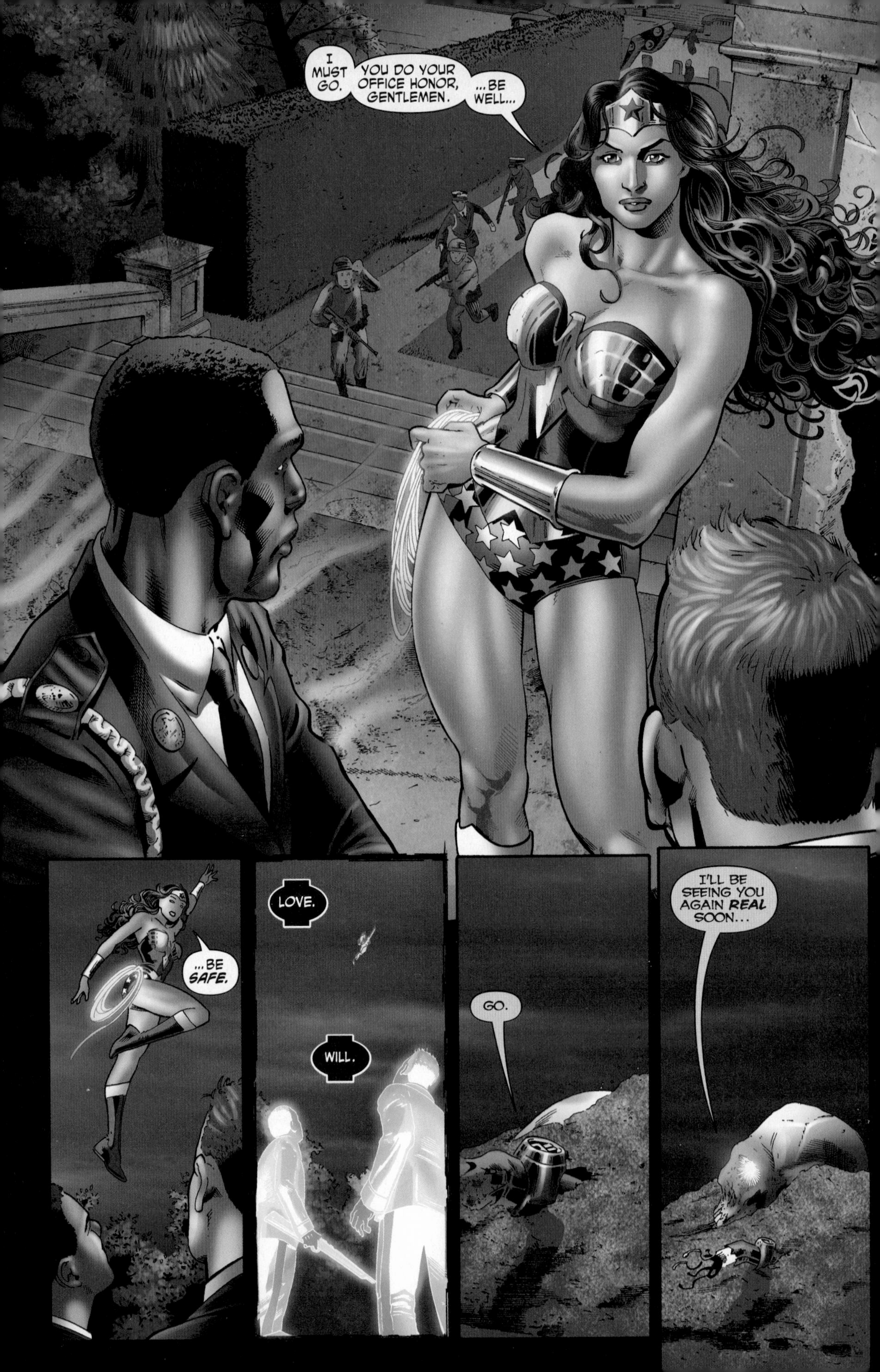
I MUST GO.
YOU DO YOUR OFFICE HONOR, GENTLEMEN.
...BE WELL...
...BE SAFE.
LOVE.
WILL.
GO.
I'LL BE SEEING YOU AGAIN REAL SOON...

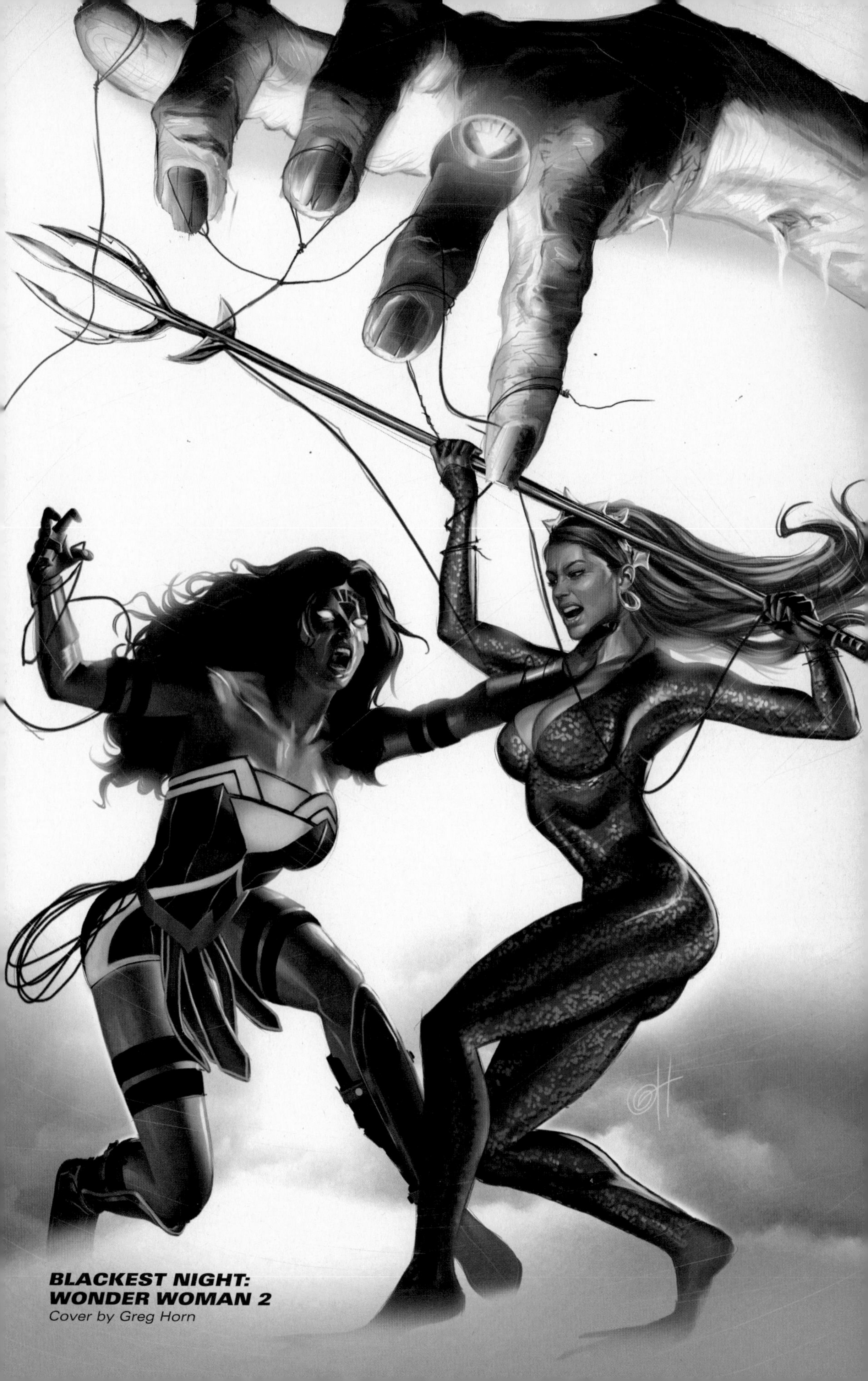

BLACKEST NIGHT: WONDER WOMAN 2
Cover by Greg Horn

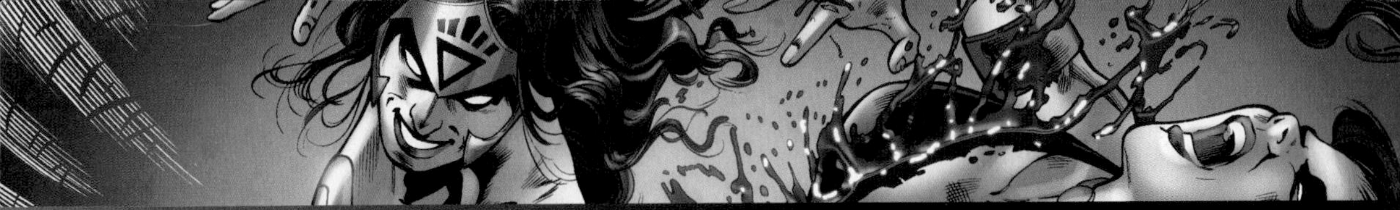

BLACKEST NIGHT: WONDER WOMAN
CHAPTER TWO

GREG RUCKA
WRITER

NICOLA SCOTT
EDUARDO PANSICA
PENCILS

JONATHAN GLAPION
EBER FERREIRA
INKS

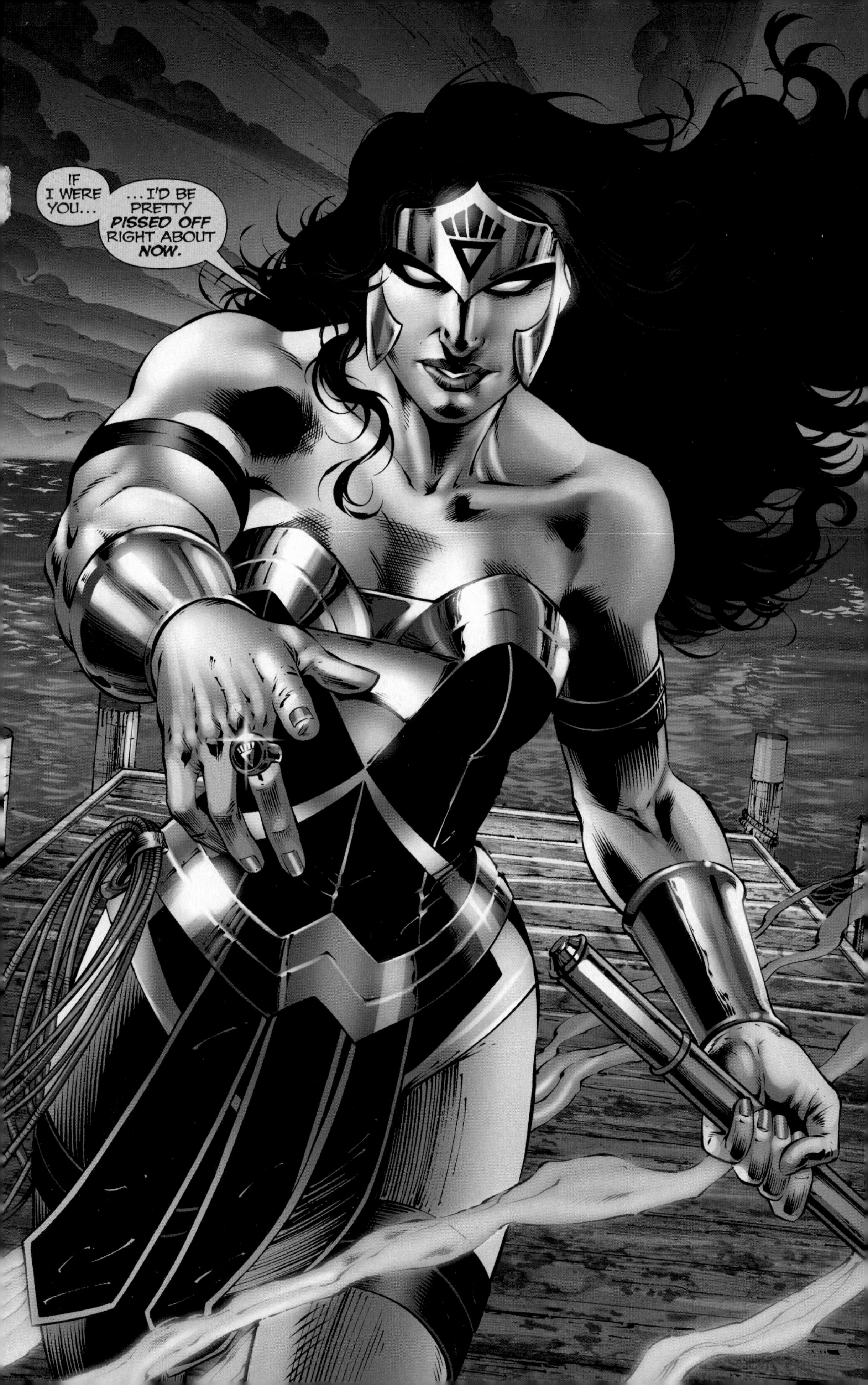
IF I WERE YOU...
...I'D BE PRETTY PISSED OFF RIGHT ABOUT NOW.

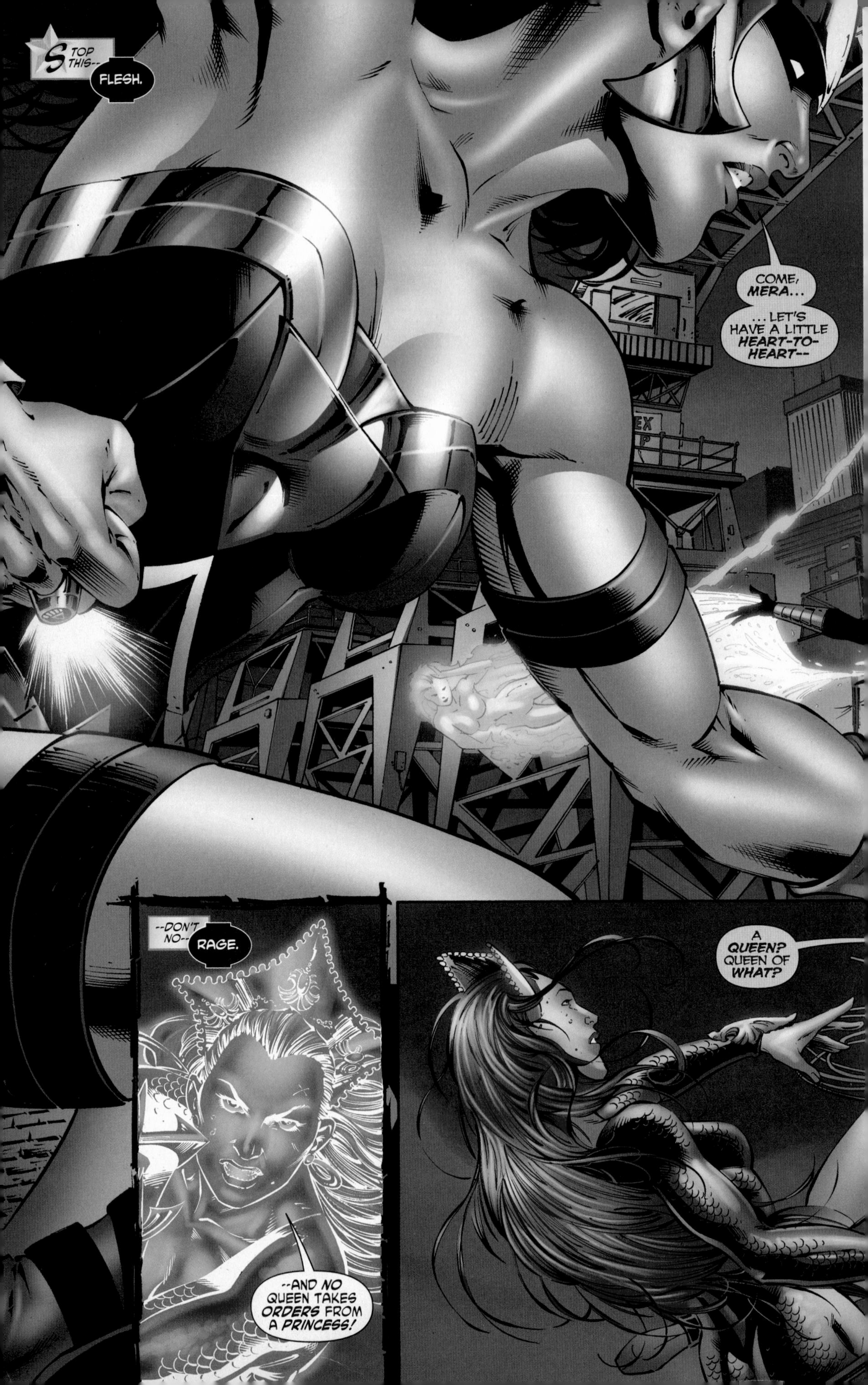
STOP THIS--
FLESH.
COME, MERA...
...LET'S HAVE A LITTLE HEART-TO-HEART--
--DON'T NO--
RAGE.
--AND NO QUEEN TAKES ORDERS FROM A PRINCESS!
A QUEEN? QUEEN OF WHAT?

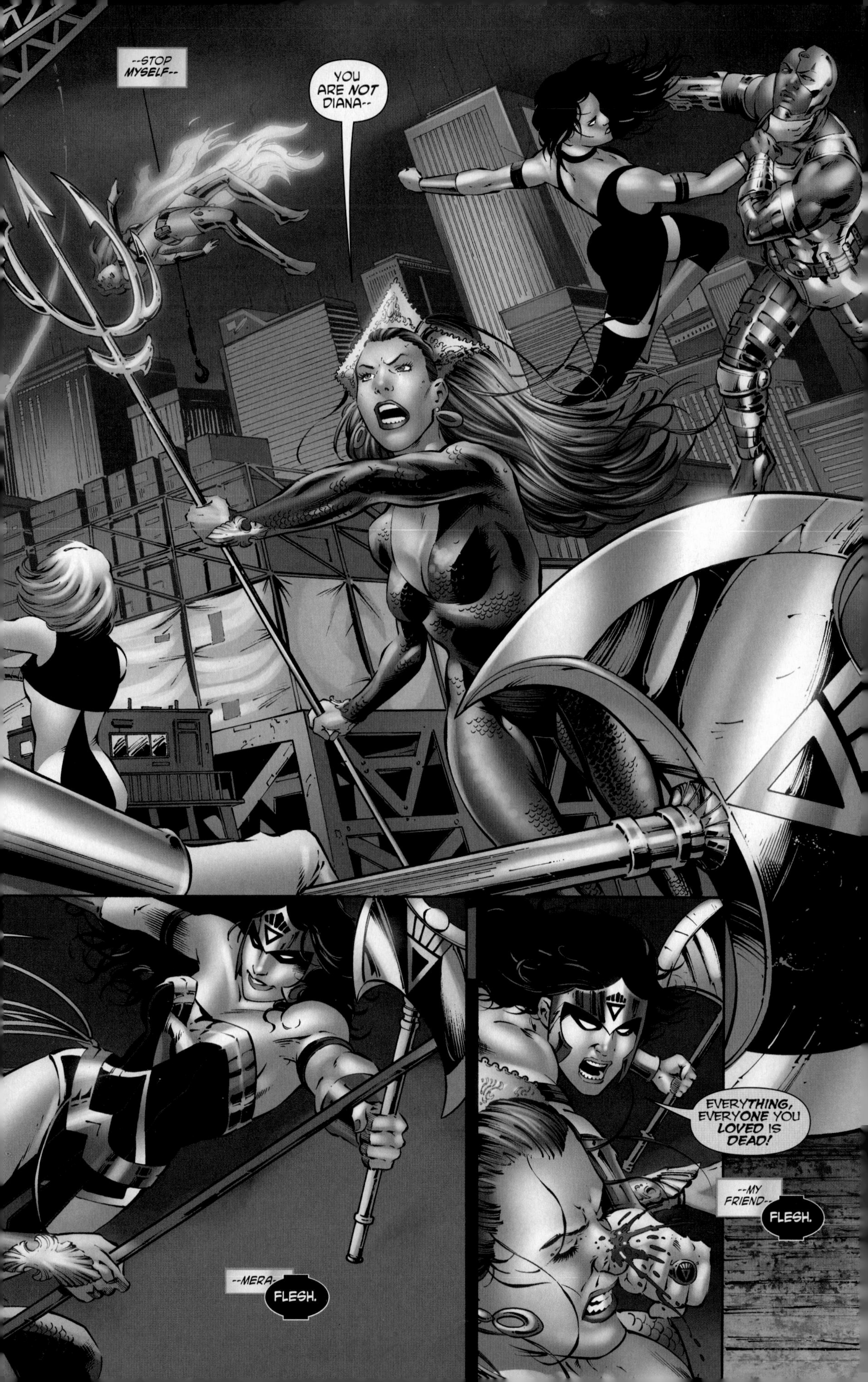
--STOP MYSELF--
YOU ARE NOT DIANA--
--MERA--
FLESH.
EVERYTHING, EVERYONE YOU LOVED IS DEAD!
--MY FRIEND--
FLESH.

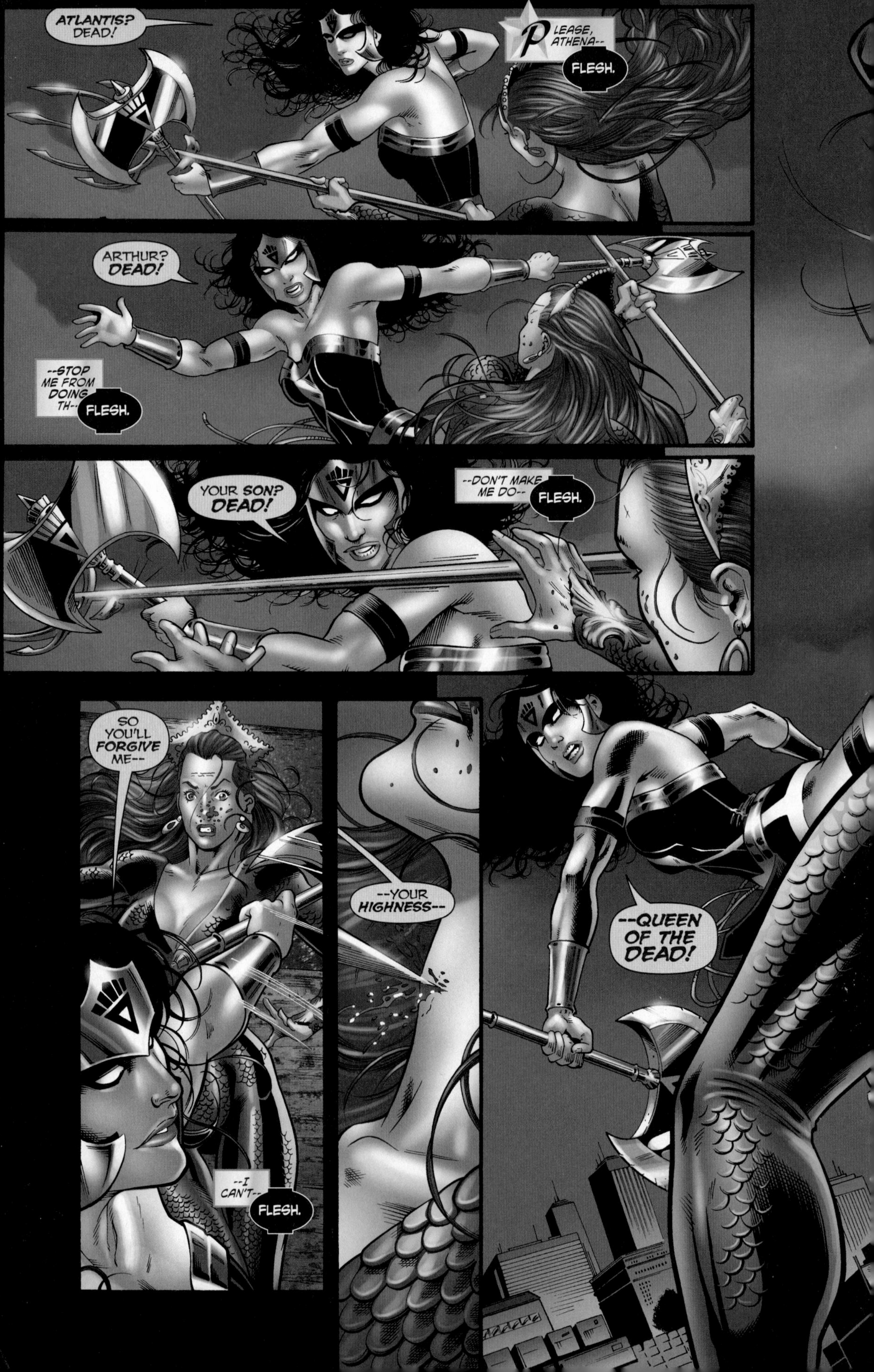

ATLANTIS? DEAD!
PLEASE, ATHENA--
FLESH.
ARTHUR? DEAD!
--STOP ME FROM DOING TH--
FLESH.
YOUR SON? DEAD!
--DON'T MAKE ME DO--
FLESH.
SO YOU'LL FORGIVE ME--
--I CAN'T--
FLESH.
--YOUR HIGHNESS--
--QUEEN OF THE DEAD!

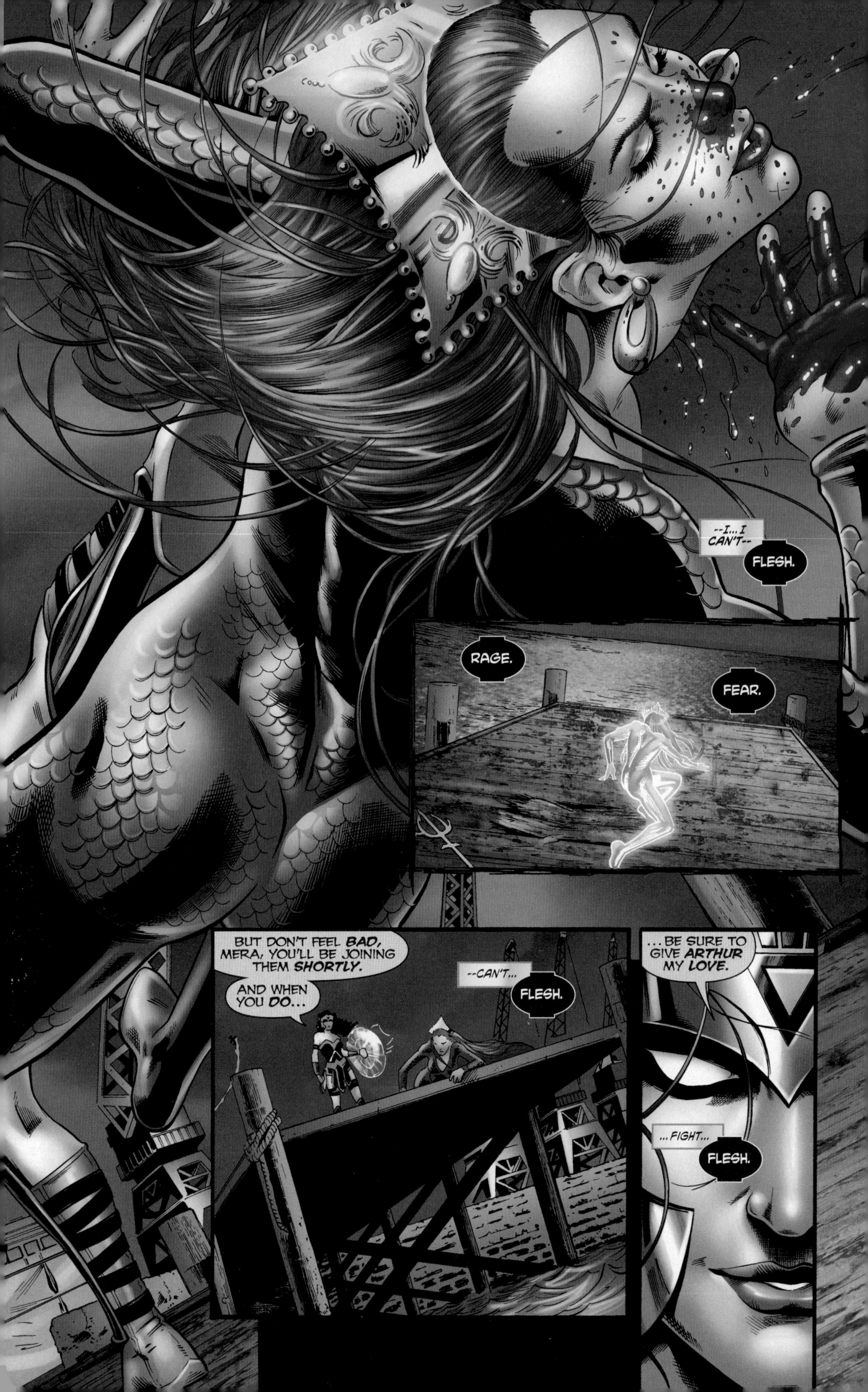
--I... I CAN'T--
FLESH.
RAGE.
FEAR.
BUT DON'T FEEL BAD, MERA, YOU'LL BE JOINING THEM SHORTLY.
AND WHEN YOU DO...
--CAN'T...
FLESH.
...BE SURE TO GIVE ARTHUR MY LOVE.
...FIGHT...
FLESH.

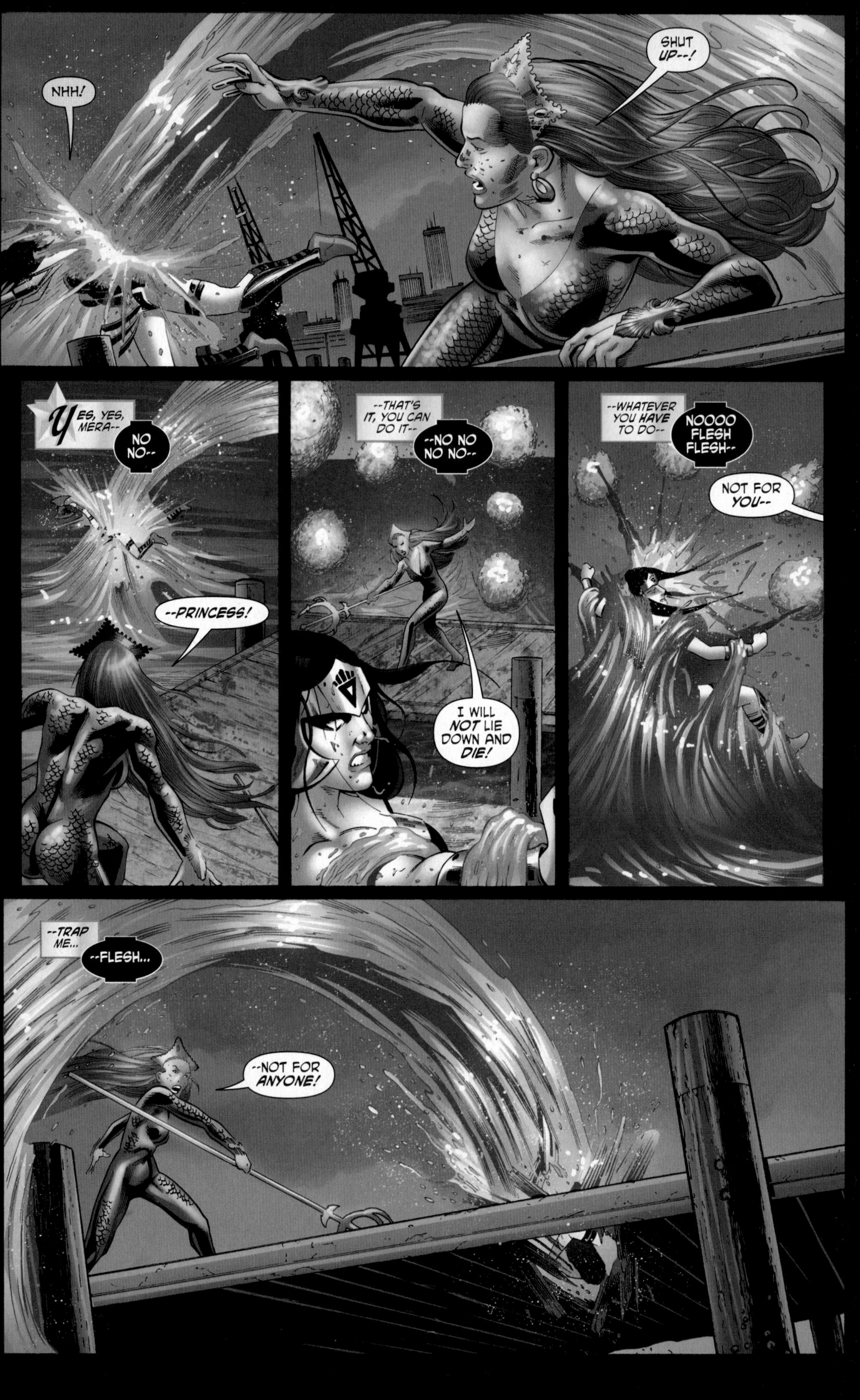
NHH!
SHUT UP--!
YES, YES, MERA--
NO NO--
--PRINCESS!
--THAT'S IT, YOU CAN DO IT--
--NO NO NO NO--
I WILL NOT LIE DOWN AND DIE!
--WHATEVER YOU HAVE TO DO--
NOOOO FLESH FLESH--
NOT FOR YOU--
--TRAP ME...
--FLESH...
--NOT FOR ANYONE!

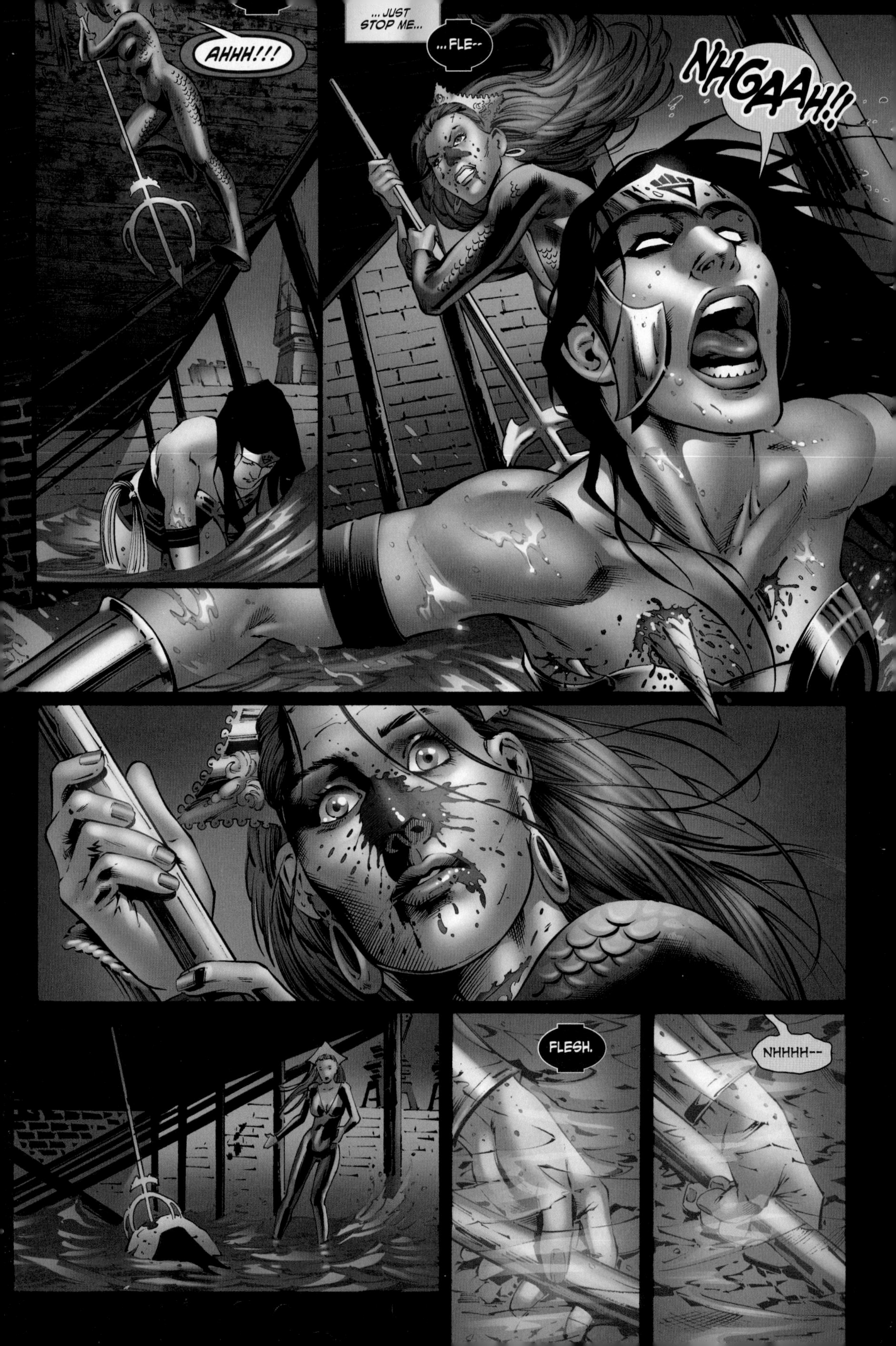

AHHH!!!
... JUST STOP ME...
...FLE--
NHGAAH!!
FLESH.
NHHHH--

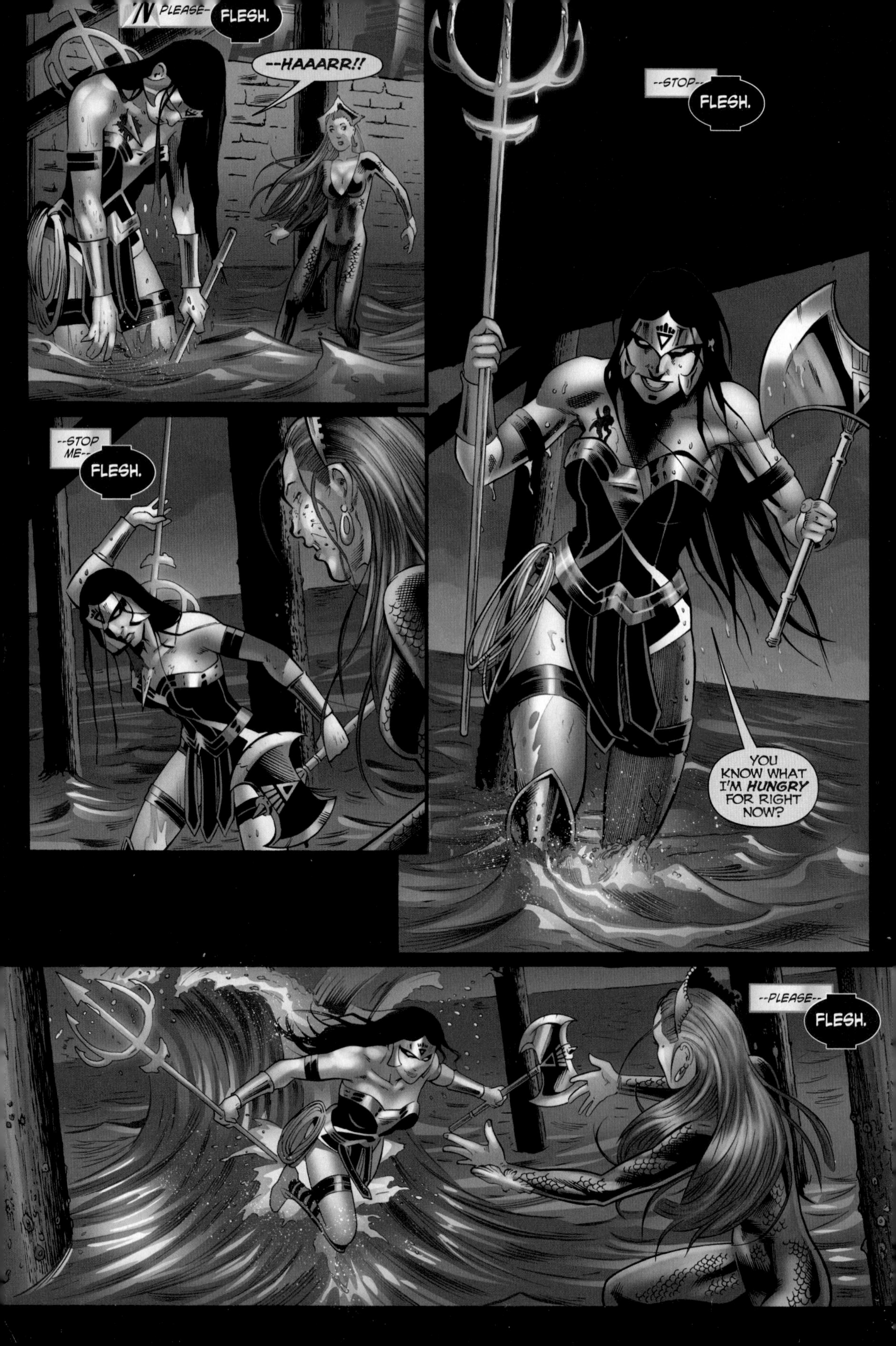
--PLEASE--
FLESH.
--HAAARR!!
--STOP--
FLESH.
--STOP ME--
FLESH.
YOU KNOW WHAT I'M HUNGRY FOR RIGHT NOW?
--PLEASE--
FLESH.

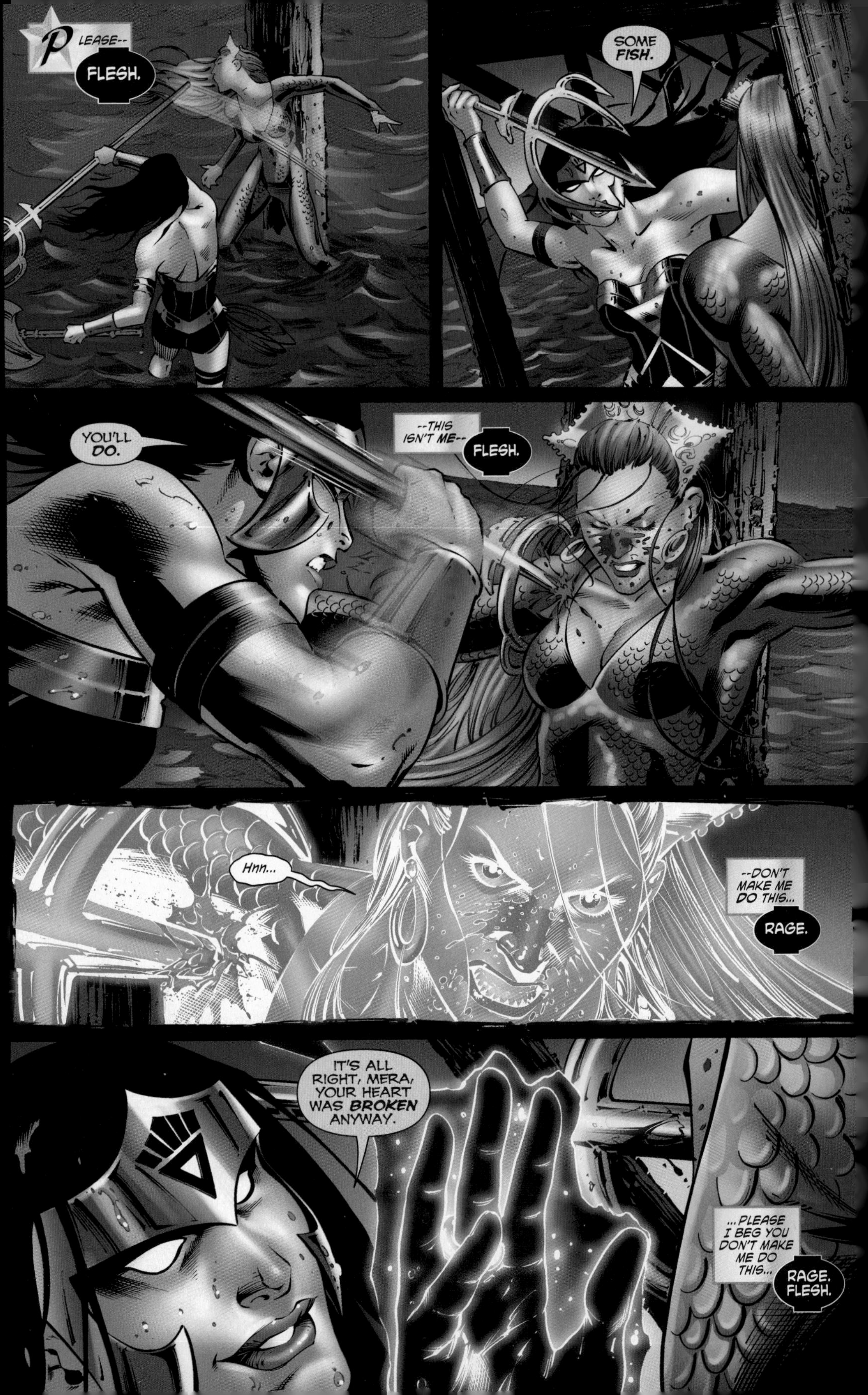
PLEASE--
FLESH.
SOME FISH.
YOU'LL DO.
--THIS ISN'T ME--
FLESH.
Hnn...
--DON'T MAKE ME DO THIS...
RAGE.
IT'S ALL RIGHT, MERA, YOUR HEART WAS BROKEN ANYWAY.
...PLEASE I BEG YOU DON'T MAKE ME DO THIS...
RAGE. FLESH.

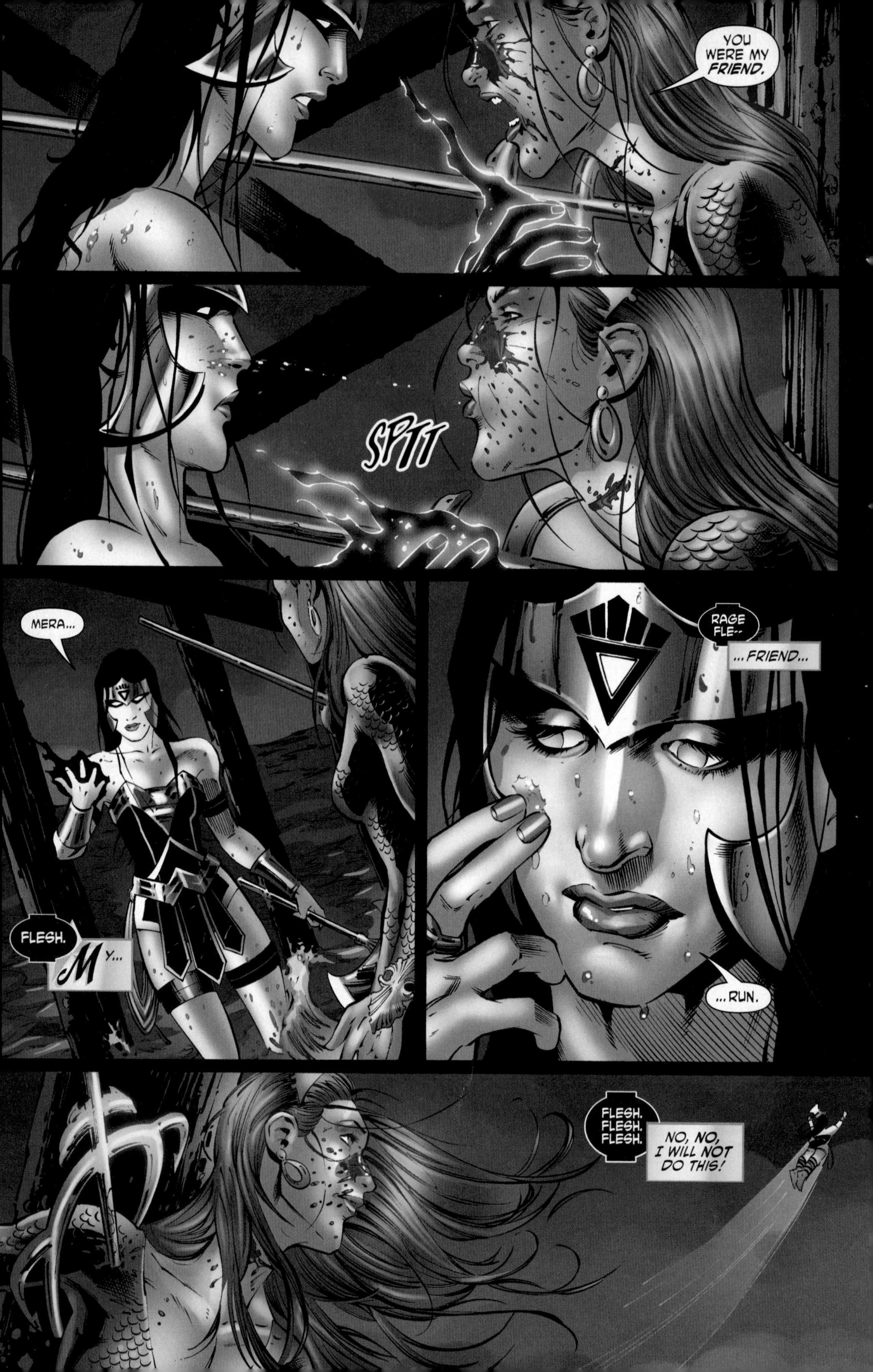
YOU WERE MY FRIEND.
SPTT
MERA...
FLESH.
MY...
RAGE FLE--
...FRIEND...
...RUN.
FLESH. FLESH. FLESH.
NO, NO, I WILL NOT DO THIS!

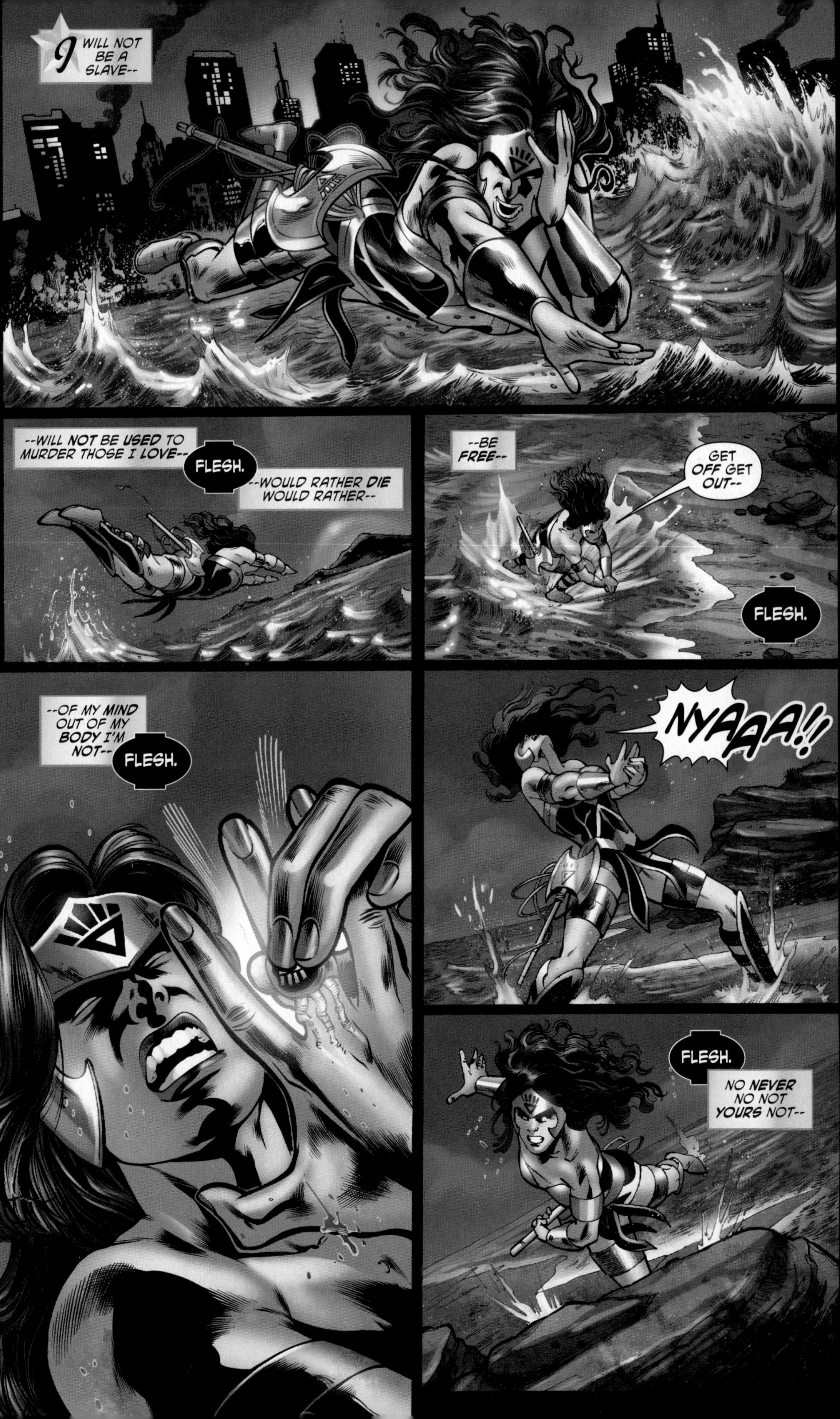
I WILL NOT BE A SLAVE--
--WILL NOT BE USED TO MURDER THOSE I LOVE--
FLESH.
--WOULD RATHER DIE WOULD RATHER--
--BE FREE--
GET OFF GET OUT--
FLESH.
--OF MY MIND OUT OF MY BODY I'M NOT--
FLESH.
NYAAAA!!
FLESH.
NO NEVER NO NOT YOURS NOT--

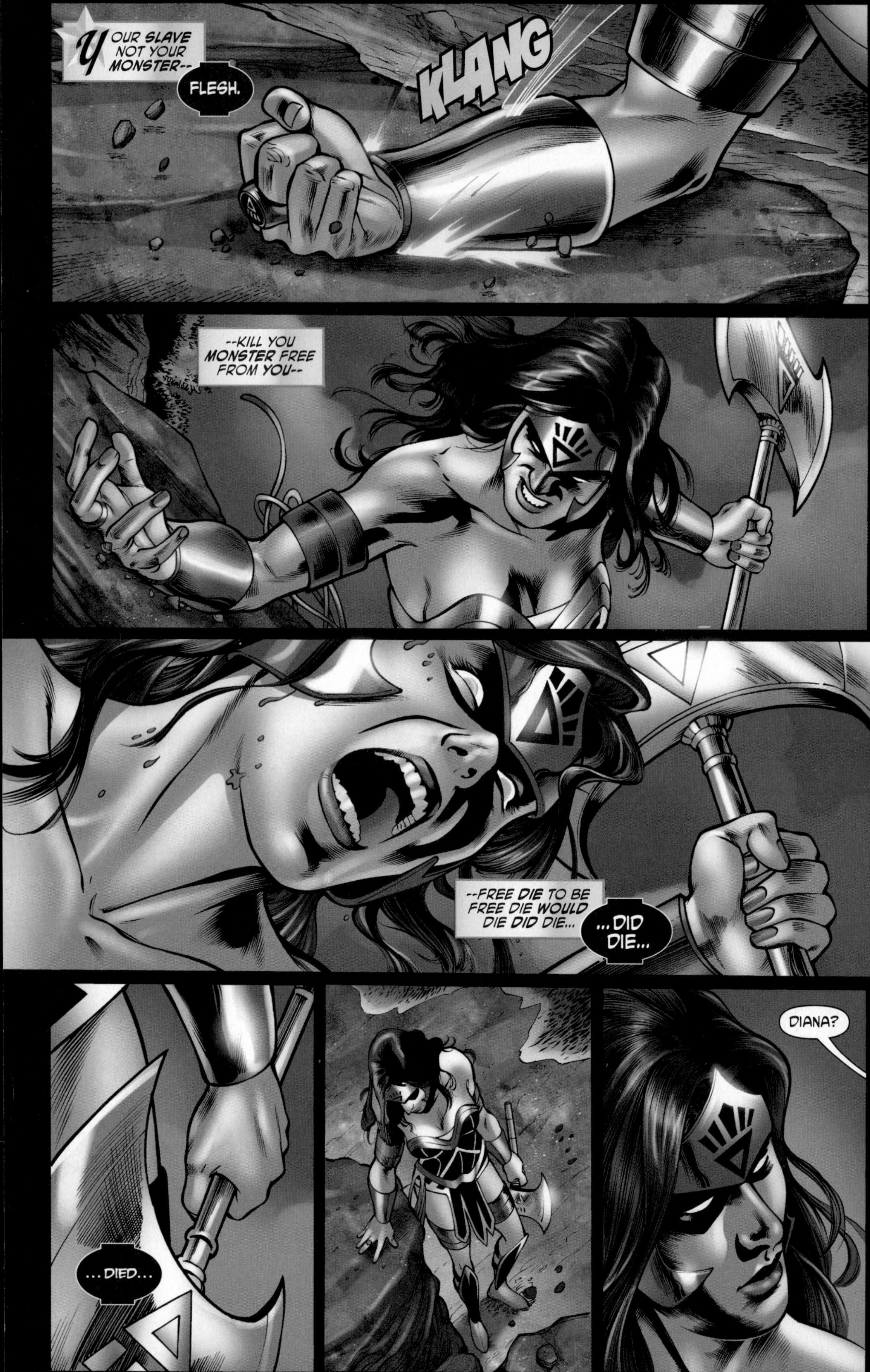
YOUR SLAVE NOT YOUR MONSTER--
FLESH.
KLANG
--KILL YOU MONSTER FREE FROM YOU--
--FREE DIE TO BE FREE DIE WOULD DIE DID DIE...
...DID DIE...
...DIED...
DIANA?

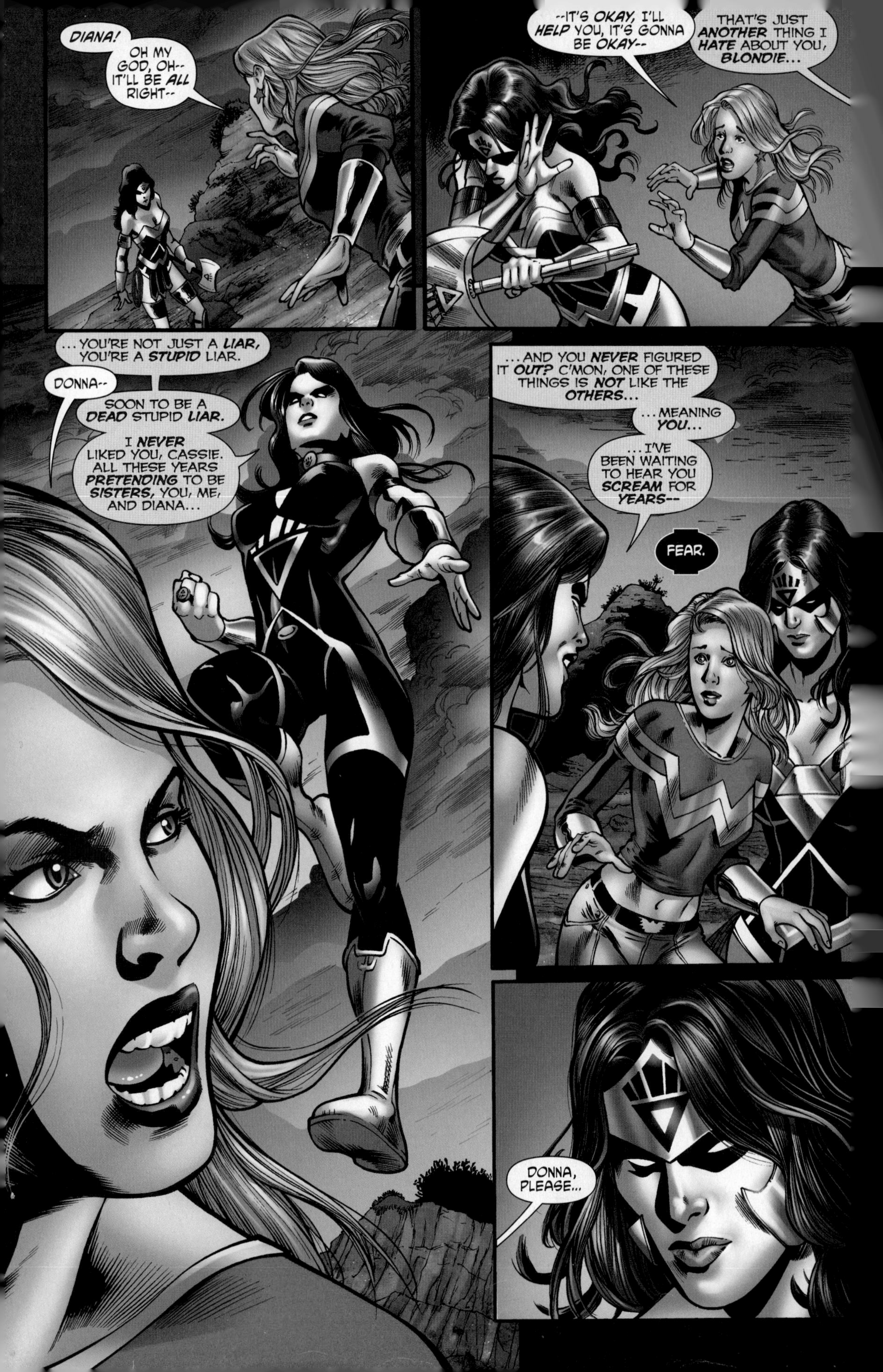
DIANA!
OH MY GOD, OH-- IT'LL BE ALL RIGHT--
--IT'S OKAY, I'LL HELP YOU, IT'S GONNA BE OKAY--
THAT'S JUST ANOTHER THING I HATE ABOUT YOU, BLONDIE...
...YOU'RE NOT JUST A LIAR, YOU'RE A STUPID LIAR.
DONNA--
SOON TO BE A DEAD STUPID LIAR.
I NEVER LIKED YOU, CASSIE. ALL THESE YEARS PRETENDING TO BE SISTERS, YOU, ME, AND DIANA...
...AND YOU NEVER FIGURED IT OUT? C'MON, ONE OF THESE THINGS IS NOT LIKE THE OTHERS...
...MEANING YOU...
...I'VE BEEN WAITING TO HEAR YOU SCREAM FOR YEARS--
FEAR.
DONNA, PLEASE...

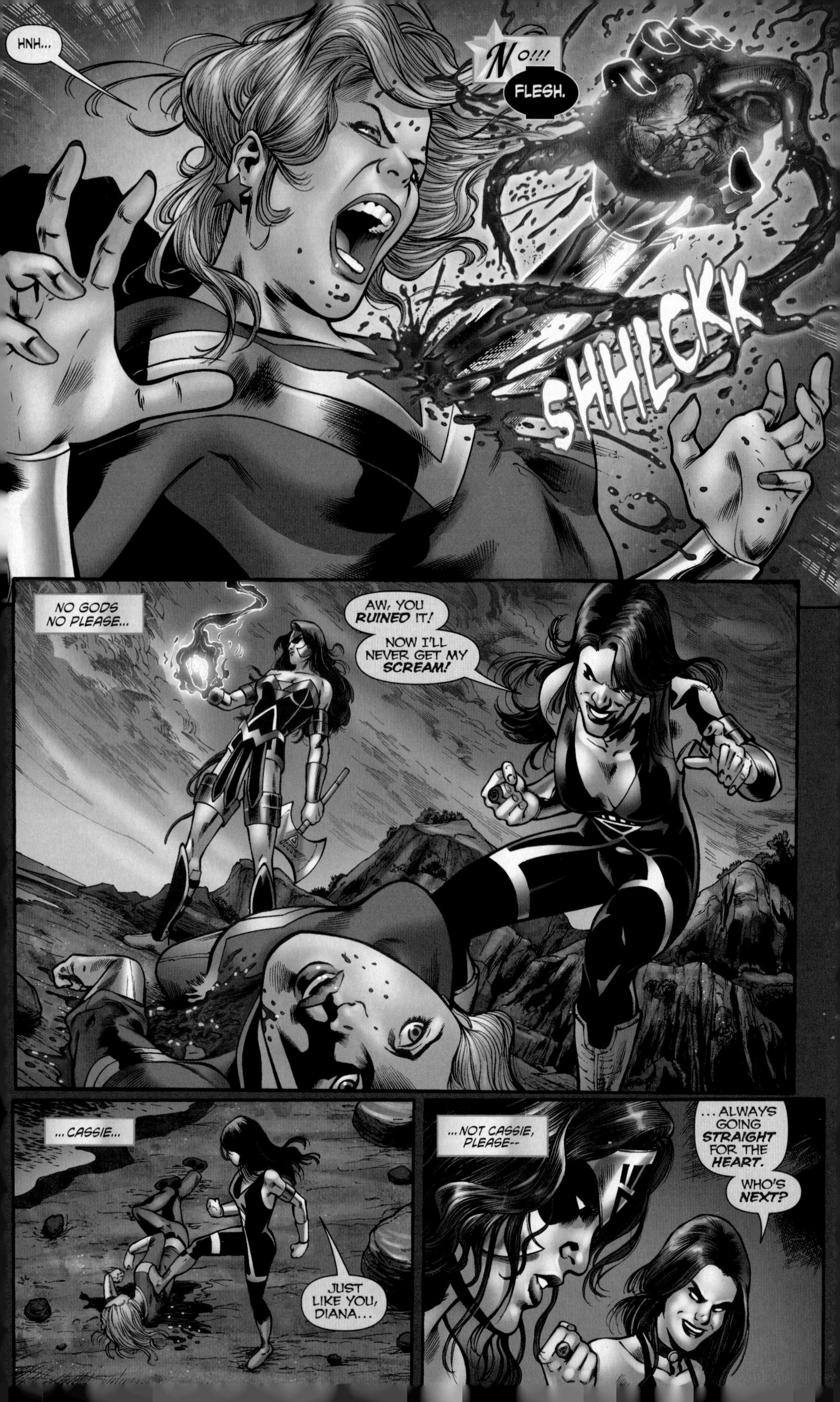
HNH...
NO!!!
FLESH.
SHHLCKK
NO GODS NO PLEASE...
AW, YOU RUINED IT!
NOW I'LL NEVER GET MY SCREAM!
...CASSIE...
JUST LIKE YOU, DIANA...
...NOT CASSIE, PLEASE--
...ALWAYS GOING STRAIGHT FOR THE HEART.
WHO'S NEXT?

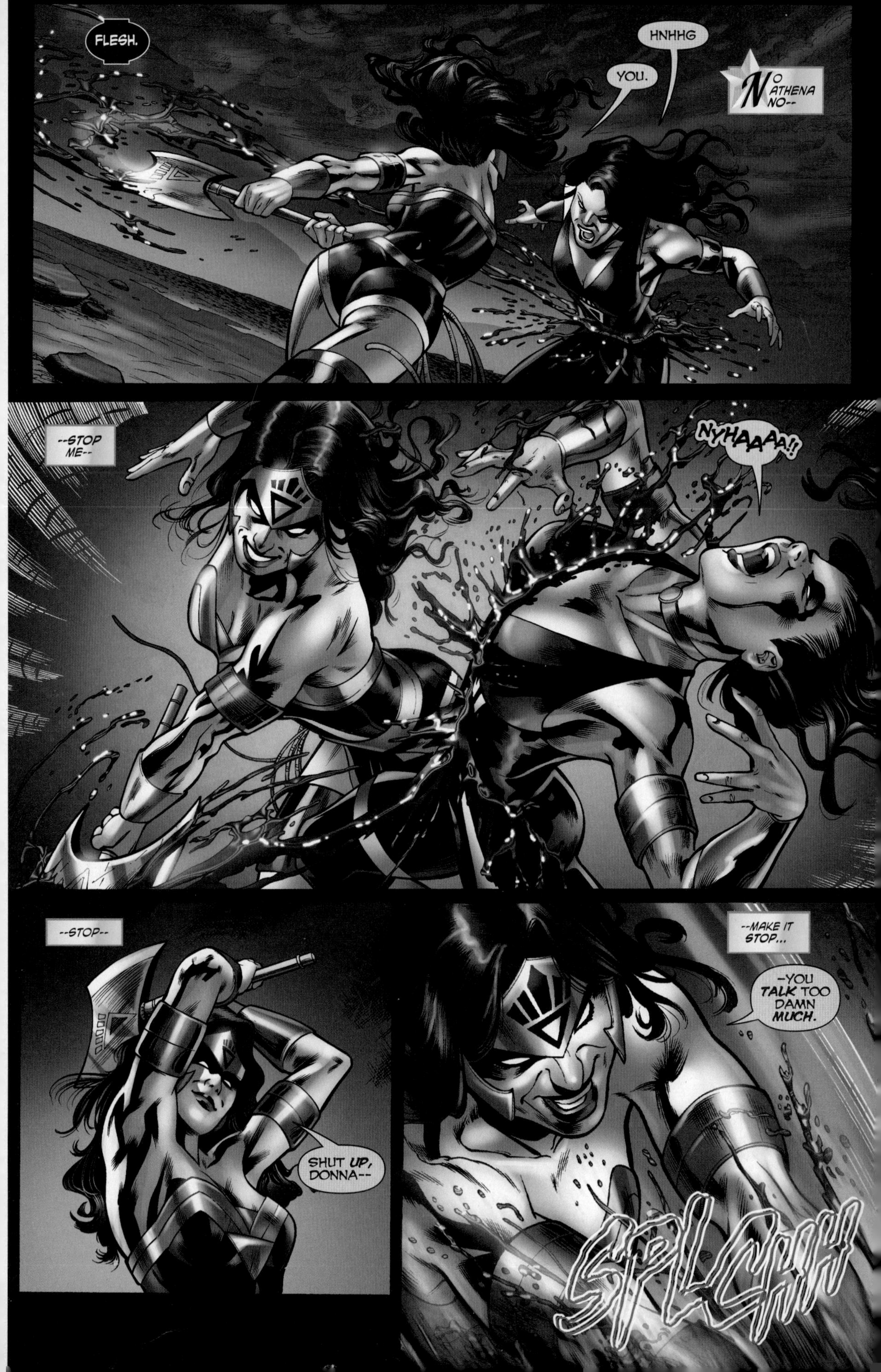
FLESH.
HNHHG
YOU.
NO ATHENA NO--
--STOP ME--
NYHAAAA!!
--STOP--
SHUT UP, DONNA--
--MAKE IT STOP...
-YOU TALK TOO DAMN MUCH.
SPLCHH

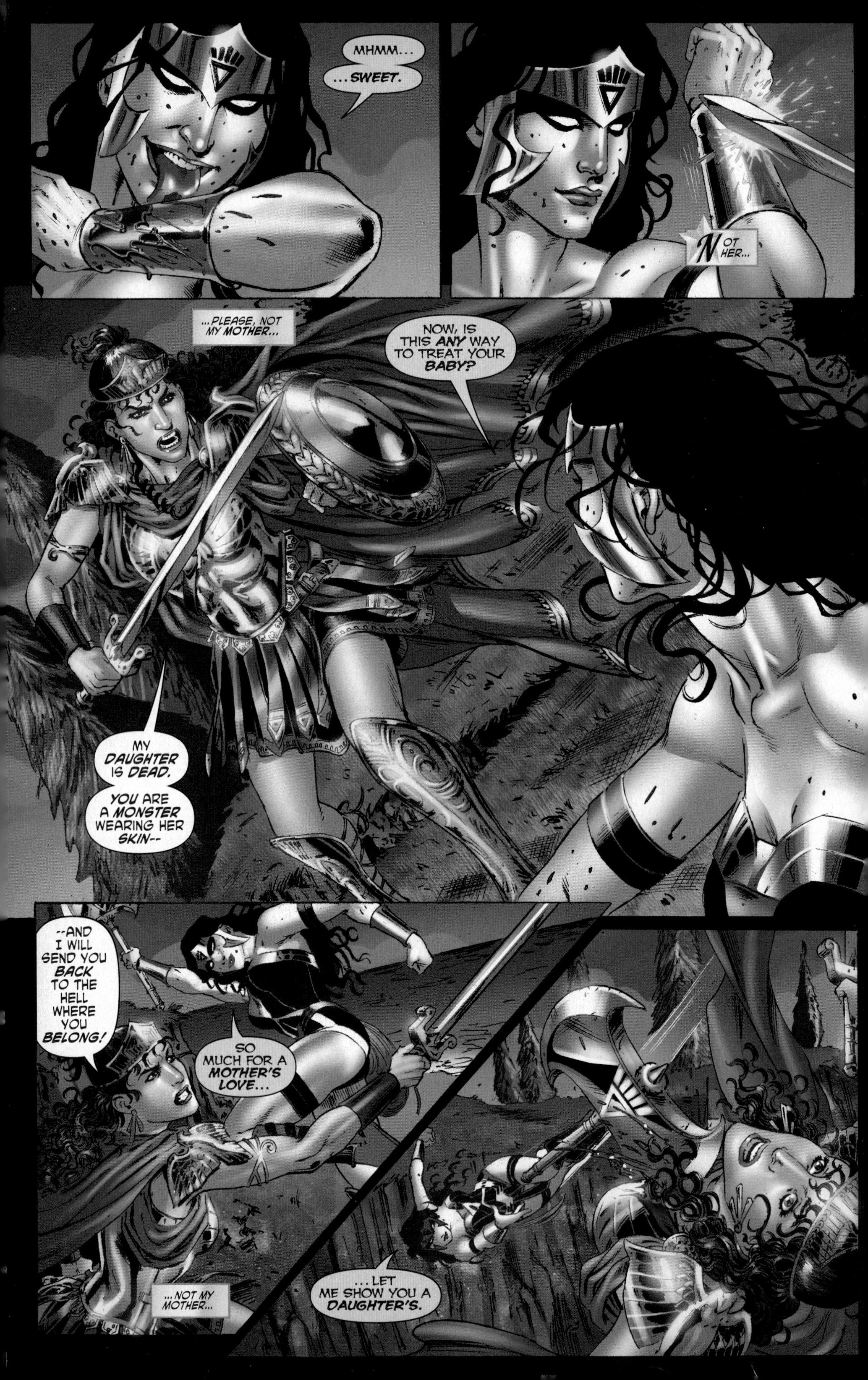
MHMM...
...SWEET.
NOT HER...
...PLEASE, NOT MY MOTHER...
NOW, IS THIS ANY WAY TO TREAT YOUR BABY?
MY DAUGHTER IS DEAD.
YOU ARE A MONSTER WEARING HER SKIN--
--AND I WILL SEND YOU BACK TO THE HELL WHERE YOU BELONG!
SO MUCH FOR A MOTHER'S LOVE...
...NOT MY MOTHER...
...LET ME SHOW YOU A DAUGHTER'S.

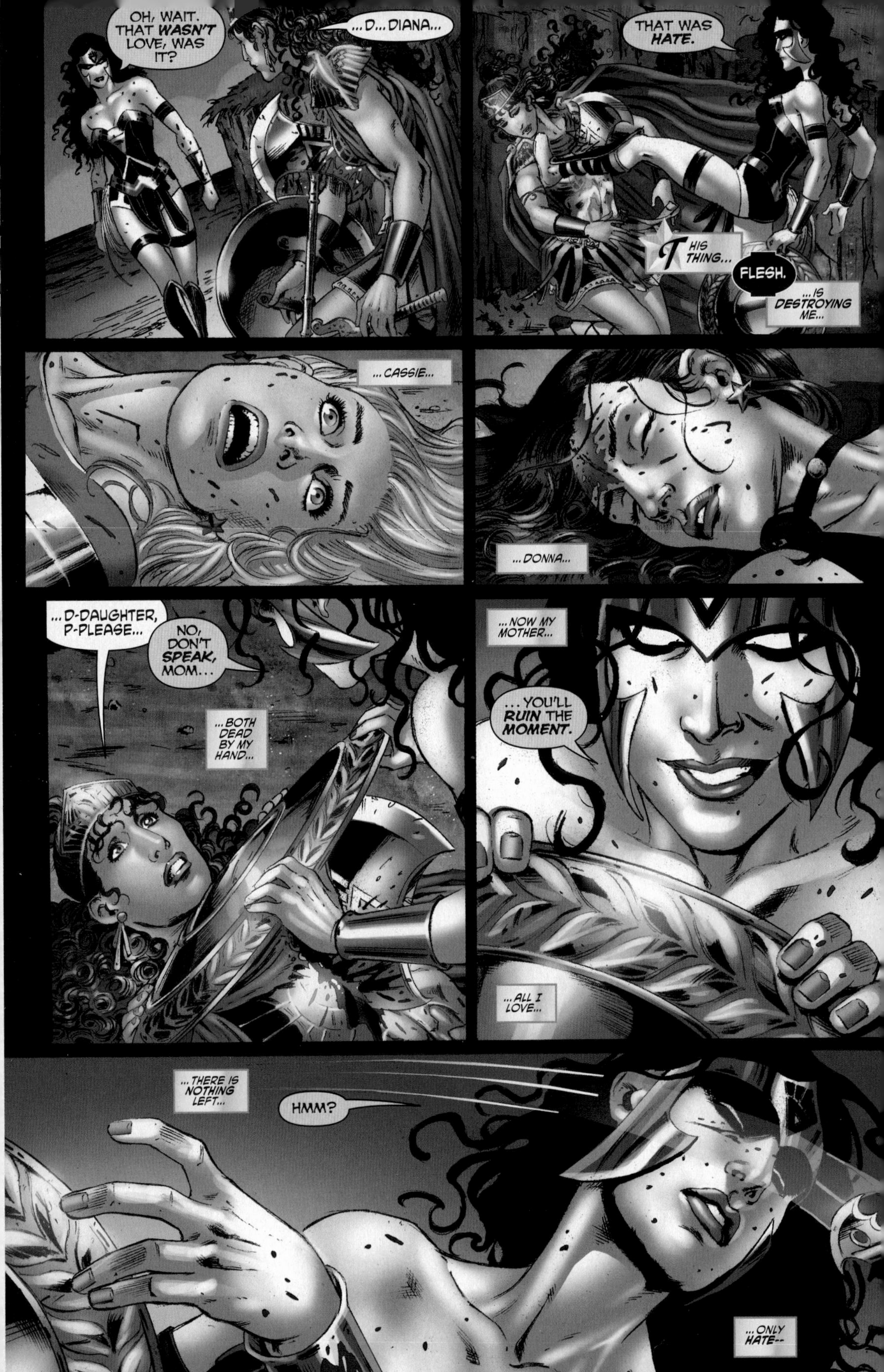
OH, WAIT. THAT WASN'T LOVE, WAS IT?
...D...DIANA...
THAT WAS HATE.
THIS THING...
FLESH.
...IS DESTROYING ME...
...CASSIE...
...DONNA...
...D-DAUGHTER, P-PLEASE...
NO, DON'T SPEAK, MOM...
...BOTH DEAD BY MY HAND...
...NOW MY MOTHER...
...YOU'LL RUIN THE MOMENT.
...ALL I LOVE...
...THERE IS NOTHING LEFT...
HMM?
...ONLY HATE--

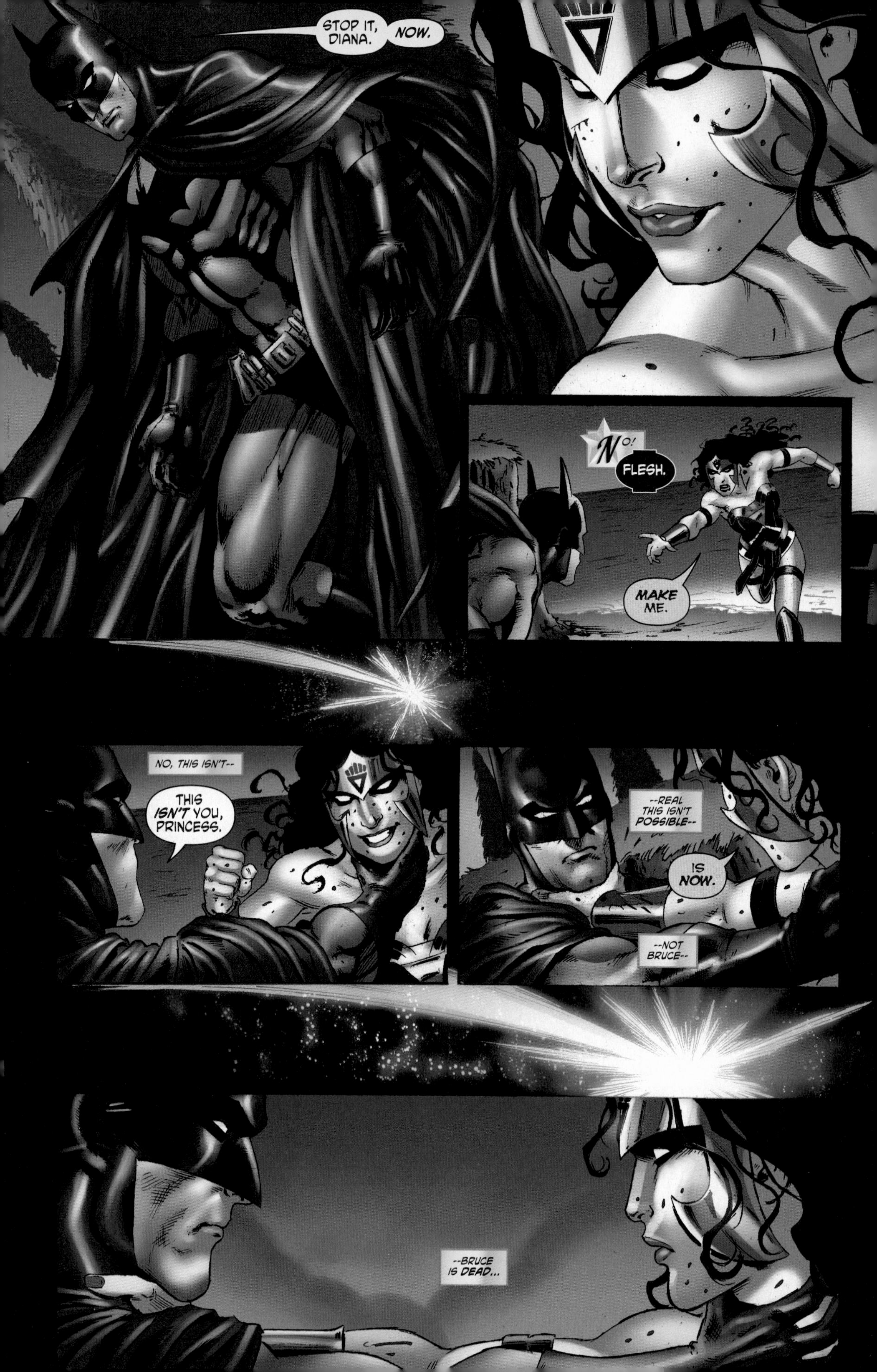
STOP IT, DIANA.
NOW.
NO!
FLESH.
MAKE ME.
NO, THIS ISN'T--
THIS ISN'T YOU, PRINCESS.
--REAL THIS ISN'T POSSIBLE--
IS NOW.
--NOT BRUCE--
--BRUCE IS DEAD...

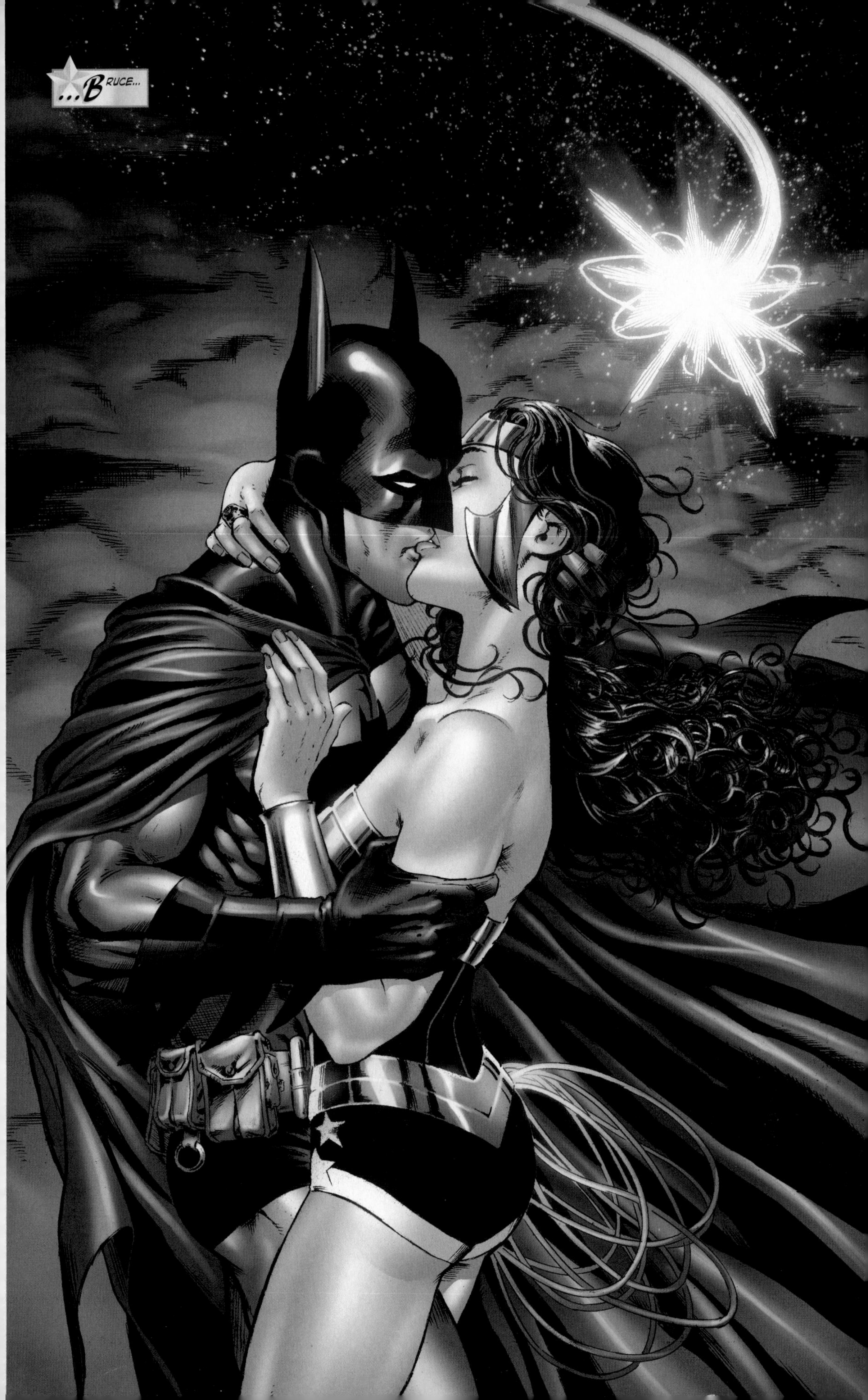
...BRUCE...

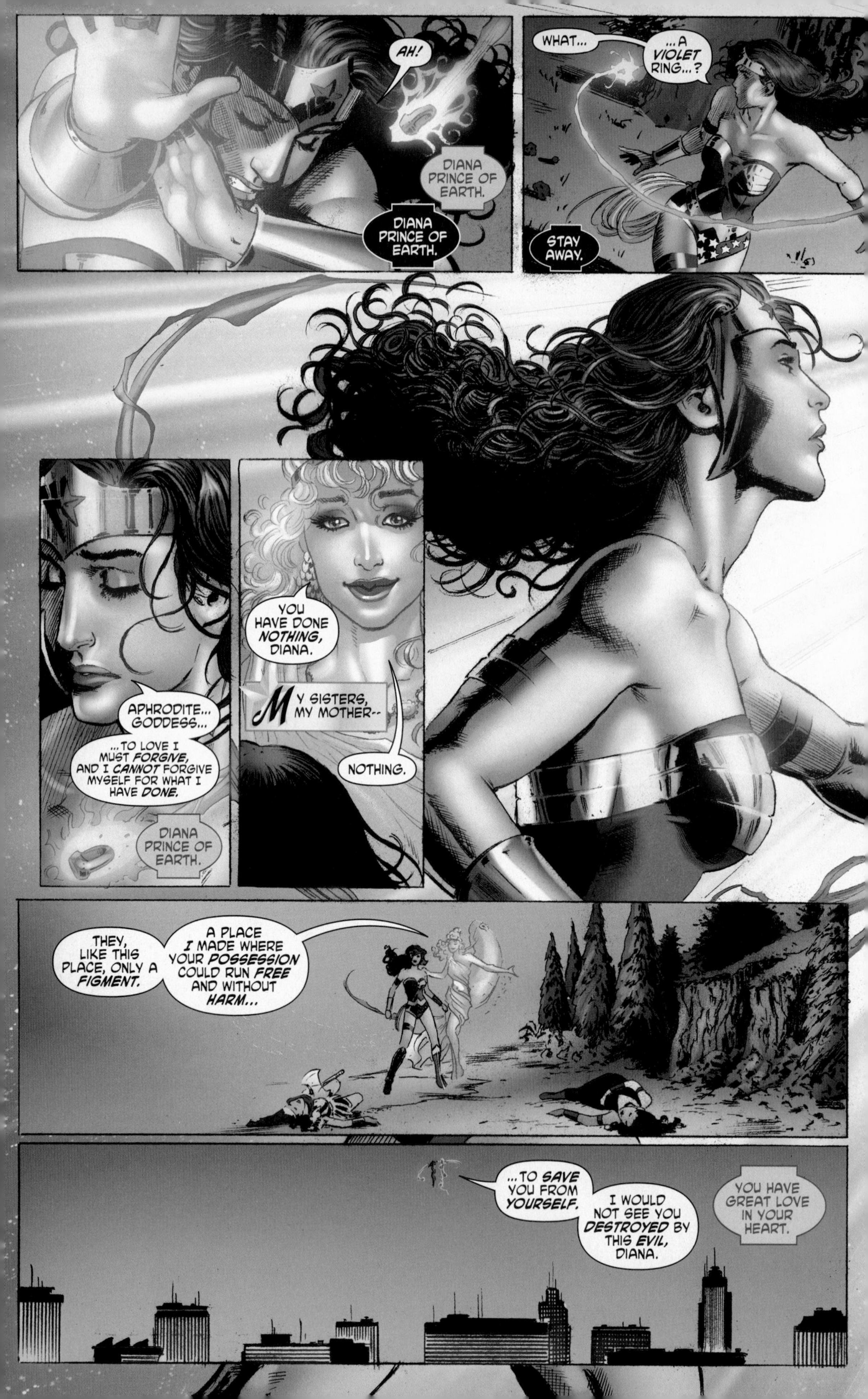
AH!
DIANA PRINCE OF EARTH.
DIANA PRINCE OF EARTH.
WHAT...
...A VIOLET RING...?
STAY AWAY.
APHRODITE... GODDESS...
...TO LOVE I MUST FORGIVE, AND I CANNOT FORGIVE MYSELF FOR WHAT I HAVE DONE.
DIANA PRINCE OF EARTH.
YOU HAVE DONE NOTHING, DIANA.
MY SISTERS, MY MOTHER--
NOTHING.
THEY, LIKE THIS PLACE, ONLY A FIGMENT.
A PLACE I MADE WHERE YOUR POSSESSION COULD RUN FREE AND WITHOUT HARM...
...TO SAVE YOU FROM YOURSELF.
I WOULD NOT SEE YOU DESTROYED BY THIS EVIL, DIANA.
YOU HAVE GREAT LOVE IN YOUR HEART.

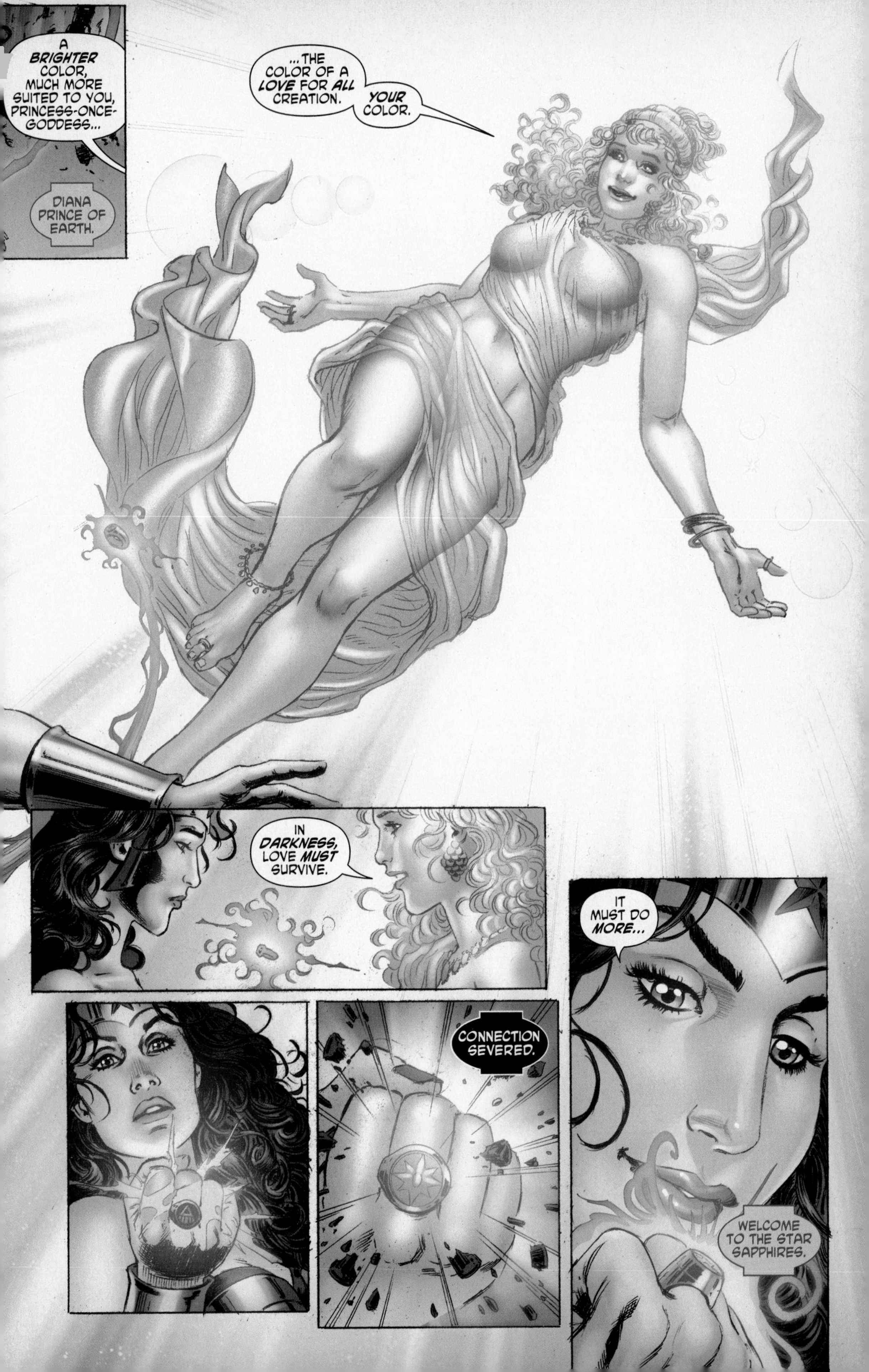

A BRIGHTER COLOR, MUCH MORE SUITED TO YOU, PRINCESS-ONCE-GODDESS...
DIANA PRINCE OF EARTH.
...THE COLOR OF A LOVE FOR ALL CREATION.
YOUR COLOR.
IN DARKNESS, LOVE MUST SURVIVE.
IT MUST DO MORE...
CONNECTION SEVERED.
WELCOME TO THE STAR SAPPHIRES.

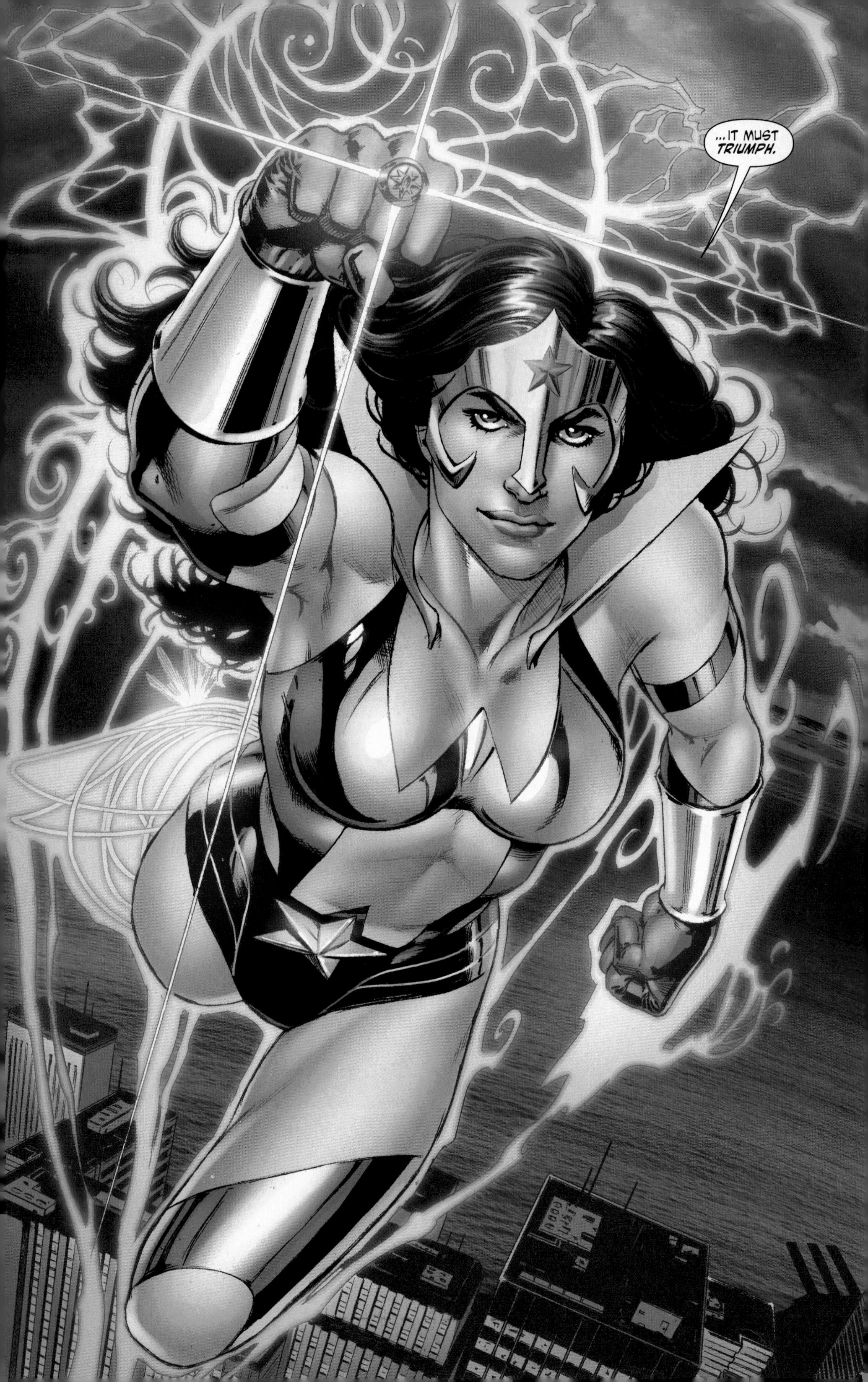
...IT MUST TRIUMPH.

BLACKEST NIGHT:
WONDER WOMAN 3
Cover by Greg Horn

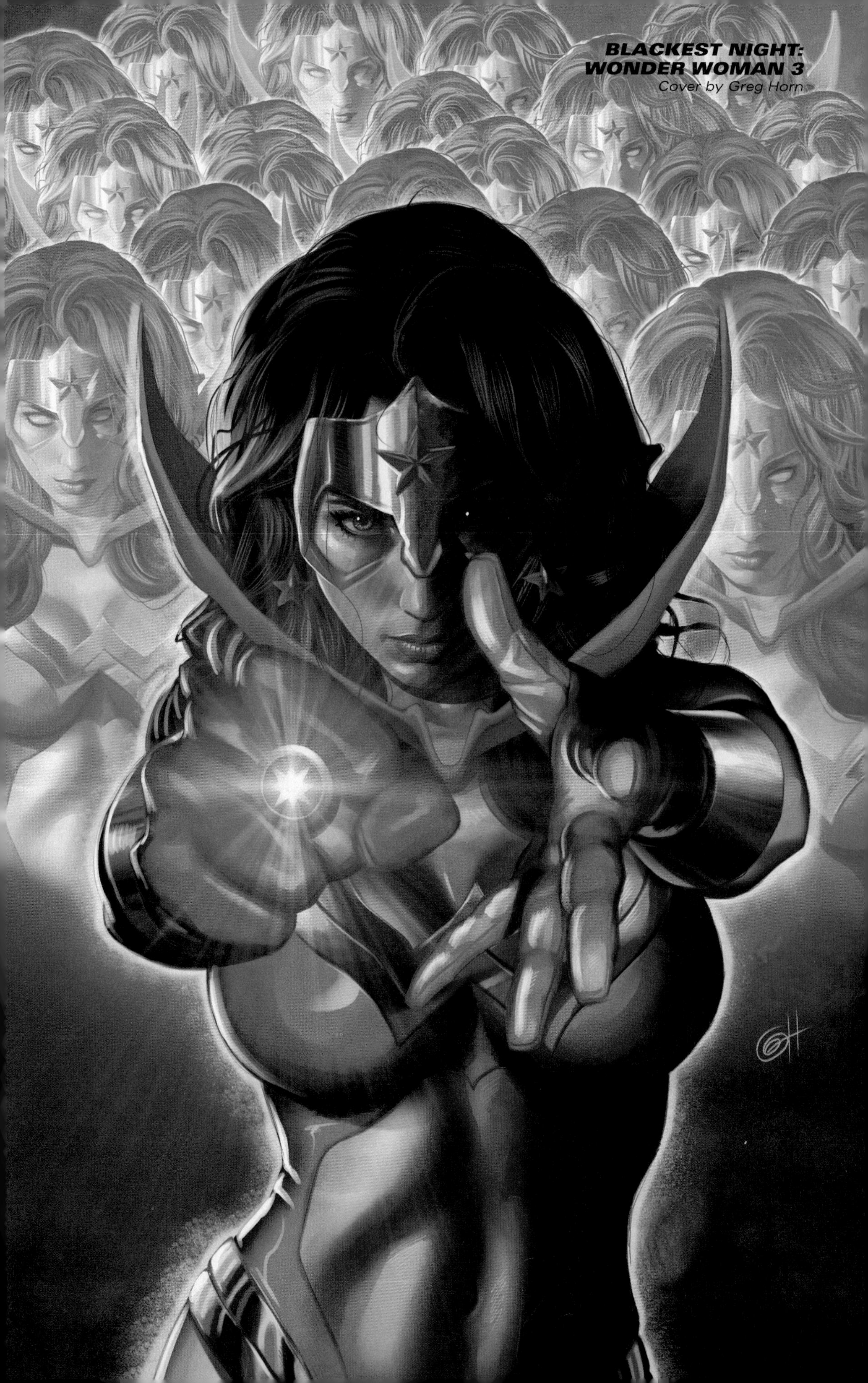

BLACKEST NIGHT: WONDER WOMAN
CHAPTER THREE

GREG RUCKA
WRITER

NICOLA SCOTT
PENCILS

JONATHAN GLAPION
INKS

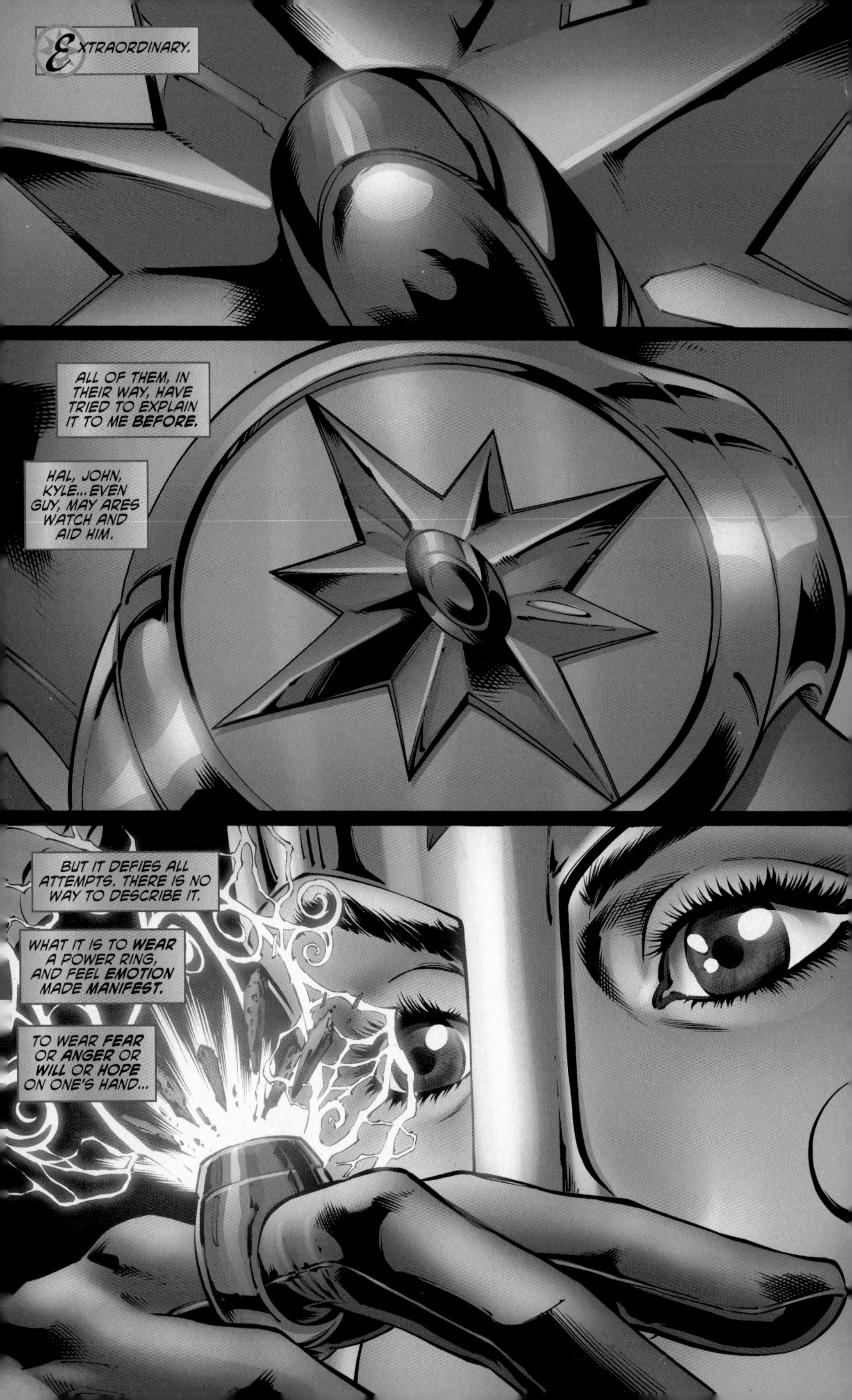
EXTRAORDINARY.
ALL OF THEM, IN THEIR WAY, HAVE TRIED TO EXPLAIN IT TO ME BEFORE.
HAL, JOHN, KYLE...EVEN GUY, MAY ARES WATCH AND AID HIM.
BUT IT DEFIES ALL ATTEMPTS. THERE IS NO WAY TO DESCRIBE IT.
WHAT IT IS TO WEAR A POWER RING, AND FEEL EMOTION MADE MANIFEST.
TO WEAR FEAR OR ANGER OR WILL OR HOPE ON ONE'S HAND...

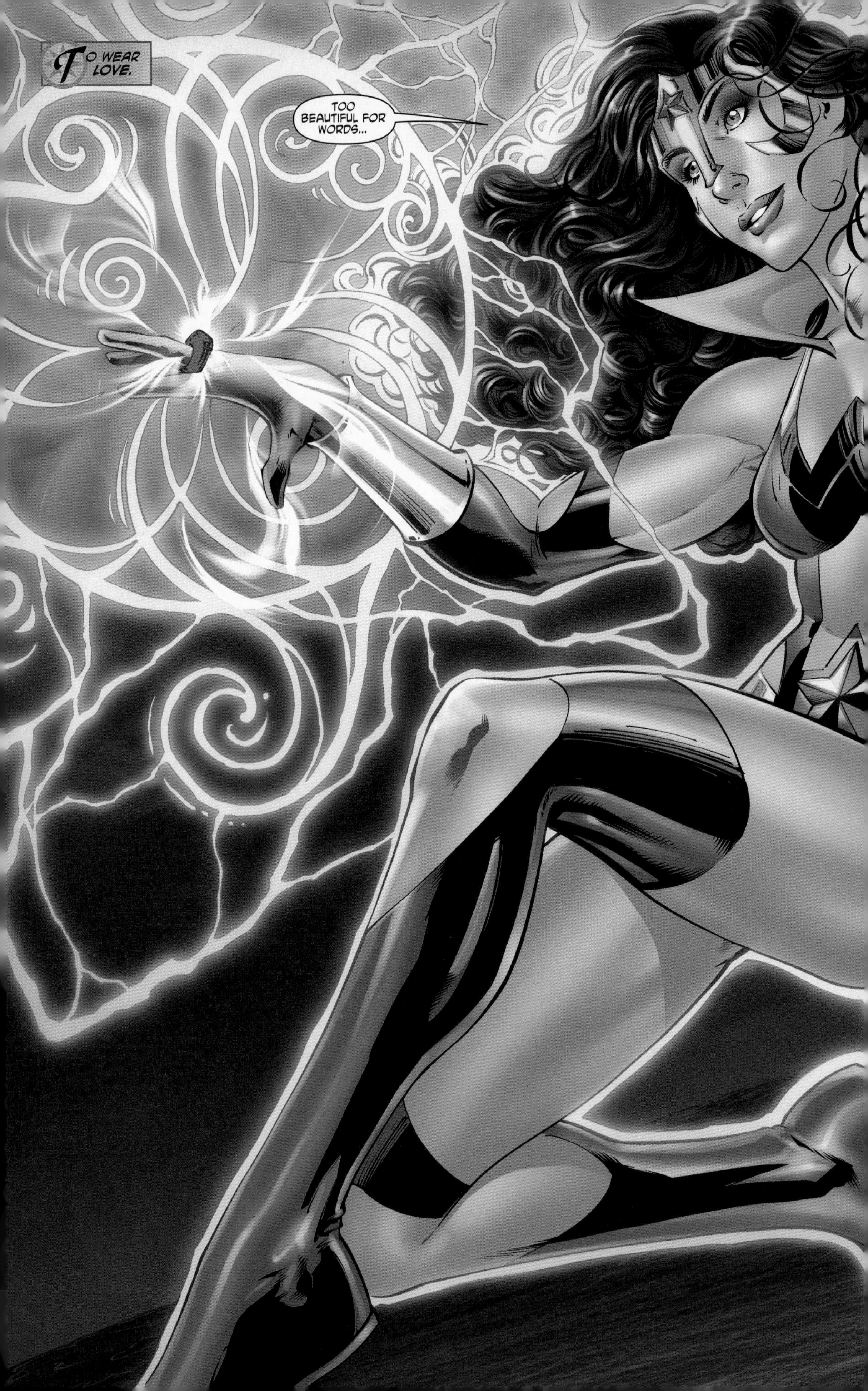
TO WEAR LOVE.
TOO BEAUTIFUL FOR WORDS...

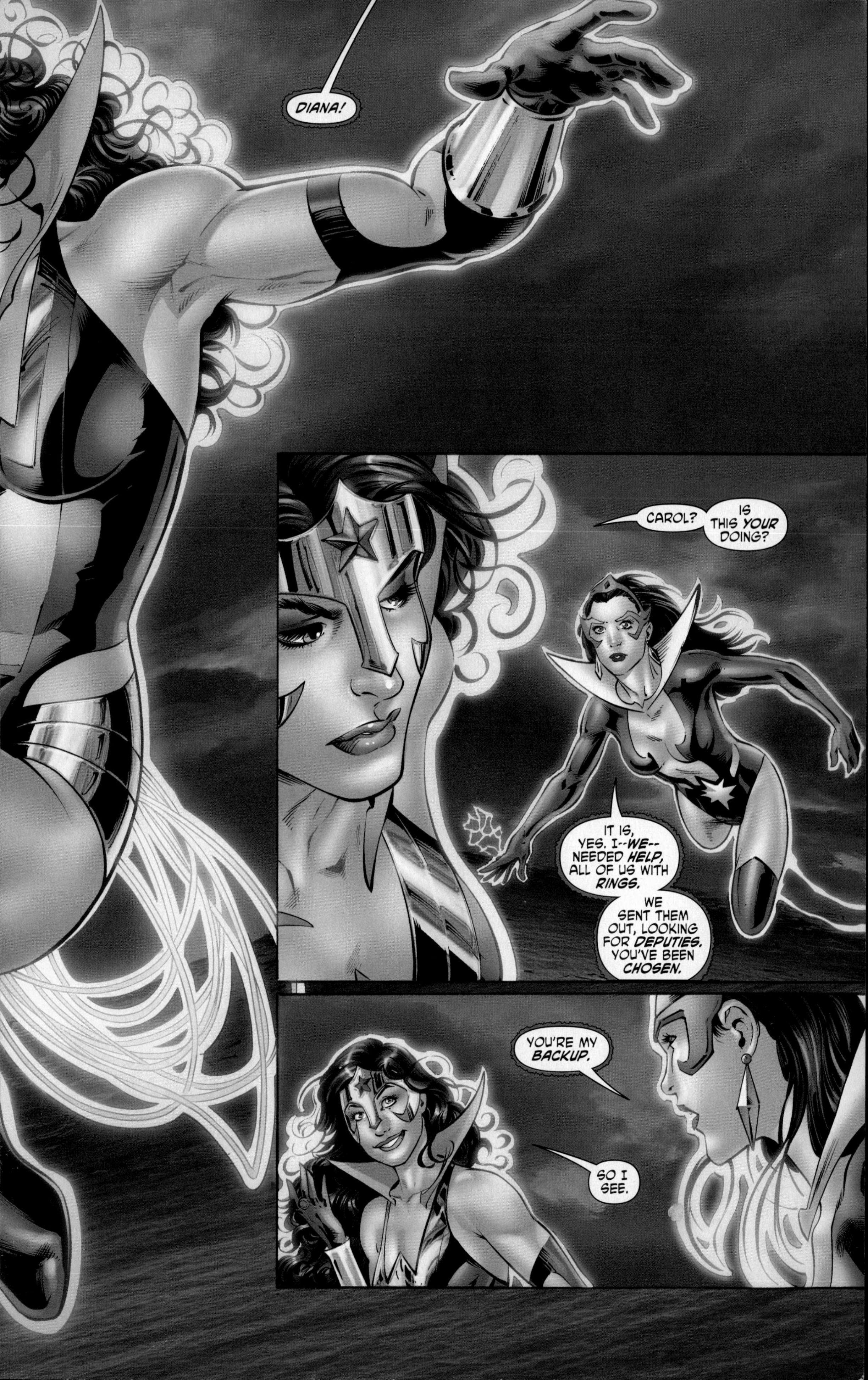
DIANA!
CAROL?
IS THIS YOUR DOING?
IT IS, YES. I--WE--NEEDED HELP, ALL OF US WITH RINGS.
WE SENT THEM OUT, LOOKING FOR DEPUTIES. YOU'VE BEEN CHOSEN.
YOU'RE MY BACKUP.
SO I SEE.

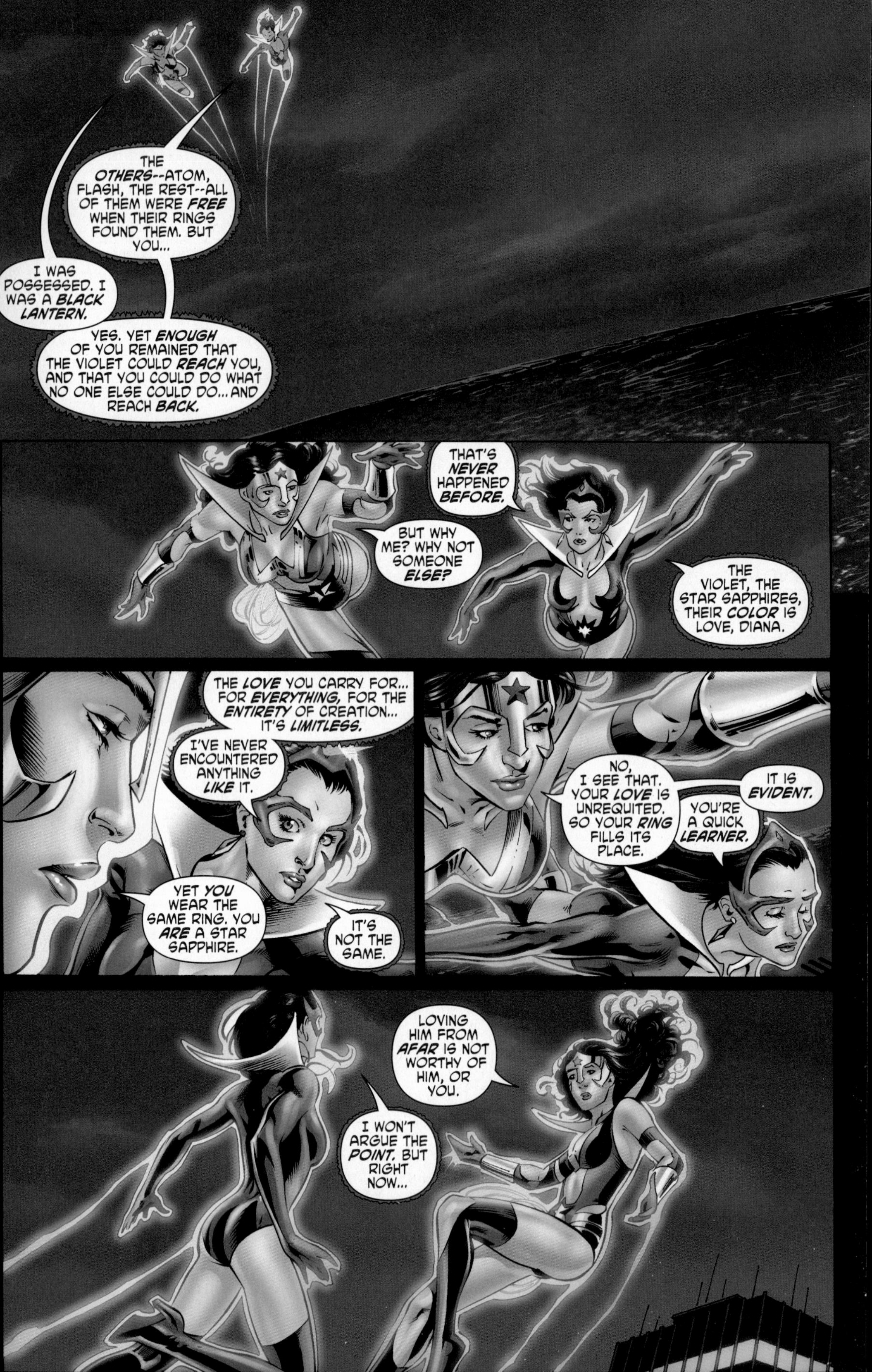
THE OTHERS--ATOM, FLASH, THE REST--ALL OF THEM WERE FREE WHEN THEIR RINGS FOUND THEM. BUT YOU...
I WAS POSSESSED. I WAS A BLACK LANTERN.
YES. YET ENOUGH OF YOU REMAINED THAT THE VIOLET COULD REACH YOU, AND THAT YOU COULD DO WHAT NO ONE ELSE COULD DO... AND REACH BACK.
THAT'S NEVER HAPPENED BEFORE.
BUT WHY ME? WHY NOT SOMEONE ELSE?
THE VIOLET, THE STAR SAPPHIRES, THEIR COLOR IS LOVE, DIANA.
THE LOVE YOU CARRY FOR... FOR EVERYTHING, FOR THE ENTIRETY OF CREATION... IT'S LIMITLESS.
I'VE NEVER ENCOUNTERED ANYTHING LIKE IT.
YET YOU WEAR THE SAME RING. YOU ARE A STAR SAPPHIRE.
IT'S NOT THE SAME.
NO, I SEE THAT. YOUR LOVE IS UNREQUITED. SO YOUR RING FILLS ITS PLACE.
IT IS EVIDENT.
YOU'RE A QUICK LEARNER.
LOVING HIM FROM AFAR IS NOT WORTHY OF HIM, OR YOU.
I WON'T ARGUE THE POINT. BUT RIGHT NOW...

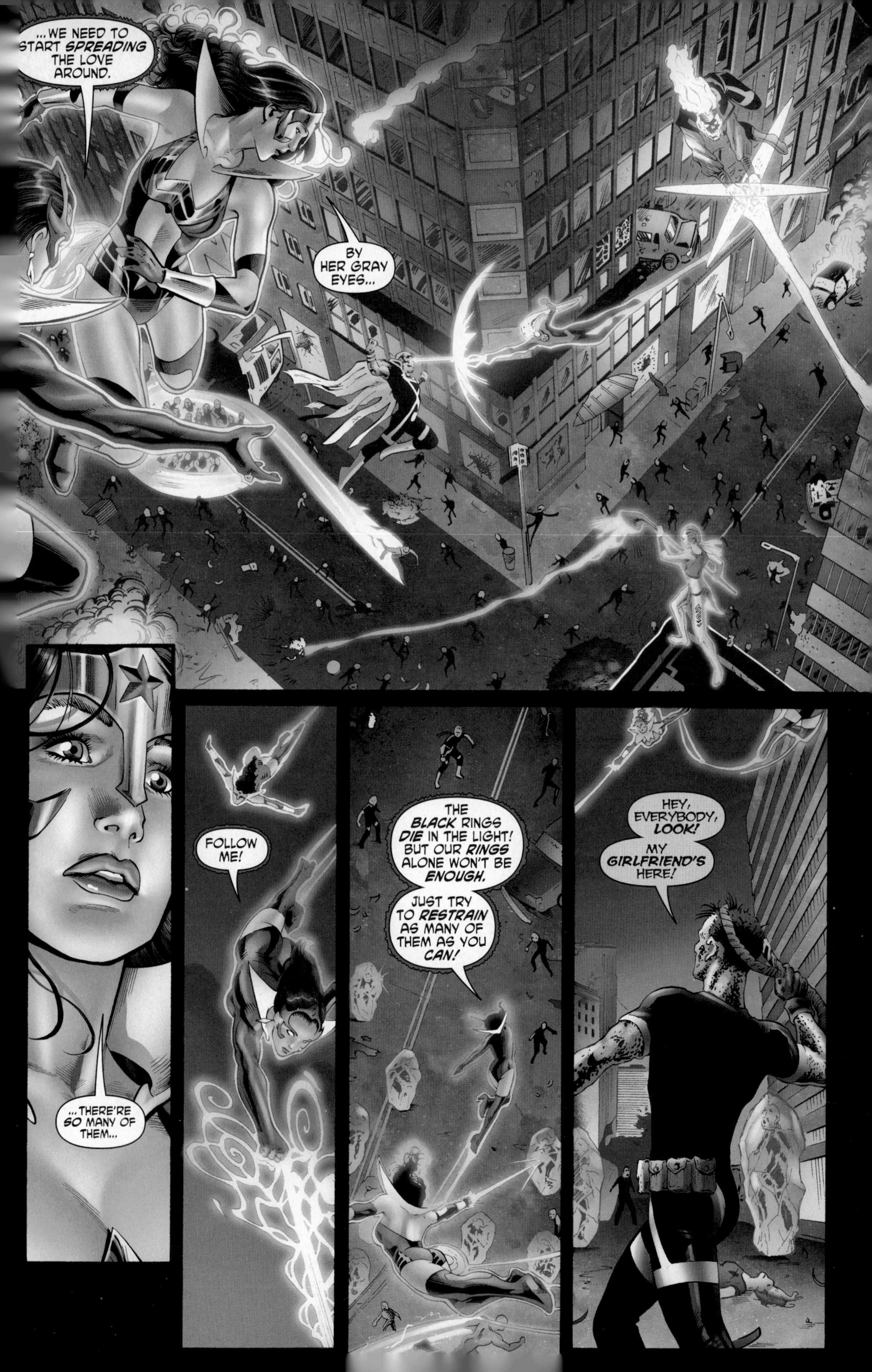
...WE NEED TO START SPREADING THE LOVE AROUND.
BY HER GRAY EYES...
...THERE'RE SO MANY OF THEM...
FOLLOW ME!
THE BLACK RINGS DIE IN THE LIGHT! BUT OUR RINGS ALONE WON'T BE ENOUGH.
JUST TRY TO RESTRAIN AS MANY OF THEM AS YOU CAN!
HEY, EVERYBODY, LOOK!
MY GIRLFRIEND'S HERE!

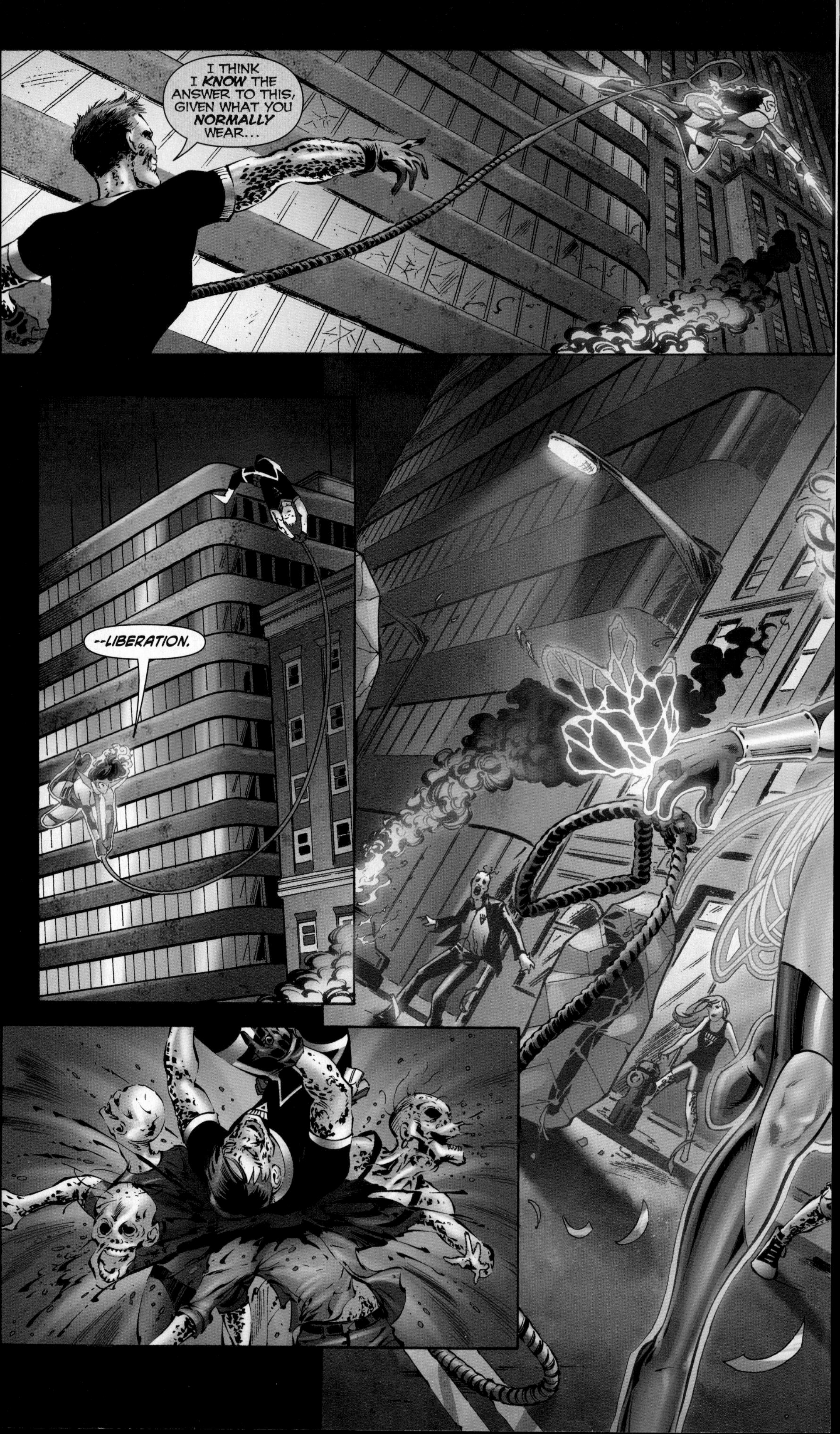
I THINK I KNOW THE ANSWER TO THIS, GIVEN WHAT YOU NORMALLY WEAR...
--LIBERATION.

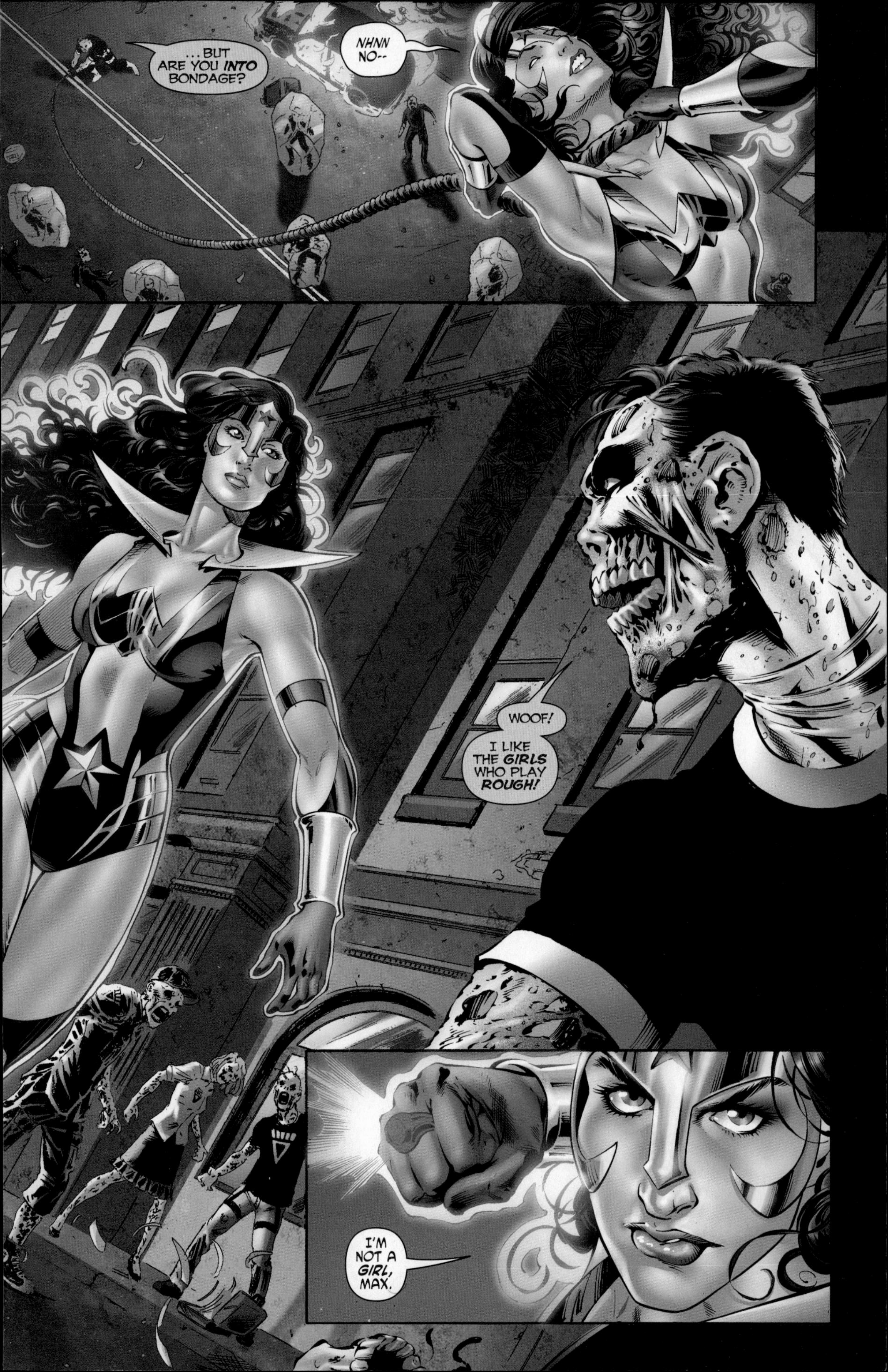

...BUT ARE YOU *INTO* BONDAGE?
NHNN NO--
WOOF! I LIKE THE *GIRLS* WHO PLAY *ROUGH!*
I'M NOT A *GIRL*, MAX.

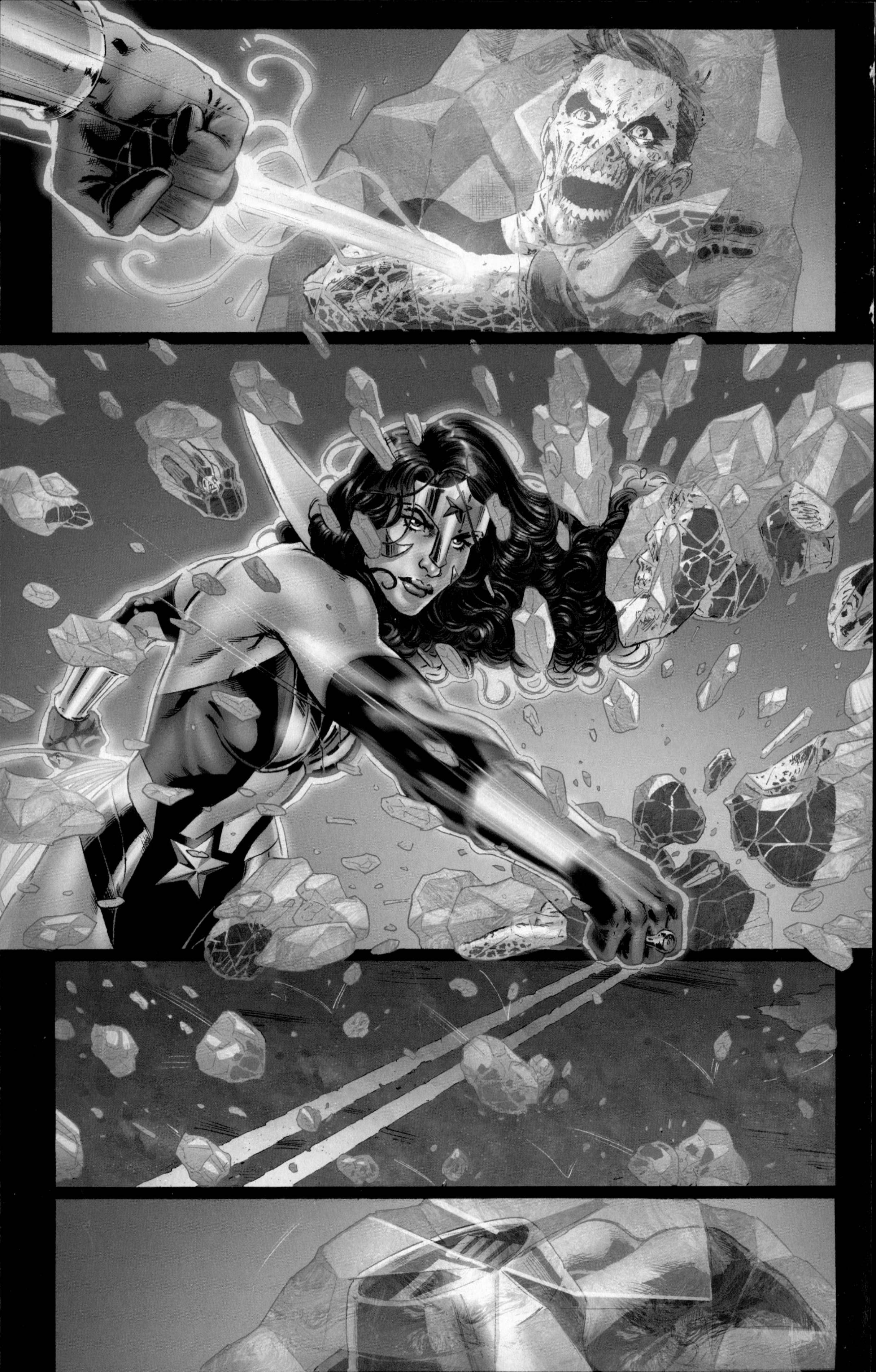

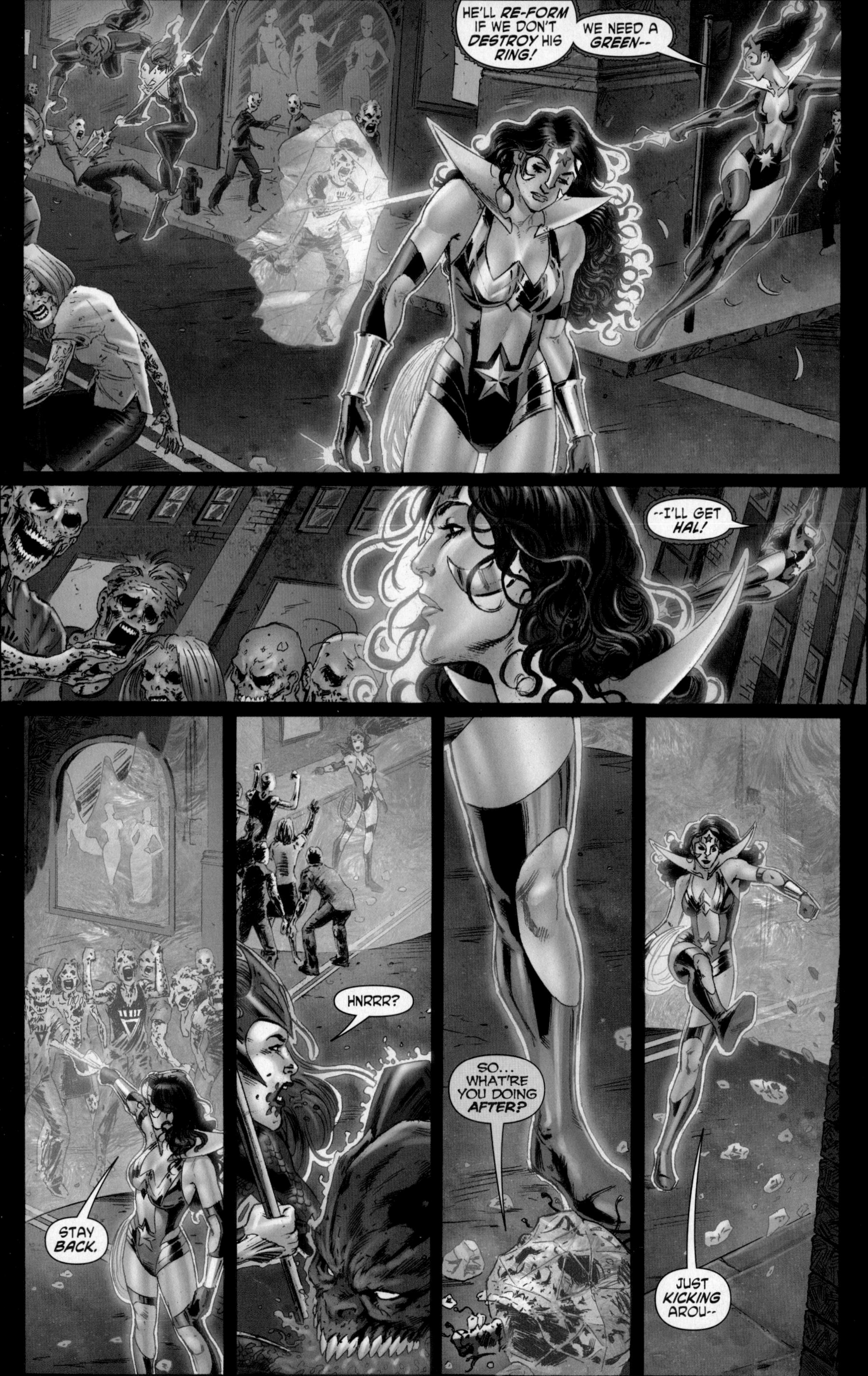
HE'LL RE-FORM IF WE DON'T DESTROY HIS RING!
WE NEED A GREEN--
--I'LL GET HAL!
STAY BACK.
HNRRR?
SO... WHAT'RE YOU DOING AFTER?
JUST KICKING AROU--

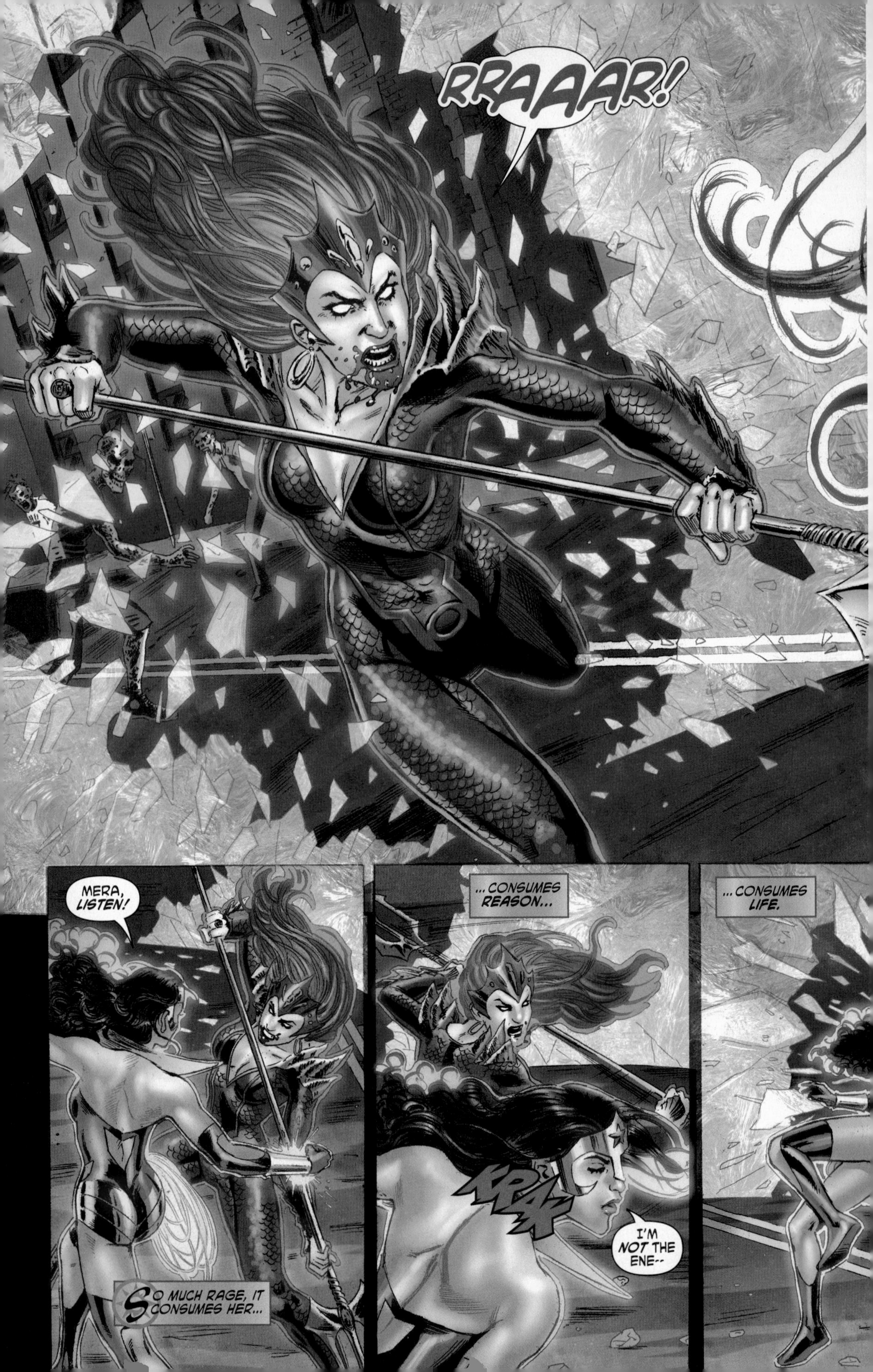
RRAAAR!
MERA, LISTEN!
SO MUCH RAGE, IT CONSUMES HER...
...CONSUMES REASON...
KRAK
I'M NOT THE ENE--
...CONSUMES LIFE.

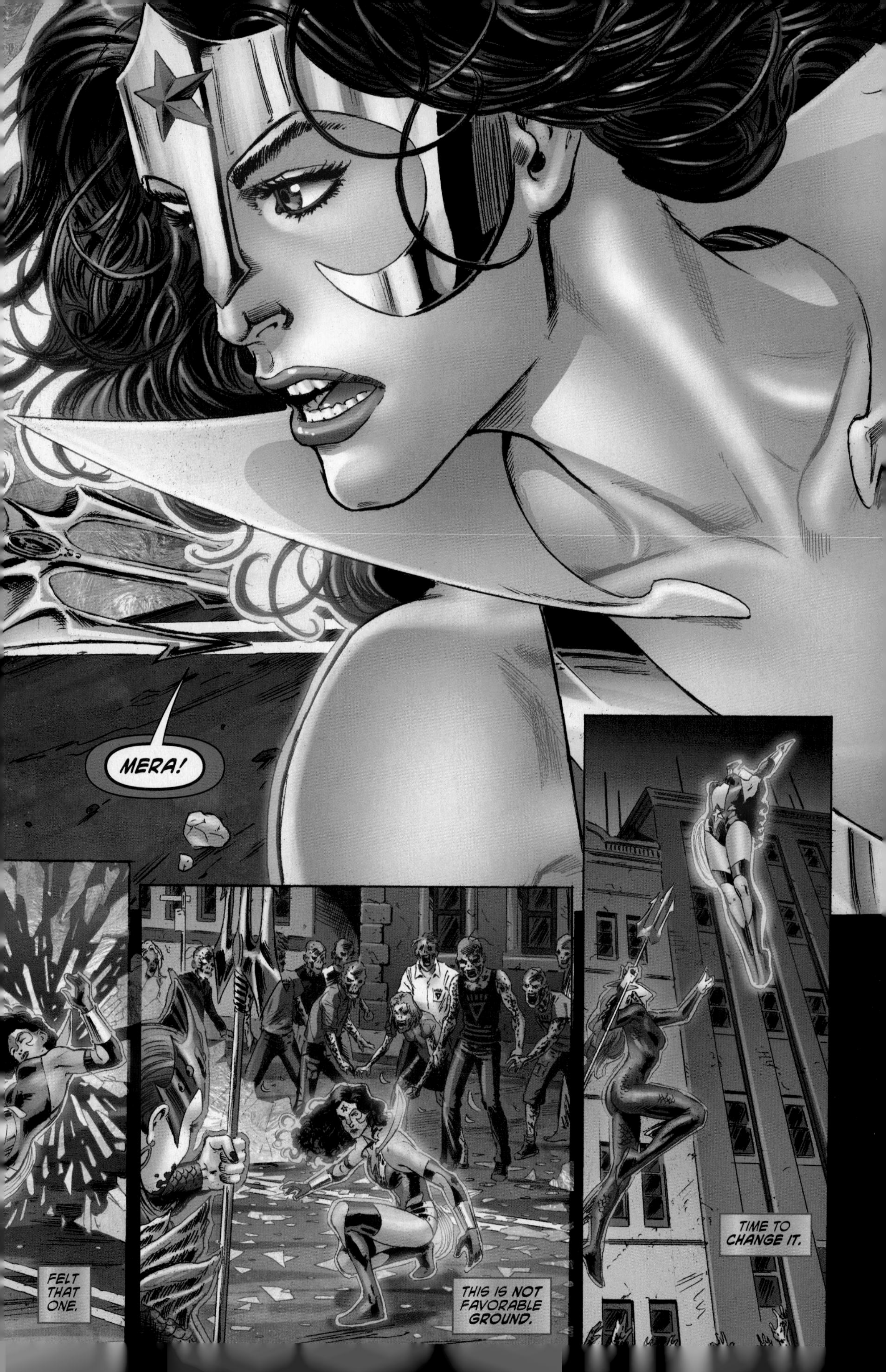
MERA!
FELT THAT ONE.
THIS IS NOT FAVORABLE GROUND.
TIME TO CHANGE IT.

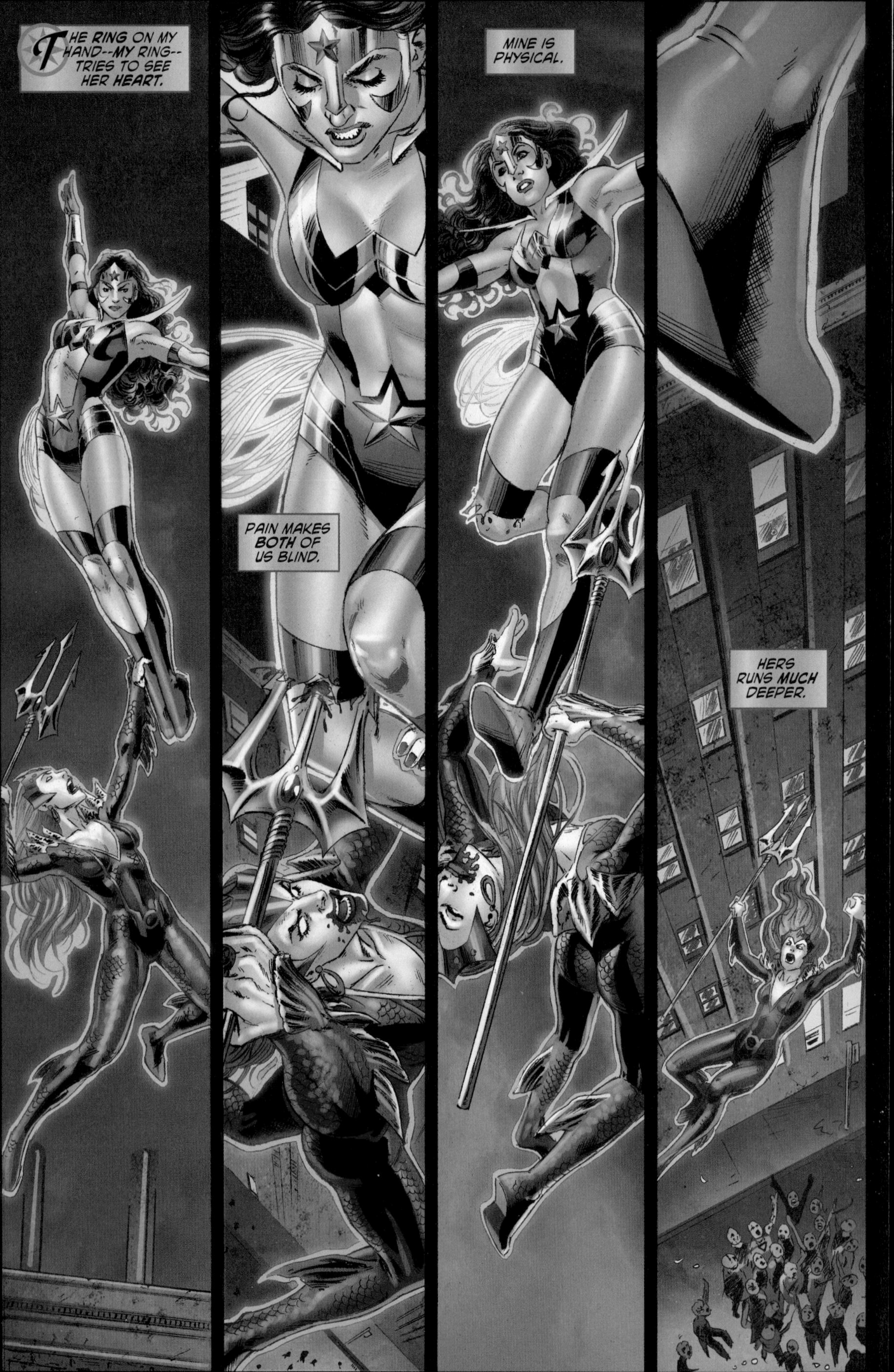
THE RING ON MY HAND--MY RING--TRIES TO SEE HER HEART.
PAIN MAKES BOTH OF US BLIND.
MINE IS PHYSICAL.
HERS RUNS MUCH DEEPER.

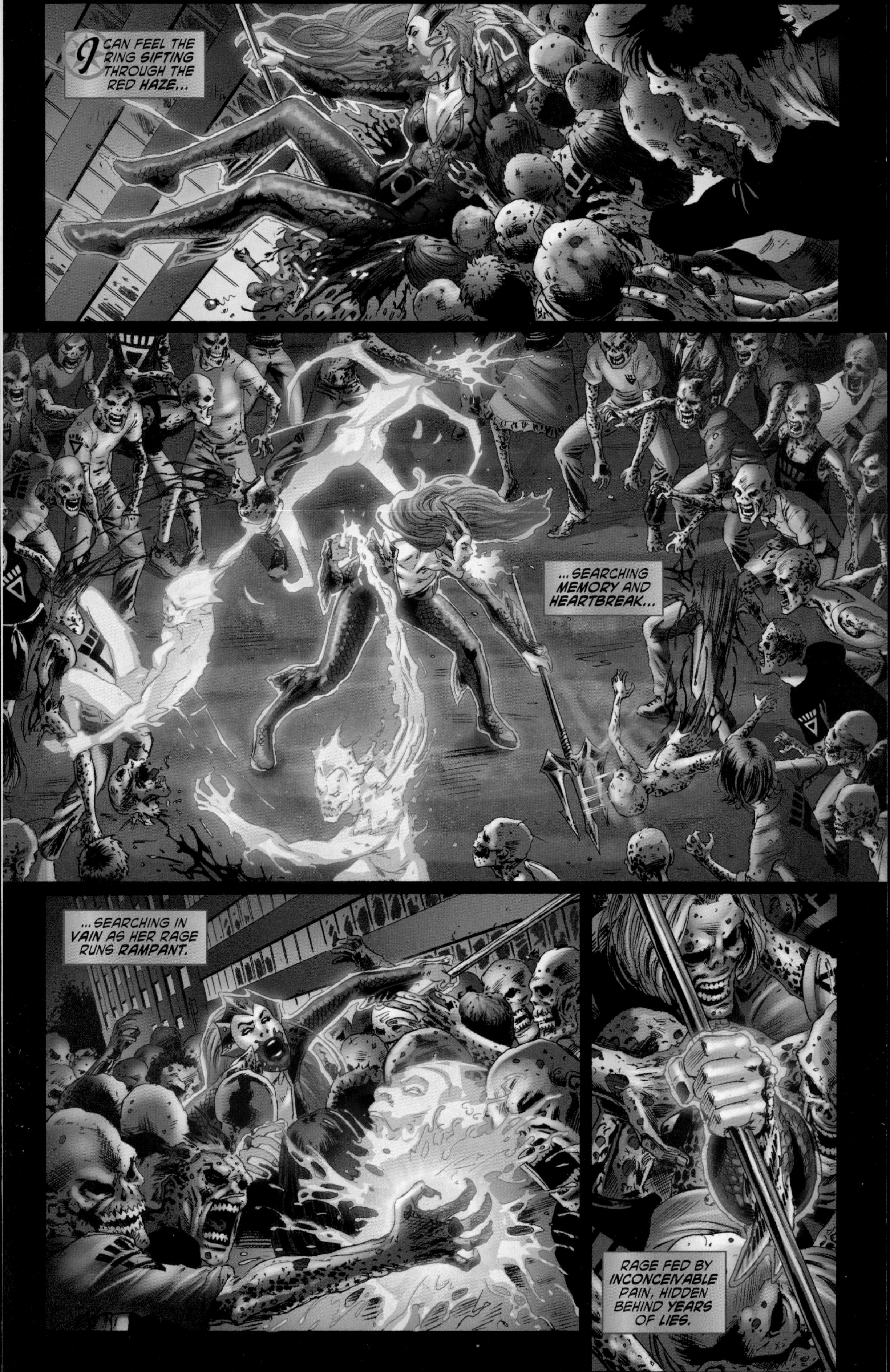
I CAN FEEL THE RING SIFTING THROUGH THE RED HAZE...
...SEARCHING MEMORY AND HEARTBREAK...
...SEARCHING IN VAIN AS HER RAGE RUNS RAMPANT.
RAGE FED BY INCONCEIVABLE PAIN, HIDDEN BEHIND YEARS OF LIES.

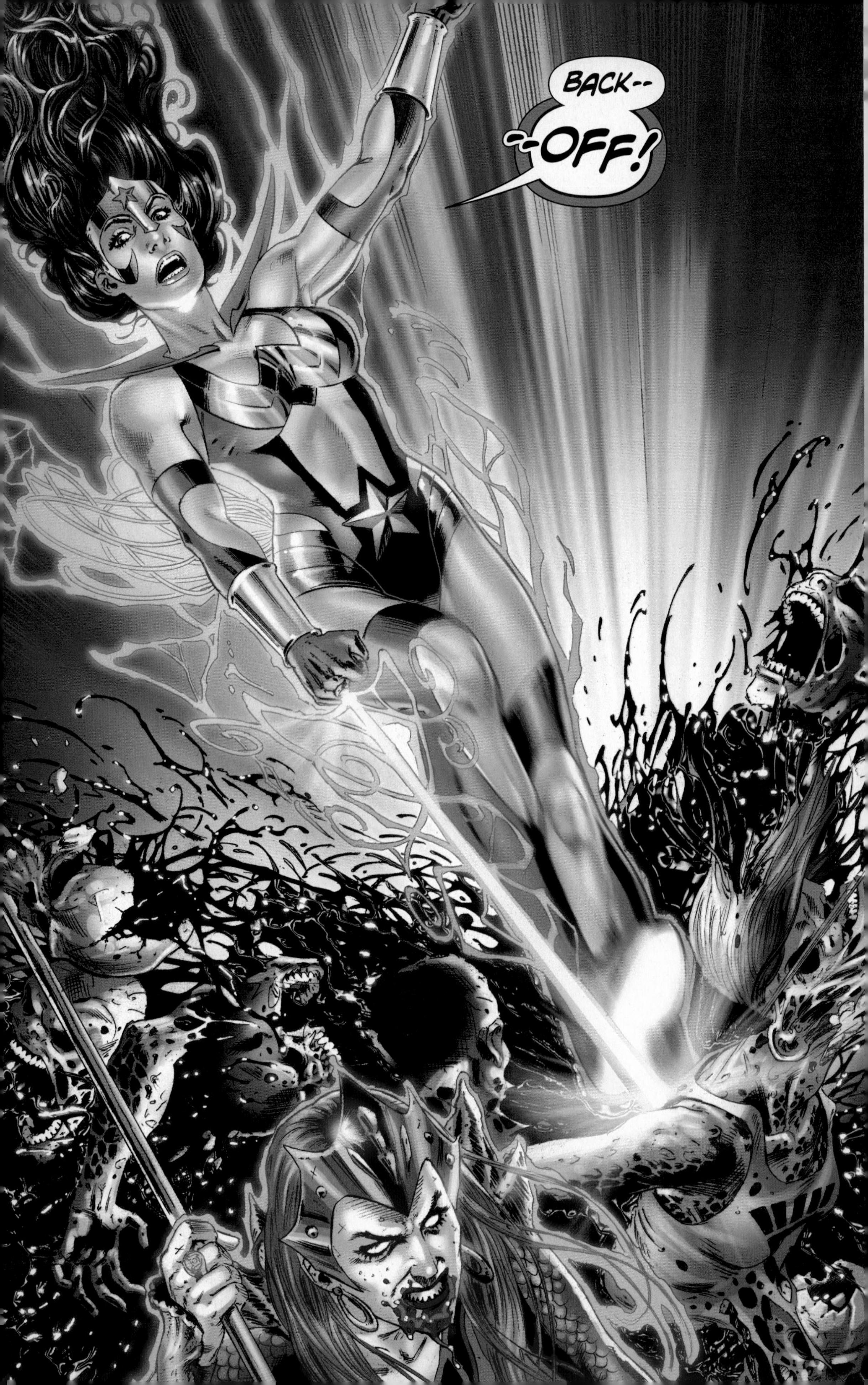
BACK--
--OFF!

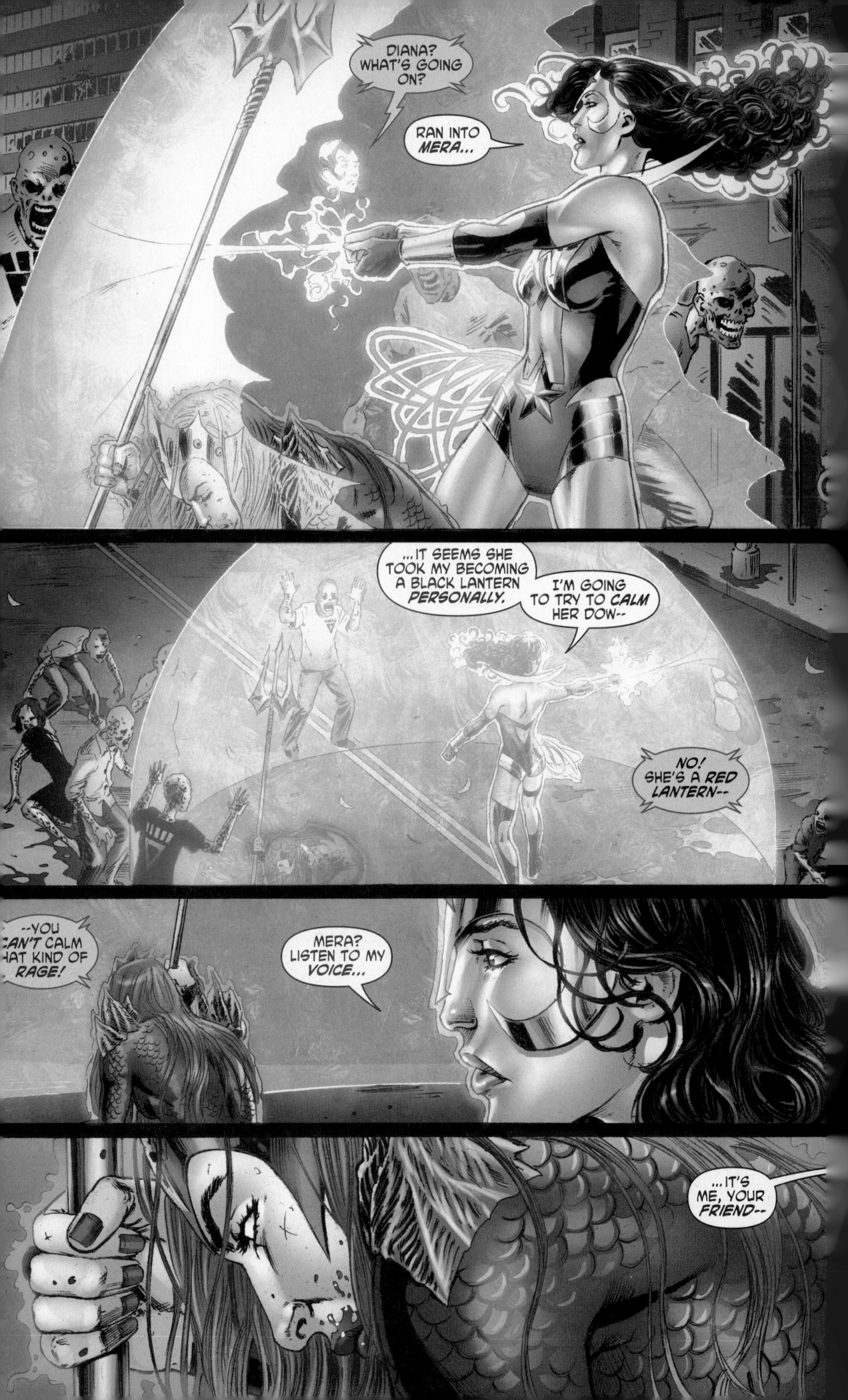
DIANA? WHAT'S GOING ON?
RAN INTO MERA...
...IT SEEMS SHE TOOK MY BECOMING A BLACK LANTERN PERSONALLY.
I'M GOING TO TRY TO CALM HER DOW--
NO! SHE'S A RED LANTERN--
--YOU CAN'T CALM HAT KIND OF RAGE!
MERA? LISTEN TO MY VOICE...
...IT'S ME, YOUR FRIEND--

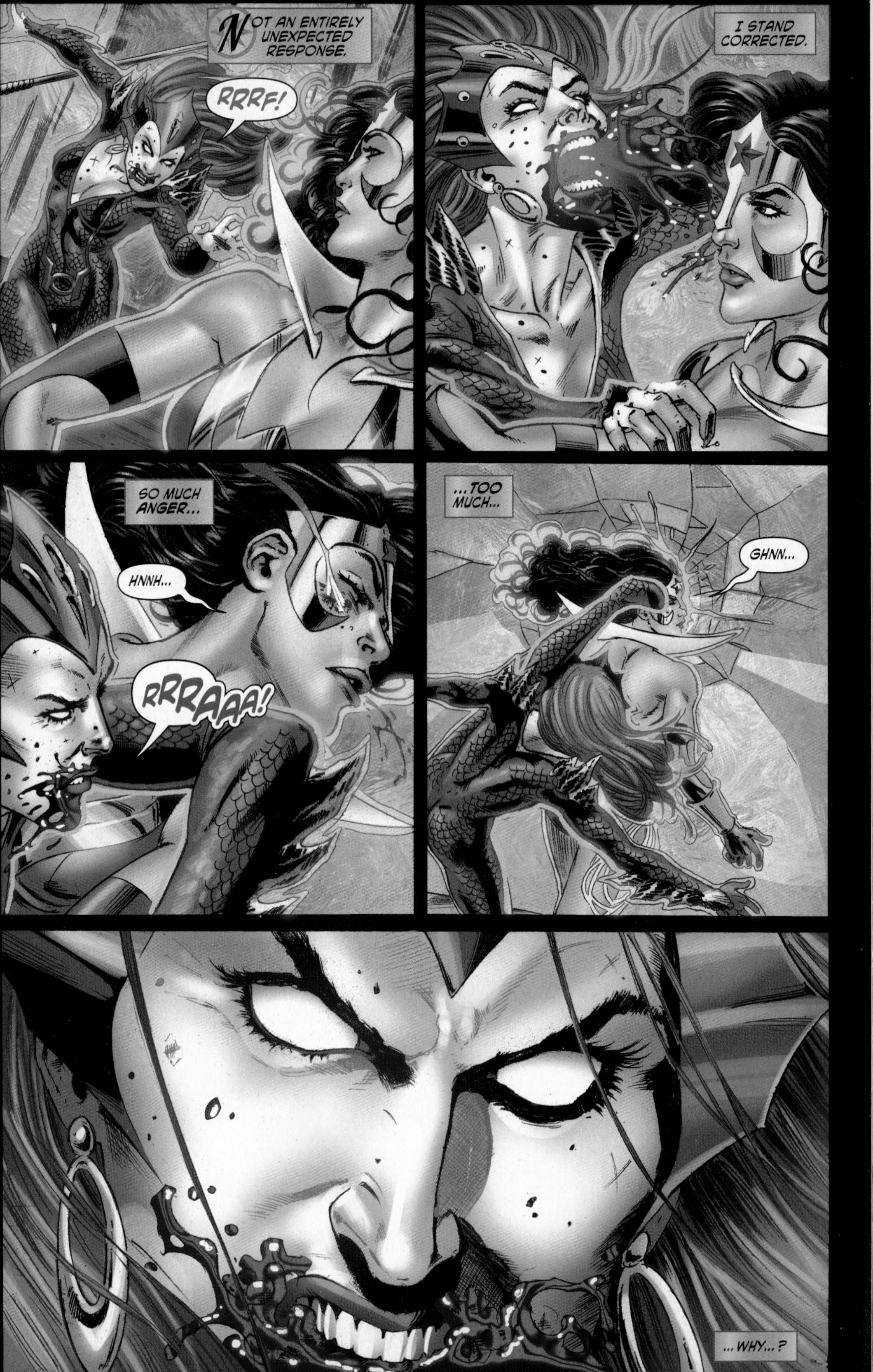
NOT AN ENTIRELY UNEXPECTED RESPONSE.
RRRF!
I STAND CORRECTED.
SO MUCH ANGER...
HNNH...
RRRAAA!
...TOO MUCH...
GHNN...
...WHY...?

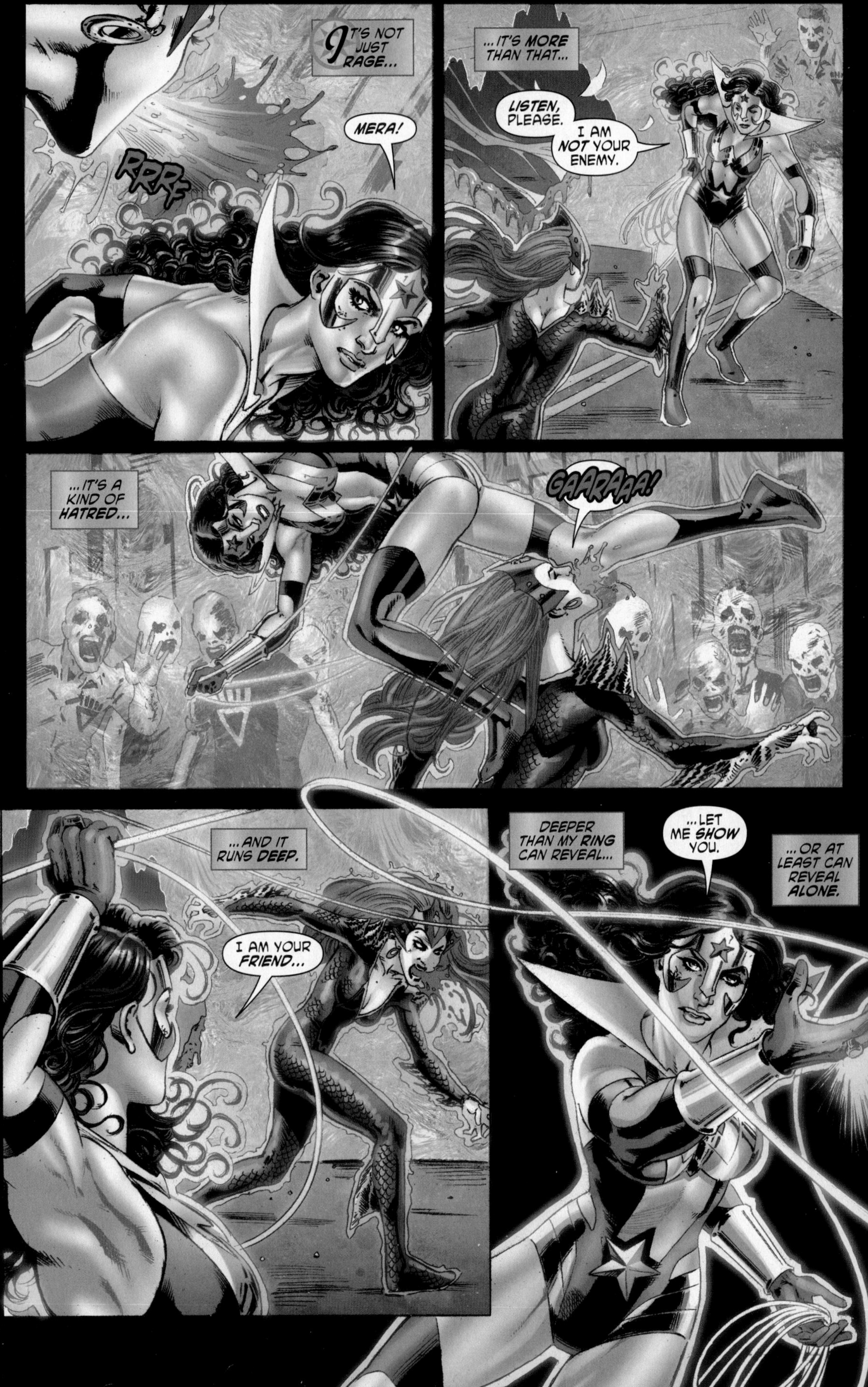
IT'S NOT JUST RAGE...
MERA!
RRRF
...IT'S MORE THAN THAT...
LISTEN, PLEASE.
I AM NOT YOUR ENEMY.
...IT'S A KIND OF HATRED...
GAARAAA!
...AND IT RUNS DEEP.
I AM YOUR FRIEND...
DEEPER THAN MY RING CAN REVEAL...
...LET ME SHOW YOU.
...OR AT LEAST CAN REVEAL ALONE.

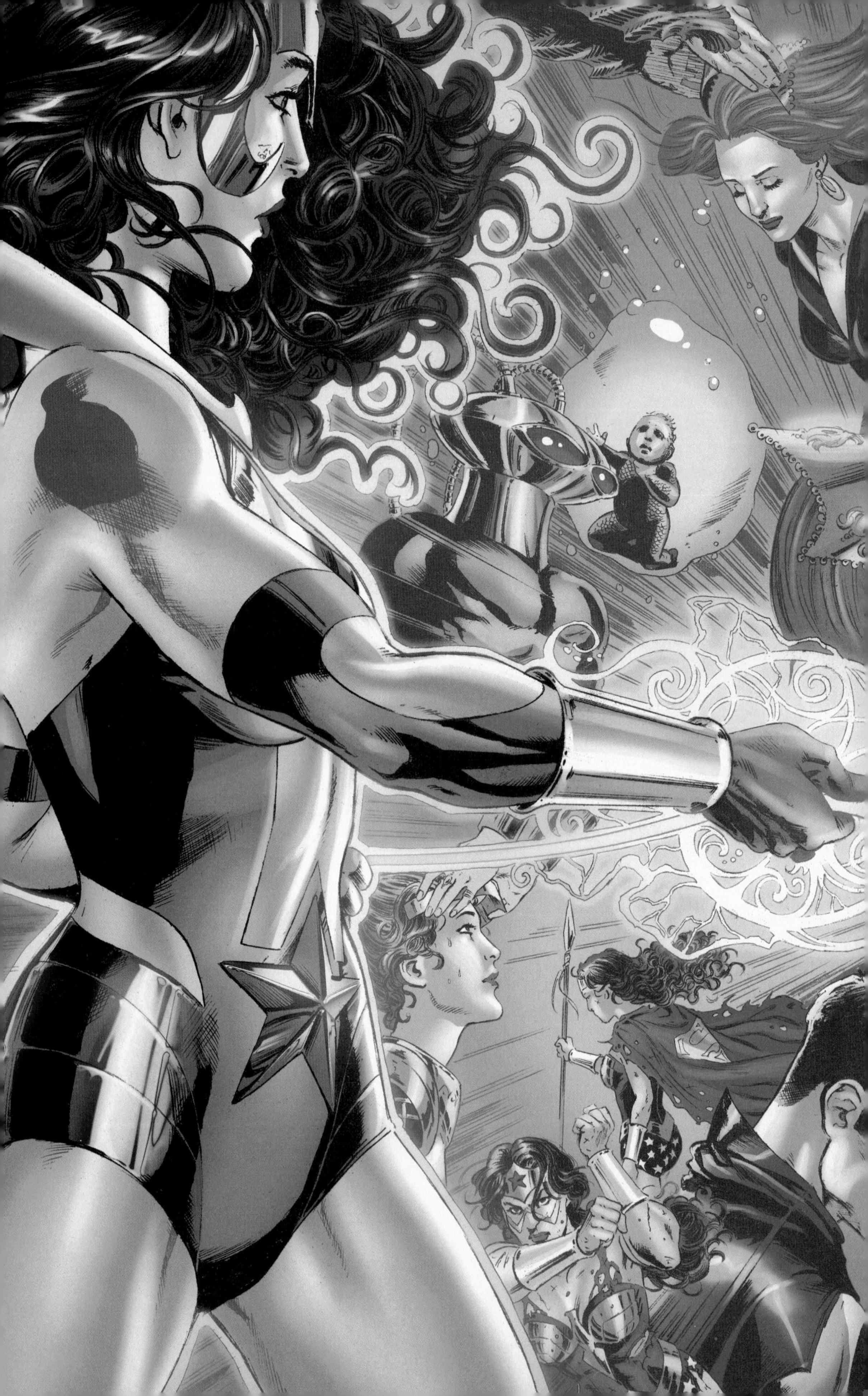

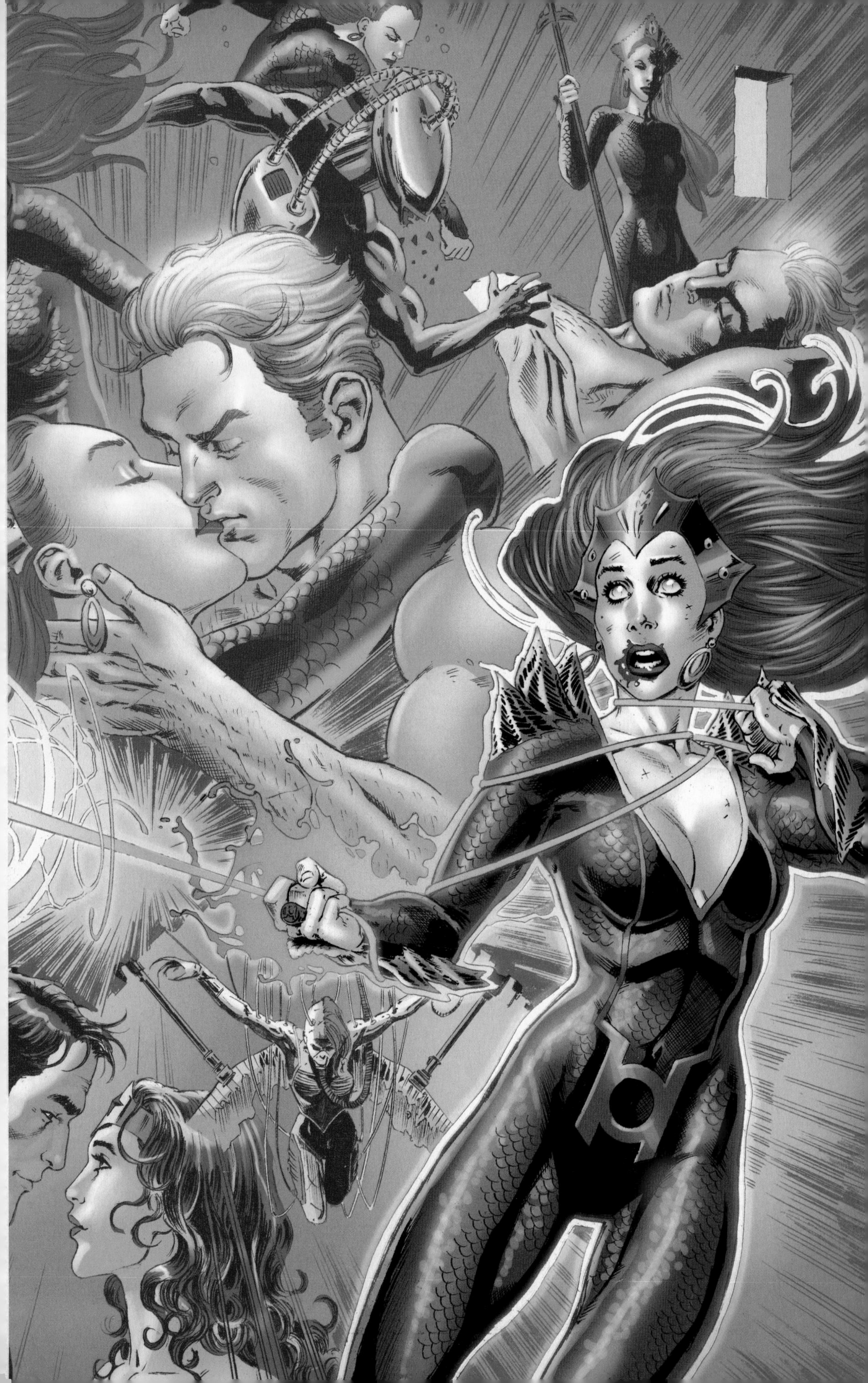

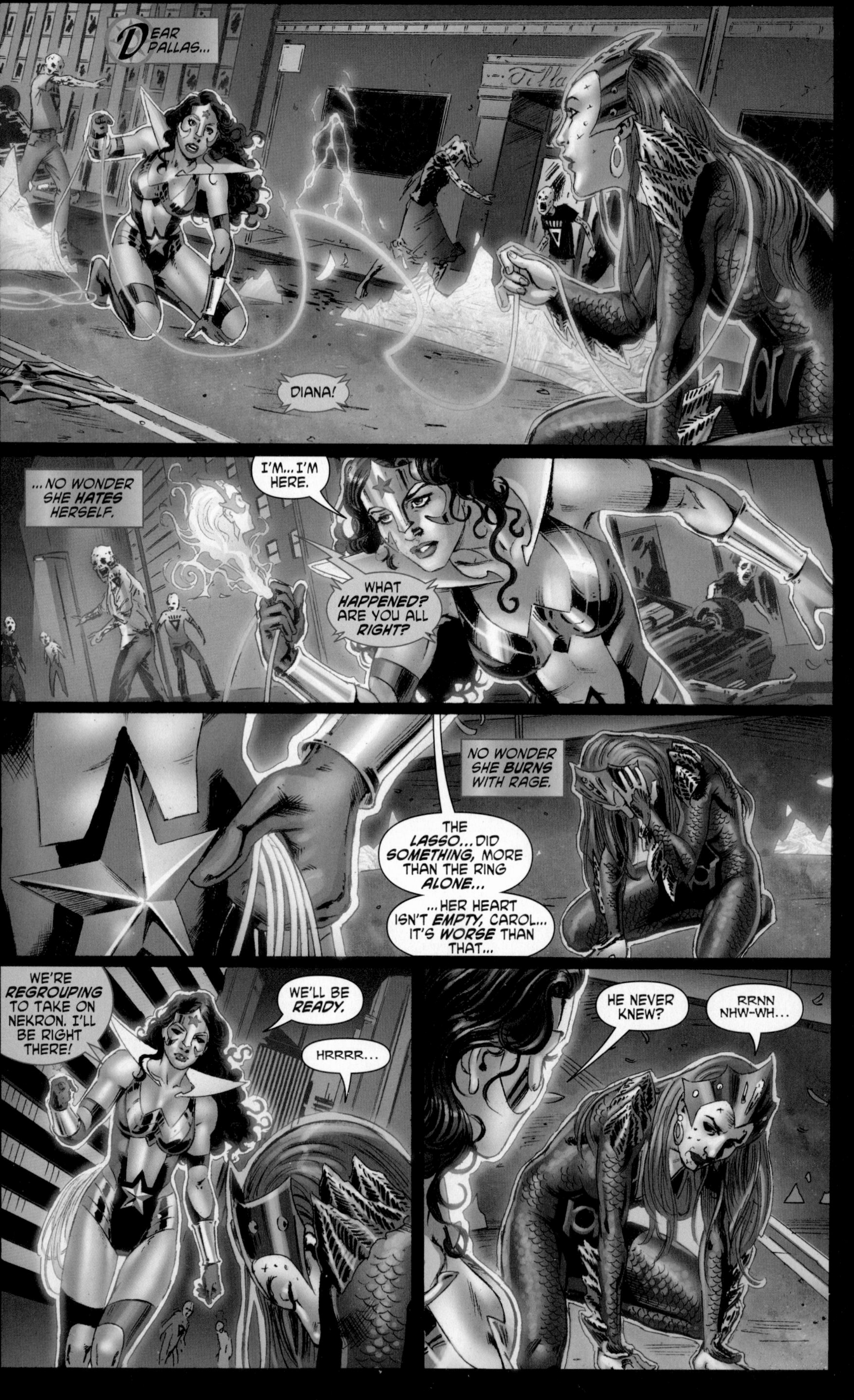
DEAR PALLAS...
DIANA!
...NO WONDER SHE HATES HERSELF.
I'M... I'M HERE.
WHAT HAPPENED? ARE YOU ALL RIGHT?
NO WONDER SHE BURNS WITH RAGE.
THE LASSO... DID SOMETHING, MORE THAN THE RING ALONE...
...HER HEART ISN'T EMPTY, CAROL... IT'S WORSE THAN THAT...
WE'RE REGROUPING TO TAKE ON NEKRON. I'LL BE RIGHT THERE!
WE'LL BE READY.
HRRRR...
HE NEVER KNEW?
RRNN NHW-WH...

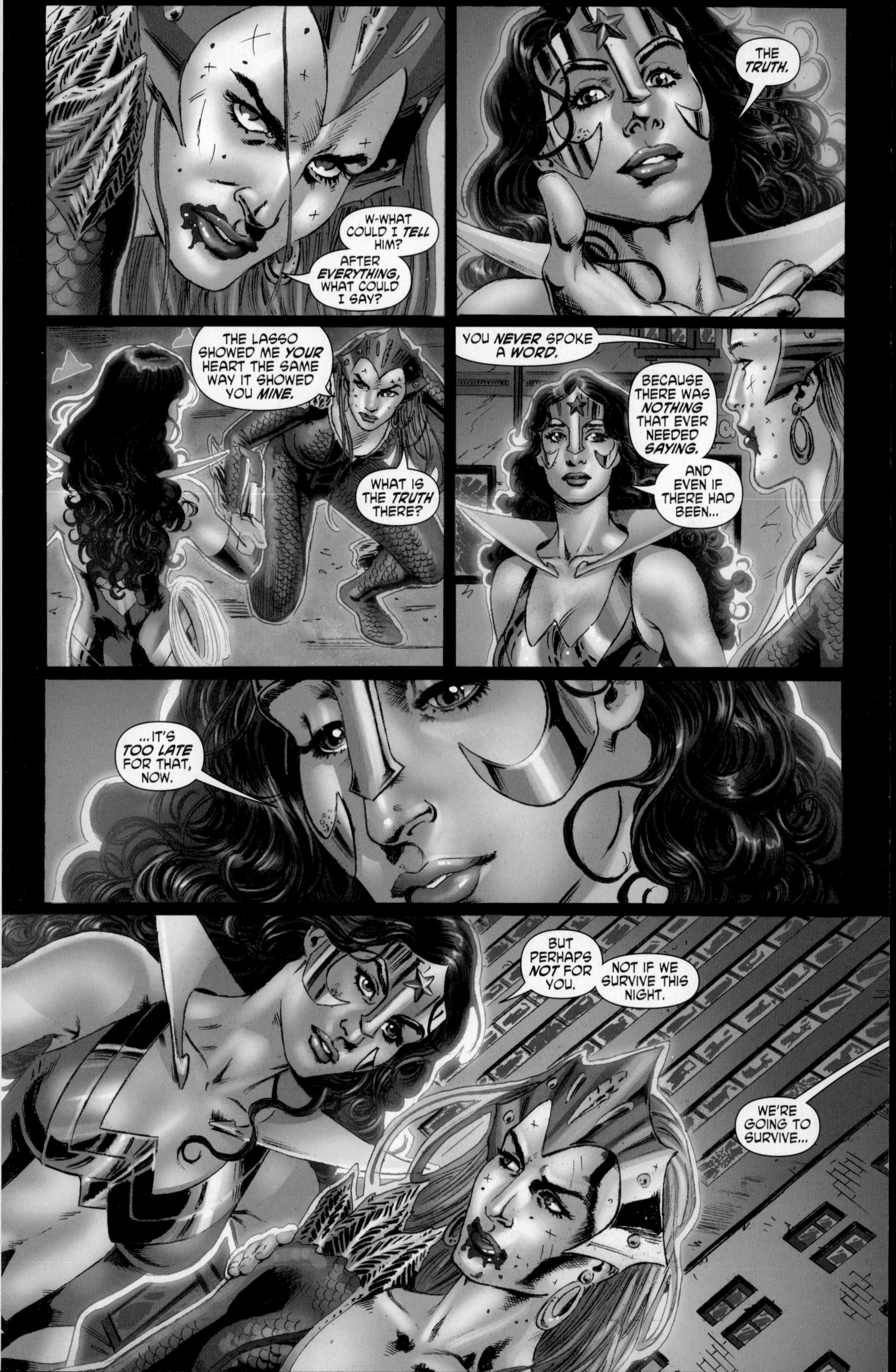
W-WHAT COULD I TELL HIM?
AFTER EVERYTHING, WHAT COULD I SAY?
THE TRUTH.
THE LASSO SHOWED ME YOUR HEART THE SAME WAY IT SHOWED YOU MINE.
WHAT IS THE TRUTH THERE?
YOU NEVER SPOKE A WORD.
BECAUSE THERE WAS NOTHING THAT EVER NEEDED SAYING.
AND EVEN IF THERE HAD BEEN...
...IT'S TOO LATE FOR THAT, NOW.
BUT PERHAPS NOT FOR YOU.
NOT IF WE SURVIVE THIS NIGHT.
WE'RE GOING TO SURVIVE...

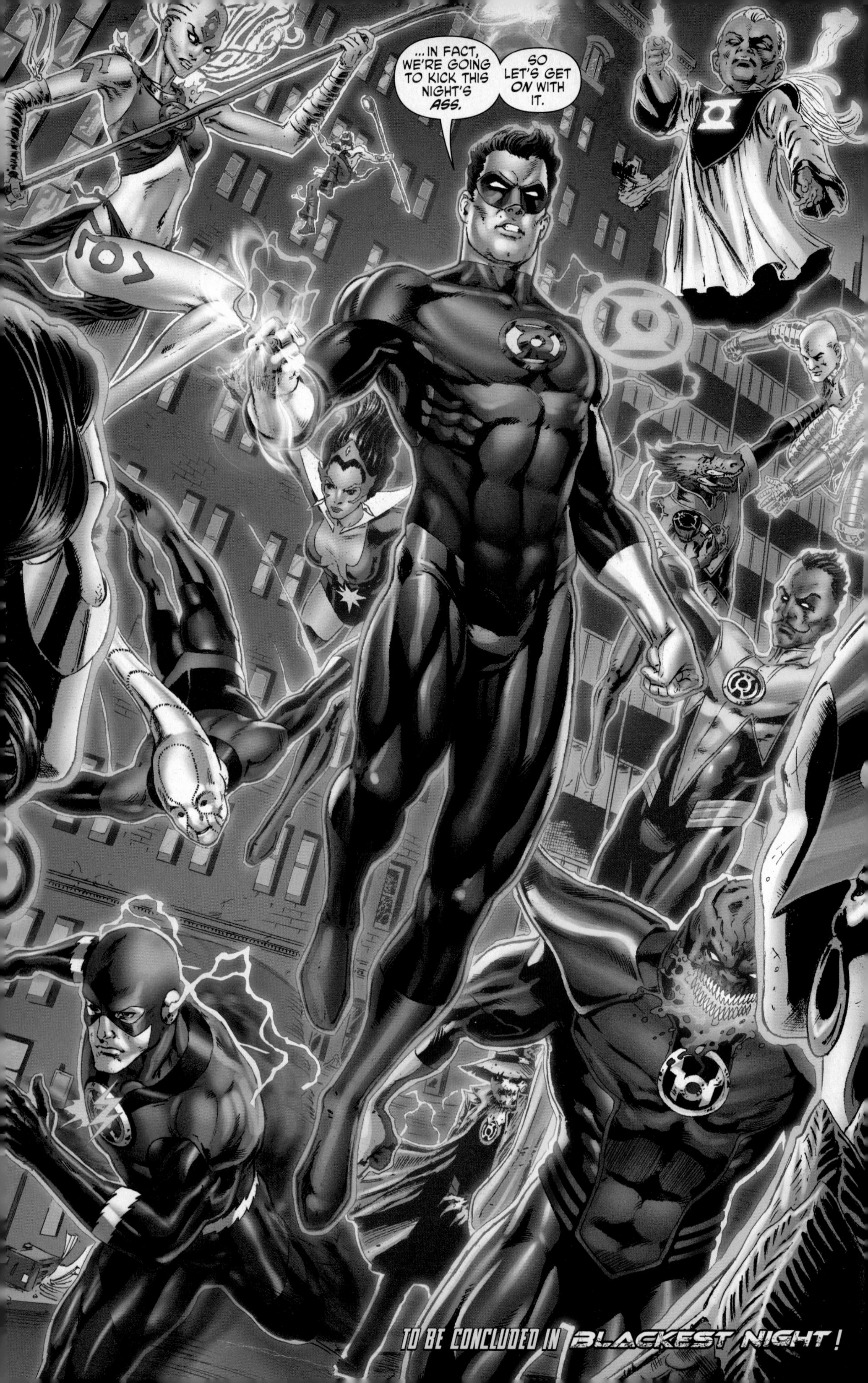
...IN FACT, WE'RE GOING TO KICK THIS NIGHT'S ASS.
SO LET'S GET ON WITH IT.
TO BE CONCLUDED IN BLACKEST NIGHT!

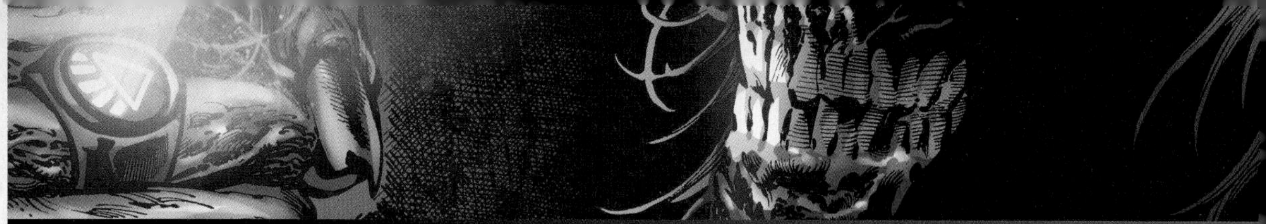

BLACKEST NIGHT
BLACK LANTERN CORPS
VOLUME TWO
VARIANT COVER GALLERY

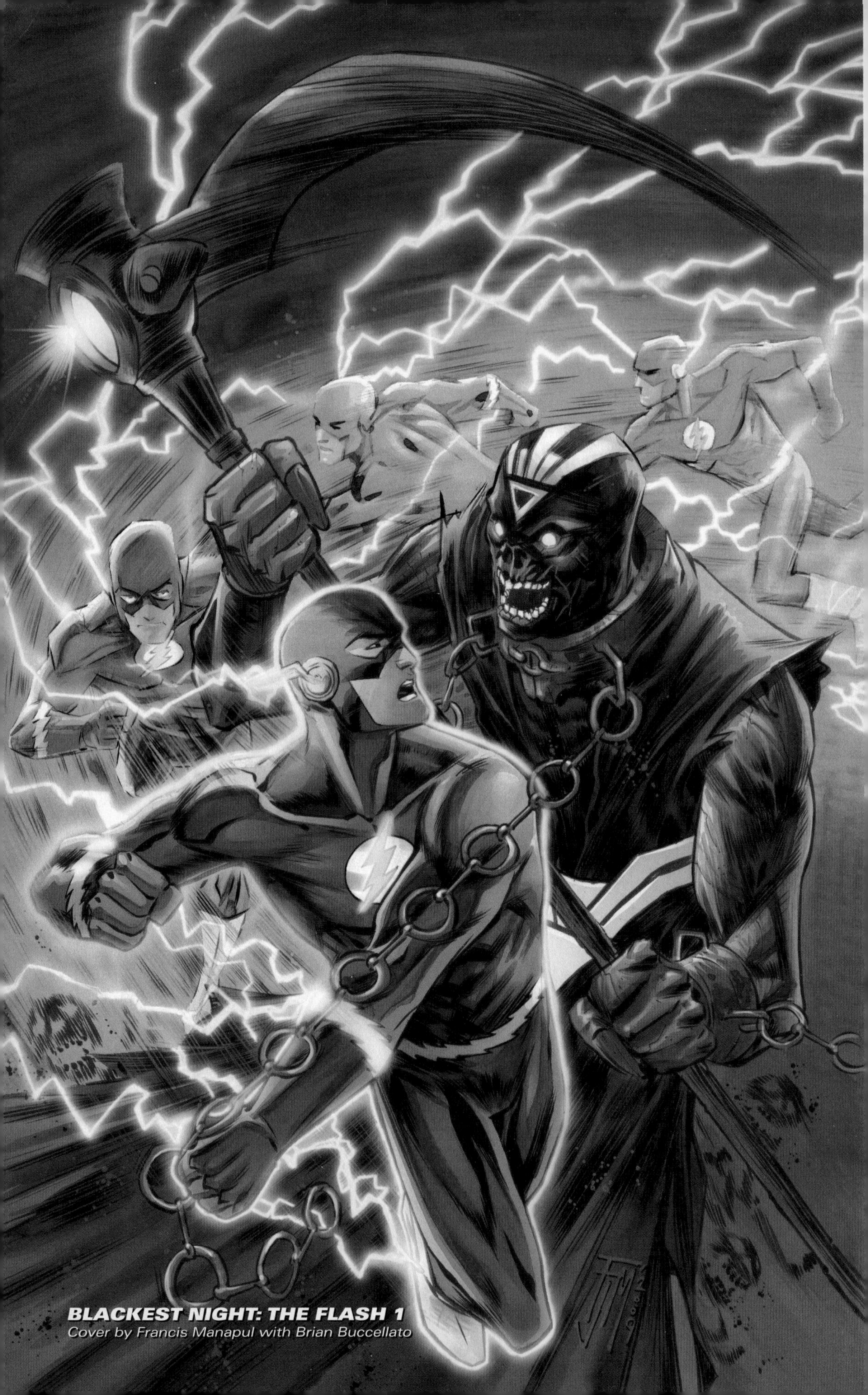

BLACKEST NIGHT: THE FLASH 1
Cover by Francis Manapul with Brian Buccellato

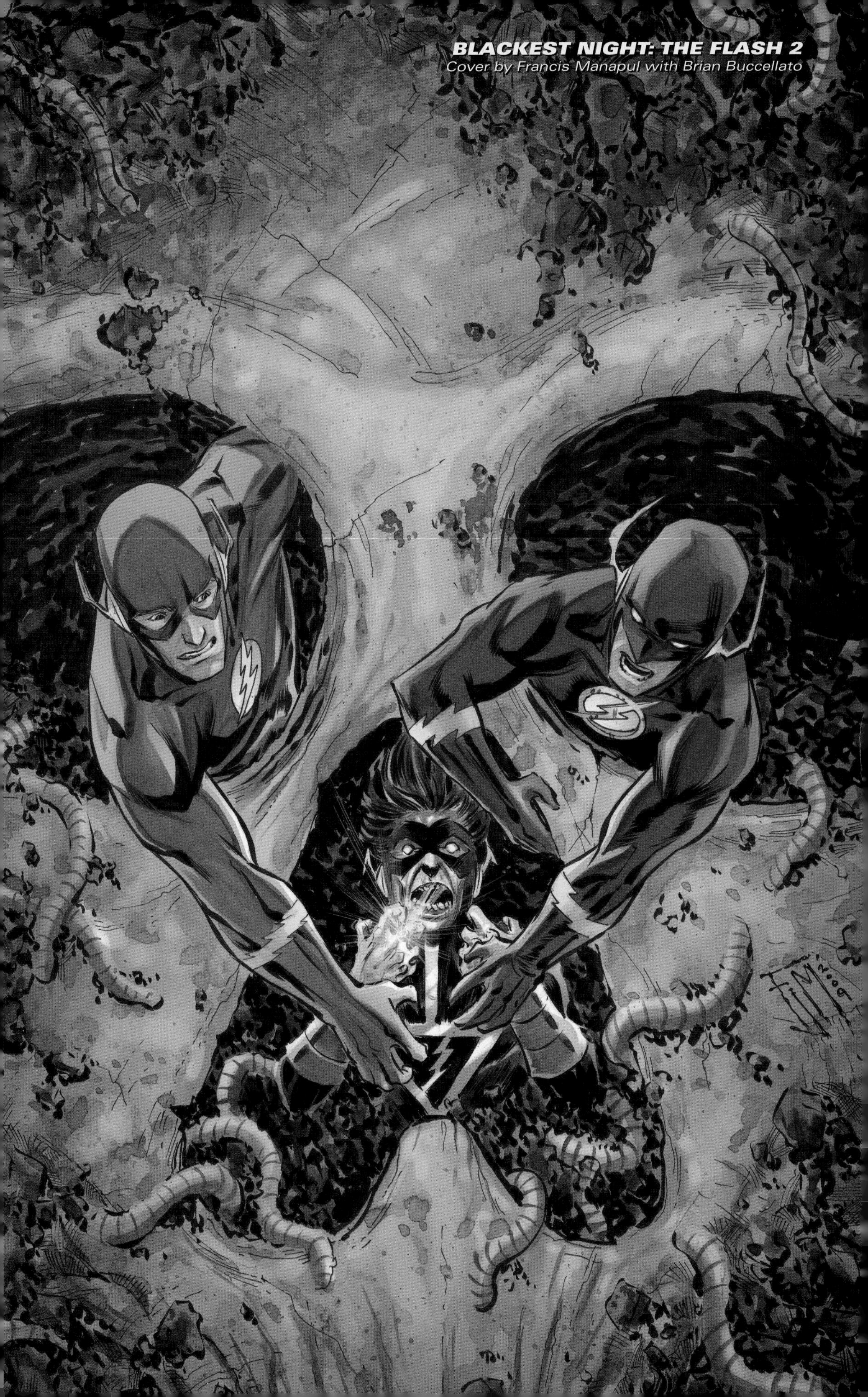

BLACKEST NIGHT: THE FLASH 2
Cover by Francis Manapul with Brian Buccellato

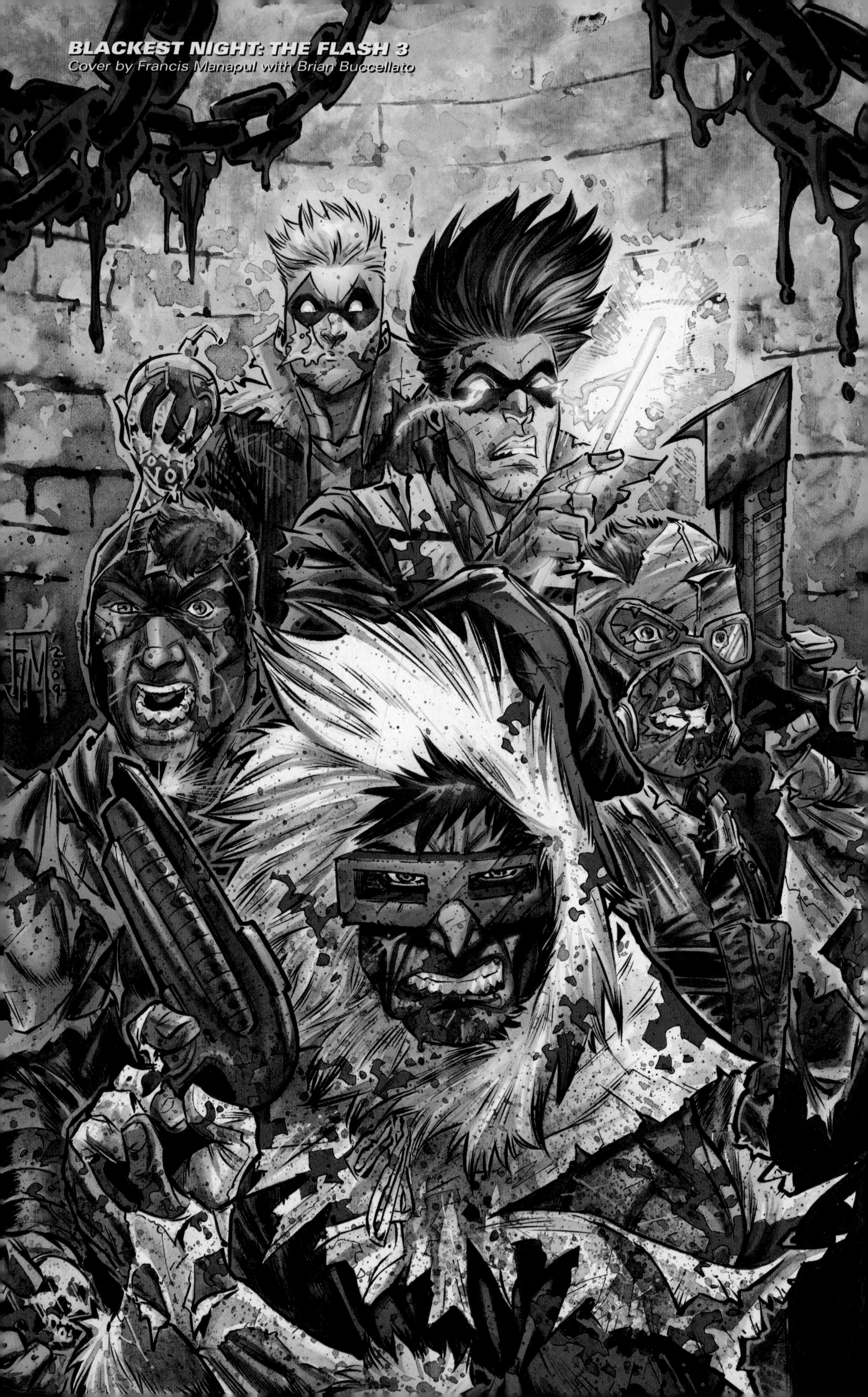

BLACKEST NIGHT: THE FLASH 3
Cover by Francis Manapul with Brian Buccellato

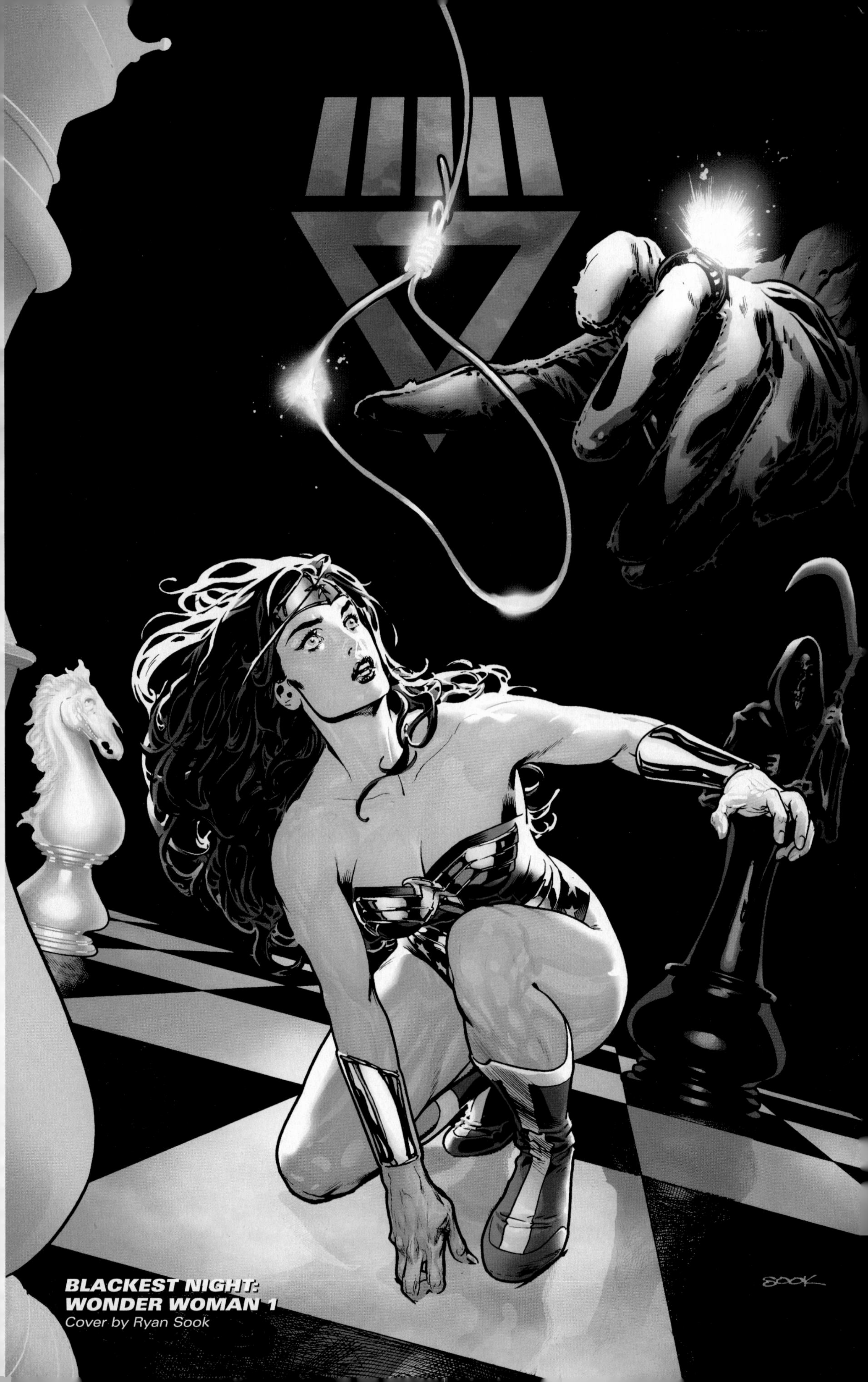
SOOK

**BLACKEST NIGHT:
WONDER WOMAN 1**
Cover by Ryan Sook

BLACKEST NIGHT:
WONDER WOMAN 2
Cover by Ryan Sook

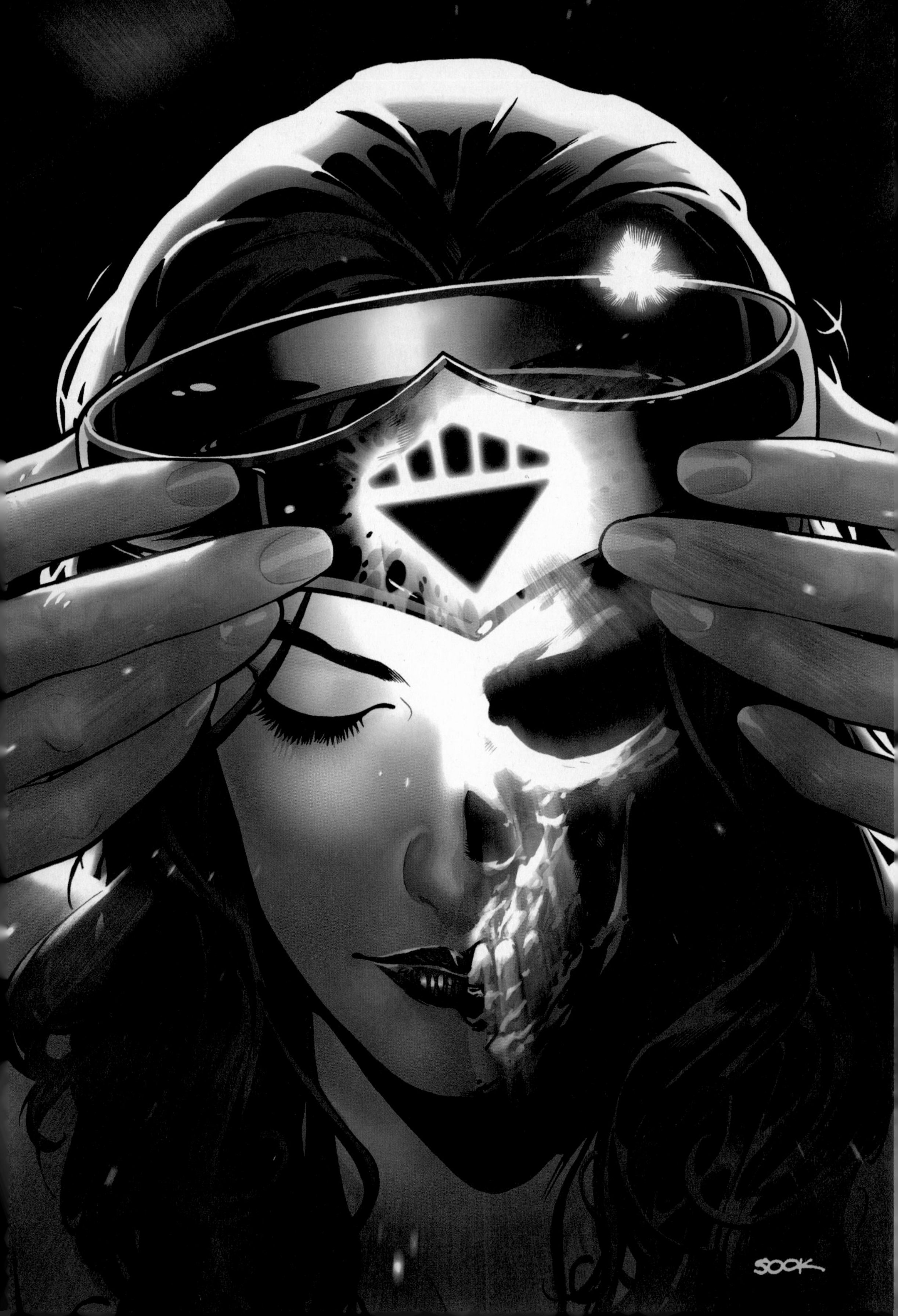
SOOK

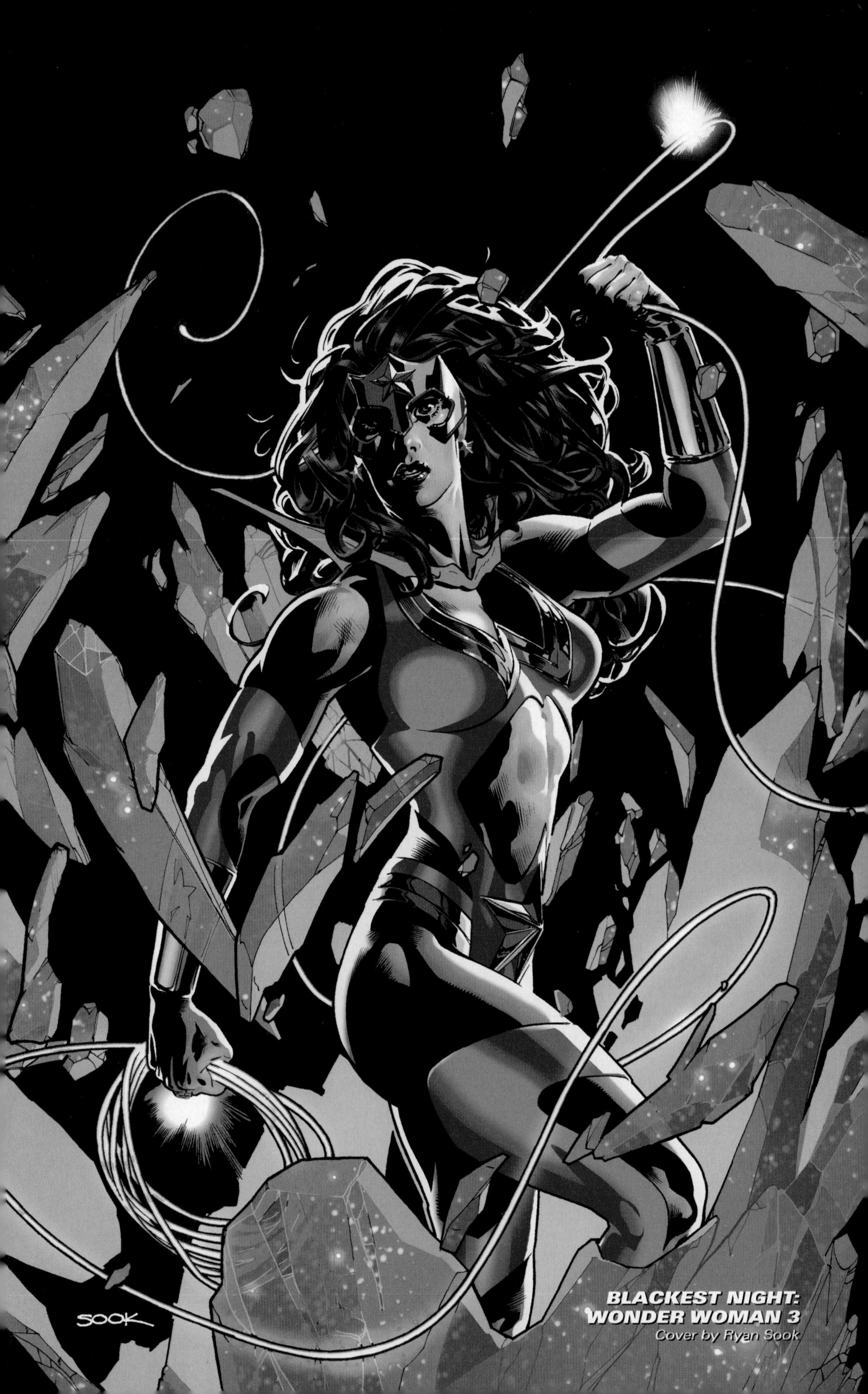
SOOK

BLACKEST NIGHT: WONDER WOMAN 3
Cover by Ryan Sook

BLACKEST NIGHT: JSA 1-3

Covers by Eddy Barrows with Nei Ruffino

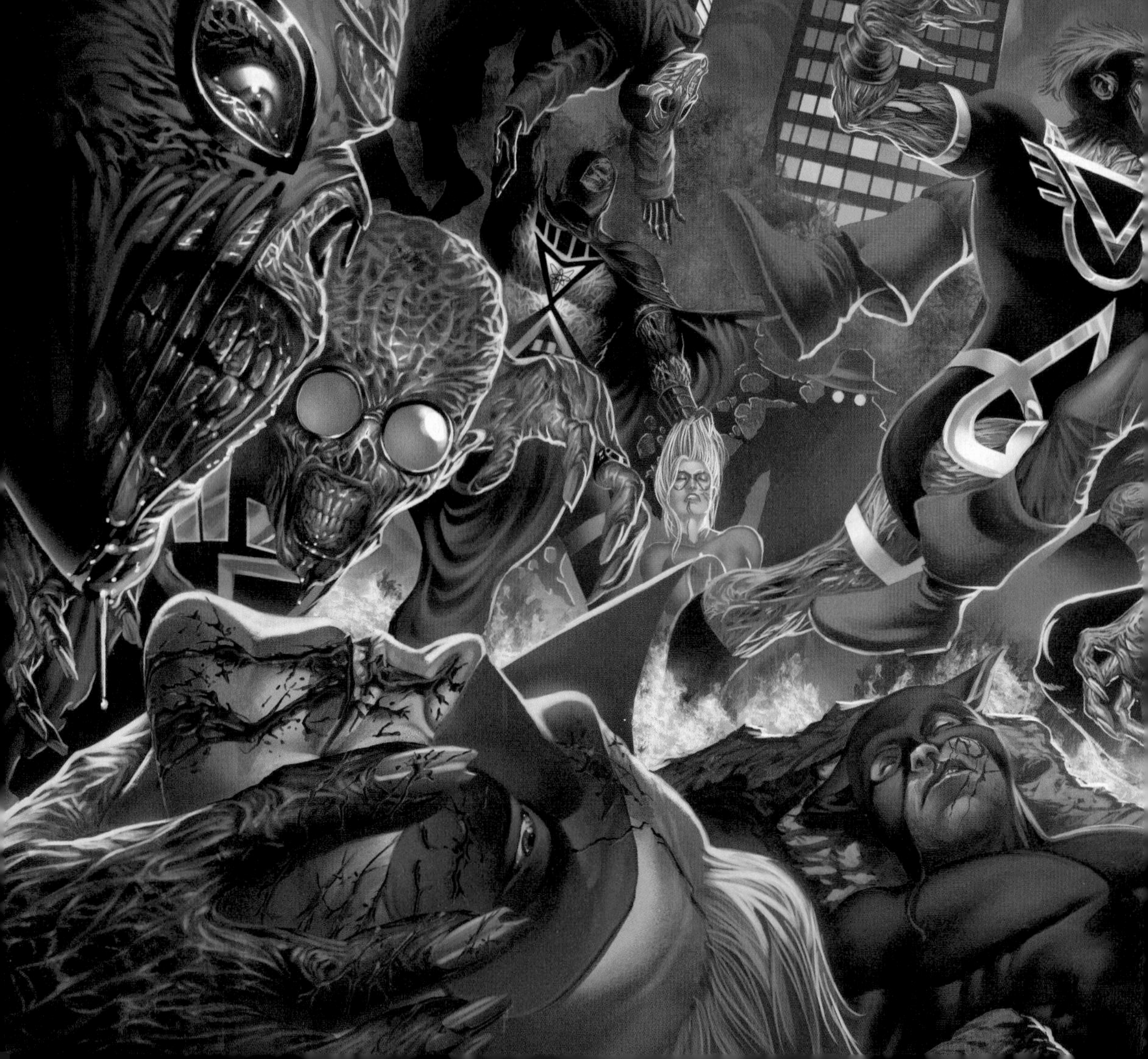

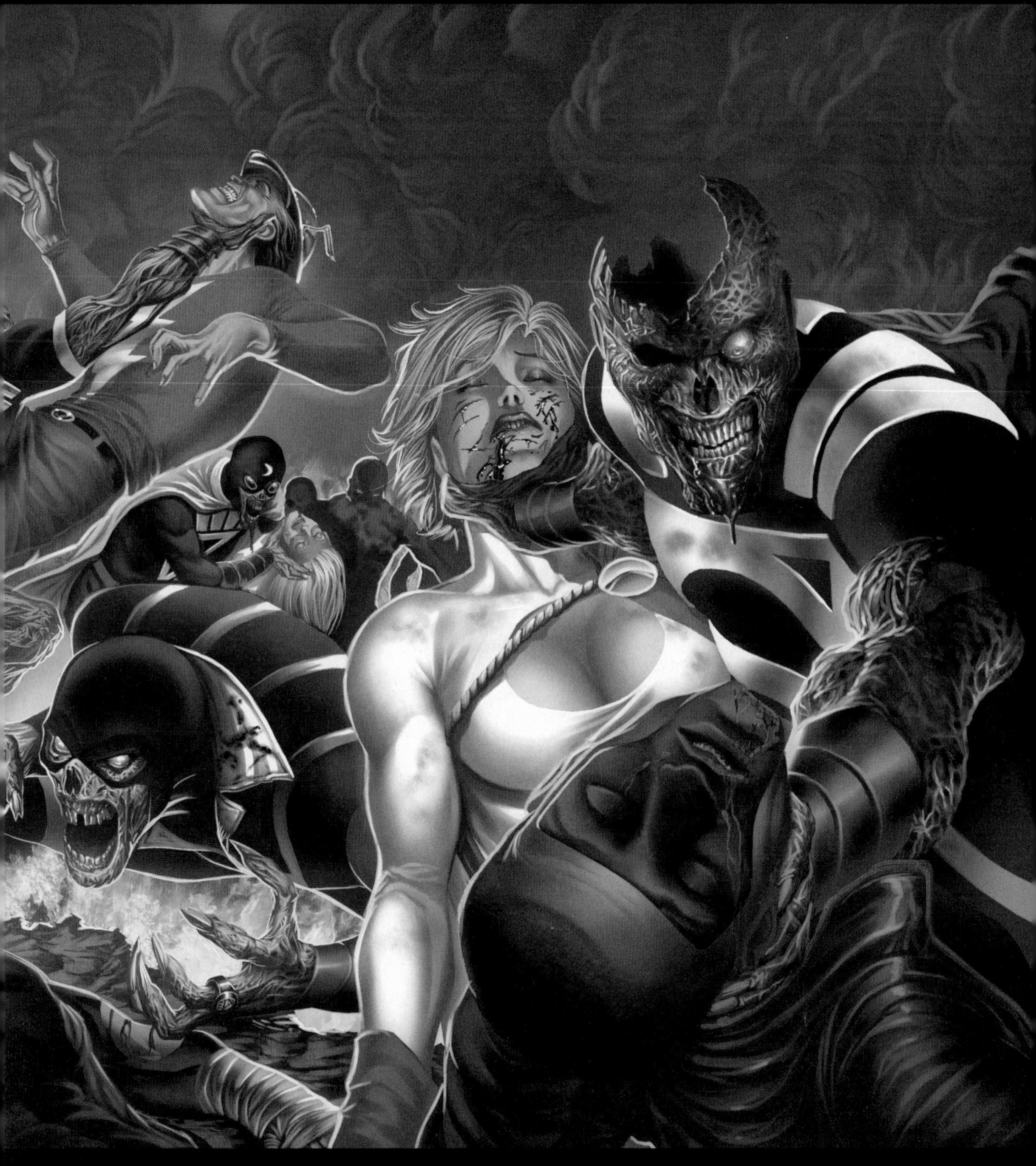

BLACK LANTERN REVERSE-FLASH

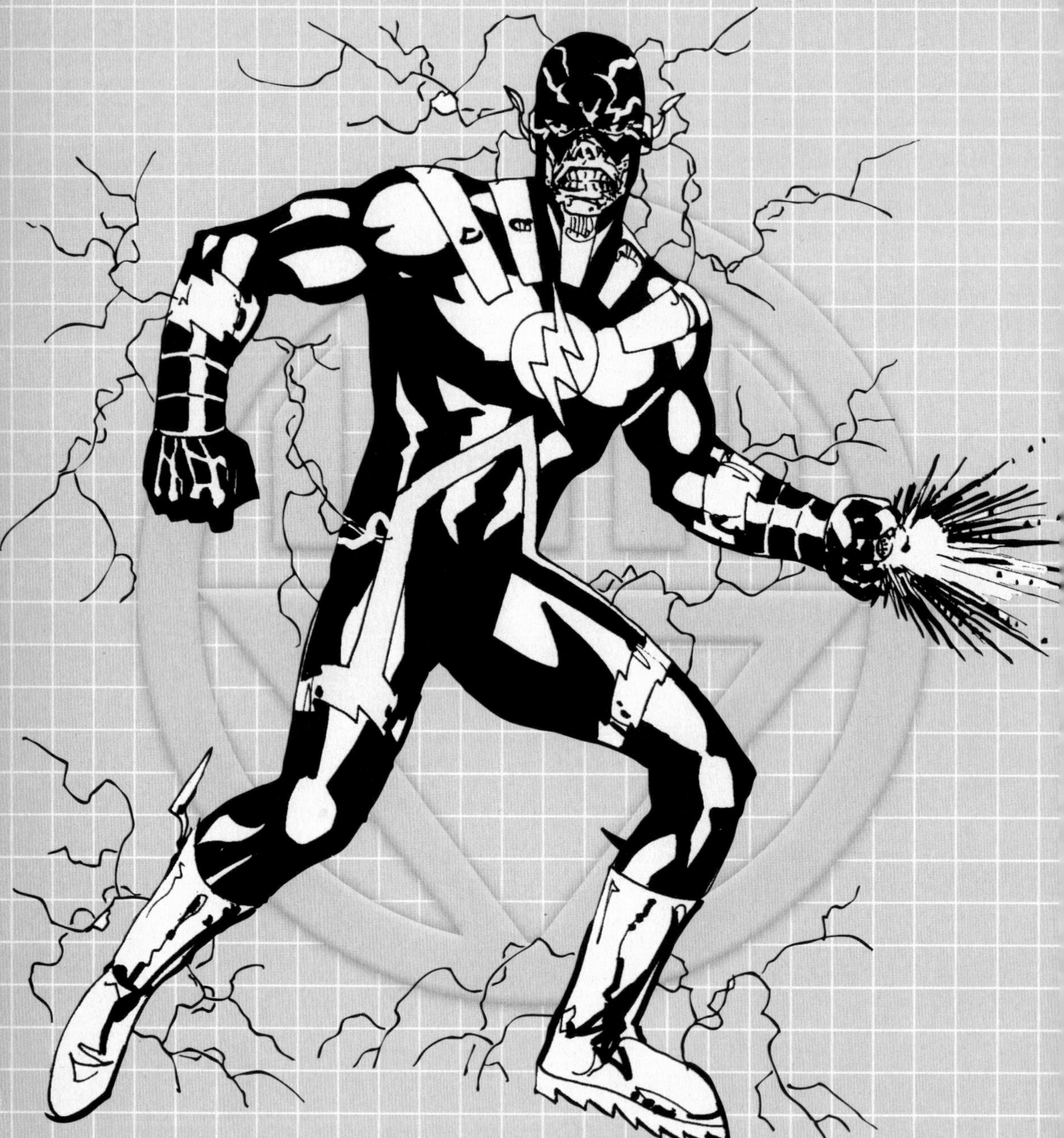

ALTER EGO: EOBARD THAWNE / PROFESSOR ZOOM
PROFESSOR ZOOM WAS KILLED AFTER THE FLASH BROKE HIS NECK. A RESURRECTED PROFESSOR ZOOM, NOW CALLING HIMSELF THE BLACK FLASH, SEEKS HIS REVENGE AGAINST BARRY ALLEN.

Design by Scott Kolins

BLACK LANTERN
KID FLASH

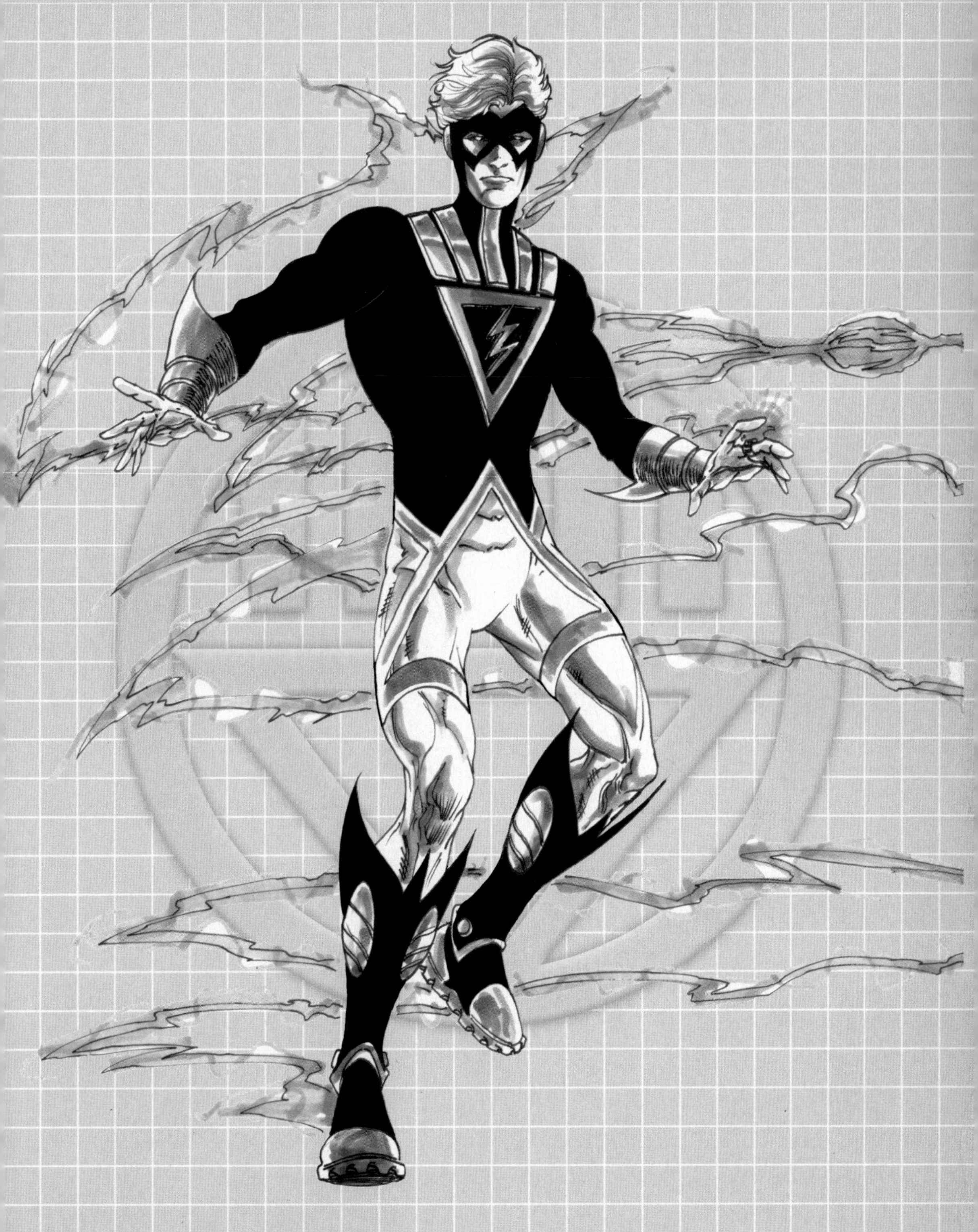

ALTER EGO: BART ALLEN
AFTER BECOMING THE FLASH, BART ALLEN WAS KILLED BY THE ROGUES AFTER THEY WERE ABLE TO RENDER HIM POWERLESS. BART LATER RETURNED TO LIFE AS A TEENAGER, BUT HIS DEATH ALLOWED HIM TO RECEIVE A BLACK LANTERN RING FROM NEKRON.

Design by Joe Prado

BLACK LANTERN JSA

Designs by Joe Prado

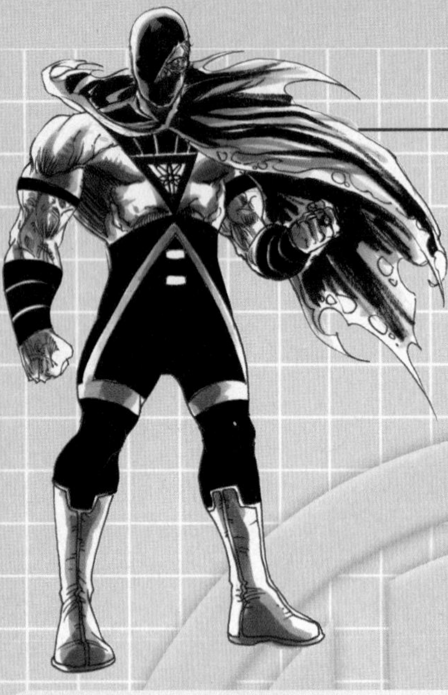

BLACK LANTERN ATOM

ALTER EGO: ALBERT "AL" PRATT

ONE OF THE ORIGINAL MEMBERS OF THE JSA, AL PRATT SACRIFICED HIS LIFE IN AN EPIC BATTLE WITH EXTANT DURING ZERO HOUR.

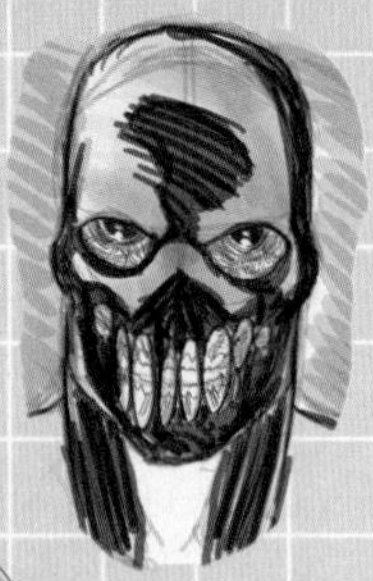

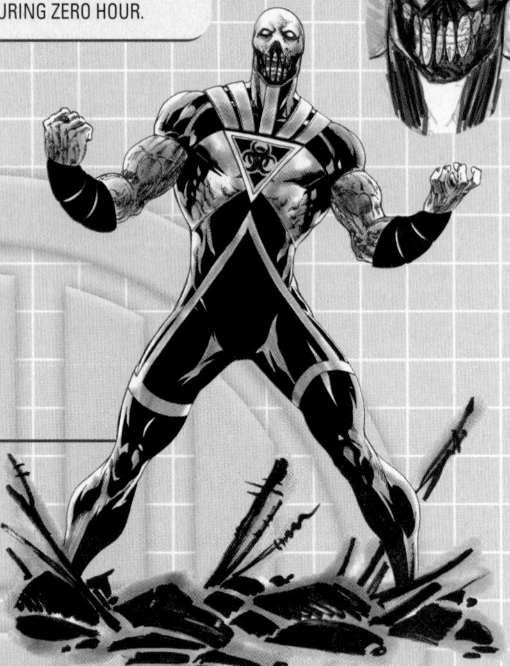

BLACK LANTERN DAMAGE

ALTER EGO: GRANT ALBERT EMERSON

ABLE TO CAUSE MASSIVE EXPLOSIONS, GRANT WAS A POWERFUL MEMBER OF SEVERAL TEAMS INCLUDING THE TITANS, THE FREEDOM FIGHTERS, AND EVENTUALLY THE JSA. HIS HEART WAS RIPPED OUT BY JEAN LORING, IMMEDIATELY TRANSFORMING HIM INTO A BLACK LANTERN.

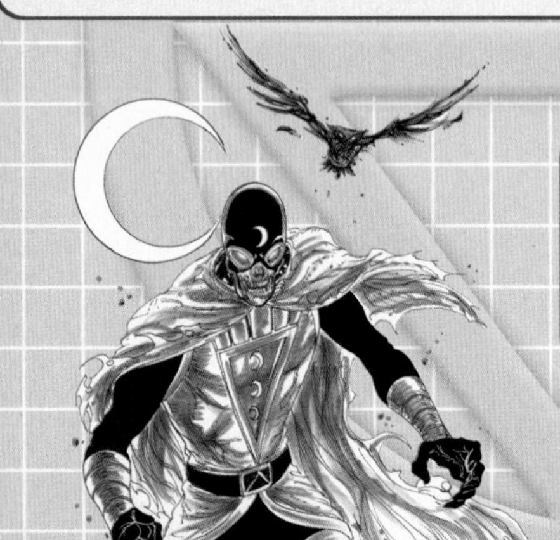

BLACK LANTERN MR. TERRIFIC

ALTER EGO: TERRY SLOANE

ONE OF THE SMARTEST MEN OF HIS GENERATION, TERRY SLOANE COULD ACCOMPLISH ANYTHING HE PUT HIS MIND TO, UNTIL THE SPIRIT KING SLEW HIM WHILE POSSESSING THE BODY OF HIS TEAMMATE AND FRIEND, THE FLASH.

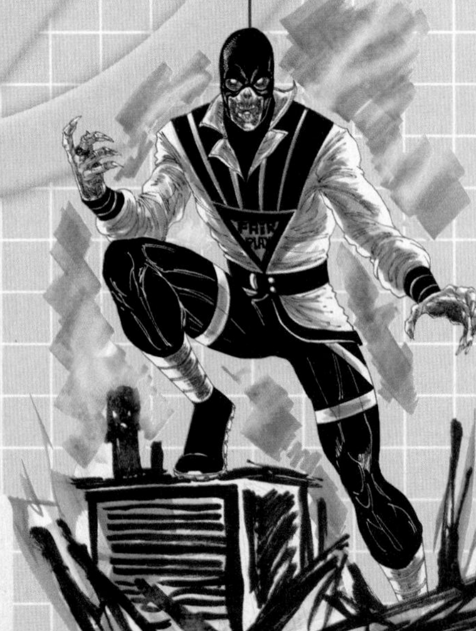

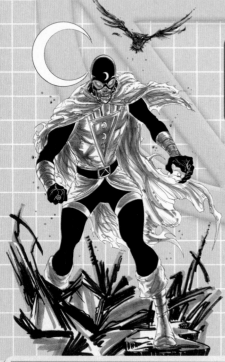

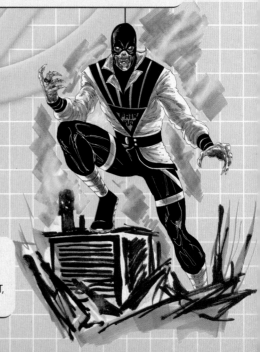

BLACK LANTERN DOCTOR MID-NITE

ALTER EGO: CHARLES MCNIDER

BLINDED BY A GRENADE, THE GOLDEN AGE DOCTOR MID-NITE DISCOVERED THAT HE COULD SEE PERFECTLY IN THE DARK. LIKE HIS TEAMMATE AL PRATT, MCNIDER DIED IN THE BATTLE AGAINST EXTANT DURING ZERO HOUR.

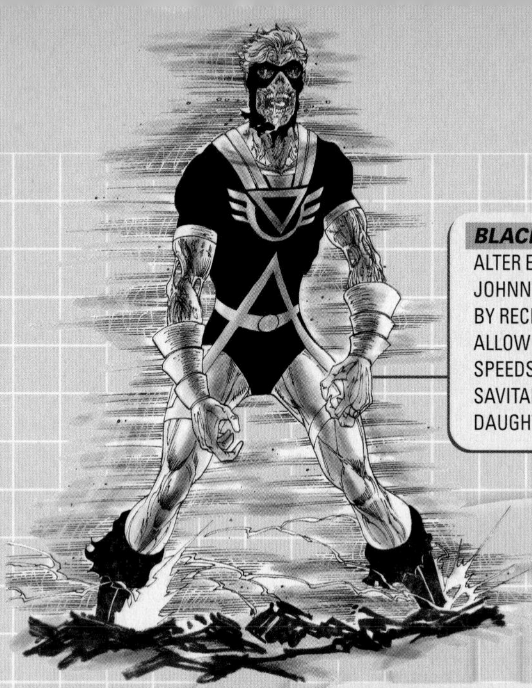

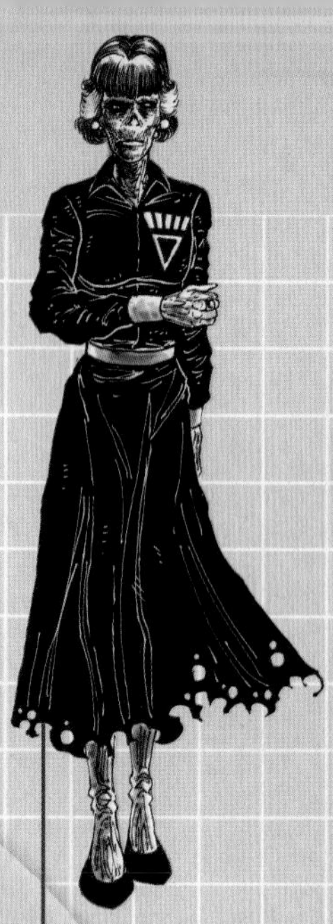

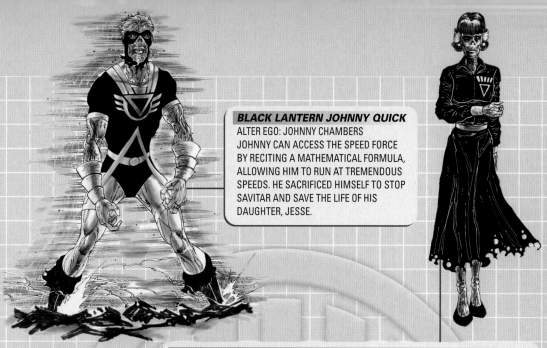

BLACK LANTERN JOHNNY QUICK

ALTER EGO: JOHNNY CHAMBERS

JOHNNY CAN ACCESS THE SPEED FORCE BY RECITING A MATHEMATICAL FORMULA, ALLOWING HIM TO RUN AT TREMENDOUS SPEEDS. HE SACRIFICED HIMSELF TO STOP SAVITAR AND SAVE THE LIFE OF HIS DAUGHTER, JESSE.

BLACK LANTERN EARTH-2 LOIS LANE

ALTER EGO: LOIS LANE

EARTH-2 LOIS LANE DIED FROM AN UNKNOWN ILLNESS AFTER LEAVING A DIMENSION WHERE SHE LIVED WITH EARTH-2 SUPERMAN, ALEXANDOR LUTHOR, AND SUPERBOY-PRIME. AFTER RETURNING AS A BLACK LANTERN, SHE HEADS TO SMALLVILLE TO WREAK HAVOC.

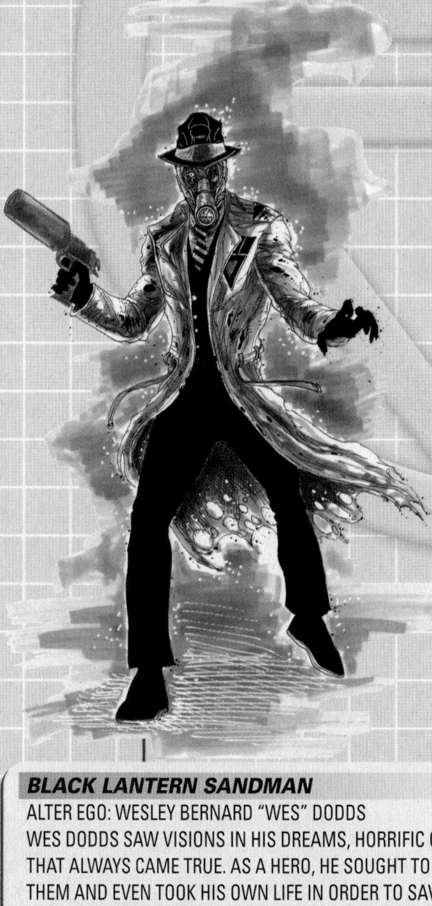

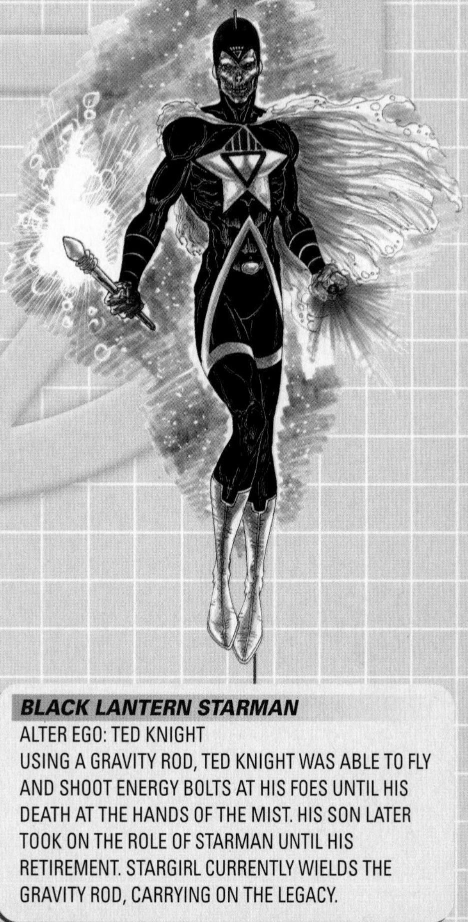

BLACK LANTERN SANDMAN

ALTER EGO: WESLEY BERNARD “WES” DODDS

WES DODDS SAW VISIONS IN HIS DREAMS, HORRIFIC ONES THAT ALWAYS CAME TRUE. AS A HERO, HE SOUGHT TO PREVENT THEM AND EVEN TOOK HIS OWN LIFE IN ORDER TO SAVE THE LIVES OF THE MANY. HIS SIDEKICK SANDY HAS SINCE TAKEN UP HIS ROLE AS THE HERO SAND.

BLACK LANTERN STARMAN

ALTER EGO: TED KNIGHT

USING A GRAVITY ROD, TED KNIGHT WAS ABLE TO FLY AND SHOOT ENERGY BOLTS AT HIS FOES UNTIL HIS DEATH AT THE HANDS OF THE MIST. HIS SON LATER TOOK ON THE ROLE OF STARMAN UNTIL HIS RETIREMENT. STARGIRL CURRENTLY WIELDS THE GRAVITY ROD, CARRYING ON THE LEGACY.

BLACK LANTERN THE FIDDLER
ALTER EGO: ISAAC BOWIN
ABLE TO HYPNOTIZE PEOPLE WITH MUSIC FROM HIS FIDDLE,
BOWIN WAS USED TO GETTING WHAT HE WANTED UNTIL HE
WAS FORCED TO JOIN THE SUICIDE SQUAD. WHEN HE FAILED
ON A MISSION, HE WAS EXECUTED BY DEADSHOT.

BLACK LANTERN BRAINWAVE
ALTER EGO: HENRY KING SR.
BRAINWAVE POSSESSED IMMENSE
PSYCHO-TELEKINETIC POWERS. WERE
HE STILL ALIVE TODAY, HE'D BE PROUD
TO LEARN THAT HIS SON HAS
FOLLOWED IN HIS FOOTSTEPS, TAKING
UP THE MANTLE OF BRAINWAVE.

No cracks on
the mask

BLACK LANTERN PSYCHO-PIRATE
ALTER EGO: ROGER HAYDEN
IN PRISON, HAYDEN LEARNED OF THE EXISTENCE OF
THE MEDUSA MASK. AFTER GAINING POSSESSION OF IT,
THE MASK DROVE HIM INSANE. THE MEDUSA MASK
CONTROLS EMOTIONS AND IS A FORMIDABLE WEAPON
FOR THE BLACK LANTERNS. HAYDEN WAS VIOLENTLY
DESTROYED WHEN BLACK ADAM PUSHED THE MEDUSA
MASK CLEAR THROUGH HAYDEN'S HEAD.

BLACK LANTERN
WONDER WOMAN

ALTER EGO: DIANA PRINCE
WONDER WOMAN IS ONE OF THE HEROES TO RECEIVE A BLACK RING AFTER
"BATMAN'S" RESURRECTION AS A BLACK LANTERN.

Design by Joe Prado

BLACK LANTERN
DONNA TROY

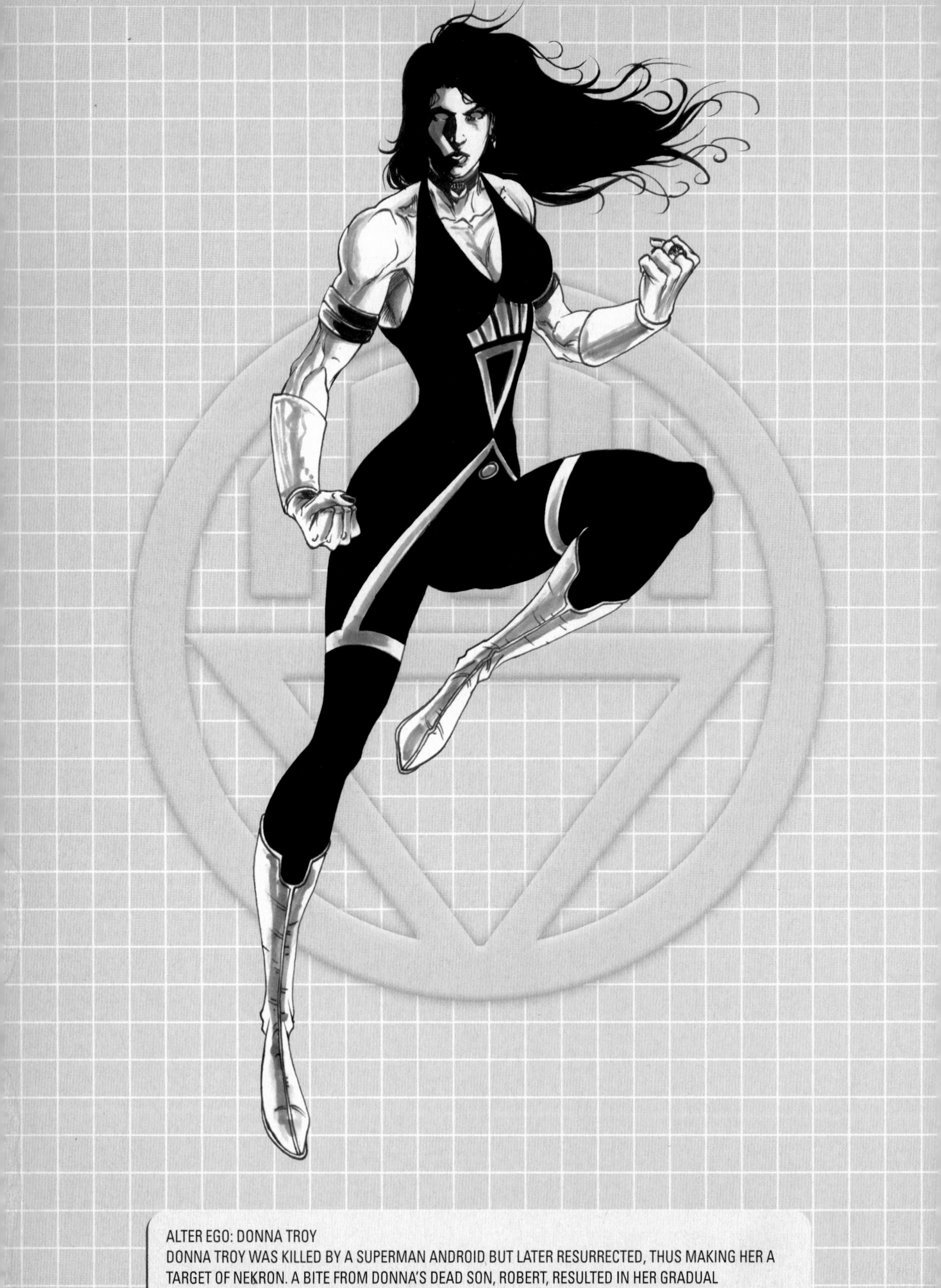

ALTER EGO: DONNA TROY
DONNA TROY WAS KILLED BY A SUPERMAN ANDROID BUT LATER RESURRECTED, THUS MAKING HER A TARGET OF NEKRON. A BITE FROM DONNA'S DEAD SON, ROBERT, RESULTED IN HER GRADUAL TRANSFORMATION INTO A BLACK LANTERN.

Design by Joe Prado

BLACK LANTERN
MAXWELL LORD

ALTER EGO: MAXWELL LORD IV
TO STOP HIM FROM COMMITTING FURTHER EVIL ACTS, WONDER WOMAN SNAPPED MAXWELL LORD'S
NECK. AS A BLACK LANTERN, HE SEEKS OUT WONDER WOMAN FOR REVENGE.

Design by Joe Prado